THE
Long Term Care
CRISIS

For
Carroll Cox Estes
whose life challenges us toward
commitment to long term care and
a vision of empowerment

THE
Long Term Care
CRISIS

Elders Trapped
in the No-Care Zone

Carroll L. Estes
James H. Swan
and Associates

Linda A. Bergthold
Elizabeth A. Binney
David S. Carrell
Monica J. Casper
Adela de la Torre
Carolinda Douglass
Patrick J. Fox
Sheryl C. Goldberg
Charlene Harrington
Susan E. Humphers
Stanley R. Ingman
Lorraine M. Kramek
Carol C. McKetty
Ellen M. Morrison
Douglas S. Sebesta
Pamela Hanes Spohn
Augusta M. Villanueva
Juanita B. Wood

Ida VSW Red, Editor

SAGE Publications
International Educational and Professional Publisher
Newbury Park   London   New Delhi

For information address:

SAGE Publications, Inc.
2455 Teller Road
Newbury Park, California 91320

SAGE Publications Ltd.
6 Bonhill Street
London EC2A 4PU
United Kingdom

SAGE Publications India Pvt. Ltd.
M-32 Market
Greater Kailash I
New Delhi 110 048 India

Printed in the United States of America

Library of Congress Cataloging-in-Publication Data

Estes, Carroll L.
    The long term care crisis: elders trapped in the no-care zone/
Carroll L. Estes, James H. Swan and . . .
        p. cm.
    Includes bibliographical references and index.
    ISBN 0-8039-3992-2. — ISBN 0-8039-3993-0 (pbk.)
    1. Community health services for the aged—Economic aspects—
United States. 2. Aged—Long term care—Government policy—United
States.   3. Aged—Long term care—Economic aspects—United States.
4. Aged—Medical care—Government policy—United States. 5. Aged—
Medical care—Economic aspects—United States. 6. Hospitals—
Prospective payment—Social aspects—United States. I. Swan,
James H.   II. Title.
RA564.8.E9 1993
362.1'9897'00973—dc   92-30579

93 94 95 96 10 9 8 7 6 5 4 3 2 1

Sage Production Editor: Diane S. Foster

Contents

Acknowledgments

The research that forms the core of this volume is the result of a genuinely collaborative effort of the coauthors with the assistance of many colleagues among the faculty, fellows, and staff of the Institute for Health & Aging (IHA) and the Department of Social and Behavioral Sciences. We are deeply indebted to the foundations that funded the research. Our first and greatest acknowledgment is to the Pew Charitable Trusts, the Robert Wood Johnson Foundation, the Meyer Charitable Trust, and our project officers, Brent Roehrs, Jeffrey Merrill, and Marty Lemke. For almost a decade, Brent Roehrs, our project officer at Pew, rendered invaluable support and encouragement to the community studies reported here. More than any other person, she made the research possible as well as the quality and quantity of work we produced. Our discussions with Rebecca Rimel and Charles Rooks of the Pew and Meyer Charitable Trusts, respectively, were instrumental in sharpening our focus. The Amon Carter Foundation, the Hoblitzelle Foundation, and the Hogg Foundation contributed to the Texas portion of the project. Philip R. Lee provided essential guidance as Co-Investigator of the research. We thank Dean Jane Norbeck and our colleagues in the School of Nursing for providing an academically challenging environment for the study. The Koret Foundation generously contributed space and other resources for this and the long line of IHA research on long term care that informs this volume. In particular, we would like to acknowledge Joe Walsh, Mel Mogoloff, Steven Dobbs, and Michael Papo.

This book is in no small part due to the leadership of its project directors. We were fortunate to have the commitment, energy, and intellectual talents of Linda A. Bergthold as Project Director from July 1, 1985, to June 30, 1988, and Juanita B. Wood during the final 6 months of the study. Without their dedication and unflagging interest, we would not have been able to complete a study of this magnitude. Juanita Wood's courage in bringing the study to a successful conclusion was heroic.

The magnitude and complexity of the research, containing within it a study of seven provider types, 12 communities in nine metropolitan areas (SMSAs), and three case studies, required an extremely able staff. More than 25 IHA faculty, fellows, and research assistants contributed to the study at some time during the 3½ years of work involved. The research benefited greatly from the enthusiasm and tireless efforts of the project staff, including Pamela Hanes Spohn, Sheryl Goldberg, Elizabeth Binney, and Rachel Steinhart. Robert Alford's consultation was invaluable in clarifying our thinking, "unpacking" research questions, and working through the most difficult issues of research design. He also contributed substantially to the initial conceptualization and revisions of Chapter 2 on the restructuring of the nonprofit sector. Virginia Hodgkinson of Independent Sector provided an infinite fund of knowledge for our work on the nonprofit sector. Leslie Kish provided crucial help in understanding the sampling and weighting issues for the data analysis. Lee Clarke and Al Immershein offered advice on conceptualizing the organizational and political aspects of the theoretical framework for the project. They have each provided leadership in additional publications using project data.

The large number of publications resulting from this work, including 20 articles and this book, is due in no small part to the ability of the study to attract the talents of pre- and postdoctoral fellows who trudged through almost endless data analyses and drafts of articles as part of their research training at the IHA and the Department of Social and Behavioral Sciences. The Pew Charitable Trusts, National Center for Health Services Research (NCHSR), and National Institute on Aging (NIA) provided fellowship support. Pew Fellows Julie Buhler, Adela de la Torre, Lorraine Kramek, Stanley Ingman, Bruce Solomon, Andrew Szasz, Augusta (Toti) Villanueva, and Walter Wong; NIA Fellows Lisa Binney, Patricia Flynn, and Susan Humphers; and NCHSR Fellow Ellen Morrison all made important contributions to the work included in this volume. We greatly appreciate the willingness of IHA faculty members Charlene Harrington and Patrick Fox to contribute to chapters of this volume. Graduate student Meryl Rappaport contributed to the final report and to additional publications of the project. John Loeb and Lynn Kotranski of the Philadelphia Health Management Corporation (PHMC) provided us with helpful statistics collected in the PHMC health survey and special data runs on the elderly from the Philadelphia case study. Monica Casper and Carol McKetty, graduate students in the Department of Social and Behavioral Sciences, contributed new material to original chapters that enriched this volume. In particular, Carol McKetty literally has devoted months to extensive and exhaustive library searches and to a competent and careful reading and suggested revisions of many chapters of the book. Sue Humphers assisted in developing and revising the Introduction. Lisa Binney contributed ideas and data for the section on social services in Chapter 12 on community-based services as well as relentless hours of designing instruments, conducting interviews, and making the initial presentation at the Gerontological Society of America of the 1991 elite survey reported in Chapter 13.

We could not have accomplished this project without significant help from several extremely competent statisticians. Victor Leino, Steve Preston, and David Carrell each contributed to the analysis during different phases of the study. Vida Jones contributed in multiple ways to the success of this institute project.

Each of the coauthors of this volume personally owes a great debt to the long hours, late nights, and early mornings of our original data manager, Rachel Steinhart, and to Hilary Nouri, who served valiantly as project assistant during the research phase until baby Ashley arrived. We particularly want to acknowledge Patrick Henderson, whose word-processing, detailed checking of text revisions, graphic capability, and great humor carried this project to a successful conclusion.

Editing the entire manuscript required that Ida Red coordinate and negotiate with multiple coauthors. The work was formidable, and the fruits of her care and patience will be much appreciated by readers of this volume. Andrew Ghazai, Scott Hood, Sue Churka-Hyde, and Norton Twite deserve special thanks for computer assistance and help in various aspects of the original report preparation. Literature searching and reference librarian services by Sandra J. Swan were particularly helpful.

Meredith O'Connor and Barbara Paschke supported us with humor and took care of all matters, great and small, while our attention turned to finishing this work. To Marie Christine Yue, we owe thanks for overall support in facilitating our immersion in and completion of what has become a long and intense effort. Additional research staff, including Carolinda Douglass, Aroha Page, Margi Stuart, and Betsy Robinson, continue the work we have started in a number of ongoing research projects.

We especially appreciate the cooperation of the study respondents, who completed 1,786 interviews, and the commitment of the agency directors and designated respondents of the seven types of service providers who provided study data through telephone interviews. The interviews with more than 150 key informants in Philadelphia, Seattle, and San Francisco and with 100 state and local policymakers added important depth to the telephone survey data from providers.

The long and arduous process involved in completing the book required time away from our families and other sacrifices. Carroll Cox Estes provided inspiration as mentor and author in her own right, and Barbara Roberts's competent work was a constant reminder of the urgent and profound importance of a national commitment to universal long term care. To our children, Duskie Lynn Estes and Michael Joseph Swan, we owe a special debt of gratitude for their love and continuing support.

Carroll L. Estes
James H. Swan

Introduction

The access of older persons to health and social services changed profoundly in the 1980s and early 1990s. Efforts to contain health care costs, federal deregulation, technological advances, and changes in health care reimbursement transformed the site and duration of medical care. Contributing to this transformation were intensifying competitiveness in the health care market, an increase in the number of proprietary providers and in their market share, growth in the number of chains and other multifacility organizations, implementation of the prospective payment system (PPS) for Medicare hospital reimbursement, and introduction of the resource-based relative value scale (RBRVS) as the basis of Medicare physician payment.

The PPS, implemented between 1983 and 1985, is a single policy change with as impressive an impact on health care provision as the initial implementation of Medicare and Medicaid in 1965. The PPS profoundly affected the ways in which health care is provided to older Americans. Medicare and Medicaid expanded access to health care for the elderly and the poor, whereas the PPS drastically altered the way in which the Medicare program is implemented. One of the most important effects of the PPS is that the locus of care for elderly and chronically ill patients has shifted from the hospital to ambulatory care settings and to the community. As a consequence, the community-based delivery system has undergone major changes in the way services are organized and delivered. The study reported in this book reveals a widening gap between services that are available and services that are appropriate to the care needs of the elderly. Reaching crisis proportions, this care gap—or no-care zone—in the community-based long term care system reflects the increasing problems of access to the nonmedical services necessary for the chronically ill elderly to retain some level of independence and autonomy.

Health Care Markets and the PPS

The health care market is far more competitive than it once was. Numbers of proprietary providers have increased in all areas of the health industry. Both the number and the proportions of service organizations that are parts of chains and multifacility systems, rather than freestanding independent providers, have increased dramatically. The market dominance of nonprofit providers of health and social services, which have historically offered the majority of formal (paid) care, is being challenged by proprietary providers. To remain viable, nonprofit providers have been forced to behave more like for-profit providers and adopt the practices of commercial business, such as marketing and advertising, fees and copayments for services, and the tightening of eligibility criteria.

The PPS has permanently affected the provision of hospital care to the elderly by imposing admission-based payment, depending on diagnosis. Although this policy is targeted to acute care hospitals as an effort to contain the rapidly escalating costs of inpatient care, the PPS has created ripple effects on non-hospital-based providers of health and social services. The community-based long term care system involves health and social services other than acute hospital care. It consists of formal (paid) and informal (unpaid) providers. The formal system comprises organizational and individual providers, such as nursing homes, home health agencies, adult day-care centers, senior centers, durable medical equipment companies, social workers, home health aides, and physical, occupational, and speech therapists. The informal component of the community-based long term care system comprises the family members and friends who provide the large majority of community-based care. The effects of the PPS are disconcertingly similar across the remarkably diverse and fragmented components of the delivery system.

Background and Aims

The research that forms the core of many chapters in this volume was conducted within the context of the PPS. The diagnosis-related group (DRG) impact study, formally titled *Organizational and Community Responses to Medicare Policy: Consequences for Health and Social Services for the Elderly*, was conducted between 1985 and 1988 at the Institute for Health & Aging (IHA), University of California, San Francisco. Additional data collected during subsequent research in 1990 and 1991 are introduced to set the context for the 1990s.

The DRG study is one of a series of IHA research efforts focused on policy outcomes (Table I.1) conducted over a decade and a half. These projects studied the state, local, and organizational consequences of federal and state policy changes in a turbulent era for health and social services, commencing with the new federalism under the Nixon administration (Figure I.1). Tracing the outcomes of nearly 20 years of policy has required numerous shifts in research concept, focus, and technique. The DRG project is one of a set of large-scale, multidisciplinary research projects with strong threads of similarity but implemented to examine the effects of different policy changes occurring at various points of time.

The IHA policy-outcome projects focused on either the state or the community level, and some projects included both levels (Figure I.1). Three studies surveyed all 50 states, whereas others employed smaller samples of between 5 and 10 states and a subsample of communities within them. The 5 states in the DRG study that is the focus of this book were included in all of the IHA policy-outcome projects. While some of the IHA community studies included as many as 40 localities, a smaller sample of 9 communities was incorporated in five of the IHA studies, including the DRG project, to permit the inclusion of a larger probability sample of providers for each community.

The objectives of the DRG study were to

1. document how one national policy (the PPS) directed at one type of organization (hospitals) influenced a variety of other types of community service provider organizations;
2. document actual changes in staffing, budgets, clients, services, and organizational structure of seven types of health and social service providers in the acute and long term care continuum of services for the elderly during the 1984-1987 period;
3. examine the relationships between and among different types of organizations in the same community, such as hospitals, nursing homes, home health agencies, hospices, senior centers, adult day-care centers, and community mental health centers;
4. address questions concerning the effects on services of the changing structure of health care delivery and the changing relationships

TABLE I.1 IHA Research Projects on Policy Outcomes

Project	Policy-Outcome Research Problem
Aging Policies Project	
Funding Practices, Policies, and Performance of State and Area Agencies on Aging (1976-1980)	Effects of state policy choices under new federalism on aging services
Fiscal Crisis Project	
Fiscal Crisis and Tax Revolt: Impacts on Aging Services (1980-1982)	Effects of state-level fiscal crisis and tax revolt on aging services
Long Term Care Project I	
Correlates of Medicaid Expenditures and Utilization in 50 States (1980-1984)	Effects of public policy changes and budget cuts on long term care in early 1980s
Long Term Care Project II	
Comparative Study of Long Term Care in Eight States (1980-1983)	Effects of state policy choices in Medicaid and income programs (SSI) on long term care services
Nonprofit Community Project	
Public Policy, Private Nonprofit Sector, and Delivery of Community-Based Long Term Care Services for the Elderly (1982-1985)	Effects of federal retrenchment and increased state discretion on nonprofit organizations serving older persons in the community
Long Term Care Project III	
State Medicaid Nursing Home Policies, Utilization, and Expenditures (1985-1987)	Effects of state policy choices in Medicaid on long term care services in the mid-1980s
DRG Study	
Organizational & Community Responses to Medicare Policy (1985-1988)	Effects of medical cost-containment policies (PPS) on delivery system of community services to the elderly
Long Term Care Project IV	
Home Health and Nursing Home Market Analysis (1989-1991)	Effects of state policy choices in Medicaid on long term care in the late 1980s
Access and Community Care	
Community-Based Long Term Care for Postacute and Chronically Ill Elderly (1989-1992)	Effects of the PPS and of public policy changes since 1987 on community-based long term care

between the public, nonprofit, and investor-owned health care sectors; and

5. compare different community responses (uniformities and variations) to a common policy change.

Theoretical Model

This research draws on a variety of theoretical sources in the fields of organizational and health services research. Specifically, it elaborates a model of how federal policy change affects the community and posthospital service system (Figure I.2). In this model, the PPS is a contextual factor, generating profound effects on the system, although the PPS is treated as a constant for the 1986-1987 period of the DRG project. Other policies, generally at the state level, obviously vary by state. Even for the federal Medicare program, however, varying decisions are made by fiscal intermediaries operating in different geographic regions of the United States. Nevertheless, policy is examined primarily in terms of how it affects and operates through the provider organizations.

Market characteristics are examined at the community level. Although the metropolitan areas (SMSAs as defined in the 1980 census) contain diverse localities, and although in three cases they contain twinned cities (now defined as separate metropolitan statistical areas, or MSAs by the Bureau of the Census), each of these metropolitan areas is assumed to constitute one general market area for long term care and other community service providers in the study. Variables operationalizing market characteristics are measured at the level of the community. Particularly important among market variables are those that measure health system capacity and competition.

Organizational characteristics operate at the level of the organization but are influenced by market characteristics. Chief among organizational characteristics examined are organizational size, tax status, multifacility (system) membership, and payment sources. Size represents a variety of concepts, including complexity and resources. Larger organizations tend to be more internally complex, to organize services and provision differently, and to be more routinized than smaller entities. Larger organizations tend to have more resources, in terms of the variety and number of services provided, providers employed, and resources that can be mobilized to repel threats or take opportunities.

Tax status is important in view of the growing privatization of health care provision and the hypothesis that differences between nonprofit and for-profit providers are disappearing (isomorphism). System membership is important because of the growing influence of chains and multifacility organizations. Public funding sources are vitally important, especially in the context of public policy changes in recent years. For example, agencies paid by Medicare may be

FIGURE I.1 Policy Changes and Research Projects

Policy Changes	IHA Community Studies	IHA State Studies
1976 New federalism (Nixon) HMO Act	1976-1980	1976-1980
1978 Taxpayer revolt in the states (Prop. 13 fiscal crisis)		1978-1982
1980 Omnibus Reconciliation Act • Medicare restrictions on home health visits lifted	1980-1982	1980-1983 1980-1984
1981 Omnibus Budget Reconciliation Act (OBRA) • Block grants • New federalism • Budget cuts • Deregulation • High interest rates	Recession (1981-1982)	
1982 Tax Equity and Fiscal Responsibility Act	1982-1985	

1982 (Continued)
Tax cuts
More state discretion
Reductions in federal share of Medicare
State changes AFDC/Medicaid

1983
PPS introduced under Medicare
(Social Security Amendments)

1984
Implementation of PPS
(all hospitals)

1985
Gramm-Rudman-Hollings
Deficit Reduction Act

1987
OBRA nursing home and home
health quality improvements

1988-1991
Medicaid expansion for
low-income groups

1992
Medicare physican payment

States developing programs to deal with increasing numbers of medically uninsured (1983-1985)

1985-1988

1985-1987

1989-1992

1989-1991

SOURCE: Institute for Health & Aging DRG study (1986, 1987).

affected by Medicare policy initiatives such as the PPS, even though they are not the direct targets of such policy.

Prospective payment system policy effects occur at the level of the organization. Specific effects on agencies differ by organization, depending on both market and organizational characteristics. For some analyses, PPS policy effects were considered as dependent variables. Effects were measured by asking organizational respondents whether DRG-based hospital payment had affected them in a number of ways (e.g., in terms of clientele and client service needs or in terms of services provided). Specific types of PPS policy effects are discussed for each type of provider in chapters throughout the book.

Outcomes occur at the organizational level. Service, client, staffing, and budgetary outcomes are affected by market characteristics, organizational characteristics, and PPS policy effects. Various analyses also specify relationships among the types of outcome measures. All multivariate analyses employ models that fit within the outlines of the general model, allowing outcomes reported to be conceptualized within its bounds. In addition, qualitative and other analyses not employing multivariate methods, such as that of the community case studies, use the general model as a conceptual structure.

Methods

The Institute for Health & Aging study of community-based care was conducted in a sample of state and metropolitan areas to maximize representation of the organizations within the sites examined. The states and metropolitan areas from which providers are drawn are San Francisco/Oakland and San Diego, California; Miami and Tampa/St. Petersburg, Florida; Philadelphia and Pittsburgh, Pennsylvania; Dallas/Ft. Worth and Houston, Texas; and Seattle, Washington.

These locations were chosen for several reasons. The study sites represent geographically diverse sections of the United States, have large populations of older persons, and vary in policies and programs in aging. The sample is biased toward the larger, more populous and more generous states within different regions of the country. The states in this study assure regional diversity and diversity of welfare generosity, sociodemographics, and state economic considerations—all factors that affect expenditures for and use of long term care services. The communities represent 9 of the 24 largest metropolitan areas in the nation and 9 of the 11 largest metropolitan

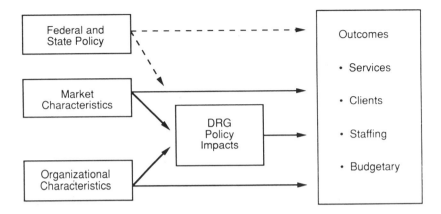

Figure I.2. General Model of Posthospital Community Service System in an Era of Federal Policy Change

areas in the sample states. Because the states and metropolitan areas have been incorporated in previous and ongoing IHA policy-outcome studies, inclusion of the same sites in the DRG study permits the examination of changes occurring over time.

Study data were drawn from several sources: (a) telephone survey interviews with probability samples of hospital discharge planners and six types of service provision organizations, conducted in the spring of 1986 and a second time in the fall of 1987; (b) telephone interviews with state and local policymakers and representatives of major provider associations, conducted in 1988; (c) detailed case studies in three communities in 1988; and (d) secondary data obtained for 1985 from a variety of sources, including U.S. Bureau of the Census area resource files and nursing home directories from the five states. In all, nearly 2,000 interviews were conducted. The response rates for the telephone survey of the providers were exceptionally high: 81% in 1986 and 91% in 1987.

Two major categories of health and social service providers were interviewed by telephone. Nursing homes, home health agencies, and hospices were chosen as community-based service settings (postacute care organizations) in which the elderly receive care immediately upon discharge from the hospital. Adult day-care centers, community mental health centers, and senior centers were selected as community-based services that generally serve elderly clients with less acute and more chronic needs than in the immediate posthospitalization period. The sample of organizations was randomly selected for each community from a comprehensive listing of each provider type. Agency directors, or their designated representatives, were interviewed by telephone for 30 to 60 minutes regarding their organizational structure, relationships with other organizations, staffing patterns, service patterns, clients, and revenue sources as well as the effects of the PPS and other policies on their operations. The data collected cover the time period of 1984 to 1987.

The research discussed in this volume has a number of unique features:

- The findings document the ways in which the hospital PPS has influenced an array of community-based providers of posthospital and other community-based care.
- Of all known studies of the effect of the PPS, this is the only one that attempts to investigate systemic effects across the delivery system.
- The conceptual framework of the work examined identifies recent outcomes of public policy in terms of community-based care and investigates a series of alternative explanations for the outcomes. In addition to PPS effects on clients, services, staff, and organizational viability, the study examines how other major effects of the PPS have shaped the structure of U.S. health care: privatization, organizational complexity, and competition as well as how other policy changes (e.g., Medicare regulations and state policies) influence community service agencies.
- By relating closely to previous research conducted at the Institute for Health & Aging, the book provides a historical and longitudinal perspective on the changing effects of policy over a lengthy period of time: 1978 to 1988.
- Both medical and social service providers are examined, permitting an understanding of trade-offs among and between these services and among provider organizations representing the entire continuum of care from acute to long term care.
- Attention is given to the viability and contributions of nonprofit service organizations in the context of changing relationships between the public, nonprofit, and for-profit sectors in health care.
- The consequences of cost-containment policies are linked to issues of access to care, particularly access limits and barriers to community-based care for older persons.

The primary goal is to assess how federal and state health care cost-containment policies in the 1980s, principally the PPS, affected the network of posthospital care organizations in a sample of communities and states. Specifically, the focus is on how the PPS affected these organizations and how the community-based long term care system changed after implementation of the PPS.

Part I, "Overview," introduces the broad context in which posthospital health services for the elderly are delivered. This introductory part describes the changing structure of community-based care in light of the economic and political forces acting upon it. The deleterious consequences of this change on access to posthospital services are discussed. Chapter 1, "Prospective Payment Revolution and Long Term Care," describes the community-based long term care system and the effects of policy changes on that system. The political and economic environments in which health care delivery takes place are described, and the literature on the effects of the PPS on hospital care and community-based care is reviewed. Chapter 2, "Restructuring of the Nonprofit Sector," examines the major changes occurring in the U.S. political environment and in the mission, structure, and composition of nonprofit sector organizations. Special emphasis is given to nonprofit health and social service providers for the elderly.

Part II, "From Hospital to Community," discusses the intended and unintended effects of the PPS, first from the perspective of hospital discharge planners and then from the perspective of providers of community-based health services. Chapter 3, "Discharge Planners as Gatekeepers to Community Care," presents acute hospital discharge planning as a gateway to posthospital care and documents the increasing difficulty discharge planners face in placing elderly patients in community-based settings. Chapter 4, "Does Out of the Hospital Mean Out of Luck?" provides empirical evidence of increasing demand for posthospital services as well as an increasing supply of clients who are sicker and in need of more intensive services in the period after implementation of the PPS. Chapter 5, "Service Paradox," documents the changes undertaken by community-based service providers to contend with the changing characteristics of clients who are older and sicker and thus in need of greater assistance than prior to the PPS.

Part III, "Home Health and Nursing Home Care," describes profound changes in the Medicare-certified home health and nursing home sectors of the community-based long term care system in the period following implementation of the PPS. Shortened lengths of stay in hospitals mean that home health agencies and nursing homes are increasingly likely to provide care to an elderly population with greater needs immediately upon hospital discharge. Chapters 6, "Metamorphosis of Home Health Care," and 7, "Nursing Homes

Under Prospective Payment," provide evidence of the increased demand for care placed on community organizations and the ways in which the organizations have changed in response to new demands. Chapter 8, "Access to Nursing Home and Home Health Services," takes a sweeping look at access to home health and nursing home care. The concept of access is critically evaluated and examined in terms of availability, acceptability, and attainability. These three components of access are used throughout the chapter to probe the issue and examine how Medicare and Medicaid, for example, affect access.

Part IV, "Elder Care and the Community," emphasizes the need for critical debate on the issue of posthospital care: What does it comprise? Whose needs does it serve? What do these changes mean for the chronically ill elderly who are far more likely to need social support services rather than the medical services reimbursed by Medicare? Chapter 9, "Informalization and Community Care," reviews the literature and discusses research findings that document a shifting trend in the responsibility of community-based care for the elderly from formal providers to family members and friends. Chapter 10, "Access in Peril," questions the changing legitimacy of social services and medical services and the implications for access to care. In Chapter 11, "Community Variation in Policy Implementation," the authors use survey data from the research to examine inter-community variations in demand for and access to posthospital care. The implications of this trend for public policy are discussed. Chapter 12, "Waves of Change," reviews more than a decade of research from 1978 to the current time documenting the shifting burden of care to the community-based long term care system as a result of declining federal responsibility for the provision and funding of human services.

Part V, "The Future," which is the final part, examines the prospects for change in the way health and social services are organized, delivered, and financed. Early findings from research currently taking place at IHA, which follows in the tradition of the research reported here, reveal that access to care for older persons is becoming increasingly constrained, particularly as state and local governments struggle for fiscal viability. In Chapter 13, "Policy Elites and Fiscal Crisis," the authors describe the early results of current IHA research on the views of policymakers about the future of services for the elderly in times of fiscal austerity. Chapter 14, "Empowerment Imperative," examines societal trends and the role of philanthropy and describes major levels of intervention to promote the empowerment of older persons. Chapter 15, "No-Care Zone and Social Policy," discusses the challenges to the posthospital system posed by the structural changes in community-based care described in previous chapters. Further, this chapter considers broad policy issues and theoretical implications raised by these changes. The policy implications raised in earlier chapters are summarized, and recommendations are made.

Finally, the Appendix is provided to serve as a resource guide to the policies that have affected the provision of community-based services.

CHAPTER **1**

Prospective Payment Revolution and Long Term Care

I view health care . . . in this country as a house of cards. You can add cards at the bottom: Medicaid expansions. You can add cards at the top: Medicare catastrophic. It is still a house of cards. A house of cards can stand in a quiet room, but it cannot stand where there is wind . . . the wind of unmet need . . . the wind of public dissatisfaction . . . the wind of demographic change . . . the wind of cost. . . . This house of cards cannot stand in this wind.

Deborah Steelman (in the Pepper Commission, 1990b, p. 6)

▼

Health care for the elderly encompasses a wide range of services. These include acute, chronic, skilled nursing, ambulatory, short-term, long-term, and socially oriented community-based personal care. The current "system" of publicly and privately financed service provision for the elderly is highly fragmented, and the many factions are often in direct competition for dwindling public support. This service system relies on a multitude of diverse funding mechanisms, both private and public. To a lesser extent, the system also relies on the provision of uncompensated care by what may be called the private sphere: formal in-home supports and informal caregiving. Dramatic changes and growth have taken place in the home health industry and innovative and alternative care strategies such as adult

---

NOTE: The authors of this chapter are Douglas S. Sebesta, Carroll L. Estes, Sheryl C. Goldberg, and Carol C. McKetty.

day health care and social day care have been developed. Nevertheless, for many elderly persons, access to a full array of medical and social health services continues to be restricted.

Problems with the delivery of health services to the elderly stem from and reflect both the organizational predicament that plagues the U.S. health care system and the fiscal crisis of the U.S. economic state. Posthospital services and long term care are transacted within a pluralistic, competitive market where proprietary and corporate interests require sizable reimbursements for services delivered. Solvency within the marketplace demands a margin of profit (Harrington, Newcomer, Estes, & Associates, 1985). This situation has been dramatically underscored by the policy, economic, and organizational changes of the past decade. For posthospital and long term care, in particular, prospective payment under Medicare has promoted changes that are virtually revolutionary.

Organizational, Policy, and Economic Changes in U.S. Health Care

In the 1980s, the health care system operated in a context of growing concern over the federal deficit, the shift in funding away from socially oriented to more medically oriented services, and the enactment of cost-containment policies that encourage shortened lengths of hospital stay. Organizational, policy, and economic changes have greatly affected posthospital services and long term care in the United States, raising concerns about care gaps and a possible no-care zone (Estes, 1987b, 1987c; Estes, Wood, et al., 1988; Loth, 1987).

Posthospital Services and Long Term Care

Access to both short-term posthospital care and long term care is integral to the health and independence of many sick and disabled elderly people. A system of nonacute care should include a full "range of services that addresses the health, personal care, and social needs of individuals who lack some capacity for self-care" (Kane & Kane, 1982, p. 4). Ideally, both short-term posthospital care and long term care encompass a continuum ranging from institutional medical care to community-based social services and personal care.

Although patient access to services encompassing this full array of medically and socially oriented care options is supported by the needs of the elderly, a biomedical model and fiscal constraints have limited the type and number of services provided and focused public funding on acute medical care. This bias against long term care financing has promoted the development of institutional and medically oriented community-based services at the expense of social and personal care programs targeted to persons with limitations due to disability and chronic illness (Joe, 1989; Mahoney, Estes, & Heumann, 1986).

Medicare and Medicaid were originally established to meet the acute medical needs of the elderly and poor. Medicare has largely retained this acute care bias by explicitly denying coverage for custodial care (Kane & Kane, 1987), as evidenced by Medicare reimbursements of only $600 million for nursing home care compared with $48.5 billion and $17.1 billion, respectively, for hospital and physician care (Waldo, Levit, & Lazenby, 1986).

Although, during the early 1980s, home health care constituted the fastest growing component of Medicare spending, eligibility requirements limit reimbursement to only intermittent acute medical, largely posthospital care, excluding benefits targeted to longer term non-medically oriented custodial and personal care (Kane & Kane, 1987).

Medicaid, on the other hand, has largely become a long term care support program for the impoverished institutionalized elderly. Reimbursement requirements maintain a medical bias and preserve the traditional centrality of the nursing home industry as the base and largest component of publicly supported posthospital and long term care. Often thought of as a safety-net program for the poor and elderly, Medicaid offers inadequate funding for home health services and provides little assistance in maintaining independence (Williams, Gaumer, & Cella, 1984).

As a result of the acute care and institutional biases of publicly financed programs, the bulk of responsibility for long term care is left to the sick elderly themselves and to their families. Because the U.S. system of posthospital and long term care is fragmented, inadequately financed, and focused on skilled care needs and institutionalization, personal and family monies must be used to finance needed nursing home, home health, and personal care. The majority of elderly people requiring long-term institutional care are, in the end, left permanently dependent on the State. Approximately two thirds (67%) of all patients who enter nursing homes deplete their personal savings and become dependent on Medicaid funds for care (U.S. House of Representatives, 1987b). Because Medicare and Medicaid do not adequately cover nonacute in-home services, access to services that would allow elders to remain independent at home is limited.

Policy and Legislative Changes
in Health Care Financing

The major political, economic, and ideological factors that have guided health policy and legislation must be clarified to assess the organization, delivery, and access of posthospital services and long term care. During the early 1980s, health planning and federal economic policy took a radical shift. The legacy of concern over access and quality that characterized the 1960s gave way in the 1980s to an emphasis on cost containment and competition (Estes, 1988; Wallace & Estes, 1989).

Even as spending for the nation's health care continued to consume an increasingly large proportion of the gross national product (GNP), rising at an average rate of 14.8% annually between 1980 and 1988 compared with an average 4.6% annual growth rate for the general consumer price index (Consumer Price Index, 1989), the Reagan administration committed itself to the neoliberal economic principles of market competition and the conservative neoindividual ethic of personal responsibility (O'Connor, 1973, 1984). Policies were designed to deregulate health care services, decentralize authority and financial support in public health and social programs, and promote a tax structure that would be economically favorable to corporate investment in health care under the ideological rhetoric of fiscal and organizational efficiency. The Reagan administration argued that the policies would assure a system of high quality and of choice and reasonable costs.

Although these strategies were introduced to promote economic stability, the Reagan legacy is an enormous federal deficit. As a result, federal policy and budgetary planning for health and social services have been increasingly constrained within an environment of massive deficit spending and the runaway costs of medical and military spending (Estes, Gerard, Zones, & Swan, 1984). Fiscal austerity included a reduced federal investment in domestic and social needs, while supply-side corporate tax incentives stimulated the growth of for-profit health care in efforts to privatize what had theretofore been federal responsibility for services. Policy objectives increasingly focused on cost containment, cost sharing, and restrictive benefit coverage.

The Health Care Market

The economic policies of the early 1980s were premised on the viewpoint that U.S. economic problems were caused by too much regulation and too much government. The administration contended that skyrocketing costs would be contained by rejecting State welfare policies and embracing deregulated, decentralized, and competitive market models. Reagan's "new federalism" aimed to decrease the federal role in health and welfare by shifting responsibility to the state and local levels or away from government entirely. Redirection of federal outlays for a variety of health and social service programs into block grants was designed to place programs closer to the people (Estes, Newcomer, & Associates, 1983; Nelson, 1986).

In addition to forfeiting the centralized control of funding policy, deregulation removed existing legislative restrictions that had previously retarded the development of for-profit health care. This state subsidization of new sources of private profit (Bergthold, Estes, & Villanueva, 1990; Estes & Wood, 1986) enlarged the medical-industrial complex (Bergthold et al., 1990; Relman, 1980) and created serious competition for public financing between for-profit and nonprofit corporations.

Fiscal Crisis and Austerity Spending

With an economic recession, a shrinking federal tax base, high peacetime military costs, unemployment, and the increased use of subsistence health and social service programs by the growing number of disenfranchised Americans, the federal government experienced protracted budgetary problems (Harrington, Newcomer, et al., 1985). The overriding strategy of new federalism was to attempt to reverse the gains made in health and social welfare policy during the 1960s (Estes et al., 1984). State governments have been barely able to maintain a positive fiscal status during this period of federal budgetary restraint and new federalism. State and local governments have been forced to restrict health and social services and to increase the burden borne by the recipients themselves (Wood, Fox, Estes, Lee, & Mahoney, 1986).

In sum, the social welfare policies of the 1980s were enacted during a period of proclaimed fiscal austerity characterized by (a) deficit spending and the enactment of emergency controls mandating reduced federal expenditures and a balanced budget (e.g., the Gramm-Rudman-Hollings Balanced Budget and Emergency Deficit Control Act of 1985); (b) a new tax structure based on supply-side economic policies; (c) the transfer of responsibility for many health and welfare programs to state and local governments; (d) sagging state fiscal resources; (e) the increased need for health and social welfare programs for the homeless, persons with AIDS, and the disabled; and (f) renewed ideological commitment to the ethic of personal responsibility.

Intended Outcomes and Adverse
Effects of Health Legislation

In 1965, when Medicare and Medicaid were enacted, reimbursement methods for both programs replicated the private insurance model of retrospective payment according to costs incurred. This indemnity structure, with payment for all costs subsequent to service delivery, provided a strong incentive to maximize the volume of health care services delivered. Inflationary public health care expenditures emerged immediately, with hospital charges being the major contributing factor (Dobson & Bialek, 1985).

Despite commissioned experiments and demonstration projects with alternative reimbursement methods (e.g., the Social Security Act Amendments of 1967 and 1972 and the 1974 National Health Planning and Development Act) and attempts at voluntary hospital cost containment, Medicare and Medicaid costs continued to escalate throughout the years of the Carter administration and to the current time. Services for the elderly, who are approximately 11% of the U.S. population, constitute 29% of health care expenditures (Dobson & Bialek, 1985).

In 1981, the Reagan administration placed the economics of health and social policy at center stage. Medicare and Medicaid were both targeted for new cost containment. Federal policy goals of access (1960s) and planning and comprehensive services (1970s) shifted to competition and efficiency (1980s) (Estes, 1991). Health care was redefined as an economic rather than a social good. The 1981 Omnibus Budget Reconciliation Act (OBRA) attempted to promote the growth (and theorized efficiency) of a market-based health care sector and to reduce federal responsibility for joint federal-state health and welfare programs. Federal contributions to state and local social services were dramatically cut through the implementation of block grants. Further, the rate of increase targeted for Medicaid was cut substantially in the first 3 years of the Reagan administration. Although federal funding for Medicaid increased between 1983 and 1987, it has not kept pace with the growth rate of medical care costs (Harrington, 1989).

In an effort to promote Medicaid cost containment, freedom of choice provisions for the selection of providers were rescinded by the 1981 OBRA. Copayments for basic services under Medicare, prohibited by federal statute prior to 1981, were condoned. Restrictions were removed and copayments became optional under 1982 amendments. In its zeal to lower the federal burden, the Reagan administration proposed cost sharing of up to 35% by health care service recipients (Kronefeld & Whicker, 1984).

In further shifting of responsibility to states and localities, more than 50 categorical programs were consolidated into nine new block grants under the 1981 OBRA. The deregulation of many of these programs also eliminated most of the federal targeting and reporting requirements. States were granted greater flexibility in determining eligibility requirements and benefit coverage, resulting in eligibility changes that reduced benefits to needy populations (Kronefeld & Whicker, 1984; Wallace & Estes, 1989). Many low- and middle-income persons in need of services were deemed ineligible for benefits. Block grants further opened the door to market competition in the health care sector (Bergthold et al., 1990). The Reagan administration philosophy, distinctly favoring the private sector, deregulation, and restricted federal funding, encouraged states to seek competitive bids from for-profit enterprises for provision of particular services under contractual arrangement.

The Omnibus Reconciliation Act of 1980 (ORA) opened the door for proprietary interests in the home health care market and eliminated many preexisting benefit restrictions (Spohn, Bergthold, & Estes, 1987-1988). Waivers granted through Section 2176 of the Omnibus Budget Reconciliation Act of 1981 permitted the provision of state-financed home health care in place of institutional long term care services for acutely ill persons (Benjamin, 1985). Even though this legislation was intended to encourage home care (Kane & Kane, 1987), approvals of waiver requests, paradoxically, have been restricted so as to contain the expansion of Medicaid dollars for noninstitutional long term care services.

The first explicit directive for implementing prospective payment emerged in the 1982 Tax Equity and Fiscal Responsibility Act (TEFRA), which directed the Department of Health and Human Services (DHHS) to prepare a plan for hospital prospective payment under Medicare. The TEFRA also limited the federal share of Medicare funding, added the Medicare hospice benefit, and encouraged the growth of health maintenance organizations (HMOs) and other comprehensive medical plans enrolling Medicare beneficiaries.

Even with TEFRA cost-containment measures, hospital expenditures continued to rise rapidly (Dobson & Bialek, 1985; U. S. House of Representatives, 1990). Title VI of the Social Security Act of

1983 provided for Medicare payment for hospital inpatient services under a prospective payment system (PPS) using 467 diagnosis-related groups (DRGs). The PPS incentives were for hospitals to decrease the length of stay of Medicare patients, to provide less intensive or more focused care, to cut back on amenities, and to aim for a cost-efficient hospital case mix. The goal was to economize by shifting costs to the posthospital and long term care systems (Chelimsky, 1985; Hughes, 1986; Kane & Kane, 1989).

With the passage of the Balanced Budget and Emergency Deficit Control Act of 1985 (Gramm-Rudman-Hollings), which mandated a decrease in the federal deficit each year, austerity spending on domestic programs became institutionalized (Wallace & Estes, 1989). Medicare, with its continuing inflationary spiral, became a renewed target for attack. To reduce the deficit and balance the budget, Congress initiated legislation that would further shift the cost of health and welfare programs to state governments and to recipients through higher premiums and deductibles.

Transformed Landscape

Recent developments in the health care industry have transformed the landscape of service delivery, access, quality, and reimbursement (Estes et al., 1984; Relman, 1980; Starr, 1982). These developments fall into three broad areas: organizational restructuring, medicalization, and the informalization of care.

Organizational Restructuring

A large component of the legislative strategy employed to contain the escalating costs of public health care is reliance on basic market forces and competition. With implementation of tax incentives and competitive bidding practices encouraging private sector involvement, proprietary institutions in the health care arena grew rapidly (Bergthold et al., 1990; Berliner, 1987; Berliner & Burlage, 1987; Institute of Medicine, 1986a; Johnson, 1985a, 1985b; Light, 1986; Salmon, 1987; Schlesinger, 1985a). Structural changes in the system included increased privatization through the establishment of for-profit enterprises as well as the further "rationalization" (Weber, 1946) of health care through the growth of large, complex, multifacility systems (Shortell, Morrison, & Friedman, 1990). In retrospect, neither privatization nor rationalization has stemmed the growth of national health expenditures or improved access to care for the elderly and poor (Alexander, Morlock, & Gifford, 1988; Ermann & Gabel, 1984; Friedman & Shortell, 1988; Rodwin, 1986; Schlesinger, Bentkover, Blumenthal, Musacchio, & Willer, 1987).

Privatization. Fiscal pressures and budget cuts, the deregulation of major domestic social programs, and policies fostering competition between the nonprofit and for-profit sectors in health care delivery (Bergthold et al., 1990; Estes & Wood, 1986) have, in combination, encouraged the advancement of proprietary interests in many areas of the health care market. The trend toward privatization is most pronounced in the home health industry (Benjamin, 1986c; Bergthold et al., 1990; Caro, 1989; Harrington, 1988; Kane & Kane, 1987; Kirby, Latta, & Helbing, 1986; Waldo et al., 1986), among nursing homes (Harrington, 1991b; Strahan, 1987), and in the hospital industry (Starr, 1982). Chapters 2 and 6 discuss the impact of privatization on home health and other community-based providers. The privatization of certain types of community-based services (e.g., unlicensed home care) resulted from the inadequacy of public reimbursement schedules for personal care and social support. Thus only people who could afford to pay for services out of pocket could purchase them, except for poor clients living in states where they were covered by Medicaid.

Rationalization. Rationalization, or the increasing complexity of the organization and structure of the health care industry, is characterized by four separate dimensions: horizontal integration, vertical integration, isomorphism, and fragmentation.

Horizontal integration reflects the transcendence of consolidated, multiple institutional, regional, or national chains over single, freestanding community agencies. Both nonprofit and for-profit chain ownership has proliferated, especially in the nursing home industry (Harrington, 1991b; Kane & Kane, 1987; LaViolette, 1983). In the current economic climate, nonprofit organizations benefit from tax advantages and access to the procurement of tax-exempt bonds, whereas proprietary concerns have successfully raised the necessary capital for expansion by issuing public stock (Berliner & Regan, 1987; Estes, Harrington, & Davis, 1992; Harrington, 1989; Strahan, 1987). Hospitals have experienced a move to system membership for similar reasons (Shortell et al., 1990). The home health industry has likewise experienced growth and structural changes (Estes, Swan,

Bergthold, & Spohn, in press; Evanswick, 1985; Grazier, 1986; Salvatore, 1985; Wood, 1985-1986). In a multi-institutional system of care, evaluations and decisions often reflect regional or national priorities rather than the concerns of local entities or communities.

Vertical integration is a movement within the health care industry to consolidate multiple levels of care within one organizational system. For example, acute care hospital, nursing home, home care, and ambulatory care entities may all be merged and managed by one parent corporation (Brody & Persily, 1984; Estes & Lee, 1986; Evanswick, Rundall, & Goldiamond, 1985; Kane & Kane, 1987, 1989; Starr, 1982). Another facet of vertical integration is the diversification of investments into affiliated business ventures, such as the control of pharmaceutical suppliers and respiratory therapy companies by proprietary nursing home chains (Starr, 1982; Swan & Harrington, 1985). With the ability to offer services at multiple levels of inpatient, outpatient, and formal community-based care, hospitals and nursing homes, often the centers of emerging verticalized systems, can better control patient flow and mix and maximize reimbursement schedules by passing patients down through the variety of Medicare- and Medicaid-funded care options.

Isomorphism is a "process of homogenization" (DiMaggio & Powell, 1983, p. 149) that occurs when individual organizations within a population of organizations (e.g., hospitals) are encouraged or forced to resemble other organizations of the same type under the same or similar environmental conditions (Hawley, 1968) as a result of changes in law (policy) or cultural expectations (DiMaggio & Powell, 1983). An important issue in health care is the extent to which there are real differences between nonprofit and for-profit institutions and providers and how being part of vertically and horizontally integrated multifacility systems affects the behavior of health providers (Chapters 6 and 8; Estes, Harrington, & Davis, 1992; Estes et al., in press).

The fiscal stability of health care institutions within the nonprofit sector has been challenged by a number of the policy objectives of cost containment and new federalism. These objectives include the decreased availability of public monies during times of mandated budgetary reductions, the introduction of major cost-containment policies, the decline of corporate charitable contributions to the nonprofit sector (Estes et al., in press), cutbacks in the rate of increase in health services, absolute cuts in social service funding, and shifts in the preference of state financing away from the nonprofit toward the proprietary sector (Estes & Alford, 1990; Estes & Wood, 1986). As a result, many nonprofit health care institutions have been forced to embrace expansionary growth and engage in for-profit ventures (e.g., subsidiaries) to remain solvent in the new competitive health care marketplace (Estes, Binney, & Bergthold, 1989; Salamon, 1983; Wood, 1985-1986). Further blurring the boundaries between the for-profit and nonprofit health care sectors, multihospital systems (and others) have begun to combine for-profit and nonprofit organizational structures to maximize capital and reimbursement options and to increase their competitive market share (Goldsmith, 1984). The contractual management of community hospitals by for-profit enterprises is an illustration of this phenomenon (Estes et al., 1992).

The continued and exacerbated fragmentation of health care services for the elderly is reflective of the multiple levels of government (federal, state, and local) involvement as well as the excessive numbers of categorical programs and funding sources (both proprietary and charitable) involved in the regulation and financing of care (e.g., Medicare, Medicaid, Supplemental Security Income, Older Americans Act, Title XX, Social Services, Veterans Administration). The current organizational structure also works against the delivery of coordinated, comprehensive, cost-efficient services by maintaining separate administrative and funding mechanisms for acute, ambulatory, and long term care; institutional and community-based care; and medically oriented and nonmedical care (Estes, 1986; Harrington, 1989; Joe, 1989; Wood & Estes, 1985). In addition, most payment sources now require the unbundling of comprehensive services, using reimbursement schedules based on single discrete (marketable) services (Estes, 1986; Estes & Wood, 1986). Fragmentation of services and funding sources also heightens the competition between institutional providers of services. This results in the unnecessary duplication of services, increased administrative and structural costs, and an unwieldy and confusing bureaucratic system difficult for both providers and clients to negotiate (Zawadski, 1983). Chapters 2 and 12 further describe and delineate specific aspects of organizational restructuring, particularly in terms of the effects on home care and discharge planning.

Medicalization

The term *medicalization* has been widely used to define the changing nature of health care at various conceptual levels (Binney, Estes, & Ingman, 1990; Conrad & Schneider, 1980; Zola, 1986). One macrolevel perspective focuses on the construction of contemporary social reality within a pervasive medical definition of self. The biomedical model (with its emphasis on pathology, disease, and the degenerative body) is viewed as having become a major institution of social control, framing the interpretation and regulation of life from the moment of conception until death (Crawford, 1980; Foucault, 1975; Zola, 1988). The concept applied in this sense refers to the increasing influence of biomedicine and medical practice in regulating various aspects of the life course (e.g., childbirth, adolescence, and aging) and in redefining social problems previously conceptualized in nonmedical social and structural terms (e.g., substance abuse and lack of community support for the elderly and poor).

Medicalization can also refer to the propensity of the health industry and the medical profession to unquestioningly maximize rapidly developing high technology and to follow an imperative to extend life regardless of the cost (Illich, 1976; Zola, 1986). One way to view this emphasis on high technology in the care of the elderly is that it is a product of the expansionary needs of an industry based on profit, competition, and specialization. In a system of third-party reimbursement, the development and implementation of medical technology often has more to do with market forces and resource allocation than with the needs of those who are ill (Enders, 1986). Competitive forces among specialized physicians and acute care hospitals, together with the increased demographic trend toward longevity, have opened up a lucrative market, targeting expensive and sophisticated medical and surgical interventions to the aging population (Fuchs, 1990). The three fastest growing categories of physician practice reimbursed through Medicare Part B are the most specialized and technologically intensive: cardiovascular disease, radiology, and ophthalmology (Lee & Ginsburg, 1988). General and family practice, general surgery, and internal medicine, on the other hand, are the three slowest growing categories of physician practice reimbursed through Medicare Part B (Lee & Ginsburg, 1988).

A third way to view medicalization is in terms of industry organization, policy development, and service provision. The concept defines "the process by which services for the elderly are increasingly brought under the domain and rationality of biomedicine, and elements of the community delivery system are increasingly drawn towards the provision of medically oriented services" (Binney et al., 1990, p. 762). Prevailing planning and finance strategies thus increasingly identify acute medical institutions as the organizational centers for the health and social service needs of the elderly (Brody & Magel, 1989). This view minimizes the importance of low-technology needs, such as research and equipment to reduce hearing and mobility impairment (Zola, 1988). The preeminence of the physician as gate-keeper in the authorization of services under Medicare ensures that reimbursement is made for services designated as "medically necessary" within the biomedical model (Binney et al., 1990). Medicaid benefits also reflect a biomedical primacy. In 1986, only 3.5% of Medicaid spending, or $1.5 billion, went to home health care, while $16 billion went to nursing home care (Harrington, 1989).

Early discharges of Medicare beneficiaries from acute care settings as a result of cost-containment measures during the 1980s, together with cutbacks in federal funding for community-based care, have forced the targeting of available public resources toward the short-term medically based home care needs of persons with acute illness rather than toward a continuum of care for chronically ill persons or those living with nonmedical impairments (Mahoney et al., 1986; Wood & Estes, 1990). With the advancement of medical technologies allowing the use of sophisticated equipment in the home environment, the emerging home health industry also has been able to capitalize on Medicare policy and finance changes, further medicalizing community-based services (Bergthold et al., 1990; Estes & Wood, 1986; Spohn et al., 1987-1988).

The medicalization of health and social services for the elderly, although benefiting persons suffering from acute medical problems, has been damaging for persons whose needs cannot be met by technological and biomedical solutions. Geriatric literature provides numerous examples of the inappropriate application of medical care when social supportive services are needed (Binney et al., 1990). Further, although biomedicine has been successful in gaining better control over fatal diseases and has increased longevity, prevalence rates of comorbidity and disability have risen (Verbrugge, 1989). Reliance on technological fixes ignores the social and psychological dimensions of the health needs of the elderly and the ethical questions about the long-term consequences of this type of health care (Zola, 1988). Chapter 12 on services addresses the implications of medicalization on specific community-based services, and Chapter 6 explores the medicalization of home health services.

Informalization

Informalization of care refers to the transfer of labor functions from the formal sector to the informal sector, or the shift of labor from persons working within the paid labor force to those working outside it (Binney, Estes, & Humphers, 1989; Estes & Wood, 1986;

Redclift & Mingione, 1985). The informalization of nonacute care for the elderly became a policy priority under the Reagan administration. The success of the prospective payment system in reducing the average length of hospital stay together with federal funding cuts heightened the importance of unpaid, informal caregiving (Estes, 1986; Estes & Binney, 1988; Stark, 1987a; U.S. House of Representatives, 1988b). Approximately 80% of all health and social services and long term care to the elderly is supplied informally by relatives, friends, neighbors, and volunteer agencies (Brody & Brody, 1989; Caro, 1989; Soldo, 1984). Women provide the vast majority of this unpaid labor. In 1985, 80% of the elderly with severe disabilities lived in the community rather than in skilled care facilities. More than 70% of these persons relied exclusively on unpaid sources of home and community health care (U.S. Senate, 1989).

Typically, the burden of providing care falls to family members. Informal care is usually provided to elderly men by wives younger than they are. Because the majority of married women are widowed by age 65 (Brody & Brody, 1989), informal care (if available) usually comes from daughters or other female relatives and sometimes from unmarried women and unrelated caregivers (Bergthold et al., 1990; Binney et al., 1989; Manton & Soldo, 1985; Soldo & Myllyluoma, 1983). Apart from the emotional and psychological toll of informally supplying care to parents and grandparents (Brody, 1985), the social cost of this increased burden on the lives of the caretakers is major. Household economies increasingly require the entry of women into the work force, but the demands on daughters and other female relatives serving as informal caregivers will lessen their social security tax contributions, thus lowering their future benefit levels (AARP Andrus Foundation, 1989; Estes & Wood, 1986).

Informal caregiving has been shown to be important in preventing institutionalization—a fact that has not been overlooked by policymakers in this era of limited funds for community-based services. Single, divorced, or separated persons living alone have a 10 times greater chance of institutionalization than those who are married (Butler & Newacheck, 1981). Various studies discussed by Kane and Kane (1987) indicate that a growing proportion of the elderly population does not have family within close enough reach to provide needed care. Many elderly people do not have any relatives on whom to rely and thus have limited options (Branch & Jette, 1983; Soldo, 1984; Stoller & Earl, 1983; Weissert, 1982). Consequently, underfunded volunteer agencies have been overtaxed trying to provide for clients without access to informal support. Issues of access to services are discussed in Chapter 3.

Impact of the Medicare
Prospective Payment System (PPS)

The repercussions of the Medicare prospective payment system (PPS) are far reaching. Hospital admissions, lengths of stay, and, consequently, occupancy rates have shown evidence of change. Changes taking place in the hospital setting have, in turn, precipitated change in the nonhospital arena. Although the shift taking place cannot be attributed solely to the Medicare PPS (Chelimsky, 1985; Goldberg & Estes, 1990; Guterman & Dobson, 1986; United Hospital Fund, 1986), the impact of the new payment system has been undeniably significant.

The PPS and Inpatient Care

The PPS accelerated the trend toward declining lengths of stay for elderly patients in acute care hospitals (Gornick & Hall, 1988; Prospective Payment Assessment Commision [ProPAC], 1990). Data from the Medicare Statistical System show that the average length of stay for Medicare patients in short-stay hospitals decreased 17% from 1984 to 1986 (Coe, Wilkinson, & Patterson, 1986; Guterman, Eggers, Riley, Greene, & Terrell, 1988; Hatten & Gibson, 1987; Iglehart, 1986). According to American Hospital Association data (ProPAC, 1988, 1990), the average length of stay for patients over age 65 dropped from 10.1 days in 1982 to just under 8.8 days in 1985. Between 1985 and 1989, hospital length of stay for the same group increased slightly to and stabilized at just over 8.8 days (ProPAC, 1990). ProPAC surmises that hospitals have reached the limit of their ability to substitute preadmission or postdischarge services for inpatient services.

The advent of the PPS also brought about an unexpected decline in hospital admissions (Hatten & Gibson, 1987; ProPAC, 1988; Sloan, Morrisey, & Valvona, 1988). Reports on the Medicare Statistical System data set show admissions falling 11.3% in the first 3 years under the PPS (Guterman et al., 1988; Hatten & Gibson, 1987). Admissions for all age groups combined have fallen annually since 1983, averaging a 2.1% per year decrease for the years 1984 through 1989 compared with an average 1% per year increase between 1978 and 1983. The rate of admissions of persons 65 and over rose slightly each year between 1987 and 1989, after a dramatic drop in 1985, but remains far below pre-PPS rates (ProPAC, 1990). The annual change in the rate of hospital admissions for the elderly averaged 4.8% between 1978 and 1983 (prior to the implementation of the PPS) and decreased by almost 1% per year between 1984 and 1989 (ProPAC, 1990).

Declining lengths of stay coupled with fewer admissions have, of course, contributed to diminished occupancy rates. The rate in community hospitals declined from 76% in 1981 to 69% in 1984 (ProPAC, 1986). During the first eight months of 1986, the average occupancy rate for hospitals was less than 64% (ProPAC, 1987b).

Changes in Physician Practice

Although large data sets lend themselves to easy recognition and statistical analysis of changes taking place at the institutional level, changes in physician practice cannot be overlooked. Physicians, as gatekeepers to the hospital, have adjusted their behavior to effect institutional changes.

The prospective payment system has had a pronounced impact on physician decisions concerning inpatient care. In a national sample of more than 4,000 physicians, 64% reported pressure to discharge patients sooner than they would prefer, and 73% reported pressure to shift diagnostic testing to outpatient settings (Rosenbach & Cromwell, 1985). A survey of 648 members of the American Society of Internal Medicine (ASIM, 1988) indicates that internists believe that the PPS has lessened the quality of patient care. Mirroring the findings of Rosenbach and Cromwell (1985), the ASIM survey shows 63% of physicians reporting premature discharge of patients. Nurse shortages (54%), delays in necessary hospitalizations (55%), and improper Peer Review Organization denials (68%) were cited as additional factors contributing to declines in the quality of care (ASIM, 1988).

Neu and Harrison (1988), in a study conducted for the Rand Corporation, report that, although average length of stay in acute care hospitals declined after implementation of the PPS (from 9.8 to 7.8 days in the study sample), there was no evidence to support the claim that patients were being discharged "quicker and sicker." Neu and Harrison note that, not only did an increase in the number of readmissions to hospitals from skilled nursing facility (SNF) care (as might be expected if patients were sicker at discharge) not occur, but that there was "a clear positive correlation between home health care use in a state and average hospital lengths of stay" (Neu & Harrison, 1988, p. ix). The most important finding of the Rand study is that the PPS is associated with "a 20 percent rise in the rate with which patients are discharged from the hospital with instability," which, combined with other discharge-related phenomena, has raised death rates 0.2 and 0.9 percentage points (Kahn, Draper, Keeler, et al., 1992, p. xi).

Quality Versus Utilization

The Peer Review Organization (PRO) represents one of Medicare's two principal quality assurance programs, the second being Medicare's conditions of participation (ProPAC, 1990). While the PROs are not, strictly speaking, elements of the prospective payment system, the two work in tandem to attempt to effectuate cost savings. Although the role of the PROs has been touted as "quality control," they have focused on utilization rather than on quality (Institute of Medicine [IOM], 1990).

Much of the research on inpatient care and the PPS has explored the issues of quality, access, and cost. Researchers have speculated that PPS incentives might lead to shifting expensive or complicated cases to other hospitals or to shortening care to the point of jeopardizing full patient recovery (ProPAC, 1990). The U.S. Senate Special Committee on Aging (1985) claims that the discharge status of Medicare patients has been altered under the PPS and that seriously ill patients are being inappropriately and prematurely released from hospitals. Indeed, multiple admission for certain kinds of cases may indicate that quality of care during the first admission was compromised (ProPAC, 1990). The findings of studies on the readmission of Medicare patients have, however, been somewhat inconsistent.

In monitoring changes in utilization and quality of care in 729 hospitals before and after implementation of the PPS, DesHarnais and associates (1987) found that the prospective payment system reduced hospital utilization for Medicare patients, but the authors detected no deterioration in quality of care. In a California study (California Hospital Association, 1986), the PPS was not found to be affecting the readmission rate at most hospitals. And, contrary to expectations, hospital readmission rates among Medicare patients in nursing homes did not rise after the introduction of the PPS (Neu & Harrison, 1988). Schramm and Gabel (1988), however, found that hospital readmission rates for all patients increased under the prospective payment system, but at a lower rate than in the years previous to the implementation of the system. Fueling the Senate claim, the Health Care Financing Administration (HCFA) reported almost 5,000 cases of premature discharge and inappropriate transfer between October 1983 and May 1985 (Kusserow, 1986).

Sager, Leventhal, and Easterling (1987) report that hospitalizations among Medicaid-reimbursed nursing home patients increased by as much as 72% after implementation of the PPS. The researchers suggest that physician "manipulation" of the PPS is resulting in the rehospitalization of nursing home patients prematurely discharged from acute care settings. Guterman and associates (1988) report that the average severity of illness at both admission and discharge was greater in the PPS period than before the prospective payment system was implemented. ProPAC (1990) reports that, between 1979 and 1983, 30-day readmission rates increased, on average, slightly more than 2% annually, and, between 1984 and 1986, annual increases averaged 1.3%. Since 1986, however, readmission rates have fallen, and, in 1988, readmission rates were lower than in 1984 (ProPAC, 1990).

Kotelchuck (1986) argues that, because there is neither a universal definition of quality of care nor a data collection system to monitor it, quality outcomes of the PPS are in question for some 29 million older Americans. She believes strongly that the most valid indicator of quality of care is patient health status outcome following discharge, and she emphasizes that research on the experiences of beneficiaries under the prospective payment system "must not stop at the hospital door" but continue throughout an illness episode (Kotelchuck, 1986).

The Institute of Medicine (1990) offers a definition of quality of care and proposes a strategy for improving quality under Medicare. The institute defines quality of care as "the degree to which health services for individuals and populations increase the likelihood of desired health outcomes and are consistent with current professional knowledge" (IOM, 1990, p. 4).

The PPS and Posthospital Care

Changes in hospital and physician provision of care to the elderly under the prospective payment system are having a domino effect on other parts of the health care system (Guterman et al., 1988; Wood & Estes, 1990). In fact, the change in location of care from acute care settings to alternative sites is one of the major consequences of the prospective payment system. Much of the research to date shows that the PPS has increased the demand for medically oriented skilled nursing care after discharge from the hospital. Shorter than optimal hospital lengths of stay among Medicare patients have resulted in sicker persons returning home and entering nursing homes and other posthospital institutions (Shaughnessy & Kramer, 1990).

Harrington and collegues (Chapter 7) find that most nursing home administrators in 1986 and 1987 experienced some impact of the prospective payment system (Institute for Health & Aging [IHA], 1986, 1987). Three fourths of the respondents reported higher acuity ratings among patients and the necessity for provision of higher levels of care than had been the case in 1984. In response to the increasing acuity levels of patients, more than half of the facilities reported adding high-intensity skilled nursing care services.

In fiscal year 1984, hospitals operating under the PPS were almost 3 times more likely to discharge Medicare patients to skilled nursing facilities (SNFs), intermediate care facilities (ICFs), or home health agencies than were non-PPS hospitals (U.S. General Accounting Office [GAO], 1986). Insofar as the discharge of patients from hospitals to other health care institutions (rather than to the home) indicates continued need for formal care, the increased rate of discharges to SNFs suggests that patients being discharged from hospitals operating under the PPS are generally sicker than patients being discharged from non-PPS hospitals. Postacute services are being used as substitutes for the hospital at the end of a stay (ProPAC, 1990).

A national study conducted by Rand (Neu & Harrison, 1988) documents a significant change in the percentage of Medicare patients using posthospital SNF or home health care between 1981 and 1984-1985. Almost 17% of patients discharged from an acute care hospital in the 1984-1985 period used one or another of the services noted above compared with only 12% in 1981. Between 1981 and 1984-1985, the total number of SNF users increased by nearly 28%. Furthermore, Medicare-reimbursed SNF care took on a shorter term, less "chronic" character after the introduction of the PPS, and the average number of home health visits per user rose from 12.8 to 14.1 during the study period (Gornick & Hall, 1988; Neu & Harrison, 1988; Shaughnessy & Kramer, 1990).

Guterman and associates (1988) report that the number of beneficiaries using home health care services following hospitalization rose 55% between 1981 and 1985 across all age groups and geographic locations. The Rand study (Neu & Harrison, 1988) document the fact that older patients are more likely to use posthospital care than are younger patients, women more than men, and that a few diagnosis-related groups (DRGs) account for the bulk of discharges to posthospital care.

Van Gelder and Bernstein (1986) cite a 1985 U.S. Department of Health and Human Services report that suggests a fairly strong relationship between shortened hospital stays and the use of home health care (U.S. DHHS, 1985). In five of the six large urban communities studied, home health care providers reported having to deliver more intensive care than had been the case in the past. Measures of the increased intensity include more visits per case, more weekend visits, longer visits, more daily visits, and growth in the number of patients with high-tech equipment to be managed. Between 1986 and 1988, the rate of use of home health care services fell, but only due to increased denial rates for Medicare coverage after all-time high use in 1986 (ProPAC, 1990). Medicare expenditures for home care rose by 13.6% between 1988 and 1989 after improvements in the administrative process led to a new spurt of utilization (ProPAC, 1990).

Between 1981 and 1985, use of skilled nursing facilities increased by 23% and SNF admissions as a percentage of hospital discharges rose by 65% (DesHarnais, Kobrinski, Chesney, Long, Ament, & Fleming, 1987; Feder, Hadley, & Zuckerman, 1987; Lyles, 1986; Van Gelder & Bernstein, 1986; Wood & Estes, 1990; Wood et al., 1986). While the provisions of the Medicare Catastrophic Coverage Act of 1988 were in effect, admissions of Medicare beneficiaries for SNF care increased by 57% (ProPAC, 1990).

Conclusion

The adequacy of formal posthospital community-care services in meeting the needs of the elderly remains questionable. A former Deputy Administrator of the Health Care Financing Administration stated that there would not be a problem with premature discharge if there were appropriate and available "receptor providers" to which patients could go (Willging, 1986). Early discharge is not necessarily inappropriate, but follow-up services in the community are often unavailable or substandard (U.S. Senate, 1985). In effect, the new payment system may be placing extraordinary strains on existing health and social service providers in the community (Kinoy, Adamson, & Sherry, 1988). Reductions in inpatient care following the implementation of the prospective payment system have increased the demand for home care and nursing home care, but in many communities these systems are overburdened. They were, in fact, overloaded even before the advent of the prospective payment system. With the possibility of care gaps developing in the community system because of the inability to meet the demands of severely ill discharged patients (Sankar, Newcomer, & Wood, 1986), elderly persons may be in danger of falling into a no-care zone (Goldberg & Estes, 1990; Kotelchuck, 1986).

Early case reports uncovered problems for patients requiring heavy medical care and trying to gain access to SNFs and home health care under the PPS (CHA, 1986; Heinz, 1986). The availability of institutional posthospital care services was judged to be "inadequate to marginal" (U.S. GAO, 1987b). Other major barriers to posthospital care were reported to be Medicare rules and regulations as well as patient needs for complex skilled services (Chelimsky, 1985, 1987; U.S. GAO, 1986, 1987b). Access to nursing home care has become more limited as the illness acuity levels of earlier discharged hospital patients have increased, thus requiring more complex treatment from highly trained professionals with expertise in gerontology (Hing, 1987a; Shaughnessy, Kramer, & Schlenker, 1987; U.S. GAO, 1983). In a national study on "transitional care" or subacute care in hospitals, just over 5% of Medicare patients spent one or more days as subacute patients (Manard, Gong, Meicel, & Kupperman, 1988). More than half of these patients (55%) were waiting for skilled nursing home placement.

With the importance of postacute care services heightened under the PPS, hospitals have begun to branch out in the health care marketplace (McCreary, 1986). In a clear demonstration of vertical integration, the PPS has accelerated the growth of hospital-based "step-down" or "short-term long term care" (Brody & Magel, 1984), with significant increases in the provision of home health services, inpatient posthospital care services, hospice services (ProPAC, 1986), and hospital swing beds (Guterman et al., 1988). A further consequence of the PPS is the change in the location of care from the acute care setting to alternative (outpatient) sites. In effect, an estimated 21 million days of care have been transferred annually since the early days of this policy (Stark, 1987a).

The effects of the prospective payment system are far reaching, even revolutionary. The shock waves of the policy reverberate through many parts of the health and social service systems. The PPS has shifted a large portion of the provision of care to alternative community-based services (Harlow & Wilson, 1985; Wood & Estes, 1988, 1990), expanding the importance of the concept of the continuum of care. The full spectrum of health care and social services must now be taken into account when considering appropriate services for the elderly patient. The purpose of this entire volume is to explore multiple facets of posthospital services and long term care in light of the trends identified in this chapter. The exploration begins in the next chapter with consideration of the restructuring of the nonprofit sector.

CHAPTER 2

Restructuring of the Nonprofit Sector

For-profit health care . . . and the resultant corporatization of the "not-for-profit" firms is removing health care from those Americans most in need. The exclusion of this population from necessary services appears to be related to a systematic attempt to curtail public consumption of health and other formerly public resources. The implications of this corporate transformation portend further breakdown of family and community caring networks, which may harm all "consumers" of health care, not only the poor.

Whiteis & Salmon, 1990, p. 129

▼

The 1980s initiated a period of major challenge and change for nonprofit sector institutions and organizations (Estes & Bergthold, 1989; Hodgkinson, Lyman, et al., 1989), yet there has been little empirical research on these changes and their effects on community-based services. Despite much academic and popular attention to theories of crisis and the welfare state (Habermas, 1975; O'Connor, 1987; Offe, 1984), the nonprofit sector (NPS) has been largely ignored in these debates, with a few exceptions (Estes & Alford, 1990; Ostrander, Langton, & Van Til, 1987; Wolch, 1990).

The private nonprofit, voluntary, independent, or third sector is a vast and amorphous collection of diverse entities including (a) organizations providing goods or services to their members (e.g., voluntary associations), (b) funding agencies and private philanthropic organizations (e.g., foundations), (c) nonprofit service agencies, and (d) churches. These organizations usually have either a 501(c)(3) or

---

NOTE: The authors of this chapter are Carroll L. Estes and Elizabeth A. Binney.

(4) tax code designation for tax-exempt organizations (i.e., public charities with annual revenues of less than $5,000). Because more than half of both the employment and the revenues of the nonprofit sector are in health and social services, anything that broadly affects this sector can be expected to affect health and social services, including postacute and long term care services. Similarly, changes affecting nonprofit health and social services have implications for the nonprofit sector as a whole. Moreover, events and conditions that affect the government (the State) and the corporate sectors also have substantial implications for the nonprofit sector (Estes & Alford, 1990; Estes et al., 1989).

Public policy as well as political and economic conditions in the 1980s have profoundly affected nonprofits. The changes that have transpired are tantamount to a restructuring of the nonprofit sector, potentially threatening to unravel it (Estes & Alford, 1990; Estes & Bergthold, 1989; Estes et al., 1989). Empirical evidence of these changes is found both internally and externally to the nonprofit sector itself. External indicators include changes in federal- and state-level policy, including tax codes and subsidies, in addition to rhetorical, legal, and other challenges to the legitimacy of nonprofit sector institutions. Internal indicators are changes occurring within individual nonprofits, such as labor restructuring and the unbundling of services. Both types of indicators reflect economic, political, and ideological aspects of struggles and crises occurring within and between elements of the nonprofit sector and the corporate and State sectors of society.

Crisis and the Nonprofit Sector

The literature dealing with State theory and crisis theory largely overlooks the nonprofit sector (NPS), and few scholars of the nonprofit sector deal with the topic of crisis. An exception is Peter Hall, who argues that there is (a) a crisis *of* the nonprofit sector due to Reagan rhetoric claiming that the State has inappropriately usurped the responsibilities of the private sector and backed by policies of deregulation and domestic budget cuts; (b) a crisis *within* the nonprofit sector, as reflected in internal pressures for increased "management, professionalization, and entrepreneurship"; and (c) a crisis of "nonprofit scholarship" (Hall, 1987, pp. 12-13). Hall cites the limits of pluralist assumptions about the NPS and calls for abandoning the rhetoric that the sector is independent of the State (Estes & Alford, 1990; Ostrander et al., 1987; Salamon, 1987a, 1987b).

Important issues concern the interrelations of the State and corporate sectors with the nonprofit service sector under conditions of fiscal austerity and political struggle. The nonprofit health and social service sector is an arena for economic, ideological, and political struggles that have consequences for social policy and service provision at the local level. A key problem is understanding how crisis tendencies in these sectors are displaced into and processed through the reorganization and restructuring of nonprofit sector health and social services.

A review of policy and funding shifts during the 1980s indicates that the legitimacy problems faced by government (e.g., declining public confidence) have contributed to legitimacy crisis tendencies in the nonprofit sector as well (Estes et al., 1989). The nonprofit sector tends to function as a buffer, absorbing crisis tendencies of both the State and the corporate sectors through cutback or expansion (Estes & Alford, 1990). The way the nonprofit sector is used and how it fares depend on the sociohistorical situation (e.g., specific constructions and manifestations of crisis and political struggle). In addition, in an area such as health, the restructuring of the corporate sector vis-à-vis the State and the nonprofit sectors is one potential solution to crisis tendencies in the economic, political, and/or social realms (Estes & Alford, 1990). An example is the group of changes in State policy used in the early 1980s to encourage the expansion of for-profit health and social services, which had traditionally been controlled by nonprofit providers. These changes abruptly altered the climate in which nonprofits operate and contributed to a restructuring of major parts of the delivery system.

Consistent with U.S. exceptionalism and a weak State, the government has fulfilled three significant roles identified by Jürgen Habermas (1975) in relation to the economy. Recast in terms of health and social services, the State has (a) created productive opportunities for private capital through civil laws and regulations protecting the market (public policy promoting and financing private rather than public institutions); (b) limited its own activities in health and social services to those that complement the market (not engaging in direct service provision for the most part) and encouraged the entry of new proprietary forms of organization in the human services; and (c) engaged in market-replacing activities by subsidizing the costs of an increasingly inaccessible, private, and highly profitable health care system that feeds the continued growth of a large and powerful medical-industrial complex (Habermas, 1975).

According to the most recent data (1987), the NPS share of the total U.S. national income of $3.8 trillion is approximately 6.5%, or $247 billion, which includes $86.5 billion in assigned value for volunteers (Hodgkinson & Weitzman, 1989). Hodgkinson and Weitzman (1989) estimate that there are 1.3 million NPS organizations (5.9% of all U.S. entities—1987 data) including nearly 350,000 churches. The sector accounts for 8% of earnings of the total national labor force, or $217 billion. This represents estimated 1987 earnings of about $13 million and 6 million volunteer workers, or 10.7% of the total (paid and unpaid) work force (Hodgkinson & Weitzman, 1989).

Boundary Problems and Contested Domain

The legal, economic, and political status of nonprofit sector entities is the object of considerable conflict and challenge (Alford & Estes, 1987). The nonprofit sector has been created legally by the U.S. tax code; economically, by State and private sector funding; politically, by participatory pluralism and a limited welfare state; and sociocultturally, by the values and ideology of individualism. With deregulation, budget cuts, and the resurgence of market ideologies in the 1980s, nonprofit service organizations found themselves in a problematic situation. A full assessment of the consequences is complicated by the rapidity of changes taking place and the growth of mixed organizational types that combine nonprofit and for-profit entities.

One result is a blurring of the boundaries between the nonprofit and for-profit sectors that has profound consequences for the economic, political, and ideological fortunes of entities operating in the nonprofit sector. With the addition of new and mixed organizational models (e.g., health corporations) that combine nonprofit entities and proprietary subsidiaries, nonprofits have been pressed (if not coerced) to create and seek out their own forms of profit making—a phenomenon heretofore considered antithetical to the mission or raison d'être of the nonprofit sector (Skloot, 1987). Multiple pressures and demands on the corporate, State, and nonprofit sectors have led to behaviors and actions on the part of nonprofit organizations that have augmented the blurring of the boundaries between the sectors and contributed to the current restructuring of the nonprofit sector.

As nonprofits have increasingly found themselves under attack, the contradictions in the organizing principles underlying the nonprofit sector have become increasingly apparent. The societal functions of the nonprofit sector have traditionally been portrayed in terms of providing (a) a variety of partially tested social innovations;

(b) countervailing definitions of reality and morality; (c) a "play" element for society (e.g., novelty, beauty, recreation); (d) directly expressive groups; (e) social integration by buffering and linking groups that might otherwise be in competition with each other; (f) new ideas about social behavior through voluntarism; (g) educational experiences; (h) an embodiment of mystery, wonder, and the sacred; (i) mechanisms of personal growth and expression; (j) a source of "negative feedback" with regard to other institutions of society; (k) support to the economic system of society; and (l) a latent resource for all types of goal attainment in the interest of the society as a whole (Smith, 1983).

A hallmark of the 1980s was that these traditional functions of the nonprofit sector began to appear outdated and idealized and were challenged as being less reflective of reality than ever before. Observers both outside and within the sector have observed that the perception and practice of some of these functions have been questioned, seriously eroded, and, in some cases, subjected to outright attack. The pressures for rationalization of the behavior of nonprofits have contributed to professionalization of staff, increased reporting requirements, and regulatory restrictions in the sector. The emergence of professional nonprofit careers and management has raised serious concerns as to the potential loss of power for voluntary nonprofit boards in contrast to the increasing power of paid staff. William E. Simon once even warned that professional staffers were becoming "new class reformers" who were attempting to change society in "collectivist" ways (Simon, 1980).

In the health arena, the nation's oldest federated charity, the United Hospital Fund, sponsors Mission Matters, a program devoted to reminding nonprofit hospitals of their distinguishing characteristics and their unique community and human values, the long-term commitment to communities and community service, special governance and accountability to the community, the tradition of institutional voluntarism, and the bond between the community and providers (including nonprofit employees and volunteers). In response to the challenges to nonprofit hospitals occurring with the growth of pro-market ideology and policy, the fund urges voluntary hospitals to retain their special character and mission as nonprofits to set themselves apart from their for-profit counterparts (Seay & Vladeck, 1988; United Hospital Fund, 1987a, 1987b).

One major result of the turbulent environment of the 1980s has been intense organizational change within the nonprofit sector. Increasingly, nonprofit organizations have shown the need for flexibility, as illustrated by the high level of organizational change (Clarke & Estes, 1992; DiMaggio & Powell, 1983; Powell & Freidkin, 1987). The degree to which changes in goals, management, and structure are successful depends in part on their incorporation or acceptance by the State (through legal and regulatory support or challenge), the corporate sector (through political support or challenge), and the public (through support of or challenges to the legitimacy of nonprofits). At the core of these organizational changes for nonprofits are contradictions that have been created by shifting and diminished sources of support, multiple constituencies, lack of objective accounting measures, and the often politicized goals of nonprofits (Powell & Freidkin, 1987) in the face of a mandate to maintain a charitable mission.

One signal of the environmental uncertainty facing nonprofits is the 1980 founding and growth of a major national organization, Independent Sector (IS), to promote giving, volunteering, and not-for-profit initiative. The IS has attempted to stimulate interest in and knowledge about the "voluntary spirit" (O'Connell, 1983). It has collected data and promoted research on the nonprofit sector (Hodgkinson & Weitzman, 1984, 1986, 1989).

Two Nonprofit Sectors

Researchers have recently noted the shifting boundaries and "fading distinctions" between nonprofits and for-profits in the face of changes in the political and economic environment. Van Til (1987, 1988) and Ferris and Graddy (1988) note that increased dependence on government funding and commercialization efforts by nonprofits have resulted in behavior by nonprofit organizations that mirrors that of proprietary sector entities. As this kind of isomorphism occurs (Clarke & Estes, 1992), an increasing number of questions are raised concerning the appropriateness of public policies intended to support the nonprofit sector (Estes & Alford, 1990). The proper way to classify and treat the nonprofit sector as a whole, and various elements within it, is being debated both within and outside the sector. The very diversity of organizational types within the nonprofit, third, independent, or voluntary sector, long cited as one of its major contributions to pluralism (and thus deserving of special protection) (Douglas, 1983), has become a focal point of contention. Lines drawn in this debate reflect, in microcosm, the internal and external indicators of the restructuring of the nonprofit sector. The debate concerning just what the third sector does and should constitute is, itself, contributing to a restructuring.

Some scholars have recently concluded that there are, in reality, two independent sectors and that they are increasingly at odds with and threatening to each other (Hansmann, 1988; Salamon, 1988). The first independent sector, the philanthropic or donative sector, represents the charity-supported organizations at risk of losing the protections necessary for their continued functioning because of the emergence of a second independent sector—the commercial nonprofit sector, which derives most of its revenues from the sale of goods or services. These commercial nonprofits have been portrayed as threatening the legitimation and continued support of the entire sector because of their changing functions and behavior. One scholar has even suggested that steps might be taken by the philanthropic nonprofit sector to disassociate itself formally from this second nonprofit sector to protect the existing privilege and function of the first nonprofit sector (Hansmann, 1988). The effect of such a separation would be to alienate from the sector an entire corps of service providers, many in health care, that currently constitute more than half of the sector. The threat to the nonprofit sector, internalized in this way, represents a major contradiction. That is, scholars and leaders of the sector itself, in reassessing and realigning their perspectives and interests to protect the sector, may, in so doing, be forced to sacrifice core principles and key participants.

Health and Social Service Subsectors

Within the nonprofit sector, the health and social service components are important for several reasons. First, they represent a significant proportion of the activity of the nonprofit sector; together, they constitute 62% of both the operating expenditures and the employees of the nonprofit sector (Hodgkinson & Weitzman, 1989).

Second, the restructuring of nonprofit health and social services is of particular interest because nonprofits represent the majority of the providers of essential human services to the elderly and other age groups. According to one national study, nonprofits provide more than half (56%) of all community social services delivered and nearly half (44%) of all community health services (Salamon, 1987b). Further, the majority (71%) of hospital beds in the United States are under nonprofit ownership (United Hospital Fund, 1987b).

A third reason for examining health and social services is the magnitude of their cost and public expenditures for them. In particular, the provision of health services is extremely costly and represents a growing percentage of the nation's gross national product (now approaching 14%), with public expenditures approximating $800 billion. In addition, in 1980, nearly half of all publicly provided health dollars went to nonprofit sector institutions, and the majority of publicly provided social service dollars went to nonprofit organizations (Estes & Wood, 1986). Therefore the support of nonprofit organizations by government expenditures has understandably been targeted as a major political and economic issue, particularly in the context of cost containment and fiscal constraint.

Fourth, with 40% of the nation's multibillion-dollar health bill paid (and thus guaranteed) through public financing, health services are of growing interest to the corporate sector because of their revenue potential, particularly in the current intensely competitive environment in which market expansion is essential to profit making. Nonprofit health and social services may therefore be more susceptible to crisis tendencies (e.g., attacks) than other components of the nonprofit sector, given that they provide a large proportion of socially necessary services. Health and social services provide an important lens through which to view trends and conditions affecting nonprofit sector services.

Nonprofit health entities are by far the largest component of the nonprofit sector as measured by current operating expenses ($134 billion, or 51% of total nonprofit sector expenditures), wages and salaries ($61 billion, or 62%), and number of employees (3.4 million, or 46%). Nonprofit social and legal services rank third in the total sector in terms of current operating expenses ($28 billion, or 11%), wages and salaries ($13 billion, or 11%), and employees (1.2 million, or 16%) (Hodgkinson & Weitzman, 1989).

National Trends and the Nonprofit Sector

The 1960s were a period of unprecedented growth for nonprofit services compared with total personal consumption expenditures and total services (Hodgkinson & Weitzman, 1989)—the share of expenditures for nonprofit services increased from 13.7% to 17.5% (1960-1969). After 1970, the proportion of nonprofit expenditures for all services remained fairly stable at 18% (Hodgkinson & Weitzman, 1989). A period of expansion followed between the mid-1970s and early 1980s (specifically, 1977-1982) in which nonprofit health and social services grew rapidly (with health growing an average of 20.9% and social services 12.5% per year). In 1982, federal funding declined sharply. Between 1982 and 1984, the annual growth rate for nonprofit health and social services slowed to 10.5% and 7.8%, respectively (Hodgkinson & Weitzman, 1986). The Independent Sector estimates that annual funds for the nonprofit health subsector grew more than 200% between 1977 and 1987. Health grew more rapidly than any other nonprofit subsector. In contrast, in the nonprofit social and legal services, "a decline was particularly noticeable" between 1977 and 1984 (Hodgkinson & Weitzman, 1989). The social and legal services share of all independent sector annual funds dropped from 10.2% to 8.4% but rose again slightly by 1987, to 9.1% (Hodgkinson & Weitzman, 1989).

The U.S. government share of total revenues in the nonprofit health subsector increased slightly, climbing from 32% in 1977 to 35% in 1984 (a proportion that remained stable to 1987). The government share in the social and legal services subsector declined significantly, however, falling from 54% in 1977 to 44% in 1984. By 1987, the government provided only 41% of the total annual support for nonprofit sector social and legal services (Hodgkinson & Weitzman, 1986, 1989). Reflecting this trend, social service outlays declined from 1.5% to .84% of the GNP between 1976 and 1992 (Estes, 1991). The decline in government support of major elements of the nonprofit sector was due largely to federal budget cuts between 1982 and 1987 as well as to subsequent deficit reduction efforts (Abramson & Salamon, 1986).

Equally important changes affected other sources of support for the health and social service subsectors. For social and legal services, there was an increase in the proportion of payments from fees and charges (rising from 9.5% to 13.7% between 1977 and 1987) as well as in the proportion of funds from private contributions (rising more modestly from 31.9% to 33.9%). For health services, payments from both the private sector and the government increased, but funding from philanthropy declined from 9.7% to 6.7% of total support during the same decade (Hodgkinson & Weitzman, 1989).

In addition to reductions in federal funds and changes in sources of support, five major trends of the 1980s have been identified in relation to the nonprofit sector (Estes & Wood, 1986). Three are general trends and two are specific to nonprofit health and social services. The relatively severe economic problems of corporate America constitute the first trend, characterized by lower profit rates than in the two previous decades, increased competition, and the weeding out of weak, inefficient businesses through unprecedented numbers of bankruptcies, mergers, and corporate consolidations. These economic conditions increased corporate pressures to search for new sources of profit, including the expansion of business into potentially lucrative areas of health and in-home services that formerly were largely the province of nonprofits.

Alterations in the interpretation and structure of the tax code represent a second trend. The 1986 tax reform legislation in effect eliminated the tax advantage for charitable contributions for many low- and moderate-income individuals by eliminating the charitable deduction for nonitemizers. Experts have warned that this could mean the loss of billions of dollars in contributions and millions of hours of contributed volunteer time for nonprofit organizations (Auten & Rudney, 1985; Clotfelter, 1985; Lindsey, 1987; Schiff, 1987; Schiff & Weisbrod, 1986). While data are insufficient to assess the actual impact of the 1986 Tax Reform Act, Clotfelter notes that "simulations based on estimated models of individual giving suggest . . . a reduction in total giving . . . on the order of 15 percent below what would otherwise have been contributed" (Clotfelter, 1989, p. 114). Further, the $750 billion in tax cuts for wealthy individuals and corporations in the 1981 Economic Recovery Tax Act dampened the advantages of tax-free contributions to nonprofits.

Third, opposition to nonprofit organizations from small business has been growing, commencing with a report by the Small Business Administration (U.S. SBA, 1983) criticizing what it called the unfair advantages given to nonprofits with which small businesses must compete. The SBA advocated circumscribing the ability of nonprofits to engage in any commercial activity whatsoever. This proposal resulted in a struggle over the heretofore ambiguous definition of "commercial activity." In addition, the SBA initiated a multistate program to inform the general public about the unfair advantage afforded nonprofits by the tax code. This move dramatically escalated public interest and media coverage of the issue. As recently as 1991, the Business Coalition for Nonprofit Competition pressed for eliminating the nonprofit tax exemption for activities for which a commercial counterpart exists (Independent Sector, 1991).

A fourth trend more specifically affecting health and social service nonprofits is the deregulation initiated by the Carter administration and accelerated by the Reagan administration. Deregulation has both facilitated and quickened the entry of proprietaries into nonprofit sector home care and medical services on the assumption that increased competition will reduce costs.

A fifth factor is the implementation of austerity and federal cost-containment policies and, more recently, deficit reduction measures that have seriously affected nonprofit organizations of all types, especially service agencies. More specifically, hospital prospective payment and reimbursement policies aimed at cost containment under the $90 billion Medicare program have altered the type and amount of health services traditionally provided by nonprofits.

An emerging literature illustrates how these trends are affecting nonprofit organizations (Skloot, 1987). Broad social trends are reflected in a series of empirical indicators of a restructuring of nonprofit health and social service components (Estes, 1986; Estes & Wood, 1986). Restructuring is expected to have serious ramifications for the nonprofit sector as a whole. An important feature of this restructuring is that parts of the nonprofit service sector are competing with each other in unprecedented ways. For example, large nonprofit hospitals now opening their own home health agencies are competing with smaller, preexisting freestanding nonprofit community home health agencies. Nonprofit service agencies are being disciplined to act like for-profits; inefficient nonprofits are being weeded out; and there is a potential domination of the nonprofit health and social service field by new forms of mixed agencies that combine nonprofit with for-profit modes and multi-institutional systems of care (via vertical and horizontal integration).

Indicators of Restructuring

The restructuring of the nonprofit health and social services is demonstrated by a number of specific empirical indicators—indicators that also provide evidence for a theory about the role of the nonprofit sector in the context of broader economic, political, and social crisis trends (Estes & Alford, 1990). External indicators, such as tax law changes, are located at the macro level, hence outside of an individual organization. Internal indicators, such as high staff turnover or high organizational death rates, exist primarily at the nonprofit organizational level, although the pressures for internal changes may originate externally. Both types of indicators can be broadly associated with crisis tendencies in the political, ideological, and economic arenas of society.

External Indicators

External indicators of the economic crisis tendencies that have contributed to the restructuring of nonprofits involve a series of challenges concerning the status, identity, and treatment of the nonprofit sector. Tax code and regulatory changes and legal challenges have significantly affected nonprofit sector status and activities.

Political and Ideological Challenges

Encouraged by the political climate of the Reagan administration, government and business entities mounted a campaign to narrow definitions, eliminate what they term "unfair competitive advantages," and erect prohibitions against the entry and continued operation of nonprofit sector organizations in areas considered the domain of the proprietary sector (U.S. House of Representatives, 1988a; U.S. SBA, 1983). For example, in response to regulatory changes resulting from 1986 tax reform legislation, the small business advocacy group (the Business Coalition for Nonprofit Competition) has organized to contest the formal tax status of various types of nonprofits. In some cases, businesses successfully challenged the legal right of nonprofits to operate in activities that compete with proprietaries (e.g., for-profit health clubs versus the YMCA). Additionally, the Small Business Administration encouraged federal agencies to set aside contracts exclusively for small businesses (by definition excluding nonprofits). Further, the U.S. Office of Management and Budget (OMB) guidelines (Circular A-76) now require nonprofits to add an amount to federal contract bids equal to the taxes a for-profit bidder would pay so as to make the bids comparable. Only if the bid is still below that of the proprietary vendor can a nonprofit be awarded a contract (Skloot, 1987).

Federal law holds that nonprofit earnings directly tied to their exempt mission are not taxable. Business advocacy groups, however, are increasingly pushing for a narrow definition of "related income" and aggressive policing of nonprofit sector activities by the IRS (Skloot, 1987). Voluntary hospitals are a particular focus of concern, with more than a dozen states and localities scrutinizing and reevaluating their tax-exemption policies (Seay & Sigmond, 1989). For example, in 1986, the Utah State Supreme Court upheld a Utah county tax assessor's challenge to a 1980 state law that granted property tax exemptions to nonprofits. The court ruled that, if a hospital did not demonstrate that they provided free care to indigents in an amount equal to the exemption, it no longer had a right to the exemption (Friedman, 1988; Seay & Vladeck, 1988; Traska, 1988). This ruling followed a lengthy legal and political battle in which the court set ambiguous guidelines for exemption, and a coalition of hospital and nursing home groups failed to achieve statewide consensus regarding the standards and procedures for meeting the guidelines. This decision not only affected Utah hospitals but also signaled to other states and localities that new sources of revenue might be lying untapped in the form of a challenge to the charitable status of nonprofits.

In the case of *Burlington, Vermont, v. the nonprofit Medical Center Hospital of Vermont*, the city and its socialist mayor billed the hospital $2.8 million in property taxes, based on the argument not only that the hospital must render 50% of its services free to be considered charitable and that more than half of its revenue had to derive from private philanthropy but also that a charitable organization must be free of private inurement. This last point raised a new challenge to nonprofits, most of which depend on professional management to remain viable yet are open to accusations that the compensation received by management is tied to the performance of the organization (Friedman, 1988). These and other suits have led to initiatives challenging the tax status of nonprofits, including a Florida proposal for a sales tax on hospital revenues tied to their level of indigent care and a federal proposal by Representative Pete Stark (1987b) to tax the investment income of nonprofits. Both are moves that nonprofits argue will hamper their ability to provide indigent care.

Additionally, in the early 1980s, the IRS proposed new regulations to clarify the Tax Reform Act of 1976, limiting the conditions under which nonprofits may lobby so severely as to bring that practice to a virtual halt. As originally proposed, the regulations would not only have severely increased the administrative and monitoring costs of foundations that make grants to any potentially liable nonprofit organization but also could have caused these funding sources to stop making grants to such organizations entirely, further jeopardizing nonprofits (Broaddus, 1987). Although these regulations were modified to limit their extreme impact on nonprofits (Smucker, 1991), they nevertheless have had a chilling effect on the voice of these entities.

In some cases, incorporation and tax laws are being amended on the federal and state levels to circumscribe nonprofit activities and to clarify and delimit the nature of the organizations themselves. This has occurred because, after a century of existence under broad and general legal status, the nonprofit sector began to be populated in the 1950s with large numbers of commercial nonprofits—nonprofits with income deriving primarily or exclusively from the sale of goods or services (Hansmann, 1980, 1987a, 1987b). Some of these entities evolved from formerly donative (largely charitably financed) nonprofits as well as from donative nonprofits that expanded into ancillary profit-making activities. In response to this commercialization or proprietarization, both tax and organizational law changes reflect attempts to move from a unitary notion of nonprofit organizations to differentiate among various types (see Simon, 1987, for a full summary of federal tax distinctions and restrictions). For example, both New York (in 1970) and California (in 1980) passed legislation differentiating types of nonprofits—New York into categories of (a) clubs, (b) charities, and (c) business with a public or quasi-public objective and California into categories of (a) religious, (b) secular-mutual benefit, and (c) secular-public benefit—each with increasing strictness of fiduciary standards and constraints.

On the federal level, the law has moved in a similar direction, taking at least three forms. First, the doctrine of charitable immunity in tort and labor law has all but been eliminated for nonprofits. Second, tax and regulatory law has begun to distinguish among different activities carried on by individual nonprofits, making them liable for income tax or postal charges on unrelated commercial activities. And, third, tax and regulatory law differentiates between certain types of nonprofits, with the 1986 Tax Reform Act denying exemption to two important categories of organizations formerly classified as 501(c)(3)—life and health insurance companies—causing Blue Cross/Blue Shield, for example, to lose its status as a nonprofit (Hansmann, 1987a, 1987b).

Legal challenges to the nonprofit sector are primarily due to economic interests, often with small- and medium-sized businesses attempting to halt or reverse what they consider the unfair economic advantages enjoyed by nonprofits competing in their markets. The legal challenges are intended to protect the economic feasibility and livelihood of private enterprise. The exact nature of the competition from nonprofits is under debate, however (e.g., Are service fees, a longtime source of income, ipso facto an indicator of commercial activity?). Also debated is the extent to which changes in the behavior of nonprofits reflect infiltration into these traditional activities by private business (DeVita & Salamon, 1987).

These conflicts signal the political and ideological content of the challenge to nonprofit organizations. Legislative lobbying and persuasion have been effective tools, along with legal challenges. Both federal and state government have participated in these activities in the name of efficiency, rationality, fiduciary responsibility, and decentralization of control. The ideological rhetoric of the Small Business Administration and allied groups emphasizes core values of competition, freedom, individualism, and, above all, fairness, while attacking the tax and other "advantages" accorded nonprofits (Hopkins, 1987). These ideological attacks, which have mobilized popular and political support from the business community and policymakers, have had significant economic impacts (Skloot, 1987). The ideological struggles threaten broad effects on public giving and volunteer time and also may have influenced the decline in corporate giving as a proportion of total charitable giving, which peaked at 5.8% in 1984 and declined to 4.7% in 1987 (Hodgkinson & Weitzman, 1989).

Economic Challenges

The decline in federal funding presents a direct economic challenge to the nonprofit sector, particularly to social services. The importance of federal support to the viability of the nonprofit sector is shown by the fact that, in 1980, the government share of funding for the nonprofit sector as a whole approximated $40.8 billion, or 35%, of the sector's total revenue. Some components of the nonprofit sector are particularly dependent on federal sources. Social services, for instance, depended on federal support for 55% of its total revenue in 1980, while medical care received government support for 36% of its revenue. In both cases, the government share outdistanced the support from private contributions and represented the largest single source of support except for private payments (Abramson & Salamon, 1986).

The most significant economic challenge to nonprofit services came in the form of the Reagan administration's federal spending reductions in fields in which nonprofit organizations are active. For example, the president's budget proposal for 1987-1989 represented $78 billion below the levels that would have existed had fiscal year (FY) 1980 spending levels been maintained (i.e., a net reduction of about $26 billion, or 25% per year over the 3-year period beginning in 1987) (Abramson & Salamon, 1986). Estimates of the direct impact on nonprofits were grim, particularly because of the extent to which government has relied on nonprofit organizations to deliver publicly funded services. Indeed, full implementation of Reagan's proposals would have meant a decline of 55% in the support received by social services (Abramson & Salamon, 1986).

It is noteworthy that these proposals followed a 4-year period of austerity (FY 1982-1986), during which the nonprofit sector had already suffered extensive reductions in federal support. Compared with FY 1980 levels, the inflation-adjusted value of federal spending in fields of extensive nonprofit activity (exclusive of Medicare and Medicaid) declined by $70 billion between 1982 and 1986, with yearly reductions of about $14 billion, or 14% (Abramson & Salamon, 1986).

Social services absorbed the largest losses of government support during the FY 1982-1986 period—a loss of $12 billion, or about $2.4 billion per year. By 1986, there had been a decline of 40% in federal support to social services compared with 1980 levels (Abramson & Salamon, 1986). In a decade comparison (1977 to 1987), Hodgkinson and Weitzman (1989) indicate that government support of social and legal services declined from 54.3% to 41.4%. This decline was compensated for by increases in the use of fees and charges (rising from 9.5% to 13.7%) and in private contributions (rising from 31.9% to 38.7%) as a proportion of total annual funds during the same decade.

Nonprofit health care entities as a whole received significantly increased federal support during the 1977-1987 decade, which reflected the rising cost of health financing primarily for hospital care through Medicare and Medicaid. For example, data for 1982-1986 show that nonprofit community health services suffered losses of $2.1 billion (–37%) at the same time that nonprofit financing through Medicare and Medicaid increased more than $22 billion (+23%) (Abramson & Salamon, 1986). Between 1977 and 1987, the proportion of annual payments to nonprofit health entities rose slightly from government (from 32.4% to 35.1%) and from the private sector (from 49.1% to 50.1%) while the proportion from individual contributors declined from 9.7% to 6.7% (Hodgkinson & Weitzman, 1989). The major exceptions to the 1980s federal cuts in services were Medicare and Medicaid. Acute medical care costs have continued to grow well above inflation and, with them, federal funding for the medical-industrial complex. Community health and community mental health centers and services present a different story. These services received policy treatment similar to that experienced by the social services—a near starvation diet.

In summary, with the primary exception of the financing of nonprofit hospital care through Medicare and Medicaid, overall federal funding of nonprofit social and health services has generally declined. Abramson and Salamon (1986) estimate, for example, that this drop exceeded 27% between 1980 and 1985 spending levels, which reflects the severe cuts in the 1981-1982 period. In light of the federal deficit, general economic conditions, and their loss of favor with business and some policymakers, nonprofits are unlikely to receive substantial (if any) increases in federal support in the near future.

Although there is agreement that government actions during the 1980s threatened the viability of nonprofit sector entities and forced many changes, there is disagreement about the cause. Some believe that government did not intend to weaken or threaten the nonprofit sector (Hall, 1987; Salamon, 1987a, 1987b). If budget cuts, challenges to the tax subsidies of nonprofits, reductions in tax incentives for giving and volunteering, and more stringent requirements on reporting, record keeping, commercial activities, and lobbying were not explicitly designed to weaken the nonprofit sector, they have, nevertheless, combined to strengthen and reinforce the proprietary sector in areas of historic dominance by nonprofits.

Economic challenges to the nonprofit sector are occurring on the state level as well. These are likely to continue if states experience fiscal problems of increasing intensity. States are struggling with budget deficits, recession-induced tax revenue reductions, and rising Medicaid spending (which grew almost 10% in 1991 alone). Legislative initiatives to place sales taxes on services, to repeal selected categories of tax exemption, and to impose service fees on nonprofits, for example, represent potential avenues for the augmentation of state revenues that are tempting "targets of opportunity" to both state and local lawmakers (Independent Sector, 1991).

Another external indicator of potential nonprofit sector difficulty is in the area of charitable giving. Part of the conflicting and contradictory nature of the nonprofit sector is reflected in changes in (a) corporate giving, (b) private giving, and (c) voluntary participation. As part of the rhetoric surrounding new federalism budget cuts, the private sector (both individual and business) was called upon to make up for declining federal support of human services. Many of the same legislators, politicians, and other notables who pressed for increased private sector support also, however, supported the Tax Reform Act of 1986, which nonprofits lobbied against because of the perceived negative effect that changes in the charitable deduction might have on individual giving and volunteering (Auten & Rudney, 1985; Clotfelter, 1985; Lindsey, 1987; Schiff, 1987; Schiff & Weisbrod, 1986).

Presidential and administrative rhetoric suggested that the private sector, especially philanthropy, fill the gap (Eisenberg, 1987). The debate over the private sector's assumption of responsibility in areas that have been traditionally public responsibility has serious economic, political, and ideological dimensions. For example, the "direct benefit doctrine," a notion that has pervaded corporate philanthropy from its inception, has renewed importance. Lawsuits upholding shareholder objections to corporate charity have created a broader interpretation of the direct benefit doctrine by which corporations could justify charitable contributions as long as the giving could be shown to have a direct benefit to the corporation. Increased pressures on corporations (e.g., mergers, takeovers, and divestitures that raise control issues) are expensive and have multiplied the number of shareholders, highlighting the fact that "the community" is only one constituency, and an amorphous one at that.

Corporate contributions, as a percentage of net corporate income before taxes, have varied with the changing economic and political climate. Steadily rising from .84% to 1.10% of pretax net income between 1955 and 1964, contributions declined slightly in the 1970s. Between 1980 and 1989, however, corporate contributions grew from .99% to 1.82%, although they peaked at 2.2% in 1986 and then declined (Greene, 1990). Nearly two thirds (64%) of the 1.6 million corporations reporting net income did not report any charitable contributions (1982 data, Hodgkinson & Weitzman, 1989). The limited proportion (one third) of corporations making charitable gifts has not changed since the 1977 study of the Internal Revenue Service (Hodgkinson & Weitzman, 1986). Of interest, manufacturing companies contribute more than half (51%) of all corporate contributions (Hodgkinson & Weitzman, 1989), even though they declined from 11% to 9% of all companies with net income. Corporate charitable contributions, including company grants to sponsored foundations, reached $5.6 billion in 1989 (Greene, 1990). Corporate contributions represented 4.7% of total giving (1987 data, Hodgkinson & Weitzman, 1989).

Individual giving patterns are another empirical indicator of the economic situation facing nonprofits. Recent data from the Independent Sector indicate that the 1980s brought increases in both per capita individual charitable contributions and contributions as a percentage of personal income. In constant dollars, per capita giving grew from $197 in 1960 to $341 in 1987. In real terms, this was a 37% increase, reflecting "the highest increase since the decade of the 1960s when it increased 30 percent" (Hodgkinson & Weitzman, 1989, p. 7). Individual contributions were 2.16% of personal income according to the latest figures.

As the source of about one fourth (27.3%, or $97.8 billion) of the total funds of the nonprofit sector (Hodgkinson & Weitzman, 1989), private giving alone cannot be expected to offset the effects of federal budget reductions, especially because religious contributions constitute about three fourths of this total. To meet the expected future funding gaps in fields of nonprofit activity as a result of anticipated

federal budget limitations, private giving would have to grow six-
or sevenfold (Abramson & Salamon, 1986). This is clearly unrealistic.

Funding trends in the past decade accelerated the pressures on
nonprofit service providers. To survive, they would need to increase
fees, reduce charity care, contract their "unprofitable" services or
clients to minimize costs, target profitable services or clients, and
devise other major strategies (e.g., merge with another organization
or change their tax status).

Internal Indicators

Internal indicators of the restructuring of nonprofit health and
social services have been identified for the 1983 to 1990 period (Estes,
1986; IHA, 1986, 1987). As early as 1984, eight processes of restructuring appeared to be under way with respect to community health
and social service delivery. Several of these are described in more
detail in Chapters 1, 5, 6, and 12. They are

1. privatization of human services via the expansion of proprietaries into
    potentially profitable areas of medical and social services;
2. competition between for-profit and nonprofit providers as they vie for
    referrals, market share, and profits;
3. expansion and diversification of provider organizational forms aimed
    at the rationalization of service provision, including vertical integration
    across services (e.g., the linkage of hospital, home health, and hospice
    organizations); horizontal integration across single industries; and the
    development of hybrid tax status entities (mixed forms of nonprofit and
    for-profit tax status);
4. labor restructuring, including the increased use of part-time and con-
    tract workers;
5. medicalization of social services due largely to reimbursement schemes
    (e.g., Medicare and Medicaid) that accord preference to medical over
    social services in terms of public financing and to the greater potential
    profitability of medical services in contrast to social services;
6. fragmentation of service delivery by unbundling and selling single ser-
    vices, which are more billable and profitable than comprehensive services;
7. reemergence of tiered systems of care with the targeting of clients and
    services and polarization between organizations serving clients who can
    afford to pay privately versus those serving clients who cannot afford
    to pay privately; and
8. informalization, wherein services of hospitals and community agencies
    are being transferred out of the formal delivery system into the informal
    family system (mainly to women).

The examination of these transformative processes and their consequences constitutes a major research agenda, of which this book is one small part. The potential effects of these restructuring processes include high nonprofit organizational death rates, reductions in staff salaries and benefits, de-skilling, high staff turnover, burnout, and a trend toward careerism and professionalism in which organizational survival and efficiency goals override service goals. When increased energy and expenditures are devoted to organizational survival and rationalization of services, products, and markets, attention to service goals is necessarily altered, most likely in the direction of the dilution of goal primacy to the organization.

Conclusion

The external and internal indicators of restructuring in the nonprofit health and social services described above illustrate some of the struggles existing within the nonprofit sector and between this sector, the corporate sector, and the State. These indicators point to the structural vulnerability of the nonprofit sector, in terms of both its functions and its bases of support.

The role, the very existence of the nonprofit sector in the U.S. economy, and the relationship of nonprofits to the State and corporate sectors are all in question. The external and internal indicators of change described above signal a shift in the economic and legitimacy bases of nonprofits and growing pressures to place efficiency and market goals above mission and service goals. The more nonprofits succumb to efficiency goals under heightened competition, the more vulnerable they become to accusations that they do not deserve their special status and tax treatment (Estes et al., 1989). Nonprofit sector entities may be seen, simultaneously, as aids to and as drags upon the economy. The intense political and ideological struggles of the 1980s are witness to this contradiction.

Advocates argue that the nonprofit sector's essential role justifies a societal commitment to values that are irreducible to economics (e.g., pluralism and individual expression) and to State policies that safeguard and protect private giving, volunteering, and the independence of the nonprofit sector. Insistence on these elements forms the necessary ideological armamentarium for nonprofit sector proponents in their efforts to secure continuing public support and legitimacy for the sector. The plethora of congressional hearings and private and governmental commissions on public-private responsibility and relations highlights the nonprofit sector as a battleground for both anti-State and pro-State forces (Estes & Alford, 1990). The economic, political, and ideological contradictions surrounding the nonprofit sector do not lead to simple analysis or easy answers.

One such contradiction is inherent in a major development of the 1980s in the field of health care—the creation of mixed organizational forms that combine nonprofit and for-profit arrangements. This mixing, or confounding, of tax status within an overarching corporate entity such as a hospital has increased the competition between and among nonprofits (e.g., in home health) as well as between nonprofit and for-profit health care entities. This further blurring of the boundaries weakens the case for the exceptionalism of the nonprofit service sector, rendering it vulnerable to even more aggressive attacks from the for-profit sector (Estes et al., 1989). The more nonprofits act like for-profits (e.g., rejecting clients who cannot pay), the less justification there is for special nonprofit tax status. Under such conditions, nonprofits will experience increased attacks based on the perception that they are not different than proprietaries. In consequence, nonprofits that survive may be stronger, larger, more centralized, and less likely to be locality specific and locality responsive. This would represent yet another transformation in the nature and structure of the nonprofit sector.

Subsequent chapters of this volume examine the implications of the restructuring of the nonprofit sector for access to care for older persons, beginning in the next chapter with discharge planners as gatekeepers to other services. Future work on the nonprofit sector is needed to track the impact of federal and state policy changes on the access, quality, and cost of human services.

CHAPTER **3**

Discharge Planners as Gatekeepers to Community Care

Discharge planning is a complex, multifaceted process that not only addresses clinical needs, but also considers psycho-social factors, economic factors, and community resources. Discharge planning is not merely the final discharge plan, nor is it only ensuring that a patient does not stay hospitalized one day longer than his [or her] medical condition indicates. Discharge planning is a process that requires a tremendous amount of collaboration and consideration of all factors that impact on utilization, quality assurance, and the discharge plan.

Hanson, 1986, p. 6

▼

Discharge planning has been variously defined as "any activity or set of activities which facilitates the transition of the patient from one environment to another" (American Hospital Association, 1987, p. 3), "the entire process of planning for help or services after the hospital from both formal and informal support systems" (Lurie, Robinson, & Barbaccia, 1984, p. 27), and "the assessment of a patient's financial resources and psychological and emotional characteristics in order to determine what health and social services are needed post-hospitalization" (Goldberg, 1987, p. 7).

Inherent in each definition of discharge planning is a process that involves patient assessment and posthospital care planning. This common theme might suggest that the discharge planning function

---

NOTE: The author of this chapter is Pamela Hanes Spohn (with Carroll L. Estes).

is the mechanism whereby hospitals assure that their most medically and/or socially vulnerable patients will be appropriately cared for after discharge from the hospital.

The hiring and staffing of discharge planning departments with trained professionals is a significant commitment of institutional resources at a time when most cost-conscious hospitals have been downsizing and de-skilling their professional work force as well as merging many of their patient care functions. Executive decisions to commit organizational resources to the discharge planning function, and the level of that commitment, are influenced by organizational form and structure. Specifically, "the articulated organizational mission of hospitals, i.e., tax status preference, and certain structural characteristics, e.g., the level of vertical and horizontal integration activities hospitals engage in, will influence administrators' decisions to commit organizational resources to the discharge planning function" (Spohn, 1988, p. 65). Policy issues have shaped the definition and performance of discharge planning in the aftermath of the implementation of the prospective payment system.

Impact of the Prospective Payment System

Most observers of discharge planning would agree that its function has undergone significant changes since the implementation of the Medicare hospital prospective payment system (PPS). Discharge planning has become an increasingly important activity as hospital administrators, their fiscal agents, and third-party reimbursers better understand the role it plays in the timely movement of patients from inpatient to outpatient status and, not coincidentally, within a profitable length of stay based on diagnosis-related group (DRG) reimbursement.

The recent ascension of the discharge planning function in hospitals has brought with it numerous problems, including interdisciplinary competition between nurses and social workers as well as issues relating to the competing, and often conflicting, goals of cost efficiency and quality of patient care (Boone, Coulton, & Keller, 1987; Fackelmann, 1987; Hanson, 1986; LeBrun, 1986; Rock, 1987; Young, 1987). The rise to prominence of discharge planning has also brought hospital discharge planners face-to-face with a new set of ethical dilemmas. These dilemmas involve choices between the hospital need for efficient and timely management and movement of patients and, alternatively, the patient need for appropriately timed and well-executed posthospital care plans.

The introduction of the prospective payment system also has brought about significant changes in the behavior of other key hospital personnel. Particularly, the PPS has shifted administrative decision making in the direction of activities related to the bottom line or fiscal well-being of the institution. Prior to the PPS, hospitals were reimbursed on a cost-based reimbursement system that provided no real incentives for administrators to be cost conscious. On the contrary, fiscal incentives were to provide more services and invest in highly sophisticated technology and costly equipment because these costs were all passed on to third-party payers (i.e., Medicare, Medicaid, and private insurance companies).

When the federal government shifted hospital payment from a retrospective payment system to the PPS in 1983, the financial risk for length of stay and intensity of services shifted from third-party payers to the providers of care—hospitals and their attending physicians. Therefore the new reimbursement policy, in combination with other procompetition policy initiatives, significantly altered the financial incentives of the various players in the industry, resulting in a major restructuring of the hospital sector (Berliner & Burlage, 1987; Ermann & Gabel, 1984; Freedman, 1985; Hanaway, 1986; Himmelstein & Woolhandler, 1986; IOM, 1986a; Johnson, 1985a, 1985b; Light, 1986; Salmon, 1987; Schlesinger, 1985a). This restructuring is apparent in terms of both the obvious profit-maximizing behaviors of hospitals (e.g., the unbundling and elimination of unprofitable services with the commensurate development and marketing of profitable services) and the less obvious, or less visible, rearticulation of organizational mission and goals through tax status preferences and selective admitting practices.

Hospitals are now employing a wide range of strategies, many borrowed from other corporate sectors, to compete in the health care marketplace. One strategy is the movement toward larger and more complex organizational entities or multifacility hospital systems and the integration of "step-down" or subacute services such as nursing homes, home health agencies, and hospice programs (Shortell et al., 1990).

This new mentality and the subsequent changes spawned in hospital staffing and service configurations render the function of discharge planning a particularly provocative area for investigation. Exploring the role played by discharge planning in continuity of patient care is especially fruitful, as both policymakers and analysts struggle to better understand the relationship between cost-containment policies and access to care.

The only reported research on the relationship between organizational characteristics and the decision to commit institutional resources to the discharge planning function is the IHA study (see the Introduction to this volume). The hospital-level analysis included an in-depth examination of the relationship between organizational form and structure, performance, and boundary-spanning activities relative to discharge planning and its function as gatekeeper to subacute and chronic care services (Estes, Wood, et al., 1988; Spohn, 1989). The hospital sample of 178 discharge planners consisted of 62% nonprofit, 28% for-profit, and 10% public facilities.

Across all organizational auspices, researchers found a consistently high level of affiliation with larger hospital systems and a trend toward affiliation that increased significantly between the first and second interview periods. Public hospitals increased their affiliation with larger systems from 35% to 59% between 1986 and 1987; nonprofits jumped from 48% to 58%; and for-profit hospitals increased in their tendency to affiliate from 65% to 92%.

In addition to noting the trend toward affiliating with larger hospital systems, researchers asked a series of questions about the relationships of hospitals to other health care organizations to gauge the intensity of developing interorganizational linkages. In particular, the level of vertical integration during the 2-year period was documented. It was found that 53% of the hospitals sampled in 1986 reported owning other health-related organizations and that there were virtually no differences between nonprofit and for-profit facilities in the propensity to vertically integrate subacute services. By 1987, the picture had changed—both nonprofit and for-profit hospitals reported increased ownership or contractual relationships with nursing homes from the previous year (rising from 44% to 59% and 37% to 46%, respectively), and public hospitals reported slightly fewer in 1987. Nonprofit and public hospitals were significantly more likely than for-profit facilities to have contractual or ownership relationships with home health agencies. Given that nursing home placement and home health care are the two most frequently used posthospital care services, increased interorganizational linkages can be interpreted as either an organizational commitment to the continuity of care needs of discharged patients or as a way to expedite discharges and prevent protracted lengths of stay.

Organizational Characteristics Influencing Function

In spite of the large numbers of elderly patients in virtually all acute care hospitals who, because of age and vulnerability to acute illness, constitute the most frequent users of hospital services, most facilities have no comprehensive geriatric program geared to the postacute medical, rehabilitative, and social needs of elderly patients. Discharge planning, by definition, would be included in a comprehensive package (Goldsmith, 1989). The reasons for the relatively low emphasis on this acute-to-chronic continuum of care are many, some related to the profitability of the services involved and others to the relative newness of the demand for such services at the acute hospital level.

Research findings suggest that there are major differences in the behavior and institutional outcomes of nonprofit and for-profit organizations. An equally large and growing body of literature, however, suggests that many of the historic differences between nonprofit and for-profit organizations, particularly hospitals, are disappearing in the new competitive marketplace (Bays, 1983; Clarke & Estes, 1992; Homer, Bradham, & Rushefsky, 1984; Nutter, 1984; Schlesinger, 1985a, 1985b).

Much has been written about the nonprofit sector and its unique role as a buffer between the public and for-profit sectors of the economy (Estes & Alford, 1990; Hodgkinson et al., 1989; Powell, 1987; Rose-Ackerman, 1986). The delivery of health care during the 1980s fueled a debate about the diminution of the nonprofit hospital and the concomitant rise of for-profit medicine. The debate about for-profit health care focuses on the implications of the profit motive for access to care by marginal populations such as the poor, the uninsured, Medicaid recipients, or other "undesirables" from a profit-maximizing perspective. Several indirect measures of hospital commitment to the discharge planning function can be observed, and the IHA study developed and tested an array of proxy variables to examine this phenomenon across organizational types.

Increased Budgets and Staff Allocations

Of the discharge planners in the IHA study sample, 30% reported their hospital had increased their department budget to support more discharge planning services (IHA, 1986). This level of growing commitment was consistent across hospital types. Further, more than half of the hospitals reported staffing increases after the implementation of the PPS. Similarly, when the Society for Hospital Social Work Directors (SHSWD) surveyed their membership in November 1986, 48% reported experiencing increases in staff since the implementation of the PPS. These staff increases occurred despite the fact that 58% of the hospitals had a declining patient census during the same period. Although reported budget increases were similar for nonprofit and for-profit facilities, differences were found. For example, nonprofit hospitals were significantly more likely to add new staff and services than were for-profit facilities in the sample.

Percentage of Patients Receiving Services

A multivariate analysis was conducted using the percentage of all patients receiving discharge planning services per month as an "organizational commitment" variable. The model regressed structural characteristics of hospitals (including size, the level of vertical and horizontal integration, and tax status) and patient case-mix variables (including percentage of patients over the age of 65 and percentage of low-income patients) against the organizational commitment variable. The researchers were interested in understanding whether form and structure had any relationship to hospital commitment of resources to discharge planning services.

When tax status was used as a control variable, independent of the system affiliation variable, for-profit hospitals were found to be significantly less likely than public hospitals to provide discharge planning services across the patient population. Nonprofit hospitals were also slightly less likely than public facilities to provide discharge planning services to their patients. Patient case mix was also an important determinant of the intensity of discharge planning services offered—the more elderly and low-income patients a hospital admitted, the more discharge planning it provided. Related to this finding, both nonprofit and for-profit hospitals were significantly more likely than public facilities to admit Medicare patients and less likely to admit Medicaid patients. Conversely, public hospitals were significantly more likely to admit low-income patients and less likely to admit Medicare patients. This finding of sameness in admitting practices is consistent with earlier studies that found no discernible difference between nonprofit and for-profit facilities in the tendency to shun low-income and uncompensated care patients (Bays, 1979; Biggs, Kralewski, & Brown, 1980; Lewin et al., 1976; Pattison & Katz, 1983; Sloan & Vraciu, 1983).

A limited number of studies show some level of difference between nonprofits and for-profits, finding that for-profit hospitals are less likely to receive revenues from public third parties or that they provide significantly lower levels of uncompensated care (Becker & Sloan, 1985; Ruchlin, Pointer, & Cannedy, 1973). The studies mentioned above were conducted prior to the implementation of the PPS. The findings of the IHA study, conducted after the PPS, indicate a new "DRG-induced mentality" that has the effect of further solidifying selective admissions policies in nonprofit and for-profit hospitals away from publicly sponsored low-income and uncompensated care patients. As Lewin and Lewin note:

> Patient dumping and skimming are by no means new phenomena, nor are the disproportionate charity care roles played by teaching and public hospitals. What is new is [that] the tendency to shift uninsured patients to public hospitals or to severely limit charity care has accelerated where competitive forces have escalated. The pressure to reduce unsponsored care has also intensified as hospitals in general have developed an increased preoccupation with producing "bottom lines." (Lewin & Lewin, 1987, p. 48)

Mechanisms to Increase Productivity

Of the many mechanisms an organization can employ to increase efficiency and extend its products or services to a wider market, several have already been mentioned: increased service intensity, adding new products or services, and increasing the number of workers who provide the services or goods produced. Another frequently used strategy is to increase the level of productivity of the current work force, thus allowing increased output without increasing internal resources (Szasz, 1990).

Of the discharge planners in the IHA study, 58% reported that their hospital had developed explicit standards to increase their productivity relative to the discharge planning function. The major categories of productivity standards were (a) increased work loads and speedups (e.g., increasing patient-staff ratios); (b) the imposition of various control mechanisms (i.e., increased supervision and working more closely with utilization review nurses); and (c) increased rationalization of the labor processes (i.e., instituting new personnel procedures, establishing patient classification systems, or updating procedure manuals).

The IHA findings are consistent with another large-scale study of discharge planning conducted in 1983 and 1984 by Feather and Nichols (1985). The Feather research was designed to provide information about changes in the discharge planning function during the early implementation period of the prospective payment system. More than 56% of the respondents in the Feather study reported increased work loads, with average caseload increases of 25% (Feather & Nichols, 1985). Further, only 21% of discharge planners responding reported staffing increases as compared with 52% reported in the IHA study 3 years later. Productivity or efficiency measures are increasingly used to extend discharge planning services to hospitalized patients. Whether these mechanisms are efficacious from a quality-of-care perspective remains unclear.

Chain ownership and affiliation with a larger health care system are significant predictors of the likelihood a hospital will attempt to increase productivity through efficiency measures. Further, size is a significant factor in the equation—the larger the hospital, the more likely it will institute productivity mechanisms to increase the output of the discharge planning function. An earlier analysis of the same data found that there was an inverse relationship between size and the percentage of patients to receive discharge planning. From these findings, it can be hypothesized that, to compensate for not increasing discharge planning staff, many large facilities are attempting to increase the level of productivity of their existing staff to extend services to a larger group of patients (Spohn, 1989).

Hospitals have various choices available to them to extend discharge planning services to a larger percentage of their patients: at the structural level, the choice of system affiliation and vertical integration of subacute care services, and, at the functional level, increased budget, service, and productivity measures (IHA, 1986, 1987). To summarize the findings:

- Tax status is a significant predictor of intensity of the discharge planning function with system-affiliated public hospitals providing discharge planning services to more patients than private nonprofit or for-profit facilities.
- The size of the hospital has a constraining effect on the level of discharge planning services provided—as the number of beds increases, the percentage of patients who receive discharge planning services decreases.
- Hospitals with their own skilled nursing beds provide more discharge planning services to their patients.

- The more Medicare and low-income patients a hospital admits, the more discharge planning services it provides.
- Increased money allocated to the discharge planning function is not a significant factor in the level of services provided; instead, increasing the productivity of existing discharge planning staff is the most significant factor in whether hospitals extend services to a larger group of patients (Spohn, 1989).

Organizational commitment to the discharge planning function was strongest among system-affiliated public hospitals. On average, these hospitals had larger discharge planning staffs and were more likely to institute measures to increase productivity than the private hospitals surveyed. These results suggest that public hospitals are adopting some of the known efficiencies of private hospital systems; that is, increasing the size and scope of their operations through the centralization of certain patient care functions as well as instituting mechanisms to increase the productivity of their staffs. According to the IHA data, public hospital systems are providing a significantly larger number of patients with discharge planning services. Whether this finding portends a qualitative difference in patient care outcomes is still an unanswered question. Assuming that public hospitals have a disproportionate share of the responsibility for low-income patients, an emphasis on discharge planning makes good fiscal sense.

Professional Issues

Prior to the implementation of prospective payment, most hospitals provided discharge planning services on a limited basis to meet the needs of certain high-risk patients being discharged or as a loss leader to foster positive community relations. The questionable utility of a discrete discharge planning function is related to two primary factors: (a) the seeming lack of a unique set of skills or knowledge base required to perform the role (i.e., a vague or ill-defined technology comprising low-skill activities, such as calling nursing homes and determining Medicaid eligibility) and (b) the dubious professional status of social workers who tended to fill this role.

From the social worker's perspective, discharge planning activities were considered "add-on" functions to their primary role of inpatient counseling and other more traditional social casework responsibilities. Discharge planning was thought to be a leftover task, requiring neither the unique expertise nor the professional skill of the social worker. As Davidson (1978) observes, discharge planning was the "stepchild" function of the more important casework activities considered the essence of medical social work practice.

Historically, hospital-based social workers have struggled to prove their institutional value to hospital administrators from an economic perspective; therefore any activities thought to be nonprofessional were spurned or avoided whenever possible (Kane, 1980; Kulys, 1983; Schreiber, 1981). But, with the full implementation of the PPS policy in 1984, discharge planning rapidly gained both professional and institutional legitimacy. This legitimation became structurally embedded through the 1986 Omnibus Budget Reconciliation Act requirement that Medicare-certified hospitals make discharge planning available to all Medicare patients. This mandate was the result of public pressure brought to bear on Congress by advocacy groups concerned about the potentially negative consequences of a DRG-based reimbursement system, which they asserted would cause premature and/or inappropriate hospital discharges of frail elders dumped into no-care zones (U.S. GAO, 1987b; Wood & Estes, 1988).

Therefore, in spite of a general move on the part of hospitals to unbundle and eliminate unprofitable cost centers and services, government policy required that discharge planning for posthospital care be made available to all Medicare patients whether or not it had been previously demonstrated to be a cost-efficient activity. The coercive nature of this new policy mandate increased the likelihood for organizational subversion of its intended objective: to assure continuity of care. It did not take hospital administrators and third-party payers long to realize that discharge planning, in combination with other utilization review activities, could facilitate the timely movement of patients out of the hospital, particularly when subacute services were available elsewhere.

Because of the 1986 mandate, and the increased awareness of discharge planning as a critical component of efficient patient care management, turf battles began to emerge between nursing and social work as to which profession was most appropriate to assume the role. To the extent that either social workers or nurses can define discharge planning within their professional domain, they can lay claim to the function from an organizational perspective. Social workers, in particular, have been under pressure for some time to justify the worth of their activities in cost-benefit terms. To be assigned primary responsibility for discharge planning provides them with the institutional legitimacy they have been seeking.

As early as 1977, under the Medicare Anti-Fraud and Abuse Law, Congress set forth a directive to the hospital industry to develop reporting systems that would track the various cost centers within their facilities. In response to this mandate, the Society of Hospital Social Work Directors (SHSWD) and the National Association of Social Work (NASW) formed a working task force to develop a reporting system to track the cost and volume of social work services provided in hospitals.

The result of this effort was the development of "relative value units" (RVUs), which were based on patient length of stay in the hospital and the number of social problems that the social worker dealt with at the individual patient level. Although the methodology was field tested on 4,000 patients in New England hospitals and further refined in a subsequent national study with 4,381 patients, RVUs have not been widely accepted as the methodology of choice to account for hospital social work functions. Researchers cite several limitations to the methodology, including its insensitivity to size and regional variations among hospitals and its lack of attention to specialty areas within hospitals, such as intensive care units and emergency rooms.

The most significant caveat to the RVU methodology is its lack of attention to quality-of-care issues:

> This study did not collect data on the cost or quality of social work services. The cost and quality of patient service time will be greatly affected by the qualifications of the social work personnel and other functions of the social work department. It is important that attempts to measure output be carried out in the context of clear standards for professional practice and definitions of professional functions. (Coulton, Paschall, Foster, Bohnengel, & Slivinske, 1979, p. 62)

In today's hospital environment, quality-of-care issues for social workers will most likely be judged relative to their performance in the area of discharge planning from both a process and an outcome perspective (Coulton, 1988; Coulton, Dunkle, Chow, Haug, & Vielhaber, 1988; Stearns, 1991).

Nurses, on the other hand, have been delegated increasing decision-making authority to arrange posthospital medical care services for patients in the wake of the PPS. This authority is often exercised with only a physician sign-off after the care plan has been developed. The role differentiation that has occurred in discharge planning involves separating the postacute medical care needs from the social and environmental needs of patients. In this regard, nurses have maintained firm control of the medical aspects of the discharge plan.

Rehr notes the qualitative differences between what nurses and social workers do in the discharge planning function:

> The care provided by physicians, nurses and most other health care professionals is oriented toward the individual patient. Social workers, however, are oriented toward families and systems; it is therefore logical for them to assume responsibility for influencing other professionals to recognize the importance of the family and the system in the continuing care of the individual patient. (Rehr, 1985, p. 248)

Ideally, a well-executed discharge plan involves a collaborative effort on the part of all the health care professionals who have some level of responsibility for patients while they are in the hospital.

Most studies of the discharge planning process find that social workers assume the primary role of discharge planner in the majority of hospitals, although there is some variation by ownership type with public hospitals favoring social workers and for-profit hospitals favoring nurses. In several recent surveys, between one half and two thirds of hospital discharge planners were found to be trained as social workers, ranging from the level of bachelor's degree to licensed clinical social worker (California Hospital Association, 1986; Coulton et al., 1979; Feather & Nichols, 1985; IHA, 1986, 1987; Society for Hospital Social Work Directors, 1987). Clearly, the trend in staffing the discharge planning function has been toward the use of social workers with master's degrees (MSWs). In the Feather study, half of the discharge planners interviewed were social workers; in the IHA study, 66% were MSWs and another 11% were BSWs; and, in the SHSWD study, 83% of discharge planners interviewed were master's- or higher-level social workers.

The larger the number of designated discharge planners in a hospital, the more likely they are to be social workers by training (IHA, 1986, 1987). Likewise, the larger the hospital, the more likely discharge planners are to be social workers who report to social service departments (Spohn, 1989). A further refinement of these data revealed that hospitals with formal policies delineating the roles of nurses and social workers relative to the discharge planning function were more likely to identify social workers as the primary designated discharge planners (Spohn, 1989). The turf wars between nurses and social workers have served to divert otherwise caring professionals away from what should be the primary concern of the discharge planning process—mobilizing all the necessary institutional resources available to assure the optimal level of postacute care services for hospital patients.

Three principal models of discharge planning have been observed: (a) the medical model, which "considers the medical condition of the patient, medical prognoses, availability of extended care beds, and ability of the patient to function in terms of self-care" (Schrager, 1978, p. 26); (b) the social model, which "examines the patients' personal and interpersonal resources for care after the hospital and asks whether the patient is isolated, who the caretaker will be, and other questions having to do with the social milieu of the patient as criteria for discharge planning" (Lurie et al., 1984, p. 27; see Glassman-Feibusch, 1981; Olsen & Cahn, 1980); and (c) the integrated model, which "looks at both medical and social factors, as well as others" (Lurie et al., 1984, p. 27; see Beale & Gulley, 1981; Hollingsworth & Sokol, 1978). The integrated model evidently represents the ideal type from a patient care perspective. By definition, the integrated model pays attention to the total needs of the patient and therefore requires the services of a multidisciplinary team capable of assessing and developing an appropriate and comprehensive posthospital care plan.

The results of IHA research on the issue of interdisciplinary teams and decision-making authority for discharge planning were somewhat encouraging and consistent with other studies, yet several interesting qualifiers should be mentioned in interpreting the findings. Of the discharge planners interviewed, 80% reported functioning as members of interdisciplinary teams for discharge planning purposes. Similarly, in a 1987 survey of 280 California hospital discharge planners conducted by the UCLA Multi-Campus Division of Geriatric Medicine, 86% of discharge planners reported that their hospital used a multidisciplinary team approach for discharge planning. In both studies, the disciplines most frequently involved were nursing, social work, and utilization review, with physical therapy, occupational and respiratory therapy, pharmacy, and nutrition also often mentioned.

The IHA data also showed a significant positive relationship between hospitals that used social workers as their primary discharge planners and the propensity to use interdisciplinary teams. Public hospitals were more likely to employ interdisciplinary teams in the discharge planning process than private nonprofit or for-profit hospitals. In public hospitals, the decision-making process was a collaborative one, whereas, in other settings, the physician was more likely to make the final decision as to the nature of the discharge plan (Spohn, 1989).

The findings from the IHA study portray an interesting scenario of the relationship between professional identity and discharge planning. The hospitals that produce the largest volume of discharge planning services per patient admitted (public system-affiliated hospitals) are using the combined efforts of social workers and nurses, and these professionals are working together in interdisciplinary teams to maximize the potential benefits found in a comprehensive discharge plan. In addition, when home health agency (HHA) staff nurses are located in the hospital, the discharge planning function is even more likely to be shared by nurses and social workers. These findings suggest that the integrated model of discharge planning discussed above is a distinct possibility in hospitals willing to make an appropriate commitment of resources. A counterfinding from another study shows that, although the hospitals in their sample were formally organized to deliver an integrated model of discharge planning, the discharge planning function was, in actuality, based on a medical/regulatory model driven primarily by services that are reimbursable (Lurie et al., 1984).

The disjunction between organizational goals and practice is widely understood by students of organizations. There are many possible explanations for a hospital making a commitment to an integrated approach to discharge planning and in reality providing only a limited set of services by an overworked health care professional. An understanding of the changing nature of the discharge planning function since the implementation of the PPS provides some clues as to the reasons for the apparent disjunction.

Both the intensity and the frequency of patient care needs have increased markedly since the implementation of the PPS, which has resulted in an increased demand for discharge planning services. Specifically, Medicare patients are being released from hospitals sooner, requiring more intensified levels of posthospital care (Estes, Wood, et al., 1988; Meiners & Coffey, 1985; Spohn, Bergthold, Estes, & Goldberg, 1988; U.S. GAO, 1987b). In addition, there has been a particular intensification in the demand for skilled nursing beds at the same time that the supply of, and access to, these beds has been restrained through public policy initiatives. Further, there has been a marked increase in the work load and job-related pressures of discharge planners since the implementation of the PPS (Estes, Wood, et al., 1988; Feather & Nichols, 1985; U.S. GAO, 1987b). The Feather study found that 56% of discharge planners reported increased work loads, while only 2 years later in the IHA study, 95% of discharge planners reported work load increases attributed specifically to the PPS policy.

Tasks and Activities

Simply stated, the tasks and activities of discharge planning are any, and all, therapeutic, educational, and personal care functions performed by health professionals from the time of admission to the hospital to the time of discharge. Physicians, nurses, social workers, therapists, and pharmacists all make their contributions to preparing the patient for return to the community. For the purpose of this discussion, however, the focus is limited to the activities of the designated discharge planner. Much of what discharge planners do in the conduct of their jobs is established through a priority ranking and/or high-risk screening system. In virtually all studies with a focus on discharge planning, respondents have noted the presence of a hierarchical list of criteria, established either formally or informally and used to determine who receives discharge planning services (Estes, Wood, et al., 1988; Feather & Nichols, 1985; U.S. GAO, 1987b).

Studies agree on the rank order of these criteria: (a) social or legal criteria (e.g., living situation, family situation, and guardianship and conservatorship issues); (b) specific diagnosis (i.e., DRG); and (c) presence of chronic conditions. Because of these criteria, related activities tend to focus rather narrowly on the necessary mobilization of resources to attend to specific identified problems: securing nursing home placement, getting the patient qualified for Medicaid, or calling in a home health nurse coordinator for short-term posthospital nursing care.

The second tier of activities, conducted as time permits, is related to the broader environmental needs of patients, including working with their families. This level of activity focuses on counseling, patient education, and other resource mobilization. When discharge planners in the IHA study were asked what other functions in addition to discharge planning are carried on within their departments, they responded with such activities as personal counseling, financial counseling, group therapy, service coordination, and quality assurance. This response raises interesting questions about the incongruence between what persons other than discharge planners believe to be the tasks of discharge planning and the perceptions of persons occupying the position and fulfilling the role.

At least one social work director in a large metropolitan teaching hospital in the IHA survey noted that social work education is largely to blame for the confusion about what constitutes discharge planning. To paraphrase her sentiments, all of hospital social work is discharge planning. Until this confusion is resolved, we can expect that definitions of the content of discharge planning will continue to be ambiguous yet considered an important component of the stock of services provided by hospitals.

Issues of Access

Probably the most important policy consideration planners and policymakers face in assessing the efficacy of the discharge planning function is its ability to provide the necessary transitional services from the hospital to the community (Stearns, 1991). An equally important consideration in this assessment is the extent to which the transitional services assure the safe and appropriate reintegration of patients into their homes or other more appropriate community-care settings. This outcome is largely dependent on the level of importance the hospital places on this goal and the availability of appropriate resources of acceptable quality in the community (Kenney & Holahan, 1990).

Two studies in particular have looked at the access question: the IHA research and the U.S. General Accounting Office (GAO) national survey of hospital discharge planners. A mixed bag of findings emerged. The GAO study defined access in terms of "the difficulty involved in placing Medicare patients in appropriate posthospital care following hospital discharge" (U.S. GAO, 1987b, p. 6). The majority of respondents in the GAO study felt that Medicare patients faced a number of important problems in gaining access to appropriate posthospital care. In general, respondents felt that Medicare program rules and regulations were the single most important barrier to placement in skilled nursing facilities and home health care. This reason was followed by the availability of beds and the need for complex skilled services (e.g., respiratory care) that existing community agencies and institutions were not staffed to provide. Researchers found some regional differences but, in general, access problems were consistent throughout the country.

Similar findings relative to difficulties in accessing posthospital care emerged from the IHA study, and the respondents also cited a number of community-based social services in particularly short supply since the implementation of the PPS. More than two thirds of the discharge planners surveyed found both nursing home placement and securing homemaker chore services more difficult; half reported difficulties in securing home-delivered meals; and more than one third reported shortages of such services as transportation, board and care facilities, respite services, and home health care. In the GAO study, discharge planners reported an inadequate supply of skilled nursing, intermediate care, and rehabilitation facilities. There was also general agreement that these institutional resources were much more difficult to secure than home heath care services. This conclusion is consistent with the IHA finding that 69% of discharge planners had difficulty accessing nursing home beds, but only 29% reported difficulties with home health care placement.

Hospital discharge delays have been linked to the undersupply of nursing home beds (Kenney & Holahan, 1990; Stearns, 1991). There is nationwide evidence of undersupply (Swan & Harrington, 1986; Swan, Harrington, & Miller, 1991), and, in the 1980s, nursing home bed stock increased more slowly than did the older population (Harrington, Preston, Grant, & Swan, 1990; Harrington, Swan, & Grant, 1988). Regardless of the cause, constrained nursing home markets, coupled with Medicare hospital prospective payment, have created major system-level access problems.

The IHA study also examined access issues relative to the tax status of the reporting hospitals. Nonprofit and public hospitals reported significantly more difficulty than for-profit facilities in gaining access to nursing home placements. Nonprofit and public planners also reported more difficulty accessing home health care services, but not at a level of statistical significance. Across the board, nonprofit hospitals reported more difficulty than for-profits in gaining access to services, including adult day health care, community mental health services, home-delivered meals, and homemaker chore services.

Variations in access could be the result of several important differences in for-profit and nonprofit hospitals: (a) Proprietary facilities are more tightly linked to posthospital care services through their system affiliation and vertical integration activities; (b) nonprofit hospitals may be more aggressively seeking alternative options to posthospital care and thus be experiencing more frustrations in securing them; or (c) nonprofit hospitals may have a larger percentage of elderly patients, upping the ante on the demand side of the equation. Further research into the issue of access is needed.

When the discharge planners in the GAO study were asked what potential trends they believed had affected access to posthospital care since 1982, the introduction of prospective payment at the federal level and, in some cases, state level was seen as the factor that most contributed to changes in access. Likewise, in the IHA study, 70% of the discharge planners interviewed reported that their ability to refer patients to posthospital care had grown more limited as a result of the implementation of the DRG-based payment system. Respondents were also asked to rank the policy issues with the greatest impact on their hospital since 1984. The overwhelming first choice was the PPS. The noted effects included an increase in discharge planning activities, more difficulty finding posthospital care, a shift toward more outpatient procedures, and patients being discharged too soon.

A final dimension of the access issue is discharge location. If, as most studies have indicated, patients are being discharged sooner with greater posthospital care needs, increased numbers of patients would be assumed to be receiving discharge planning services. Greater numbers of patients would also be expected to receive some type of formal service provision after hospital discharge. In the IHA study, the mean percentage of all patients who received discharge planning services per month increased from 44% in 1986 to 51% in 1987. For elderly patients, the mean increased from 64% in 1986 to 71% in 1987. Changes in discharge location were also noted between the 2 years in which data were collected. The number of discharges to nursing homes dropped slightly between 1986 and 1987 while the number of discharges to hospital-based nursing home beds rose slightly between the 2 years. Likewise, the number of discharges to board and care facilities dropped 17%. In summary, although more patients were receiving discharge planning services from the hospital, discharge plans securing any type of formal services dropped 16% between 1986 and 1987. These numbers suggest that the location of posthospital care is shifting from health care professionals and institutions to the home and family.

Answered and Unanswered Questions

Because of the recent and rapid ascension of discharge planning into a position of prominence within the acute hospital setting, relatively little empirical research has been conducted concerning the practical and theoretical nature of discharge planning. An analysis of the full content and requisite skills required to perform the discharge planning function has yet to be performed. Hence there is no clear consensus about what discharge planning is, who should receive it, who should do it, and whether it achieves either of its expressed goals—continuity of patient care or the timely movement of patients out of the hospital. As one expert on the subject notes:

> Few involved in discharge planning are able to concur on what it definitely involves. There is no widespread agreement on the level of skill and sophistication it requires; its target population; its boundaries; the roles of patient, family, social worker, nurse, and physician; or what should be done when patient needs and institutional needs conflict. (Rehr, 1986, p. 48)

Although limited in number and scope of inquiry, studies about the discharge planning function have curiously resulted in the convergence of several common themes worth noting.

- Patient care needs have increased markedly in intensity and frequency since the implementation of the PPS, which has resulted in an increased demand for discharge planning services.
- Medicare patients are being released from hospitals sooner, requiring more and intensified levels of posthospital care (Estes, Wood, et al., 1988; Meiners & Coffey, 1985; Spohn, 1988; U.S. GAO, 1987b).
- The demand for skilled nursing beds has intensified at the same time the supply of, and access to, these beds has been restrained through public policy initiatives (certificate-of-need regulations) and adverse eligibility and reimbursement policies under the Medicare and Medicaid programs (Swan & Harrington, 1990; Swan, Harrington, & Grant, 1988; Swan, Harrington, Grant, & Preston, 1991).
- The work load and job-related pressures of discharge planners have increased markedly since the implementation of the PPS (Estes, Wood, et al., 1988; Feather & Nichols, 1985; U.S. GAO, 1987b).
- The discharge planning function has gained significant institutional recognition since the implementation of the PPS. This recognition has been a mixed blessing in that discharge planning is now recognized as an important component of patient care in terms of moving patients to outpatient status in a timely fashion, but in most cases it has not been accompanied by a commensurate increase in institutional resources to achieve its stated objectives (Estes, Wood, et al., 1988; Feather & Nichols, 1985).

Factors in the external environment of hospitals as well as intraorganizational factors (both structural and administrative) might help to explain possible differences in the ways in which hospitals organize discharge planning (from both a hierarchical and a professional perspective). Differences in the level of organizational resources committed to the discharge planning function (both monetarily and in terms of staffing) also contribute to an analysis of the issue. The findings presented provide some illumination but, more importantly, suggest that further investigation into the dynamics of hospital behavior relative to discharge planning would be a provocative and worthwhile exercise.

Conclusion

Interest in hospital discharge planning has increased significantly since the implementation of the Medicare prospective payment system in 1983. At the executive decision-making level, corporate officers and hospital administrators have embraced the function as one that facilitates the early discharge of patients within a profitable DRG-determined length of stay. At the functional level, professionals who carry out the discharge planning role have attempted to provide their patients with care plans and services that assure a minimum level of safety on return to home or an alternative posthospital care setting.

The observed duality of these interests concerning the goals and outcomes of discharge planning has occurred within an institutional framework of constrained budgets and a shortage of dedicated staff to meet the increased demands brought about by the PPS. In addition, the external environment of hospitals is characterized by a conflicted public policy agenda concerned with restraining health care costs on one hand and seeking to assure quality of patient care on the other. In this environment, hospitals must make decisions about resource allocations to the discharge planning function. The organizational tensions resulting from these various special interests have been exacerbated by a significant increase in overall demand for posthospital care with a concomitant dearth of community resources available to absorb an increased volume of sicker and more vulnerable persons discharged from the hospital (Estes, Wood, et al., 1988; Fackelmann, 1987; Rehr, 1986; Swan, Harrington, & Miller, 1991).

Interpretation of the IHA findings is neither straightforward nor conclusive. The picture of discharge planning after implementation of the PPS is far from focused. The data presented here provide a small piece of a complex puzzle of policy mandates, professional prerogatives, and organizational strategies. These data are suggestive of what is happening at the community level among hospitals and the community-based services that provide posthospital care services to discharged patients. The issue clearly warrants further study.

The ultimate legitimacy of the discharge function begins at the institutional level, and all the major actors, from their own particular perspectives, consider discharge planning to be a critical component of patient care in the hospital. The differing perspectives are noteworthy. In the final analysis, well-executed discharge plans can save hospitals money and safeguard the well-being of patients. Therefore policy goals, professional goals, and organizational goals have the potential to be met simultaneously when discharge planning is supported with adequate budgets and staff. Multiple goal attainment will be possible if the concept of an integrated, multidisciplinary discharge planning process is embraced and implemented by hospital administrations and corporate headquarters.

CHAPTER **4**

Does Out of the Hospital Mean Out of Luck?

No single program provides the services or financing to accommodate the multiple long-term care needs of the elderly, and most are left to receive services at home from family and friends with little assistance from public programs.

Davis & Rowland, 1986, p. 62

▼

The stated objective of the Medicare prospective payment system (PPS) was to control escalating Medicare costs for hospital care without limiting or restricting beneficiary access to services or affecting the quality of health care (Guterman & Dobson, 1986). Changes at any one point on an interconnected system, however, usually effect at least a short-term change at other points. A number of important changes took place within community-based services immediately following the implementation of the PPS based on the diagnosis-related group (DRG) (IHA, 1986, 1987). Changes occurred, among other places, in the types of patients seeking care, access to care, and service intensity needs. More important, the agencies surveyed perceived the changes to be linked to the Medicare PPS (Estes, Wood, et al., 1988).

Among the results of the implementation of the Medicare prospective payment system is the growing number of elderly persons seeking community care when discharged from hospitals. Moreover,

---

NOTE: The authors of this chapter are Sheryl C. Goldberg and Carroll L. Estes. (Adapted and revised from the authors' article, Medicare DRGs and Post-Hospital Care for the Elderly, *Journal of Applied Gerontology, 9,* 1990, 20-25.)

these clients are in a more compromised state of health than previously seen. Not only has the demand for care in posthospital
settings risen, but the demand is for greater than usual levels of care.
Resultant barriers to entry may increase, and discharge from the
hospital may not be accompanied by access to necessary care.

Client Changes

Demographers and health service researchers have long noted the
shifts occurring in the U.S. population and have predicted that care
for elderly people will be "the biggest future growth market for most
health care providers" (Eastaugh, 1981, p. 312). The over 75 and the
65 to 74 age groups, respectively, are the two fastest growing segments of the population.

All classes of agencies included in the IHA study—nursing homes,
hospices, home health agencies, adult day centers, and senior centers—
reported increases in the numbers of clients over age 65 (Table 4.1).
Almost 90% of the adult day centers in the study, 74% of senior centers,
and 70% of home health agencies reported increases. A large number
of agencies reported increases in clients classified as "old-old," that is,
aged 85 or older. Just over half of the nursing homes and home health
agencies studied (51%) and half of the adult day centers reported
increases between 1984 and 1986 in clients aged 85 and over.

Although the proportion of elderly persons in the population has
been increasing steadily, demographic shifts would have been, at
most, a minor contributor to the changes noted over a mere 2-year
period and insignificant in explaining increased client demand. A
more plausible explanation would be that one effect of the PPS was
to increase the caseloads of older persons in the agencies studied.
Early hospital discharge shifted the burden of care to other care
providers. A test for significant differences between posthospital
(home health agencies, nursing homes, and hospices) and continuing
care providers (adult day centers and senior centers) in reported
increases in old-old clients on the heels of the implementation of the
PPS found significantly more variation in the former.

As demand for service increases relative to supply, providers are
better able to select among persons seeking care. The inability of
elders to pay for sought-after services may become an even greater
liability under these conditions.

More than one fifth of the nursing homes (21%) reported decreases
in the number of low-income patients after 1984, and, for 54% of the

TABLE 4.1   Agencies Reporting Changes in Number of Clients Aged 65 or over Between 1984 and 1986

| Type of Agency | Direction of Change | | | Total N |
	Decreased (percentage)	None (percentage)	Increased (percentage)	
Posthospital care:				
home health agency[a]	12	18	70	168
nursing home	2	72	26	195
hospice	4	54	42	24
Continuing care:				
adult day-care center	3	9	88	32
senior center	2	25	74	113

SOURCE: Data from Institute for Health & Aging DRG study, telephone surveys (1986).
NOTE: Question on instrument: "since 1984, has the number of clients aged 65 or over decreased, remained the same, or increased?"
a. We asked home health agencies and adult day-care centers about changes in clients aged 65-74, 75-84, and 85 and over and regrouped this data into 65 and over to get a comparable statistic. If an agency reported an increase in all three categories, we recoded an increase; similarly, if all three groupings had decreased or remained the same, we coded decrease or *rights* (RTS). If there were any combination or increases, decreases, or RTS, we counted it as missing data (HHA = 23; ADC = 9). It is possible that some reports of "remained the same" were washed out in our records.

home health agencies and senior centers, the number of low-income clients did not change during the 2-year period. Adult day-care centers and hospices were more likely than other types of agencies studied to report an increase in the number of low-income clients after 1984. The increasing numbers of elderly patients likely to need posthospital nursing home care under the PPS and the difficulties in providing services to those who cannot pay indicate that issues of elder access (particularly for low-income individuals) to needed health care and social supportive services have become increasingly important to monitor.

Access to Care

According to IHA study data, access to most of the agencies under investigation was restricted for some clients between 1984 and 1986. More than 80% of the respondents from each organizational type indicated that after 1984 their agencies were inaccessible for persons with one or more of the following conditions: (a) with specific physical health problems and medical care needs, (b) requiring technical support services, (c) with mental health/mental retardation/behavioral problems, (d) with reimbursement or payment-related problems, (e) requiring social supports, and (f) not meeting agency eligibility. These categories are not mutually exclusive and all categories of persons were not barred entry from all the agencies. Agencies were asked to cite up to three categories their agency could not serve.

Among home health agencies (HHAs), more than half (53%) listed low reimbursement and high cost of care as the predominant reason for not providing care to some persons. The lack or inadequacy of Medicare reimbursement was by far the major access barrier cited by HHAs. For example, if the patient does not require skilled nursing care but needs more than intermittent care, is not under the care of a physician, and is not homebound, Medicare will not cover the care. Older persons who do not meet these stringent reimbursement criteria are often denied access to needed home health care services.

Like income, the nature of one's illness and one's service needs may also become liabilities when demand for services far exceeds available supply and providers have more opportunity to pick and choose among potential clientele.

Denials by fiscal intermediaries for both home health and nursing home care markedly increased with the stricter Medicare regulations that followed the implementation of the PPS. Nursing home administrators reported denying admission primarily to patients with mental health/behavioral problems such as psychiatric disorders, specific health conditions or medical care needs such as communicable or contagious diseases, and requirements for high-tech care (Figure 4.1).

Almost two thirds of hospice directors responding to the IHA study stated that clients without adequate social supports (e.g., informal caregivers) could not be served by their agencies. It is ironic that dying persons without the aid of informal caregivers and thus perhaps more in need than others of formal supportive care are denied hospice services for reasons related to this eligibility restriction.

Adult day-care directors reported refusing access most often to persons with specific physical health problems or medical care needs such as extreme incontinence and to persons with mental health or behavioral problems such as violence exhibited toward the self or others.

The majority of senior center directors reported being unable to accommodate persons with physical health care needs beyond the scope of services usually offered by the institutions. Under this criterion, Alzheimer's patients, disabled or handicapped individuals, and persons requiring continuous one-on-one care were problematic.

Study data reflect aspects of a larger phenomenon described as the no-care zone (Estes, 1987c; Kotelchuck, 1986). The no-care zone is a concept that portrays the predicament of many older individuals

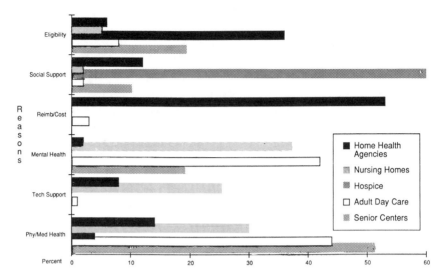

Figure 4.1. Reasons Given for Inability to Serve Some Persons by Agency Type, 1986

SOURCE: Institute for Health & Aging DRG study, telephone surveys (1986).

who are released sick from hospitals and are either intermittently or continuously in need of services and social supports, unable to pay privately for needed care, unable to meet the eligibility requirements of community-based service organizations, or all of the above. Moreover, each agency type has separate admission criteria, differing financing mechanisms, and reimbursement by payers at different rates. The absence of coordination between agency types means that there is little or no assurance that someone denied access to one agency type will necessarily be referred to and received by another.

As discussed above, as the service demand increases relative to supply, barriers to entry may be raised. Among the agencies included in the IHA study, one means of raising this barrier is through the use of waiting lists. If everyone seeking a service should have an equal chance to be placed on and selected from a waiting list, then such a device could aid in assuring eventual admission into an institution. The waiting list, however, may become only a reservoir of desirable clients, with the list serving as a mechanism for limiting access to the institution for individuals having particular characteristics.

Almost half (46%) of the adult day centers included in the study reported having started client waiting lists between 1984 and 1986;

30% of senior centers, 20% of hospices, and 7% of home health agencies reported having done the same. Adult day centers reported being forced to take action to restrict services (in the form of client waiting lists) because of space and staff limitations as well as the growing number of clients seeking services.

Nursing homes were the most likely of all provider types to report having waiting lists. Almost two thirds (64%) of the nursing homes surveyed had lists, and, in more than half the nursing homes, the waiting list grew during the 18-month period of the interviews. The shortage of nursing home beds in many areas (Harrington & Swan, 1985) may account for the high percentage of these facilities reporting waiting lists. The median waiting period was 3 weeks. Considering the condition of sicker elderly patients discharged from hospitals under the PPS and the increased number of patients in need of nursing home care (DesHarnais et al., 1987; U.S. GAO, 1987b), a 3-week wait for placement is, indeed, problematic.

Service Intensity Needs

The early discharge of patients from hospitals shifts the burden of care, in most cases, to another care provider. Older patients discharged from hospitals may no longer be in need of acute care services yet not be well enough to return home without receiving formal nursing care or other types of posthospital care. The medical care needs of elderly patients discharged early from hospitals pose new challenges to long term care providers. All five agency types included in the IHA study reported changes in the service intensity needs of clients referred for care after 1984.

Of the home health agencies in the study, 92% reported increases in the proportion of persons seeking care with high illness acuity ratings (that is, needing more hours of care per day). The HHAs also noted an increase in the number of persons requiring services immediately following discharge, needing multiple services, needing daily services, needing more than usual total hours of care, and needing more high-tech services.

The majority of nursing homes reported that persons referred after 1984 typically required higher levels of care and had higher than usual illness acuity ratings. Patients received by hospices, after 1984, were increasingly likely to require medical-technical interventions, such as intravenous therapy. The U.S. General Accounting Office (1986), Lyles (1986), and Wood and colleagues (1986) report similar findings.

Adult day-care centers reported that clients referred after 1984 required more supervision, were more likely to suffer severe functional impairments, and generally required more hours of care than had been the case in the past. Senior centers proved the exception. Considerably less than half (43%) of the senior centers studied reported receiving persons requiring "more than usual staff supervision" or more likely to have severe functional impairments. Senior centers were about half as likely as adult day-care centers to report dramatic changes in clientele. This difference would be expected given that senior centers generally serve a client population that is more active in the community.

The PPS and Elderly Clients

At the conclusion of the IHA study, agency directors were asked about their perceptions of the relationship between changes in their clientele since 1984 and the implementation of the hospital prospective payment system. Most home health agency (91%), hospice (89%), and nursing home (84%) respondents indicated a connection between client changes and the PPS. Adult day-care center directors (53%) also reported clientele changes that they attributed to the implementation of the PPS. Even senior centers (56%), which accommodate the community elderly, reported that the hospital PPS had affected clientele demands on their centers. Agencies reporting changes in clientele explicitly as a result of the PPS noted that patients were physically sicker and in need of longer than usual and higher levels of care. Among home health agencies, 95% reported negative PPS effects on clientele.

Related Policy Issues

The major changes occurring in U.S. health policy and the transformation of the health care system that commenced in the 1980s make attributing changes in health care delivery directly to the PPS reimbursement policy extremely difficult (Guterman & Dobson, 1986; United Hospital Fund, 1986; U.S. GAO, 1986). While the PPS policy is unquestionably a factor in producing shifts in the number and needs of elderly recipients of long term care services, the policy is not the only factor operating. Manley (1987) cites the changing number and composition of the elderly client population as additional elements affecting service delivery after the PPS. Other influences include an increasingly competitive health care market, the expansion of community-based long term care, the rise in the use of complex medical technologies, changes in Medicaid policies (waivers and state policies), and other modifications in Medicare policy (Lyles, 1986; U.S. COTA, 1985; Van Gelder & Bernstein, 1986).

As noted in Chapter 1, the PPS accelerated the trend toward declining lengths of stay for elderly patients in acute care hospitals (Gornick & Hall, 1988; ProPAC, 1990). Hatten and Gibson (1987) report that, under the PPS, there was a dramatic decrease in the total number of Medicare stays in addition to a drop in hospital lengths of stay. Smith and Picard (1986) conclude that the PPS produced significant reductions in average length of stay, total days, and hospital occupancy rates but did not have a significant effect on admissions. Coe, Wilkinson, and Patterson (1986) agree that the national trend toward shortened hospital stays may have been accelerated by the implementation of the PPS. These researchers report that dependency-at-discharge scores have increased in three of five studied DRGs (pneumonia, heart failure, and hip replacement) and conclude that cost-containment policies are having an impact on the health status of patients in certain DRG classes.

Many of the above studies imply that the health care needs of elderly patients discharged from hospitals earlier and in sicker condition under the PPS than was previously the case have been spilling over into other parts of the formal (and informal) care systems. Congressional committees predicted that the discharge of elders "quicker and sicker" from hospitals as a result of the Medicare PPS would increase the need for appropriate and affordable follow-up health care (U.S. House of Representatives, 1986c), specifically nursing home and home health care (U.S. Senate, 1985).

A number of research studies have investigated the impact of the PPS policy on posthospital care. The GAO documents that, in 1984, the percentage of hospital discharges for Medicare patients to home health agencies and nursing homes was approximately 3 times as high for PPS hospitals as for non-PPS hospitals (U.S. GAO, 1986). DesHarnais and associates (1987) report that, in both 1984 and 1985, significantly greater percentages of Medicare patients were discharged to home health care and to skilled nursing facilities than in years immediately prior to the implementation of the PPS. A 1985 U.S. Department of Health and Human Services report suggests a "fairly strong relationship" between shortened hospital stays and the use of home health care. In five of the six urban communities studied by the U.S. General Accounting Office (1985), home health care providers reported delivering more intensive care (i.e., longer and more frequent visits) to clients in the home after the PPS. As early as 1983-1984, there was evidence of dramatic increases in the percentage of elderly being served by local service providers and in the illness acuity levels of agency clients (Wood et al., 1986). Researchers attribute these changes primarily to the decreased length of hospital stays under the PPS. The research findings above indicate the heightened importance, since the PPS, of posthospital health care services.

The results of studies of the impact of the PPS on nursing homes are not always in agreement. More than 80% of the nursing home directors sampled by Lyles (1986) in Oregon reported increases in the severity of illness of patients and in the prevalence of clinical problems among their clients, and 65% indicated increases in the use of medical supplies (Lyles, 1986). These changes were explained, in part, by earlier hospital discharge following PPS implementation.

In contrast to the Oregon study, Lewis, Leake, Leal-Sotelo, and Clark (1987) found, in their study of the initial effects of the PPS on nursing home patients in southern California, modest case-mix differences and no changes in patient discharge outcomes (i.e., percentage dying in the skilled nursing facility or returning to the hospital).

Conclusion

Community-based agencies have been confronted by both increased demand for posthospital services and a demand for levels, intensity, and duration of care not previously experienced. Agencies report an increased number of clients aged 65 and over and 85 and over, mixed results on changes in low-income clientele, increased barriers to access in the form of waiting lists and outright refusals to serve certain types of clients, and greater service intensity needs of those referred since 1984 to posthospital and continuing care services. Finally, the majority of respondents in each agency type perceived that the foregoing client changes were linked to the Medicare PPS.

The magnitude and complexity of health policy changes during the 1984 to 1986 period make controlling for all factors that might also account for client changes impossible. Thus, in the current cost-conscious environment, the PPS may serve as a convenient scapegoat to explain the inability of agencies to provide all needed services and serve all clients. Whatever the explanation, the IHA survey suggests that, for many elderly persons, out of the hospital may mean out of luck.

CHAPTER 5

Service Paradox

[The] American health care system . . . [is] a paradox of plenty and of want, a system where some receive the benefit of the most advanced medical technologies in the world, yet many . . . families can't get help to keep a frail parent from having to go into a nursing home.
Senator Dave Durenberger (in the Pepper Commission, 1990b, p. 2)

A variety of service changes have occurred in community-based long term care for the elderly since the advent of the Medicare prospective payment system (PPS) in October 1983. Although the PPS introduced a system of scheduled, flat-fee payments based on diagnosis-related groups (DRGs) to slow the escalation of federal, state, and third-party costs for hospital care, there have been important effects on the provision of community-based services as a result of this policy (Estes, Wood, et al., 1988; Wood & Estes, 1986, 1990).

Of all aspects of community-based long term care that have been affected over the past decade, issues regarding services—including the availability and provision of different types of services as well as staffing, organizational, and other related changes—are among the most significant and least studied. It is critical at this juncture to study the nature and scope of service changes in community-based home health, adult day care, hospice programs, senior centers, and community mental health centers.

The service paradox is that, in this era of rapid technological change in medicine, the attention of researchers and policymakers

---

NOTE: The authors of this chapter are Elizabeth A. Binney and Carroll L. Estes.

has been captured by home care and other community-based sup-portive services (Benjamin, 1992). The paradox results from tradi-tional conceptions of home care that place it in the realm of informal, unskilled, inexpensive, and low-tech care—an anomaly in the cur-rent age of high-tech medical scientific revolution. Yet, as Benjamin suggests, the so-called nursing home problem (i.e., the policy bias toward institutionalization), the demographic revolution, and pol-icy fallout from cost-containment policies have all contributed to major transformations in the provision and delivery of community-based long term care.

An important factor in the changing spectrum of services is an altered perception of and reliance on biomedicine as the primary dis-cipline of value and utility for solving the problems of aging and old age in the United States. Medicine and the medical-industrial complex are dually recognized as forces in the progress of the medical manage-ment of old age and as major participants in the medical hegemony of aging. Crisis in the provision of community-based and long term care is a result of (a) the limited ability of curative medicine to ameliorate many of the conditions that affect large segments of the population and place the elderly at particular risk; (b) the course and treatment require-ments of chronic illnesses; (c) the preference of elders for home, rather than institutional, care; and (d) the effects of changes in technology on the location of many care regimens (Binney & Estes, 1988).

Changing Spectrum of Services

Perhaps the most immediate and obvious reasons for changes in the provision of community-based care for the elderly are the shifts in societal needs that have occurred in the mid- to late 1980s. First, demo-graphics altered perspectives on priorities and called into question the way societal resources are to be allocated. These changes have not only raised issues of generational equity but revised notions of filial, familial, and fiscal responsibility vis-à-vis the elderly. Along with alterations in perceptions of societal values and priorities, there have been empirical changes in need and demand for community-based long term care services.

The decline in mortality and rise in life expectancy in this century have resulted in a growing aging population that will be living longer with increased chronic illness and disability (Verbrugge, 1989). Current population data indicate that both the elderly and the oldest-old (aged 85 and over)—groups with the greatest need for acute, postacute, and long term care—will be among the fastest growing populations through the year 2020 (Manton & Suzman, 1992). Research shows, in fact, that the proportion of older people with disabling conditions is increasing over time (Rice & LaPlante, 1988; Verbrugge, 1984), indicating that the need for all types of services also will be growing rapidly into the next century. Ironically, Verbrugge (1989) and others note that mortality declines are accompanied by a significant increase in disability and that the net result of medical interventions is the addition of years of life expectancy spent in disability (Estes & Rundall, 1992). The paradox of the demographic imperative is that the medical care contributing to expanding longevity is the same care that threatens to vanquish the provision of chronic, community-based, and long term care supportive services.

Changes within the elderly population also account for changing service needs. It is well documented in this volume and elsewhere that one of the major effects of the PPS is the earlier release of acute care elderly patients in an increasingly seriously ill condition—the "quicker and sicker" phenomenon (Chapter 4; Chelimsky, 1986; DesHarnais et al., 1987; Estes, Wood, et al., 1988; Fischer & Eustis, 1988; Goldberg & Estes, 1990; Guterman et al., 1988; United Hospital Fund, 1986; Wood & Estes, 1990).

Changes also have occurred in service needs. First, the increased acute needs of posthospital patients altered the nature of demands on community care providers, particularly those caring for elders immediately after hospital discharge. Second, community providers noted that the changes in client needs created changes in the focus or spectrum of service provision. For example, even senior centers reported increased demand for medical and health services from their clientele (Goldberg, 1988), indicating that even providers who operate at some distance from acute care settings experience the effects of early hospital discharge. Third, social changes occurring during the period of PPS-related early hospital discharge, including a declining economy, geographic mobility, and women's labor force participation, have also contributed to a socially reconstructed (Berger & Luckmann, 1966; Estes et al., 1984) view of the environment in which community-based services for the elderly are delivered. Women's labor force participation is often addressed in terms of its detrimental effect on the availability of informal caregivers and its consequent threat to the continued availability and expandability of a pool of unpaid long term care service providers.

Geographic mobility is another social factor contributing to the changing face of community-based services for the elderly. Like women's labor force participation, the geographic mobility of the young, and especially those who are middle aged, is viewed as threatening the continuing care of older persons. Likewise, the declining economy is both a new and an old theme affecting the provision of services for the elderly. Compared with other issues of the past or current time, economic problems have contributed more to constraints on the provision of services through increased fiscal austerity in public financing. Cost containment, particularly in the area of social services (Estes, 1991), has especially threatened nonprofit providers (Abramson & Salamon, 1986)—the bedrock of nonmedical community-based care.

High-Technology Revolution

The challenge presented by medical technology is, at this point, not assessable in terms of its eventual impact because of innumerable uncertainties of the economy, policymaking, and many other factors. This uncertainty extends especially to the uses and impact of technology on the lives of the aged, who are the object of a disproportionate amount of debate on the rationing of high-technology allocated to the elderly in our society. With the exception of severely compromised infants and children, nowhere in the domain of medicine have science and technology come to such a crossroad as in the area of the provision of high-tech care, including home care, for the elderly. Sometimes described as a technological imperative, the necessity of using the most advanced technology to do the most good under any condition has been rendered problematic by issues of cost containment and the rationing of limited resources (Binney & Estes, 1990; Callahan, 1987; Homer & Holstein, 1990).

Nevertheless, the expansion of technology is a significant factor in the changing service environment of community-based care. Developments in technology, such as computerization and miniaturization, may be viewed benignly as altering the boundaries and limitations on the site and provision of care and allowing many technologies to be transferred to the home (Benjamin, 1992; Fox, Andersen, Benjamin, & Dunatov, 1987). From a positive perspective, this transfer is seen to achieve both the financial benefits of substituting home care for expensive hospitalization and the benefits of maintaining persons in their homes rather than in institutions.

In an alternative view, several issues are raised about the very real costs and liabilities of this expansion of high-tech care at home for both the individual and the broader service system. First, this expansion increases the need for and demands on informal caregivers. For example, the availability of an informal caregiver is sometimes a requirement for a person to become eligible for certain high-tech services to be provided in the home. Such requirements inevitably raise issues of equity and even issues of caregiver exploitation (in terms of their commitment of time, service, and liability). In this sense, technology facilitates the transfer of countless millions of hours of caregiving work to lay providers. Second, the medicalization of services places a premium on the provision of both high-tech and highly medical services and has serious implications for staffing, provider organizational structure, provider liability, and caregivers. Medicalization strongly affects the structure, organization, and financing of the entire community service system (Binney et al., 1990; Estes & Binney, 1989; Wood & Estes, 1988).

Third, changing service provision has accelerated major types of organizational change in home care and other service industries (Bergthold et al., 1990; Clarke & Estes, 1992; Estes & Wood, 1986; Estes et al., in press; Wood & Estes, 1990). In nearly all sectors of health and community-based care, the 1980s brought major transitions in organizational structure and auspice, including (a) a decline in the role of the public provider, (b) an infusion of for-profit providers into the service delivery system, and (c) a process of isomorphism, or homogenization of organizational structure and behavior (Chapter 2; Clarke & Estes, 1992; DiMaggio & Powell, 1983).

The decline of public sector provision and financing of care has profound implications not only in terms of access (the public sector has historically been a major provider of community-based health and social services, particularly to elderly persons with low and moderate incomes) but also in terms of the availability of a full spectrum of services beyond high-tech, postacute services reimbursed by Medicare. Because public providers have not been driven primarily by a concern for maximizing profits, they have, in the past, been more willing to provide less profitable services, especially nonreimbursable ones, more frequently needed by the chronically ill elderly in the community. Thus, even if the elderly could afford to increase their already high out-of-pocket costs to purchase services, the services they need may be increasingly difficult to find.

As discussed in Chapter 2, the nonprofit sector, the dominant auspice in health and social services for the first half of the 20th century (Marmor, Schlesinger, & Smithey, 1987), is also undergoing massive changes (Estes & Wood, 1986). The competition created by the expansion of for-profit providers into health and social services has fueled other organizational changes, one of which is the disappearance of differences between different types of organizations (e.g., nonprofits and for-profits) in form and function. This isomorphic phenomenon within industries, which occurs as organizations mimic one another in their attempt to survive under conditions of uncertainty, is a major under-studied development in community-based long term care (Clarke & Estes, 1992).

This isomorphic process appears to be having profound effects on services. One result is the expansion in the addition and provision of high-tech and medical-related services without a comparable expansion (and, in some cases, a reduction) in chronic care and social supportive services (Binney et al., 1990), as providers target highly profitable and reimbursable services at the expense of a comprehensive spectrum of services.

Rapid changes experienced in the home care industry include mergers, buyouts, and overall decline in the number of visiting nurse associations (VNAs), once the mainstay of the home care industry, to less than 10% of the U.S. Medicare-certified agencies (despite the fact that they provide more than 30% of all Medicare home care) (Scalzi & Meyer, 1991). These changes raise serious questions of access and quality for home care for the elderly and the disabled. Pressed by survival needs, service providers have altered both the content and the process of their service provision, often with little information or advanced preparation concerning the type or nature of new demands likely to be made of them.

Warring Dualism of Medicalization and Informalization

The provision of community-based services for the elderly in the PPS environment may be characterized as a case of the "warring dualism." This conceptualization acknowledges that the service environment is being reorganized and two complementary yet conflicting processes are occurring: medicalization and informalization.

Both public policies and technological advances have accelerated the medicalization of services provided in the community care system (Chapter 1). Providers of all types are being asked to provide more and more services outside the hospital that were once provided within it to elders whose health care needs are intensified due to shorter hospital stays (Binney et al., 1990). The medicalization of community-based services "accords legitimacy to the acute care needs while denying the legitimacy of social supportive needs of the elderly" (Wood & Estes, 1988, p. 36). The legitimation of medically related services and the delegitimation of social supportive services is taking place in a highly competitive environment in which providers are driven by funding and reimbursement requirements. Competition is occurring both within industry markets (Chapter 2) and between competing needs of other groups within society (Chapter 13). Competition and medicalization intersect in several ways in community-based care but nowhere so significantly perhaps as in service provision.

As a consequence, senior centers, hospices, adult day-care centers, and community mental health centers, as well as providers of home and nursing home care, have been required to respond to the pressures of reimbursement, competition, and demand, resulting in service-mix and service package changes that are weighted toward medical rather than social care. At stake is the availability of a continuum of care in the community and the existence of supportive services that may keep older people out of institutions. There also are specific links between the process of informalization and service provision. These links relate to both types of informalization identified in Chapter 9. The first type of informalization, the transfer of care from a more formal to a less formal provision site (in either the home or the community), has obvious implications for services. The second, the transfer of care from paid formal provision to unpaid provision by family and friends, has an equally important relationship to service provision.

Nursing home care represents a major area in which formal services might be informalized. State and federal governments are already attempting to reduce the high cost of nursing home care, particularly under Medicaid, by encouraging informal caregiving in the home. Of interest, this could have unanticipated effects on the labor market. A return to informal care of the functionally dependent might reduce the ability of women to work outside the home. For example, in estimating a model of state-level demand and supply for Medicaid nursing home care, Miller, Swan, and Harrington (1992) found that the percentage of women in the labor force had one of the strongest effects on Medicaid demand for nursing home bed days; a 1% difference in women's labor force participation is estimated to increase Medicaid demand by 3%. This finding is interpreted to mean that higher proportions of women in the labor force diminish the availability of informal supports, resulting in dramatically higher need for nursing home services. The extent to which unavailability of nursing home services keeps women out of the labor force is unknown, but the finding suggests such an effect or, conversely, that women's labor force participation may set limits on the possibilities of informalization of services now rendered in an institutional setting.

Similar relationships between women's labor force participation and home health care also apply. Because the availability of informal support is necessary for an elder who needs home care to remain at home, Swan and Benjamin (1990a, 1990b) predicted and found women's labor force participation to reduce the use of Medicare home health care due to their unavailability to provide informal support. Swan and Benjamin have not considered the question of possible effects of home health use on the labor force status of women, but there appears to be an empirically demonstrated trade-off between informalization of care and the labor force participation of women when Medicaid nursing home and Medicare home health care utilization is examined.

Changes in Community Service
Provision Under Prospective Payment

Several trends in service provision were similar across all provider types studied in both 1986 and 1987. In 1986, directors were asked whether, since 1984, they had added or dropped services, increased or decreased provision of specific types of services, and what services most frequently requested could not be provided. The same questions were asked again in 1987, measuring any changes from the previous year (IHA, 1986, 1987). Providers tended to add services to their list of available services far more frequently than they dropped them. Of services added, medical and/or high-tech services tended to be added far more frequently than social services or other services for chronically ill persons. This trend was consistent across provider types, from the most immediate postacute providers (discharge planners, home health providers, nursing homes) to providers that are more distant from the acute care hospital setting (senior centers, adult day care, community mental health centers, and hospices).

The fact that, consistently across provider types, few services were eliminated reflects the growth and extension of community care occurring in spite of the current environment rather than a fundamental change in provision strategy. There were similar patterns in the types of services selected for elimination, the vast majority of services dropped being social or custodial services. Only senior centers reported eliminating medical or high-tech services and this in large part due to budget constraints forcing the cutback of contracted health screening and clinic services. The data indicate that providers across the board were attempting to restructure service provision to meet the demands of an increasingly postacute and frail older population. Yet, in an environment constrained by cost containment, some providers were forced to consolidate and eliminate services. The majority of services cut were the less reimbursable and less profitable ones. There were almost no cases in which a medical or high-tech service was eliminated. The services requested by clients that agencies could not provide were social and custodial long term care services, ranging from transportation and meals to housekeeping/chore and social work services. This pattern suggests that the provision of a broad spectrum of services may be in jeopardy.

Home Health Care

Home health care remains one of the most empowering of the health services, enabling disabled and frail people to remain in their homes and communities by receiving assistance with health, caregiving, and other daily needs. Despite its importance, home health care is one of the most underfunded and burdened provider sectors in the health sector today. The growth in this sector over the past decade has piqued a tremendous interest on the part of policymakers, the health care industry, and the public. Consequently, home health and home care have become a major issue on the health policy agenda (Council on Scientific Affairs, 1990; Estes, Wood, et al., 1988).

Six services are covered by Medicare home health benefits: skilled nursing, physical therapy (PT), speech therapy, occupational therapy (OT), home health aide, and medical social work. To receive benefits, however, a client must be judged to have a need for at least one of the first three services; therefore a client in need only of the last three technically cannot qualify for these services under Medicare. Benjamin, Fox, Swan, and associates (1989) found high levels of need for Medicare-covered home health services (as well as other services) 6 months after hospital discharge, which is long after the usual home health spell of service. Thus the inability of elders to fit the restrictive Medicare eligibility profile disqualifies many potential users from continuing to receive the Medicare-covered services they still need (Chapter 8).

Swan, Benjamin, and Fox (1991) studied the use of Medicare services during the home health period. Although receipt of skilled nursing was much more common (79% of sample) than receipt of PT (54%), users of both received about the same number of visits of each type (7 and 6, respectively) during an average stay of 35 days. Receipt of speech therapy was very infrequent (Benjamin et al., 1989). Home health aide and OT users averaged 8 and 4 visits, respectively. That receipt of OT, but not number of visits, was related to numbers of PT visits received (or, alternatively, to length of home health period) is interpreted to mean that OT services ultimately tend to be allowed after some period of receipt of other care, particularly PT, rather than initially planned.

To examine some of the service trends occurring in home health care, a panel of practicing home health providers rated a list of specific services to differentiate services relative to one another on their degree of medicalization, although it is understood that, to be reimbursed by Medicare and most private insurance, most home health care today is medical service provision. This rating was used to analyze all aspects of service change, including services added, dropped, and requested but not provided by agencies.

In both 1986 and 1987, services added by home health agencies were likely to be highly medical (45% in 1986 and 66% in 1987) with only 21% and 15% of services added in respective years rated as low or nonmedical services. It is important to note that the rapid organizational and structural changes occurring in the home health industry are also likely to have an effect on the kinds of services agencies will provide (Clarke & Estes, 1992; Estes et al., in press). Consistent with the hypothesis of isomorphism, which suggests that nonprofit and for-profit home health providers have begun to resemble each other in the types of services they can and cannot provide (Clarke & Estes, 1992), both nonprofits and for-profits showed very little difference in the types of services added in 1986-1987. This contrasts with the 1984-1986 period, when for-profits were more likely than nonprofits to add highly medical services and nonprofits more likely than for-profits to add nonmedical services (Binney et al., 1990). Certification status predicted similar service trends. Medicare-certified agencies consistently reported that a greater percentage of the services they added were highly medical, while uncertified agencies added larger percentages of less medical services than their certified counterparts (Binney et al., 1990).

Another measure of the changing service environment, the requested services that agencies cannot provide, also supports the medicalization hypothesis and transfer of care to the informal sector. Of requested services that home health agencies could not provide in both 1986 and 1987, almost two thirds were low medical (social) services, and an additional 13% were moderately medical. Both the isomorphism of for-profits and nonprofits and the differences by certification status are again supported on this service measure. While there were differences between nonprofit and for-profit providers in the 1984-1986 period, nonprofit and for-profit home health agencies were virtually indistinguishable by 1987 in their overwhelming report of low medical services as the ones they were unable to provide. Similarly, the differences between certified and uncertified providers were reduced considerably between the 1986 and 1987 data periods, suggesting that changes in and demands on the overall service environment were beginning to have an effect on the entire industry, regardless of tax status or dependence on a particular funding source.

High-tech home health services are becoming increasingly common, specialized, and expensive, which reflects the dominant set of trends in home care. The change in the locus of heavy and high-tech care from the hospital into the home has increased the need for skilled, capable, and available home care providers; necessitated changes in the structure and organization of the providers of care, including changes in the practice patterns and assessment skills of physicians; increased the need for coordination of discharge planners, case managers, and community care providers; and entailed innumerable other major changes. Much of the impact of these changes on the cost, quality, and outcomes of care is, as yet, unknown.

Adult Day Care

Adult day care, one of the fastest growing sectors of the community-based care system, is an important alternative to institutionalization for many elders (Hedrick, 1991; Von Behren, 1986, 1988; Weissert, Elston, Bolda, et al., 1989; Wood, 1989). Although it is unclear whether adult day care is a lower cost alternative to nursing home care (Ham, 1985; Harder, Gornick, & Burt, 1986; Hedrick, 1991; Weissert, Elston, Musliner, & Mutran, 1991; Weissert et al., 1989; Wood, 1989; Wood & Ingman, 1988), there has been tremendous growth of adult day care from just 15 centers in 1973 (Wood, 1989) and 300 centers in 1978 to more than 2,000 in 1989 (Von Behren, 1989). Likewise, the estimated number of persons using adult day care increased from 5,000 to more than 70,000 persons from 1978 to 1989 (Von Behren, 1989), making the service an important component of community-based long term care. In addition, the "quicker and sicker" phenomenon of hospital discharges after the implementation of DRG-based prospective payment has placed extraordinary pressure on community providers of posthospital care and opened the way for adult day care to assume a major role in postacute care rather than its initial orientation toward the provision of chronic care (Wood, 1989; Wood & Ingman, 1988).

The organization of adult day care varies along a continuum of organizational forms, client populations, and service offerings (Conrad, Hanrahan, & Hughes, 1990; Conrad, Hughes, Campione, & Goldberg, 1987; Luken & Vaughan, 1990; Weissert et al., 1989; Weissert et al., 1991; Wood, 1989; Wood & Ingman, 1988). A traditional distinction frequently used is that of *social* versus *medical* or *health* models of adult day care (Weissert, 1976, 1977), but many authors have recently pointed out that, with growth and diversity within the industry, these terms have lost their conceptual clarity and utility (Von Behren, 1989; Weissert, 1977, 1978; Weissert et al., 1989; Weissert et al., 1991; Wood, 1989). Weissert and colleagues (1989, 1991) suggest that service mix represents one set of characteristics that can aid in distinguishing different models of adult day-care centers.

In the IHA studies, almost two thirds (62%) of adult day-care centers reported adding services between 1984 and 1986, while less than one third (31%) did so in the subsequent year. The majority of services added, such as medical therapies including rehabilitation therapy, were required to obtain Medicaid certification or to attract or retain Medicaid clients. This trend reflects the degree to which Medicaid is becoming an increasingly important source of revenue for these centers (Wood, 1989; Wood & Ingman, 1988) as well as a predictor of service availability. Adult day-care programs with at least some reliance on Medicaid as a funding source are twice as likely to have added services in 1986 than those without Medicaid.

Expansion of services was typical of the 1984 to 1987 period; only 2 of 39 agencies in each of the survey years reported dropping any services. Medical services such as rehabilitation therapies and respiratory therapies became more available by the 1987 survey. In both years of the survey, however, the most frequently requested services that agencies could not provide were extended hours and respite care, the latter being a service cited almost twice as frequently in 1987 as it was in 1986 (27% in 1986 to 44% in 1987). This trend also reflects the changing nature of adult day care and its increasingly heavy-care clientele (Wood, 1989; Wood & Ingman, 1988).

By 1987, service changes slowed down, and fewer agencies reported increases in the provision of specific core services such as health monitoring, mental health counseling, social work, and rehabilitation therapy than in the year before. Another indicator of the beginning of a period of stabilization is agency reports of effects of the PPS on services. In 1986, a higher percentage of agencies reported an effect on services (37% in 1986 to 30% in 1987). But there were important differences between the 2 years. In 1986, agencies that depended on Medicaid as a source of income were less likely to report an effect of the PPS on services than those with no Medicaid sources. By 1987, these differences had disappeared and there was no difference between the two types of agencies in the likelihood of reporting such an effect, which points to increased stability in funding sources and overall growth of the field. Medicaid funding appears to have buffered the potential effects of the PPS on adult day-care providers, whereas adult day-care centers (ADCCs) that were more reliant on private pay were more exposed to the demands of elders after hospital discharge. Because Medicaid continues to be the largest single source of funds in the industry (Weissert et al., 1991; Zelman, Elston, & Weissert, 1991), and Medicaid certification initiates the provision of more medical services, adult day-care service trends need to be followed closely with respect to the needs of chronically ill as well as acutely ill clients.

There are few data on the interrelationship between adult day care and other community health providers. Kirwin and Kaye (1991), in a regional study, have examined the range and frequency of informal, adult day care and other service and care usage by adult day clients. Their data show that there are major overlaps in the nature and frequency of the wide range of services provided by the various networks but that major types of care regularly fall through the cracks (Kirwin & Kaye, 1991). These results indicate that much more work is needed not only on the interorganizational relations between the provider networks (Estes, Wood, et al., 1988) but in terms of understanding the organization and coordination of individual care, including the role played by providers like adult day care.

Community Mental Health Centers

Community mental health centers (CMHCs) have traditionally underserved the elderly, with low proportions of center clientele being aged (Flemming, Buchanon, Santos, & Rickards, 1986). Although the aged have a lower prevalence of many psychiatric disorders than do younger populations (Bliwise, McCall, & Swan, 1987), low use of services by the elderly is in large part attributable to physical or geographic access problems (Swan & McCall, 1987). Funding and reimbursement issues also limit the scope and delivery of services (Harper, 1992; Ray, List, Clinkscale, Duggar, & Pollatsek,

1987). For example, Medicare funding excludes all freestanding CMHC services (Flemming et al., 1986).

Swan, Fox, and Estes (1989) found service budgets of CMHCs to be positively affected when their aged clientele either increased or decreased. This suggests that there may be incentives for CMHCs to specialize either on elderly clientele or on younger clientele. In light of the already extremely low representation of the elderly among CMHC client populations, about 6% in 1985 (Flemming et al., 1986), and the importance of geographic accessibility of services to the elderly, such specialization could result in extreme barriers to access for the aged.

Fox and Swan (1988) report findings of 94 community mental health centers interviewed in 1986 and 1987. Directors of CMHCs reported changes in the types of clients served, especially in the number of acutely ill elderly clients. The majority recounted providing either increased or stable levels of service to the elderly. The types of service shifts attributed to the PPS most frequently related to the need for increases in the duration of the client care period and the need for more client case management. Fox and Swan (1988) project that the trend of increases in the frequency and duration of services provided to clients as a result of DRGs will continue because of "the paucity of federal initiatives that could lead to the development of a comprehensive mental health policy for the elderly, as well as for other age groups" (Fox & Swan, 1988, p. 174).

In general, reimbursement systems are reported as inadequate and as providing disincentives for CMHCs to provide services to elderly clients. In addition, CMHCs have been moving toward a more restrictive budgetary climate; only a small number of centers in the IHA study reported recent budget increases. More than 60% of responding CMHCs reported tightening eligibility in the 1984 to 1987 period, and more than two thirds reported establishing waiting lists in that period. One result of shifting responsibility for mental health services from federal seed grants to state and local funding is wide variation in the scope and type of care offered across geographic areas, threatening access to needed services.

Senior Centers

Senior centers have rarely been considered in analyses of the impact of PPS policies or in analyses of many other federal or state policy changes. Yet, as community-based providers with an estimated 10,000-12,000 facilities offering a broad range of social, nutritional, and health services to 5 to 8 million community-resident elderly persons (Goldberg, 1988; Krout, 1989; Krout, Cutler, & Coward,

1990), these agencies are also experiencing many effects of such recent policy changes (Goldberg, 1988; Krout et al., 1990; Ralston, 1987; Wood, 1985). It is estimated that 15% of the population aged 65 and over attended a senior center in the past year. This 4 to 12 times greater use than for any other community-based service for the elderly (Havir, 1991; Krout et al., 1990; Wood, 1985) makes senior centers an extremely important locus of community care provision.

Senior centers typically provide a variety of services including health-related services (health monitoring, screening, mental health counseling), social supportive services (meals, transportation), and social and recreational programs (educational classes, art activities, exercise programs). Yet the issues of cost containment and fiscal austerity pose difficult questions for senior centers as well as for other community providers.

The IHA study of a random sample of 104 senior centers in five states and twelve communities comprised approximately 70% non-profit and 30% public centers. Due to the importance of senior centers in providing a variety of services to the community-resident elderly, it is important to understand whether organizational auspice and funding source make a difference in service delivery. The reported ability to provide particular levels and types of services is one indicator of differences in types of centers. In 1986, more than two thirds (69%) of center directors reported adding services, a figure that fell slightly (to 58%) in 1987. In both surveys, approximately one fourth of directors reported dropping services. There were, however, significant differences between public senior centers and nonprofit centers. In 1986, public agencies were much more likely than nonprofits to add services (90% to 59%) while nonprofits were much more likely to drop services (40% to 3%). Both types of centers were most likely to add health and medical care services first and then transportation and nutrition/meals. Centers that dropped services tended to drop transportation (a relatively expensive service to maintain) and socially oriented services such as outreach. By the second year of the survey, the differences between the two types of centers had disappeared. Slightly more than half of both types of providers (53% of public and 61% of nonprofit) added services, both social/recreational and health (particularly screening), and 20% to 25% of centers dropped services, primarily transportation.

Hospice Care

Hospices are another of the fastest growing community-based service providers, providing an alternative to hospital care for the terminally ill patient. Emerging in the United States in the 1970s, the hospice movement attempted to demedicalize the dying process and provide more appropriate and specialized care for the dying. U.S. hospice care took on a different organizational, if not philosophical, structure than its European forebears, with the U.S. model emphasizing home rather than institutional care. When the potential for savings in costly hospital care, especially in the last months and weeks of life, captured the interest of health policymakers, hospice became the subject of a major congressional demonstration project, the 1979-1980 National Hospice Study.

In the fervor of cost containment and without knowing the results of this demonstration, Congress made hospice a limited Medicare benefit in the 1982 Tax Equity and Fiscal Responsibility Act (TEFRA) (Mor, 1987). The hospice benefit contained a number of important restrictions designed to cap costs by (a) ensuring that there is a major contribution of informal caregiving, (b) imposing a 210-day lifetime limit, and (c) forfeiture of other Medicare benefits on election of the hospice benefit. Subsequently, hospice became an optional Medicaid benefit.

As a condition of participation in Medicare, hospices must provide a specific set of core services including physician services, skilled nursing care, medical social services, counseling, and a valid contract with an inpatient facility. Hospices must also agree to a cap on inpatient utilization (Hoyer, 1990). These limitations have greatly restricted participation in Medicare by hospice programs. The IHA sample included a disproportionately large percentage of Medicare-certified providers (42% in 1986 and 38% in 1987, due, perhaps, to the urban bias of the sample) in contrast to the estimated 22% to 30% nationally in this time period. Medicare participation remains low, although it may be reaching 40% to 50% as a result of an increase in the payment rate effective in 1990. The medicalized bias of the Medicare program has made it much more difficult for small hospices and those in rural areas to meet the core service requirements for participation (Hoyer, 1990; Mor, Hendershot, & Cryan, 1989).

One fear within the hospice movement is that, in the environment of fiscal austerity and cost containment, the inclusion of hospice benefits in publicly financed reimbursement schemes might alter the initial purpose, availability, and delivery of hospice care and services. Of concern is the changing environment of delivery—the original home and noninstitutional base of the U.S. hospice movement has given way to a major entry of hospital and other institutional providers of hospice care (Mor, 1987; Mor et al., 1989; Wong, Ingman, & Wood, 1988). The IHA sample included 25% institutional providers, lower than the estimated 27% to 45% of hospital-based providers reported nationally by other sources (Longo, McCann, & Ahlgren, 1987; National Hospice Organization, 1987). A second concern is that, as a result of the PPS, the demands being placed on hospice programs have increased. Hospices are receiving more acutely ill and heavy-care clientele in part due to the increase in high-tech interventions. There also is an increased need for intensive and more highly trained informal caregivers (Wong et al., 1988). The current payment policy, which does not differentiate case mix, may be the greatest jeopardizing factor to the full expansion of hospice service because it provides disincentives to accept heavy-care patients or clients who could exceed the 210-day limit.

Because so few of the sample hospice agencies were either public (4%) or private (8%) as opposed to nonprofit (88%) and because the sample was small in general, it was not feasible to stratify service provision on the basis of auspice or other dimensions. Nevertheless, several interesting trends were observed. In both 1986 and 1987, the services provided by hospice agencies were fairly stable in terms of the spectrum of services provided. Of the relatively few changes reported in service provision, bereavement services were most frequently added, followed by skilled services and counseling. In both the 1986 and 1987 surveys, more than half (52%) of hospices reported that their current year budgets could only support services at the same or lower levels than in the previous year in spite of their reports of both a numerical increase in demand and increases in more frail and acutely ill clients in both 1986 (71%) and 1987 (54%). As a result, the majority of hospice providers in both surveys reported that clients required more medical and more high-tech care and more staff time.

Two important trends in the provision of hospice services emerged in the 1980s. The first trend involves the process of informalization described above and in Chapter 9. The warring dualism of informalization and medicalization converges in the case of hospice services for older persons. Both mechanisms of informalization—the transfer of care from more formal to informal sites of provision and the transfer of care from formal, paid providers to informal providers—are the cornerstones of the hospice philosophy. Yet medicalization, because of the incentives of the reimbursement system and the trickle-down effects of the PPS, interacts with the processes of informalization to contribute to significant changes in the delivery of hospice services.

At least two major questions remain as important research and policy issues for the future of hospice care as a component of the community-based care continuum. The first question relates to the importance of reimbursement patterns for the availability of high quality hospice care for all who seek it. The second relates to social and cultural reluctance to accept hospice care as an appropriate and positive alternative to other care choices for the terminally ill. In recent studies, Mor and associates (1989) and Prigerson (1991) note a lack of wide knowledge about and relatively low utilization of hospice services by elderly people, despite the expressed preference of the elderly for home care and Medicare coverage of hospice services. It is critical that the factors contributing to this discrepancy and the role played by health workers (especially doctors) and family members in this outcome be better understood.

Conclusion

The nation is at a crossroad in the provision of care for the elderly. The crises of aging and aging policy have led to a debate—an intergenerational tug-of-war—over resources that have been defined as scarce and finite, with allocation issues taking precedence over questions of need and appropriateness. There has been no consensual determination of how this allocation will be made. The timetable for this decision is vague. Yet, on a de facto basis, decisions on the distribution of resources are being made constantly and often in ways that occlude underlying assumptions of deservingness and right to access (Estes et al., 1984).

Health care can be allocated on a cost-benefit basis, with persons receiving health care on the basis of the "objective" benefit of service provision for society. Alternatively, health care can be provided on a market basis, with persons who can pay for certain levels of care receiving them and others receiving either nothing or an agreed to minimal level of care. The crossroad becomes an issue when what can be provided by society, both in terms of the capacity of the community-based long term care system to offer needed services and in terms of what can be accessed—found, afforded, and scheduled—collides with competing societal needs and priorities. The needs of elders and their caregivers will clearly continue to grow, particularly in the areas of chronic, long term care, and community-based services. How society will choose to meet the needs remains unclear. Subsequent chapters explore these issues for specific types of services, beginning with home health care in the next chapter.

CHAPTER **6**

Metamorphosis of Home Health Care

As Gregor Samsa awoke one morning from uneasy dreams he found himself transformed in his bed into a gigantic insect.

Kafka, 1961, p. 67

Profound changes in Medicare policy during the 1980s have contributed to the metamorphosis of home health care organizations. In response to policy changes, these and other community-based service organizations have adopted practices that have transformed the nature of services delivered, clients served, and organizational structures. Organizational responses to policy changes can be regarded as "transformative processes" because they have drastically altered the character of the organizations delivering health and social services (Estes, 1986). Four types of transformative processes that affect home health care organizations are discussed below: privatization, medicalization, changing labor conditions, and structural changes. These processes signify profound changes in access to community-based services.

Since 1980, several changes in government policy have affected the organization and delivery of home health services. For example, Medicare-certified home health agencies (HHAs) grew in number from 1,275 in 1966 to 5,962 in 1985 (Spiegel, 1987), an increase of 367%. The proprietary segment of the Medicare-reimbursed market grew from only 43 agencies in 1972 to nearly 2,000 agencies in 1985, constituting one third of the market (Spiegel, 1987). This increase of

---

NOTE: The authors of this chapter are Susan E. Humphers, Carroll L. Estes, and Linda A. Bergthold.

more than 4,000% is largely attributed to the Omnibus Reconciliation Act of 1980 and the prospective payment system (PPS) implemented in 1983 (Bergthold et al., 1990). Medicare policy has the single greatest influence on home health care, and implementation in 1983 of the PPS for hospitals under Medicare contributed to the acceleration of changes in the home health industry. The PPS has increased the demand for home health services by causing millions of older persons to be discharged from hospitals earlier than before (Lerman, 1987; U.S. Senate, 1991). More older persons are being discharged to home health care from various service organizations (Neu & Harrison, 1988; Spohn et al., 1987-1988; Wood & Estes, 1990). Government was quick to embrace and promote privatization of the industry during the 1980s (Bergthold et al., 1990), and private enterprise has been quick to exploit reimbursement schemes.

Theoretical Orientation

One characteristic of modern society is that organizations engage in processes of bureaucratization and rationalization (Scott, 1987; Weber, 1946). Home health care is no exception, and since the 1980s home health organizations have sought to rationalize the delivery of services. This process is, however, vulnerable to external policy influences as well as to internal mandates of efficiency and outcome maximization. Organizations such as home health agencies operate in an open system and are influenced by policy changes that occur outside of the organization (Spohn et al., 1987-1988). This premise highlights the interconnectedness of the policymaking and organizational processes. The effects of public policy can therefore be explained from the perspectives of policy changes and of organizational responses to these changes.

Van Gelder and Bernstein (1986), using an environmental impact model, identify numerous policies and other forces that affect the behavior of home health agencies. Environmental forces important to an understanding of home health agency (HHA) behavior include:

- Experimental payment systems and the Medicare hospice program
- Growth of community-based care
- State certificate-of-need policies
- Medicare hospital PPS
- Private long term care insurance

- Changes in technology
- Growth of the population over age 75
- Declining mortality rates

Spohn and associates (1987-1988) specify additional policy developments and environmental forces that encourage expansion of the
home health industry:

- Medicaid policy and the bureaucratic relationships between the federal,
  state, and local governments that administer long term care programs
  and the private agencies that deliver them
- Medicare waiver-of-liability provision, claims denial rates increasing
  fourfold, and agencies opting out of Medicare home health
- Cost-containment strategies and stringent regulations adopted by the
  Health Care Financing Administration (HCFA)
- The 1980 Omnibus Reconciliation Act (ORA)
- The 1987 OBRA, which added regulations addressing the quality of care

Process of Metamorphosis

The history of home health services dates back to 1796, when the
Boston Dispensary created the first home care program. The new
service sought to avoid the welfare stigma associated with hospital care
at the time. "The sick, without being pained by separation from their
families, may be attended and relieved at home" (Irwin, 1978, p. 4, cited
in Spiegel, 1987). Public and private funding for home health care was
limited, however, until 1965 because government provided little incentive for agencies to deliver home health services. The enactment of
Medicare in 1965 and subsequent revisions of the Medicare law provided the foundation for the growth and development of home health
care. From the beginning, Medicare-reimbursed home health services
have emphasized highly skilled and medically oriented care.

At first, qualification for Medicare reimbursement of home care
required a 3-day prior hospitalization and a declaration that the
client was homebound but not so ill as to require constant care.
Further restrictions included a limit on the number of home visits for
which Medicare would pay and a deductible for which the client was
responsible. These restrictions proved so prohibitive that, between
1970 and 1975, the number of Medicare-certified HHAs declined.
Only 1% of the health care labor force was employed in the home

health sector (Kahl & Clark, 1986), and home health care accounted for less that 2% of Medicare and Medicaid reimbursements (Doty, Liu, & Wiener, 1985). In addition to limited reimbursements, regulatory barriers contributed to the lack of growth in home health services (Wood, 1985-1986). Thus, prior to the implementation of Medicare, the organizational tenor of the home health sector was set by the traditional philanthropic service-oriented visiting nurse associations (VNAs) (Balinsky & Shames, 1985; Clarke & Pinkett-Heller, 1979; Salvatore, 1985) as opposed to the entrepreneurial course that later characterized the industry.

Home health care in an era of hospital cost containment has become increasingly visible and important. While family members provide most long term care, paid caregivers provide an estimated 15% to 40% of all extended assistance (U.S. DHHS, 1990). As the level of dependency increases, so too does the use of formal (paid) home health services. Approximately 8% of moderately dependent elderly persons use home health services compared with 38% of those who are severely dependent. On the average, however, 6% of all dependent elderly persons use formal home care services, and the majority of this assistance is provided by Medicare-certified home health agencies (U.S. DHHS, 1990).

In 1989, $9.7 billion was spent on formal (paid) home care, including nursing care, home health aides, medical social services, and speech, physical, and occupational therapy. Out-of-pocket payments for home care amounted to $2.1 billion (22% of the total); Medicaid expenditures, $3.3 billion (34% of total expenditures on home care); Medicare expenditures, $2.6 billion (27% of total home care expenditures); and private insurance expenditures, $600 million (U.S. Senate, 1991). Research indicates that, although eligibility for home health services was expanded to a limited degree during the early 1980s, the changing structure of the industry may have deleterious consequences for home health consumers (Bergthold et al., 1990).

Medicare only covers home health care services for cases in which there is a need for intermittent skilled nursing care or physical or speech therapy. Specifically, to qualify for Medicare home health services, an individual must be homebound and under a physician's care. Care is generally limited to 5 days per week for 2 to 3 weeks and may include the following services: skilled nursing care; physical, speech, or occupational therapy; medical social services; medical supplies and equipment (excluding drugs); and part-time services provided by a home health aide. Services must be provided by a Medicare-certified HHA (U.S. Senate, 1991).

In 1982, there were 3,415 Medicare-certified HHAs. By 1986, this number had climbed to 5,963. Home health use leveled off and began to decrease between 1984 and 1986 (Table 6.1). The number of participating agencies, as well as the volume of visits, decreased as a result of HCFA efforts to slow growth (U.S. Senate, 1991) by tightening regulations and increasing claims denials (see the Appendix). Because Medicare home health services were increasingly restricted following the implementation of the PPS in 1983, the chronically ill, but not postacute, elderly may not be receiving needed services.

Impact of Policy Changes

The 1980 Omnibus Reconciliation Act (ORA), along with deregulation and other policies designed to promote competition, triggered unprecedented growth in the home health industry during the 1980s (Rappaport & Wood, 1989; Scalzi & Meyer, 1991). The Appendix summarizes this and other policy developments affecting the home health industry. Prior to the 1980 ORA, proprietary HHAs could participate in Medicare only if they held a state license in the state in which they operated. This restriction discouraged proprietary agency participation in the Medicare home health program. The 1980 ORA, however, allowed proprietary agencies in states without licensure to receive Medicare reimbursement. Prior hospitalization and other limits on benefits were also eliminated by this policy. As a result, more than 20 states allowed licensed and unlicensed proprietary agencies to deliver Medicare reimbursable services (IOM, 1986a), thus drastically altering the character of the home health industry. During the 1983 to 1986 period, Medicare-certified hospital-based agencies grew in number nationwide from 597 to 1,370, a growth rate of 129%. The proprietary segment of the industry grew from 471 agencies in 1982 to 997 agencies in 1983, and to 1,899 agencies by 1986, reflecting a growth rate of 90% in the 3 short years surrounding the implementation of the PPS. Nonprofit agencies grew a mere 21%, from 674 agencies to 813 agencies in the same period (Lerman, 1987). The utilization of Medicare HHA services paralleled agency growth (U.S. Senate, 1991).

Between 1966 and 1984, the proportion of the home health care market made up of VNAs declined from 40% to 12% (Salvatore, 1985; Scalzi & Meyer, 1991; Figure 6.1). Industry growth is evidenced by trends in Medicare expenditures for home health care, which have drastically increased (Table 6.1). Medicare is the major program providing attractive market incentives sufficient to cause a former cottage industry to enter the arena of big business (Spohn et al., 1987-1988). In 1987, the home market was valued at approximately $3 to 5 billion; but, by 1990, the market was projected to be worth $8 to $19 billion, an average growth rate of 13% to 17%.

Prospective payment to hospitals, implemented in 1983 through a diagnosis-related group (DRG) system, is regarded as a significant force in the growth of the home health market, particularly in conjunction with the shorter hospital stays promoted by DRGs. The purpose of the PPS was to contain the rapidly escalating costs of hospital care. Elderly patients constitute nearly one third of all short-stay hospital admissions, usually for an acute episode of a chronic illness (U.S. Senate, 1991). By encouraging hospitals to shorten inpatient stays, the PPS increased demand for posthospitalization health and social services (DesHarnais et al., 1987; Guterman et al., 1988; Neu & Harrison, 1988; Spohn et al., 1987-1988; Van Gelder & Bernstein, 1986). This payment system has had a ripple effect on the organization and delivery of community-based long-term health and social services, thereby affecting access of the chronically ill aged to care (Wood & Estes, 1990) as well as that of the elderly who are too sick to qualify for the intermittent care test (U.S. House of Representatives, 1986a). The intermittent care test requires that a patient not be so ill as to need 24-hour care but be sick enough to require periodic care.

Kenney (1991) argues that the PPS caused increases in the number of home health users and the number of home health visits in the 2-year period following implementation. The PPS produced decreases in mean length of stay in hospitals and concomitant increases in home health agency use. The proportion of Medicare beneficiaries using home health care increased more than 9%, and the number of home health visits per user of home health care increased 19%.

Given that the PPS sought to contain the costs of institutional care, home health under Medicare came to be seen by policymakers as part of the problem of rising costs. Subsequent to the implementation of the PPS, outlays for home health care constituted the fastest growing component of Medicare. Expenditures increased from $287 million in 1976 to $1.7 billion in 1984 (United Hospital Fund, 1990). The Health Care Financing Administration claimed that, as a result of PPS cost containment associated with inpatient services, the efficiency of the health care system would increase as Medicare beneficiaries were redirected toward more appropriate types of nonhospital care. Following the period of rapidly escalating home care costs,

TABLE 6.1 Medicare Home Health Services

Year	Persons Served (thousands)	Persons Served per 1,000 Enrollees	Reimbursments (millions of dollars)	Visits (millions)	Visits per 1,000 Enrollees
1975	500	22	215	11	431
1980	957	34	662	22	788
1983	1,351	45	1,398	37	1,227
1984	1,516	50	1,666	40	1,324
1985	1,589	51	1,773	40	1,279
1986	1,600	50	1,796	38	1,208
1987	1,565	48	1,792	36	1,113
1988	1,565	48	1,792	36	1,113

SOURCE: Data from U.S. Senate (1991, p. 155).

however, HCFA attempted to limit expenditures and "refused to invest in alternative services and settings" (United Hospital Fund, 1990, p. 15). Medicare home health eligibility was subsequently tightened considerably. The impact is evidenced by the decline in the number of Medicare beneficiaries receiving home care, the decline in the number of visits per beneficiary, and the decreased outlays for home care (Table 6.1). Further, between 1985 and 1986, the number of home health claims filed decreased 5% while claims denials increased 73% (U.S. Senate, 1988).

The nature of Medicaid reimbursement has also affected the home health industry. Although Medicaid law (Title XIX of the Social Security Act) does not define home health services, states are required to provide a minimum range of services, including intermittent nursing care, home health aide services, and medical supplies and equipment. States have the option of providing audiology and occupational, speech, and physical therapy. Like Medicare, Medicaid only provides home health services on the recommendation of a physician.

Expenditures for home health care in the Medicaid program grew from $13 million in 1974 to $600 million in 1983, amounting to only 2% of all Medicaid outlays for that year. Because many separate state agencies administer Medicaid funds and establish eligibility and benefit structures, substantial programmatic and design differences across states discourage many HHAs from seeking Medicaid reimbursement. For example, Medicaid vendor payments for home health care varied widely in 1984 from a low of $8,159 in Oklahoma to $522,958,000 in New York State (Spiegel, 1987).

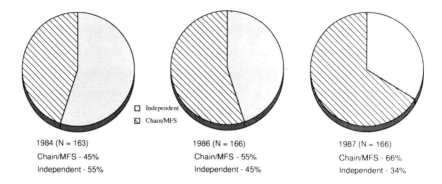

1984 (N = 163)
Chain/MFS - 45%
Independent - 55%

1986 (N = 166)
Chain/MFS - 55%
Independent - 45%

1987 (N = 166)
Chain/MFS - 66%
Independent - 34%

Figure 6.1. Changes in Home Health Organizational Structure, 1984-1987
SOURCE: Institute for Health & Aging DRG study (1986, 1987).

Current policy fails to address the long term care needs of the chronically ill population. Institute for Health & Aging research surveying home health agency administrators in 1986 and 1987 (Estes, Wood, et al., 1988) shows "a serious *lack of fit* between need for care and current policy, particularly the gap between the need for social supportive services (e.g., homemaker chore workers, shopping assistance, transportation, etc.) and Medicare's historic emphasis on medically oriented services" (Spohn et al., 1987-1988).

Several transformative processes were uncovered by the IHA study (1986, 1987; Estes, 1986), three of which are discussed below: privatization, medicalization, and changing labor conditions.

Privatization

The privatization of the home health industry is illustrated by the tremendous growth of its proprietary segment since the passage of the 1980 ORA. The proprietary segment of the industry increased from 4% of Medicare-certified agencies in 1976 to 33% in 1986 (United Hospital Fund, 1990). Privatization is identified in the "extent to which government is committed to the welfare state system of collective provision, financing, and regulation of services, as well as the degree to which a private market philosophy dominates the operation of these systems" (Bergthold et al., 1990, p. 4). The evidence clearly demonstrates that home health services have undergone extensive privatization as a result of policy changes and environmental influences.

Ideological, economic, and political forces that have promoted the privatization of home health care include

1. the shift or replacement of public and private nonprofit services by for-profit agencies;
2. the shift by HHAs from reliance on largely public funding mechanisms to private sources (e.g., insurance and private pay); and
3. the use of market criteria to distribute services in the home health sector. (Bergthold et al., 1990, p. 17)

The proprietarization or monetarization of health care, a specific type of privatization, was encouraged by the 1980 Omnibus Reconciliation Act (ORA) and the 1981 Omnibus Budget Reconciliation Act (OBRA). Both stimulated competition, deregulation, and the private provision and contracting out of services.

Bergthold and associates (1990) argue that the U.S. health care system is characterized by inadequate health and social services, an active private nonprofit sector, and a rapidly growing for-profit sector. Debate is rife as to whether privatization has negatively affected social equity. Relevant research by the Institute for Health & Aging suggests that privatization has already adversely affected socially marginal elderly consumers of health and social services in the United States. "If the consequences of privatization can be linked to the denial of service to needy clients, privatization may, indeed, represent a dark alternative to the welfare state" (Bergthold et al., 1990, p. 1). Nevertheless, government health and social service policies are encouraging privatization by transferring resources and responsibility from the nonprofit and public sectors to the for-profit sector.

Replacement

Privatization by replacement is defined as the replacement of public organizations or funding by private organizations or funding (LeGrand & Robinson, 1984). This process lacks clarity because of the level of complexity of the private nonprofit (or voluntary) sector. The nonprofit sector has long played a significant role in the delivery of human services in the United States. For example, approximately 46% of all public health care dollars and more than 80% of public social services dollars went to nonprofit organizations in 1986 (Estes

& Wood, 1986). Further, health and social services account for more than 62% of the annual resources of the nonprofit sector, constituting its largest component (Hodgkinson & Weitzman, 1988).

Despite the historic significance of the nonprofit home health sector, proprietary agencies began rapidly replacing nonprofits as a major factor in the industry during the 1980s. The number of public and nonprofit HHAs has been declining since the 1970s changes in Medicare and Medicaid created a favorable climate for proprietary home health agencies. The decline in numbers and proportion of public and nonprofit agencies accelerated during the 1980s (Bergthold et al., 1990). As a proportion of all Medicare-certified home health care agencies, nonprofit HHAs declined in number from nearly one third to less than one fourth between 1972 and 1986. During this same period, the number of hospital-based HHAs increased 105% to 1,165 agencies, while public HHAs declined 7%. During this time, for-profit HHAs increased 4,251%, to 1,871 agencies, constituting the fastest growing type of Medicare-certified agency. By 1986, proprietary agencies constituted 32% of the Medicare-certified home health agency market (Figure 6.1). In the period immediately following the implementation of the PPS, the growth rate of the proprietary segment of the industry was 93%, second only to the hospital-based agency growth rate (118%) (Spiegel, 1987). As noted, this trend came about largely as a result of the 1980 ORA, which liberalized home health benefits for Medicare beneficiaries and deregulated the industry by eliminating restrictions on Medicare certification of for-profit agencies located in states without licensure regulations.

Privatization by way of replacement has increased pressure toward organizational isomorphism (Clarke & Estes, 1992; Estes & Alford, 1990; Estes & Swan, 1988; Swan & Estes, 1990a), which is recognized by the growing similarity in the behavior of different types of organizations (e.g., for-profits and nonprofits) in a particular field such as health care. Depending on the extent to which the behaviors of different organizational types converge, isomorphism raises concerns about cost, quality, and access to services. Research has shown dramatic shifts in home health agency reliance on nongovernment funding sources and similarities between nonprofit and for-profit agencies with regard to funding behavior. For example, in the Institute for Health & Aging study (Estes, Wood, et al., 1988), only 33% of home health agencies attempted to augment their budgets by increasing their reliance on government funding, while 57% of all agencies increased fees or copayments between 1984 and 1986 (Rappaport & Wood, 1989). Nearly 70% of agencies reported having to refuse services entirely to some clients, and 27% had to refuse services to low-income clients or those lacking the ability to pay for services (Bergthold et al., 1990; Estes & Swan, 1988).

Privatization by replacement also occurs when service provision is transferred from formal to informal networks, as when the unpaid labor force (i.e., home and family) increasingly provides care. The informalization of home health care has been encouraged by the implementation of the PPS. The trend toward the informalization of care for the elderly was a pronounced policy goal of the Reagan administration, and research on home health documents the replacement of caregiving work, formerly provided in the hospital, by work provided in the home and community (Binney et al., 1989). Another dimension of privatization by replacement occurs when the costs of formal home care are transferred to the informal sector. Approximately 14% of elderly beneficiaries of Medicare home health services have out-of-pocket expenses for home care that range from $360 to $1,680 per year, depending on their level of disability (U.S. Senate, 1991). As disability levels increase to five to six limitations in activities of daily living (ADLs), however, nearly 36% of the elderly pay out of pocket for services, and 29% have services paid for by Medicare (Spiegel, 1987). These costs exclude those accrued for prescriptions and other community-based services.

Reduction

Privatization by reduction is the retrenchment of total public expenditures for a particular type of service (LeGrand & Robinson, 1984). Policies that shift the reliance of organizations from the government to private funding sources are considered to be forms of privatization by reduction. For example, recent changes in Medicare home health funding have "forced HHAs to decrease their reliance on federal funding and increase reliance on private insurance and private fees" (Bergthold et al., 1990, p. 13). Home health agency responses to public funding cuts push organizations toward isomorphism in the industry, as already noted.

Although likely to create difficulties for all providers, budget cuts tend to favor for-profit providers because they have superior access to capital and diverse markets. The nature of access to services changes with the privatization of the market. Eligibility for services is increasingly determined by ability to pay. With intensifying for-profit provision, the distribution of resources is not likely to reflect the same order of social priorities as under a predominantly public system. As Higgins emphasizes, "At the heart of the debate lies the tension between the two basic models of health care distribution—one based upon market principles and the other upon the principle of equity" (Higgins, 1988, p. 198).

Attrition

Privatization by attrition (LeGrand & Robinson, 1984) is identified by the gradual disappearance or delegitimation of public or non-profit services due to legitimacy problems of government or of the nonprofit sectors (Estes & Alford, 1990; Estes et al., 1989). Economic or political problems experienced by either of these sectors may stimulate efforts to undermine the role of that sector. One result of economic and political difficulties in the 1980s was the tendency toward legitimacy crisis for public and private nonprofit services with the private sector rapidly filling market demands when public and private nonprofit sectors stagnated (Chapter 2).

Medicalization

Empirical data indicate that, even though home health care under Medicare has always been provided with an emphasis on skilled care, the 1980s deepened the medicalization of home health services. The concept of medicalization designates "the process by which services for the elderly are increasingly brought under the domain and rationality of biomedicine, and elements of the community delivery system are increasingly drawn toward the provision of medically related, medically supportive, and/or medically oriented services" (Binney et al., 1990, p. 762; Wood & Estes, 1988).

More than three fourths (79%) of home health agencies in 1986 added new services categorized by an expert panel as highly medical or medium medical (Binney et al., 1990). Less than 22% of services added were in the low medical category. The trend toward increased medicalization of home health services was even more pronounced in 1987 when 85% of added services were classified as highly or medium medical, and only 15% were in the low medical category. These trends applied for both nonprofit and for-profit agencies, although for-profits were slightly more likely than nonprofits to add highly medical services (56% and 52%, respectively).

Home health agencies also were asked to report the types of services requested but unavailable. Data similarly support the medicalization thesis. The majority of services that agencies reported they were unable to provide in 1986 (62%) and in 1987 (60%) were in the low medical category. Again, there was little difference between non-profit and for-profit agencies in inability to provide primarily low medical services (59% and 61%, respectively) (Binney et al., 1990).

The increasing prevalence of high-tech services in the home, such as intravenous therapy, ventilation therapy, and enteral and parenteral nutrition therapies, reflects the fact that there are increasing numbers of acutely ill individuals in home settings. "It is probable that the PPS/DRG scheme is referring patients to home health care or other alternatives in a physical condition necessitating more care" (Spiegel, 1987, p. 370). This trend is likely to have negative implications for the chronically ill elderly person without a recent hospitalization.

Changing Labor Conditions

Little attention has been paid to the impact of cost-containment policies on HHA employees. The U.S. health care system employs 7 million individuals (Kahl & Clark, 1986). Health care is a labor-intensive industry in which labor costs accounted for approximately 50% of hospital budgets in 1978 (Kidder & Sullivan, 1982; Szasz, 1990). Home health care labor costs, however, account for 70% to 90% of agency budgets (Bly, 1981; Szasz, 1990). Home health agencies, adapting to a changing, dynamic policy context, are expected to "critically examine and, if possible, transform their employment practices" (Szasz, 1990, p. 3). Policy changes are likely to affect labor markets (the number and types of jobs available) and the labor process (the way in which work is organized in the workplace).

Policy changes have affected labor markets by altering the organization of work in HHAs (Estes, Wood, et al., 1988). First, increased federal funding for home health care created new medium- and low-skilled jobs disproportionately filled by women. In the lower-skilled categories, positions were filled largely by minorities. Such jobs are characterized by low wages and part-time status. Second, in response to federal policy changes, HHAs altered the labor process by intensifying work loads, increasing managerial supervision, and taking other steps to increase productivity. More than 90% of both Medicare-certified and uncertified home care agencies in the IHA study reported efforts to increase productivity in the period immediately following DRG implementation (Rappaport & Estes, 1991).

Reviewing the home health care literature, Szasz (1990) reports that agencies were advised by home health industry leaders to plan their market, operate their business strategically, stabilize their funding base and cash flow, diversify their funding sources and services, and rationalize their organizations. Acting on this advice, nonprofit VNAs and for-profit HHAs adopted similar organizational and management structures in their efforts at restructuring, diversification, fiscal consciousness, and organizational and market rationalization. "Agencies reorganized and created subsidiaries; they entered into joint ventures with other agencies and other providers; they acquired or merged with other agencies" (Szasz, 1990, p. 8). Thus HHAs adopted an awareness as an industry, and the institutionalization of home health as a market-driven field was well under way.

Growth in the job market was similarly fueled during the rapid growth of the home health sector occurring in the early and mid-1980s. The number of employees in home health care increased more rapidly than in any other health care sector after 1980 (Kahl & Clark, 1986). Labor force growth continued as cost-containment policies were implemented. Data from the IHA research reveal that 60% of HHAs added staff while only 26% decreased staff between 1984 and 1986. Jobs in home health care, however, are considerably segmented and stratified (Szasz, 1990). Agencies identified nine occupations in the sector, including physical therapist, registered nurse, speech therapist, occupational therapist, social worker, nutritionist, licensed practical nurse, home health aide, and homemaker/chore worker. There are significant wage differentials between the skilled (physical therapists and registered nurses), semiskilled (home health aides), and unskilled (homemaker/chore workers) employees. In addition, minorities are overrepresented in the low-skilled, low-paid occupations.

Patterns of growth among different home health occupations reflect Medicare certification and reimbursement status (Rappaport & Estes, 1991; Szasz, 1990). To be eligible for Medicare certification and reimbursement, an agency must offer skilled nursing, physical therapy, occupational therapy, speech therapy, medical social services, and home health aide services. The IHA research indicates that this federal regulation has guaranteed favorable market conditions for these occupations. Other home health occupations not similarly regulated "depend on the non-certified segment of home health for employment" (Szasz, 1990, p. 12). The growth of noncertified agencies, particularly between 1984 and 1986, benefited licensed practical nurses and homemaker/chore workers.

The home health labor market is characterized by part-time jobs, low wages, and low benefit packages. The majority of agencies hired some part-time employees and contracted out for other employees, thereby assuring the flexibility necessary to handle variations in patient loads. Of the employees of the agencies in the IHA study, 51% were employed part-time, and another 20% were employed on a contract basis (Szasz, 1990). Employees in the occupational categories demanding fewer skills are more likely to be employed part-time than skilled workers. Highly skilled employees, with the exception of nurses, are more likely to be employed on a contract basis.

Effects on the home health labor market were found during the cost-containment era. This is not surprising given that labor costs are the home health providers' largest expense (Kahl & Clark, 1986). Of respondents to the IHA survey, 75% reported that it was very important to keep labor costs down, and another 17% responded that it was somewhat important. A majority of providers held the line on caregiver salaries between 1984 and 1986 (Rappaport & Estes, 1991). Among strategies to keep labor costs down, respondents increased productivity, lowered the occupational skill mix, and held down employee compensation (Szasz, 1990). The nature of the labor market and restrictive federal regulations, however, limited options for cost savings other than by increasing productivity.

These findings reflect nationwide trends in the home health care labor market. One reason that HHA capacity to provide services did not necessarily increase during the period of tightened eligibility (from 1985) is that agencies cited shortages in both nursing and paraprofessional personnel (United Hospital Fund, 1990). Because patients were released from hospitals in a more acutely ill condition than in prior years, they needed more services, required daily services, and displayed higher-intensity needs. The fact that staff time per case decreased as client service needs increased points to the interconnectedness of policymaking processes and their effects on organizations and patients.

Structural Changes

The containment of health care costs by the federal government through the implementation of the PPS has encouraged the restructuring of hospitals as well as organizations providing subacute levels

of care. Restructuring has taken multiple forms, including expansions, mergers, vertical integration of services, growth of multifacility or
ganizational forms and proprietary conglomerates, and rapid growth of proprietary and institutionally based HHAs (Estes et al., in press). The provision of home health care services has been shifting toward the private sector, away from the voluntary and public sectors, as a result of policy forces. The number of proprietary home health agencies increased nearly 14 times from 1972 to 1981 and an additional 60% from 1981 to 1983. Corporate chains, controlled by industries such as pharmaceutical companies and nursing homes, are absorbing an increasing share of the market in home health care.

The restructuring of health care organizations can be viewed from two perspectives: as an effort on the part of organizations to eliminate inefficiencies and provide greater access to needed posthospital services or, alternatively, as an attempt to reduce competition and increase profits. Public policy concerning hospital care for the elderly has resulted in a significant increase in the demand for and utilization of home health care services.

Several types of structural change have occurred in the organization and provision of home health services. Structuration, rationalization, and bureaucratization, as well as competition, are products of the actions of the State and the professions (DiMaggio & Powell, 1983). *Structuration* is defined as a process of institutional definition consisting of (a) increased interaction among organizations in a field, (b) the emergence of sharply defined interorganizational structures of domination and patterns of coalition, (c) an increasing information load with which a field must contend, and (d) a developing mutual awareness among participants in an organizational set that they are in a common enterprise (DiMaggio, 1982). In addition, isomorphism is introduced to describe the process of homogenization in which one unit in an organizational population (e.g., the HHA) is encouraged or forced to resemble other units that face the same set of environmental conditions as a result of changes in law (policy), cultural expectations, or other forces (DiMaggio & Powell, 1983).

Estes and her associates argue the applicability of the theory of isomorphism to organizational restructuring in home health care. The policy environment, including Medicare law, deregulation, cost containment, and competition have altered the legitimacy and resource distributions available to home health agencies. Under pressure of strong rhetoric concerning the need to be competitive and efficient, both the privatization and the rationalization of home health care organizations may be seen as viable strategies to reduce uncertainty and ensure survival (Estes et al., in press).

Based on the work of DiMaggio and Powell (1983), three types of institutional isomorphism appear to be relevant to home health: (a) Coercive isomorphism stems from cultural expectations and pressures exerted by other organizations, political influences, and legitimacy problems, the pressures of which may be experienced as force, persuasion, or collusion; (b) mimetic isomorphism results from standard organizational response to uncertainty or forces that encourage imitation—organizations regarded as legitimate or successful are modeled, and (c) normative isomorphism is a consequence of professionalization and successful dissemination of the educational requirements and knowledge base through professional and organizational networks. Thus policies, as well as professionalization and other legal and normative pressures, contribute to the process of organizational homogenization or isomorphism. Significantly, organizational isomorphism may occur in the absence of any empirical evidence that changes so rendered are actually more efficient or efficacious than what occurred previously. Thus changes can occur for ideological, and not necessarily economic, reasons.

Estes and Swan (1988) argue that increased environmental pressures cause agencies to seek ever-creative ways of adapting. During the mid-1980s, agencies engaged in several varieties of organizational restructuring. These include mergers; multidivisional entities; addition of non-Medicare branches or divisions, often using a different tax status than the parent agency; spin-offs of new product lines; establishing formal relationships with complementary organizations; and buying and selling other agencies (Estes et al., in press).

Another aspect of structural changes is the effect of market measures on organizations. Three measures of market are operationalized in the IHA research: structure, supply, and demand. Market structure is measured in terms of competition or market structure inequality, using a Herfindahl Index. Market supply is measured by the number of agencies per capita and the existence of a state certificate-of-need (CON) program. It is hypothesized that the existence of a CON program, which is "a regulatory device to limit provider capacity and market entry," would result in less competition (Estes & Swan, 1988, p. 11). CON programs, however, also can provide the impetus for existing agencies to explore new markets and new market arrangements.

Two measures of market demand are used: the percentage of standard metropolitan statistical area (SMSA) population aged 65+

and the nursing home bed supply per SMSA population. Higher proportions of aged individuals in the population are hypothesized to result in greater demand for home health care because the aged constitute the majority of Medicare beneficiaries. Further, it is hypothesized that greater numbers of nursing home beds per population enable substitution of nursing home care for home health care, thus lowering the demand for home health care.

Estes and associates (in press) report that more for-profit agencies are entering and leaving the market than nonprofit or voluntary agencies, and the most significant organizational change is toward greater organizational linkage and system affiliation (Figure 6.1). As of 1984, 45% of agencies studied were part of chains and/or multi-facility systems (MFSs). Of the agencies in the 1986 sample, 55% reported belonging to chains or multifacility systems, and, by 1987, 66% of agencies were affiliated with chains. Although most tax status change was from nonprofit to for-profit, this type of change had leveled off by 1987. Finally, the majority of agencies sought strategies to reduce their reliance on Medicare. On average, agencies nationwide rely on Medicare for 80% of their revenue; but, between 1986 and 1987, the percentage of revenues derived from Medicare dropped to 75%.

The likelihood of change in chain and multifacility system affiliation was found to be unaffected by local market measures. Four individual agency characteristics, however, were found to be predictors of change in chain or MFS affiliation, including tax status, budget status, Medicare reliance, and market competition. For-profits were quite likely to move toward chain or MFS affiliation between 1986 and 1987. Agencies with budget decreases between 1984 and 1986 were much more likely to move toward chain affiliation and were also more likely to enter relationships with other providers, such as acute care hospitals. Budgetary problems clearly create pressures on HHAs to deal with hospitals, while preexisting affiliation eases the establishment of such relationships (Estes et al., in press). HHAs were most likely, however, to forge relationships with nursing homes—particularly in states with CON regulations.

HHAs with greater reliance on Medicare were less likely to become affiliated with a chain or MFS, contrary to hypothesis. This is consistent with Benjamin's (1986b) finding that Medicare plays a primary role among third-party payers in the home health market. Although problematic in some respects, Medicare may represent the most secure source of funding in a competitive market, thus buffering agencies from seeking protection by joining larger organizational entities. Alternatively, agencies that rely heavily on Medicare may be undesirable targets of acquisition by chains or multifacility systems. Organizational change to chain or MFS membership was found to be more likely in areas with more HHAs per population, greater competition in the market, and greater inequality in market share. Linkages with nursing homes were expected to be less likely where there were more nursing home beds per capita, illustrating a substitution effect. The reverse was found to be true, however; HHAs were more likely to form relations with nursing homes in areas with more nursing home beds. Older agencies formed relationships particularly with nursing homes and not with other provider types. Agencies that reported PPS impacts were less likely, as expected, to forge links with nursing homes and with other HHAs, perhaps "because their niche in the 'DRG marketplace' would be an advantageous one, making links to others less necessary" (Estes et al., in press).

Political, ideological, and environmental demands have invoked organizational change in home health and have shaped the direction of that change. Moves toward corporatization among most sectors of the economy in the 1980s reflect the power of corporate rhetoric and ideology as well as the legitimacy of market strategies to maximize chances of organizational survival and success. The rapid pace of organizational change in the home health industry testifies to the power of this ideology. "The growing legitimacy of organizational rationalization and efficiency motives as a basis for health organization behavior have framed and limited the conception of what are viable strategies for reducing uncertainty and securing survival" (Estes et al., in press). In addition, this trend has contributed to the declining legitimacy of forms of organization other than for-profit ones.

Conclusion

Multiple policy changes and environmental forces have affected the delivery and provision of home health care, altering organizational structures and the types of clients previously in contact with home health services. These changes have been illuminated by the research, and the following concepts have been identified: privatization, medicalization, changes in labor conditions, and structural changes.

The policy and environmental effects on home health care as a result of cost-containment policies have been profound. The uncertainty of operating in an increasingly competitive market has forced providers to adopt managerial and organizational rationalization strategies. Agencies must adopt internal controls to ensure that the cost of providing services does not exceed reimbursement. They must practice strategic market planning, diversification, and vertical and horizontal integration. The role of the federal government in encouraging HHAs to be more competitive and market oriented has been substantial. As a consequence, the "appropriate roles for government, commercial enterprise, and voluntary nonprofit organizations are all being questioned simultaneously" (Stevens, 1989, p. 3). Policy changes have encouraged the privatization and medicalization of the industry, and they have also profoundly affected the labor structure of organizations. "As government policy squeezes Medicare-certified HHAs, HHAs in turn are forced to limit services to those who need them most. Intentionally or not, policymakers may have hurt the very people they set out to help" (United Hospital Fund, 1990, p. 37). Further, perhaps the most significant and disturbing conclusion to be drawn from the IHA research is that, despite overall growth in the home health sector, there is no evidence to suggest that access and availability of services for the frail and functionally impaired elderly have improved (Spohn et al., 1987-1988).

The four transformative processes discussed above are inextricably linked. For example, the medicalization of the industry cannot be brought about without concomitant changes in agency staffing. These trends, however, are likely to have important effects on access to services for the chronically ill elderly who have had no recent hospitalization. A related set of changes occurring in the nursing home industry is the topic of the next chapter.

CHAPTER 7

Nursing Homes
Under Prospective Payment

If you have tears to shed, prepare to shed them now. We are in the presence of an institution society needs but does not wholly accept, an institution that many deplore but none can reform. It is a system grown remote from the people it was meant to protect and the communities it was meant to serve. Its humane components, left over from an earlier era, have become endangered species, while its predatory elements thrive as never before.

Margolis, 1990, p. 147

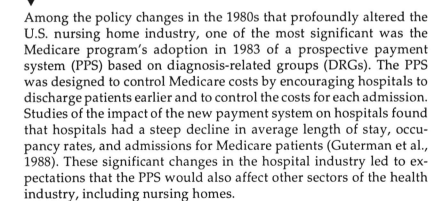

Among the policy changes in the 1980s that profoundly altered the U.S. nursing home industry, one of the most significant was the Medicare program's adoption in 1983 of a prospective payment system (PPS) based on diagnosis-related groups (DRGs). The PPS was designed to control Medicare costs by encouraging hospitals to discharge patients earlier and to control the costs for each admission. Studies of the impact of the new payment system on hospitals found that hospitals had a steep decline in average length of stay, occupancy rates, and admissions for Medicare patients (Guterman et al., 1988). These significant changes in the hospital industry led to expectations that the PPS would also affect other sectors of the health industry, including nursing homes.

NOTE: The authors of this chapter are Charlene Harrington, Carroll L. Estes, Adela de la Torre, and James H. Swan.

Medicare has traditionally limited its payments for nursing home and home care to short-term services needed for posthospital care. The prospective payment system, however, appeared to threaten conventional Medicare utilization of posthospital services. Medicare utilization of nursing home services remained at a steady rate until the implementation of the PPS, after which the number of Medicare nursing home admissions increased 23% (from 9.6 admissions per 1,000 enrollees in 1981 to 11.8 per 1,000 in 1985). Referral rates from hospitals to nursing homes also increased between 1981 and 1985 (Guterman et al., 1988). Neu and Harrison (1988) report that referrals of hospital patients to nursing homes were more likely after the implementation of the PPS than before. Although referrals increased, the covered Medicare days in nursing homes declined 20% between 1981 and 1985—from 29 days to 23 days (Guterman et al., 1988). Because Medicare represented only 2% of total nursing home revenues between 1980 and 1988, its payments alone would not be expected to have had a significant impact on the nursing home industry (Lazenby & Letsch, 1990). Because most nursing home patients are admitted from hospitals, however, the PPS effects on hospital practices can be expected to affect nursing homes and their residents (Swan, de la Torre, & Steinhart, 1990).

Other policy changes also have had important effects on nursing homes. Federal reductions in Medicaid payments to states in the early 1980s resulted in substantial efforts by states to control their costs, particularly for nursing homes (Harrington, Newcomer, et al., 1985). As a result, many states altered their reimbursement policies for Medicaid, adopted preadmission screening to limit nursing home admissions based on special criteria, and implemented policies to divert persons from seeking care in nursing homes to look at community long term care programs instead (Harrington & Swan, 1987; Harrington et al., 1988; Swan et al., 1988). At the national level, the Health Care Financing Administration (HCFA), in response to the Omnibus Budget Reconciliation Act of 1987 (OBRA), adopted stricter regulations for nursing homes and new nursing home survey procedures that focused on quality of care for residents. All of these policy changes are expected to change the nursing home industry, but few studies of their effects have been conducted.

The nursing home industry in the United States is a multibillion-dollar business, characterized by rapid growth costs and by access and quality problems (Harrington, 1991a). In 1985, 88% of nursing home residents were aged 65 years or over. About 5% of all persons aged 65 or over, and 22% of persons aged 85 or over, resided in nursing homes at any given time during that year (Hing, 1987b). The elderly are particularly likely to go to nursing homes in their last year of life. Wingard, Williams-Jones, McPhillips, Kaplan, and Barrett-Connor (1990) found 43% of their sample aged 85 years or over to have been admitted in the last year of life.

This chapter examines the general movements taking place in the nursing home industry between 1984 and 1987 following the implementation of the Medicare prospective payment system (see the Introduction to this volume). Changes in nursing homes (the unit of analysis) and the relationship of those changes to federal and state policies are examined at two points in time: between 1984 and 1986 (during the implementation of the PPS) and between 1986 and 1987 (IHA, 1986, 1987).

Nursing homes were a small cottage industry (with about 11,000 facilities and 400,000 residents) until the early 1960s, when they began to expand with the infusion of public funds from Medicaid and Medicare (Vladeck, 1980). By 1985, there were 19,000 facilities in the United States with 1.6 million beds and about 1.4 million residents (Strahan, 1987). Of these, 75% were proprietary. A growing number of facilities, 41% in 1985 as compared with 28% in 1978, were owned or operated by organizations with multiple facilities or vertically and horizontally integrated systems (Strahan, 1987). Moreover, members of the nursing home industry have been consolidating to create larger facilities and corporate ownership. By 1983, 32 corporations controlled 17% of the nursing home beds. Many of the large nursing home chains are publicly held corporations listed on the New York Stock Exchange and the American Stock Exchange and are multinational in their operation (Berliner & Regan, 1990; Strahan, 1987).

Nursing home expenditures grew by 140% between 1980 and 1989, from $20 billion to $48 billion (Lazenby & Letsch, 1990). These expenditures are particularly problematic for the Medicaid program, which paid 43% of all the nation's nursing home expenditures in 1989 (Lazenby & Letsch, 1990). Medicare's contribution to nursing home expenditures increased dramatically from its historical level of about 2% of total expenditure to 7.5% of total nursing home expenditures following the passage of the Medicare Catastrophic Coverage Act of 1988. The act was repealed in December 1989, however, and the Medicare share of total costs is expected to return to the 2% level (Lazenby & Letsch, 1990). Private insurance payments account for only about 1% of nursing home costs. Direct out-of-pocket payments made by residents constituted 44% of the total dollars spent on nursing home care in 1989.

U.S. nursing home beds have been undersupplied relative to demand (Swan & Harrington, 1986). Bed stock grew more slowly than did the aged population in the 1980s (Lane, 1984; U.S. GAO, 1983). Beds per 1,000 aged persons declined from 54 in 1978 to 52 in 1986, increased slightly in 1987, but declined afterward to the 1986 level (Harrington et al., 1988; Harrington et al., 1990). Because bed stock is a major predictor of Medicaid nursing home expenditures (Harrington & Swan, 1987), its control is important to cost constraint, whatever the bed stock per aged.

Nursing home occupancy peaked at 92% in 1984, remaining at that level since (Harrington et al., 1990), while hospital occupancy declined (Guterman et al., 1988). Nursing home referrals are directly tied to hospital admissions (Harrington & Swan, 1987). Greater Medicare nursing home admissions under the hospital PPS (Guterman et al., 1988; Neu & Harrison, 1988) were apparently offset by reductions in Medicare length of stay or by decline in nursing home admissions related to lower hospital admission rates.

The large number of Medicaid residents in nursing homes (60%-70% of patients) is directly related to the high cost of nursing home care (Swan et al., 1988) because growing numbers of patients soon exhaust their own funds and become reliant on the public program. The average annual cost of $34,000 (in 1989) results in many individuals spending down their assets within weeks of admission to a nursing home (Lazenby & Letsch, 1990). Although recent studies suggest that spend-down may be less rapid than previous estimates, a sizable proportion of total nursing home resident spend-down is nevertheless paid for by Medicaid (Liu, Doty, & Manton, 1990; Spence & Wiener, 1989). At the same time, access problems for Medicaid patients have increased because of low Medicaid reimbursement rates (Phillips & Hawes, 1988). Medicaid policies established by the states are critical in shaping the industry. Most state Medicaid programs pay nursing homes on a prospective basis by setting rates in advance, which has kept reimbursement rates low (Swan et al., 1988).

Because of the large differential in rates between Medicaid and private-pay or Medicare rates, Medicaid is not the payer of choice for most nursing homes. Many studies have documented the efforts of facilities first to select private-pay or Medicare patients and to accept Medicaid patients only when empty beds are available (Feder & Scanlon, 1980; Scanlon, 1980a, 1980b; U.S. Senate, 1984). Other facilities seek for admission patients with the least disability or need for nursing home care (except in states where higher rates are paid for more disabled patients). As a result of this practice, many facilities have reported waiting lists for Medicaid patients (Swan & Estes, 1990b) and the issue of access to nursing home beds has become critical (Chapter 8; Phillips & Hawes, 1988).

Even though nursing homes complain about the reimbursement rates paid by Medicaid, the nursing home industry is basically healthy. The price-earnings ratios in the industry varied between 14% and 18% in the years 1978 to 1984 (Moskowitz, 1983). Although some nursing home chains reported financial losses between 1987 and 1988, the industry continues to be profitable (Wagner, 1988). Manor Care and National Medical Enterprises (owning large numbers of nursing homes in 1990) showed 11.8% and 14.5% returns on equity during 1989, and many corporations reported a 22.2% return on equity during the 1980 to 1990 period (Fritz, 1990). Nevertheless, Medicaid payments, which are considerably lower than private-pay rates, contribute to access problems for Medicaid recipients (Miller et al., 1992).

Access to nursing home care becomes more difficult as nursing home residents increase in level of disability and require more complex treatment. Changes in the severity of illness and dependency of nursing home patients following the implementation of the PPS are documented in several studies (Hing, 1987b; Shaughnessy et al., 1987; U.S. GAO, 1983). Many nursing home residents need complete or partial assistance in bathing, toileting, eating, transferring, and other activities of daily living (Hing, 1987b). Large numbers of nursing home residents have problems such as urinary and bowel incontinence, decubitus ulcers, malnutrition, infections, and other conditions requiring skilled nursing care. Some facilities are now providing intravenous therapy, inhalation therapy, and other complex treatments that require extensive nursing care. As these demands increase, nursing homes need a higher level of professional nursing staff.

No issue is as difficult and controversial as quality of care in nursing homes. Many studies describe the problems that have led to deaths, permanent injury, disability, pain, and discomfort (U.S. Senate, 1974-1976). As many as one third of nursing homes are substandard in the care offered (U.S. Senate, 1986c). The U.S. General Accounting Office (1987a) found that 41% of skilled nursing and 34% of intermediate care facilities nationally were out of compliance during three consecutive inspections with one or more requirements most likely to affect patient health and safety. Although some nursing homes offer high quality of care, the wide variation and the substantial problems have created a crisis of confidence concerning nursing facilities.

The Institute of Medicine (IOM, 1986b) conducted a 2-year study on nursing home quality and regulation and urged immediate federal legislation to improve regulation. Lawsuits against the federal government (*Smith v. Heckler*, 1984) and subsequent federal rulings have shown the regulatory process to be inadequate to protect residents. Because of these problems, Congress passed and the president signed new legislation—the Nursing Home Reform Act in the Omnibus Budget Reconciliation Act (OBRA) of 1987—to make the most substantial changes in regulation since the Medicare and Medicaid programs were enacted. The findings reported here reflect the effects of the prospective payment system rather than those of OBRA 1987 because implementation of the nursing home reforms did not commence until 1990. Although the new nursing home legislation and the regulations were delayed in implementation, they are expected to improve quality of care over time.

Nursing Home Characteristics

According to the latest national nursing home survey (Strahan, 1987), there are about 19,000 nursing homes in the United States. The number of nursing home beds has been growing slowly and has not kept pace with the increasing elderly population (Harrington et al., 1990). In terms of tax status of facilities, the IHA nursing home sample of 166 facilities reflects nursing homes nationally. Almost three fourths (73%) are proprietary or investor owned; 23% are private nonprofit; and 4% are government facilities. Chain ownership and size characteristics of the sample differ from the national picture, however. There are more chains in the sample (62%) than the national average (41%), probably attributable to varying definitions of chains, the expectation that more chains are located in urban areas from which the IHA sample is drawn, and/or the fact that residential care facilities are excluded in the IHA study. Throughout the chapter, comparisons of IHA findings with data from the National Nursing Home Survey of 1985 (Strahan, 1987) require interpretation because the National Nursing Home Survey includes residential care facilities, whereas the IHA study only includes facilities classified as providing either skilled nursing or intermediate care.

The average facility in the IHA sample was about 21 years old and in 1987 reported having 49 beds certified for Medicare and 118 beds certified for Medicaid. IHA sample facilities are larger than the national average, as measured by average number of beds per facility. The average number of beds in the IHA sample in 1987 was 121, compared with a national average of 85 beds per facility. The difference in size between the facilities in the IHA sample and the national average is likely due to the fact that the facilities in the sample were drawn from large metropolitan areas.

Little change in the distribution of organizational structures among the sample facilities was expected between 1986 and 1987 given that the same facilities participated in the study both years. There were two slight but noteworthy changes, however. One is the slight drop in the total number of nursing home beds (20,141 beds in 1987 versus 20,331 in 1986—a 1% decline). This decline is consistent with the slow growth in overall nursing home bed supply and actual reductions in some states reported in another IHA study by Harrington and associates (Harrington et al., 1988; Harrington et al., 1990). The second change is the increased percentage of nursing homes becoming part of chains (62% in 1987 and 58% in 1986).

Nursing homes across the nation derive their revenue from two principal sources: Medicaid (43% of total revenues) and out-of-pocket patient payments (44%) (Lazenby & Letsch, 1990). The IHA study found for their sample facilities that 52% of facility revenues came from Medicaid and 38% from out-of-pocket payments in 1987. In the IHA nursing home sample, Medicare and private insurance each represented 5% of revenue—both slightly higher than the national average (Division of National Cost Estimates, 1987). As would be expected, nursing home revenues from all sources increased between 1984 and 1986 as well as between 1986 and 1987. Although some facilities showed declines in total revenues, on average, nursing homes showed an increase in revenues of 10% between 1986 and 1987.

As shown in Table 7.1, Medicaid revenues dropped for 14% of the facilities but increased for 58% in 1987. Medicare revenues, on the other hand, dropped for 44% of the facilities and increased for only 29% in 1987. Facilities experienced substantial fluctuation in government revenues during the 1983-1987 period, with only about 25% having stable revenues from public sources for the period. Facilities appeared to offset some of the fluctuation in public revenue with increases in private out-of-pocket charges, which more than half of the facilities reported.

Residents

The typical nursing home resident today is older and has more disabilities than ever before (Hing, 1987b; Shaughnessy et al., 1987). Nationally, about 37% of all residents are aged 85 and over. Among the facilities in the IHA study, in 1987, about 88% of residents were

TABLE 7.1 Revenue Source and Change in Revenues for Nursing Home Facilities, 1986 and 1987

Payer	Revenue Decreased[a]		Revenue Same[a]		Revenue Increased[a]		Not a Source of Revenue	
	1986 (percentage)	1987 (percentage)	1986 (percentage)	1987 (percentage)	1986 (percentage)	1987 (percentage)	1986 (percentage)	1987 (percentage)
Medicaid	19	14	30	28	52	58	0	0
Medicare	26	44	26	22	48	29	0	6
Resident (out of pocket)	NA	20	NA	27	NA	53	NA	3
Private insurance	NA	19	NA	51	NA	31	NA	46

SOURCE: Data from Institute for Health & Aging DRG study, nursing home instrument (1986, 1987).

NOTE: NA = question not asked in 1986.

a. Question on instrument: "For each of the following, please indicate whether it is a revenue source and, if so, whether that source has decreased, remained the same, or increased in total dollars in the past twelve months."

aged 65 or over, a proportion just slightly below the 1985 national average. Women constituted the majority of the residents among the facilities in the sample (averaging 76% per facility), as expected. The number of residents in the sampled facilities who may be classified as members of minority groups was higher than the 1985 national average—15% to 10%. This finding, too, was expected because the sampled facilities are located in urban areas with high concentrations of minorities in the population.

Demand for more complex care grows in nursing homes with the age and disability of patients. As medical technology and complex procedures shift the locus of care from hospital to nursing home, acuity levels rise in the latter, greatly increasing the complexity of staff duties. Ventilators, oxygen, IV feedings and medication, and special medical equipment and high technology have raised the complexity and challenge of patient care (Harrington & Estes, 1989; Shaughnessy, Schlenker, & Kramer, 1990; U.S. Senate, 1986c). Changes in technology have created complex issues of the appropriateness of procedures and applications of technology and also of the adequacy of staff training and skill levels.

Nursing home administrators were asked whether or not the profile of admitted patients had changed since the implementation of the Medicare PPS. As predicted, 78% of the facilities reported residents with increased illness acuity levels between 1984 and 1986, and 75% reported higher acuity levels for residents in 1987 than in 1986. In addition, 80% of nursing homes also reported higher levels of care required for residents in 1987 than in 1986 (Table 7.2), and 83% stated that more staff time was required. Data on higher levels of illness were further supported by hospital readmission rates. Nursing homes reported in 1987 that an average of 13% of their residents were readmitted to hospitals within 30 days and 21% within 60 days.

Of the facilities responding, 31% reported increases in the number of short-term residents in comparison with long-term residents. The average length of stay (LOS) declined 12% by 1987 from 28 months in 1986. There was some variation across states in lengths of stay, and facilities in some states reported rather large declines. In Florida, LOS declined by 22%; in Washington, by 39%; and, in Pennsylvania, by 21%. Texas was the only state where facilities reported an increase in length of stay. Overall, about 10% of the residents were discharged each month. To have shorter lengths of stay and only a slight decline in occupancy rates, facilities must have had additional admissions.

TABLE 7.2 Shifts in Care Needs Among Nursing Home Patients, 1986
and 1987

Nursing Homes	1986 (percentage)	1987 (percentage)
Institutions reporting increase in number of patients[a]		
with higher acuity ratings	78	75
requiring higher levels of care	82	80
requiring more staff time	NA	83

SOURCE: Data from Institute for Health & Aging DRG study, nursing home instrument (1986, 1987).
NOTE: NA = question not asked.
a. Percentages are the average for the facilities reporting an increase over the past 12 months.

Access

For Medicaid patients, access to nursing home care has been a long-standing and multifaceted problem. Chapter 8 of this volume examines access to posthospital care and includes an exploration of the nursing home access dilemma for the Medicaid-dependent population.

Four access measures were examined in the IHA study: average length of stay, occupancy rates, maintenance of waiting lists, and average length of wait for admission (Table 7.3). It is surprising that the overall average occupancy rate decreased slightly, from 94% in 1986 to 92% in 1987. In spite of the decline in occupancy rates, however, there was a slight increase in the proportion of facilities with waiting lists: 70% of the nursing homes in the sample reported having waiting lists in 1987, compared with 65% in 1986, but the average waiting time for admission diminished slightly between the two study years, from 74 days in 1986 to 73 days in 1987.

Nursing home administrators were also asked what percentage of their patients (1986 survey) and their revenue (1987 survey) is attributable to Medicaid. Except for Pennsylvania, Medicaid-reimbursed persons constituted more than 50% (and, in the case of Texas, nearly 60%) of the nursing home patient population in 1986. With slightly lower occupancy rates, nursing homes may have been able to admit more Medicaid residents. The percentage of residents who were paid for by Medicaid could be used as a proxy measure for Medicaid access. Unfortunately, the question posed on the 1987 instrument asks for a count of dollars rather than of people and so that data cannot be accurately compared with the 1986 data. Current literature reports, however, that nursing homes hold some beds vacant rather than admit Medicaid-reimbursed persons in the hope of getting private patients who will pay higher rates than Medicaid pays (Phillips & Hawes, 1988).

TABLE 7.3 Selected Measures of Access to Nursing Home Facilities by
State, 1986 and 1987

	1986	1987
Average length of stay (in months):[a]		
California	24	23
Florida	26	20
Pennsylvania	31	24
Texas	38	40
Washington	26	16
combined average length of stay	28	24
Average occupancy rate:[b]		
California	94%	93%
Florida	96%	95%
Pennsylvania	94%	94%
Texas	87%	88%
Washington	95%	91%
combined average occupancy rate	94%	92%
Facilities maintaining waiting lists:[c]		
California	78%	78%
Florida	43%	57%
Pennsylvania	71%	78%
Texas	55%	62%
Washington	81%	69%
total facilities maintaining waiting lists	65%	70%
Average waiting time for admission (in days):[d]		
California	51	60
Florida	88	94
Pennsylvania	82	89
Texas	105	80
Washington	72	43
Combined average waiting time for admission	74	73

SOURCE: Data from Institute for Health & Aging DRG study, nursing home instrument (1986, 1987).
NOTE: The McNemar statistical test shows no significant differences between 1986 and 1987.
a. "What is the average length of stay at your facility (in months)?"
b. "What is your current occupancy rate?"
c. "Does your facility currently have a waiting list of prospective patients?" (percentage saying yes).
d. "On average, how long a wait is there to get into your facility (in days)?"

Nursing home administrators were asked what types of residents they were unable to admit to their facilities and the reasons for not admitting such residents. Some facilities (29%) reported not admitting residents with AIDS or communicable diseases. A number of facilities

(26%) reported not admitting residents with psychiatric, mental health, or substance abuse problems. Others reported not admitting patients with special care needs such as inhalation therapy, hyperalimentation, or care requiring a full-time staff person. The primary reasons reported for not admitting such residents were related to the limitations of the staff and the facility. In other instances, state licensing regulations did not allow certain types of residents under the facility license. Chapter 4 provides a fuller discussion of these issues.

Services

Substantial increases in the illness acuity levels of nursing home residents within recent years have no doubt augmented the demand for various services. The IHA study sought to determine what changes in services, if any, were made in response to changes in resident characteristics. Facility administrators were asked to report shifts in the types of services offered.

Of the facilities responding to the query about services, 55% reported changes in the kinds of services provided (Table 7.4). Some facilities added new services; others eliminated existing services. For the most part, service changes meant addition of new services or augmented provision of existing services. In 1987, 45% of the sample nursing homes reported adding new services, and only 3% of respondents reported eliminating any service. Of facilities that provided special services, many reported increases in the amount of services provided (e.g., tube feeding, intravenous therapy, inhalation therapy, urinary catheters, discharge planning, and social work services). Large increases (19% to 52%) were reported for all services in the 1984-1986 period immediately after the PPS was implemented. The number of facilities reporting increased services of specific types were about the same in 1986 and 1987. Facilities described many of these services as acute high-tech services. These increases in services were consistent with the reports of increased acuity levels for the residents after implementation of the PPS (Shaughnessy et al., 1987; Wood & Estes, 1990). Less than one fourth (24%) of the facilities reported receiving additional revenue for provision of additional services in 1987.

Staffing

Compared with levels in hospitals, staffing levels in nursing homes traditionally have been low. Nursing homes are staffed primarily by nursing assistants with only a few professional nurses on staff

TABLE 7.4 Change in Services Provided by Nursing Home Facilities, 1986 and 1987[a]

	Does Not Provide Service		Decreased Service		Same Provision of Service		Increased Service	
	1986 (percentage)	1987 (percentage)	1986 (percentage)	1987 (percentage)	1986 (percentage)	1987 (percentage)	1986 (percentage)	1987 (percentage)
Tube feeding	15	12	2	9	32	27	51	52
Intravenous therapy	52	55	4	6	16	22	28	18
Inhalation therapy	37	36	3	7	35	37	25	20
Urinary catheters	4	2	16	12	48	55	32	31
Discharge planning	5	5	1	2	41	45	54	48
Psychogeriatric services	30	17	2	2	32	43	36	38
Social work services	4	1	4	2	40	36	52	60
Ostomy care	9	NA	6	NA	65	NA	19	NA
Decubiti services	NA	2	NA	24	NA	53	NA	20

SOURCE: Data from Institute for Health & Aging DRG study, nursing home instrument (1986, 1987).
NOTE: The Bowkers tests show no significant difference between the 1986 and 1987 periods. NA = question not asked. Question on instrument: "Has provision of the following services by your facility decreased, remained the same, or increased in the past twelve months?"
a. Percentages are averages for the facilities reporting.

(Harrington, 1991a). The IHA study examined whether nursing homes have begun to improve the ratios of professional staff in response to the increased dependency needs of residents. As the dependency levels of residents increased, most nursing homes reported that staffing levels remained the same or increased. Only a small percentage of facilities reported decreased staffing in 1986 or 1987.

The largest increases in staffing occurred between 1984 and 1986 when 47% of the facilities increased the number of registered nurses (RNs) on staff, 39% increased the number of licensed vocational/practical nurses (LVNs/LPNs), and 57% increased the number of attendants (Table 7.5). Between 1986 and 1987, more than a fourth of the facilities reported increasing the number of RNs, LVNs, and attendants. The cause for the staffing changes varied. For some facilities, the changes were consequential to a shifting of the levels of beds in the facility. Some states, including Pennsylvania, changed state level of care definitions and requirements resulting in shifts in staffing levels to accompany changes in the level of licensed beds. In other cases, states increased the nursing staff requirements for nursing homes, thus forcing facilities to add staff.

Facilities were asked to report the ratio of registered nurses, licensed practical nurses, and attendants to residents in the facilities in 1987. Consistent with national data, the total number of registered nurses reported represented 14% of the direct nursing personnel; LVNs, 20%; and attendants, 66%. Ratios of direct nursing personnel reported in the study were higher than those reported in the National Nursing Home Survey in 1985, but this was expected because the national survey sample included uncertified facilities and the IHA study sample did not.

The overall staffing ratio reported in 1986 (110 staff per 100 residents) was higher than reported for 1987 (100 staff per 100 residents). It is interesting that, although the facility administrators reported greater dependency levels among residents and the same or increased staffing within their facilities, actual staff-to-resident ratios reported showed a decline between 1986 and 1987.

Facilities appeared to focus on efforts to increase staffing productivity as a means of handling the increasing acuity of residents. In 1987, 65% of the facilities reported that staff work loads had increased. Three fourths of the facilities reported efforts of some type to increase productivity. About half of the facilities reported efforts to increase productivity through the use of in-service training and other continuing education efforts. Others reported closer monitoring of staff, more explicit job descriptions, giving more paperwork to clerks, reorganizing service delivery, increasing the number of volunteers,

TABLE 7.5 Nursing Home Facilities Reporting Change in Nurse Staffing Levels, 1986 and 1987

	Decreased Staffing 1986 (percentage)	Decreased Staffing 1987 (percentage)	Same Staffing 1986 (percentage)	Same Staffing 1987 (percentage)	Increased Staffing 1986 (percentage)	Increased Staffing 1987 (percentage)
RNs[a]	5	16	48	55	47	28
LVNs[b]	12	10	49	63	39	27
Attendants[a]	12	14	31	54	57	32

SOURCE: Data from Institute for Health & Aging DRG study, nursing home instrument (1986, 1987).

NOTE: Question on instrument: "In the past 12 months, have there been any changes in the numbers of these staff and if so, by how many have their numbers increased or decreased? a) RNs b) LVNs/LPNs c) Attendants"

a. The Bowkers test shows a significant difference between the 1986 and 1987 periods: $p \geq .001$.
b. The Bowkers test shows a significant difference between the 1986 and 1987 periods: $p \geq .025$.

and other such activities. Only a few facilities (2%) reported specific efforts to provide financial incentives to staff or to improve staff morale as a means of increasing productivity.

Of the nursing homes in the IHA study, only 24% reported having employees represented by a union. Of those reporting unionization, 18% of the facilities had RN employees who were members of a union, 38% had union member LVNs, and 96% had union member attendants. Increased work load requirements for nursing staffs did not appear to result in changes in unionization. During the 1986 to 1987 period, only a 1% increase in unionization was reported.

Policy Impact

The years 1984 through 1987, following the implementation of the PPS and other federal and state policies, were a time of great turmoil and change for nursing home providers. Nursing home administrators, when asked by IHA interviewers which policies had the greatest impact on their nursing homes (Table 7.6), most often reported the effects of the Medicare PPS. To that open-ended question, 28% of the facilities listed the PPS among the policy changes with the greatest impact on them between 1984 and 1986; 9% of the sample claimed no policy effects of any kind. Increased regulatory activities for federal certification, including implementation of new federal survey procedures; Medicare policy changes, including the Gramm-Rudman-Hollings Medicare reimbursement reductions (the Balanced Budget and Emergency Deficit Control Act of 1985 and subsequent amendments); changes in state Medicaid reimbursement; changes and restrictions in Medicaid policies; and stronger state staffing requirements were also among the policy changes reported as having had the greatest impact on the facilities in the study.

Facilities reported that the PPS changes increased the acuity level of their patients and, as a consequence, the staff work load. The increased acuity levels were claimed to have had direct effect on the kinds of skilled nursing services demanded and sometimes offered. Of greater concern were the funding problems the facilities reported experiencing. More than one third of the facility administrators considered reimbursement levels inadequate. Moreover, stricter rules had resulted in increased paperwork, claims denials, and other problems that resulted in a loss of funds. These financial problems were considered serious and were reported by many facilities.

TABLE 7.6 Policy Effects on Nursing Homes, 1986 and 1987

	1984-1986 (percentage)	1987 (percentage)
No policy effects reports	9	6
Policy effects reported	91	94
Medicare PPS/DRGs	28	24
Stricter regulation/certification	16	18
Other Medicare policy changes including Gramm-Rudman cuts	12	13
Medicaid reimbursement	12	10
Other Medicaid policies	10	6
Stronger state staffing requirements	5	8

SOURCE: Data from Institute for Health & Aging DRG study, nursing home instrument (1986, 1987).
NOTE: Question on 1986 instrument: "Please tell me which *three policy changes* or interpretations have had the greatest impact on your facility in the past two years, and what *effects* these changes have had." Question on 1987 instrument: "Please tell me what policies, or interpretations of policy, have had the greatest impact on your nursing home in the past twelve months and what that impact has been." Percentages do not equal 100% because multiple responses were recorded.

To a pointed question regarding the effect of the Medicare PPS, facility administrators were more forthcoming. The question posed was as follows:

As a result of Medicare DRG payment to hospitals in the area you serve, has your facility experienced . . . changes in the types of patients you admit; shifts in the kinds of services you provide; changes in the hours of care required per patient; changes in the numbers of short-term patients; changes in the ability to refer patients to hospitals; changes in your number of referrals from hospitals; changes in your ability to refer your patients to other agencies; or other effects? (IHA, 1986, 1987: Nursing Home Instrument)

Almost all nursing homes (93% in 1986 and 94% in 1987) reported at least some effect of the PPS on their facility. When specifically asked about the effects of the PPS, virtually every institution claimed to have been affected by the Medicare DRG payment system.

Conclusion

The decade of the 1980s was a period of change and uncertainty for nursing homes. Revenues and financial stability, residents, staffing, and access were all affected in direct relation to policy changes at the state and federal levels.

Although overall revenues for nursing homes increased during the 1984 to 1987 period, administrators reported that their revenues fluctuated substantially across payer sources. Facilities that reported Medicare and Medicaid decreases appeared to have increased their private-pay revenues to offset these changes. The revenue increase of 11% for those reporting, however, was higher than would be expected, given that the medical care inflation rate for the 1986-1987 period was about 8%. Because data on net profits and losses are not generally available, it is not possible to know whether or not the facilities experienced real financial losses, even though their revenues increased. Many facility administrators reported financial distress, which they attributed to federal and state policy changes, including the PPS and other reimbursement and regulatory policies. Perhaps the uncertainty of revenues and the problems of responding to the many policy changes created the reports of financial strain.

Facilities experienced substantial increases in the illness acuity of their residents during the 1984 to 1987 period. The majority of the facilities reported that the increased acuity resulted in greater work loads and more time spent by staff. In response to the increasing acuity level of patients, more than half the facilities reported adding new services to the nursing home, and few services were eliminated. New services included intravenous therapy, tube feedings, inhalation therapy, and other high-intensity skilled nursing care services. Thus service levels appeared to be substantially higher in nursing homes than prior to the introduction of the PPS.

Nevertheless, the increased acuity did not translate into increased staffing in terms of FTEs or a higher percentage of RNs and LVNs hired in relation to attendants. Although facilities reported that staffing levels stayed the same or increased, their reports of actual FTEs showed a slight decrease between 1986 and 1987 for staff providing direct patient care. Most facilities appeared to be increasing productivity and work loads of staff as a means of responding to the changes in acuity rather than increasing the number of staff or changing the type of staff provided.

Although the total number of beds declined slightly, the occupancy rates also declined slightly instead of increasing as would have been expected. Hospital occupancy also has declined (Guterman et al., 1988). The decline in nursing home occupancy may occur because skilled nursing referrals are directly tied to hospital admissions (Harrington & Swan, 1987). Thus the increased Medicare admissions to nursing homes reported by Guterman and associates (1988) and by Neu and Harrison (1988) apparently were offset by either the reduced Medicare length of stay and/or the overall decline in nursing home admissions related to lower hospital admission rates.

As the occupancy rates declined slightly, it was expected that access to nursing homes for Medicaid patients would increase. It is not clear that the number or proportion of Medicaid patients increased. The percentage of facilities reporting waiting lists actually increased, although the average number of days on waiting lists appears to have declined. The demand for nursing home beds continues to be greater than the supply (Swan & Harrington, 1986). Many nursing homes prefer to hold beds empty for private-paying patients rather than to fill the beds with Medicaid patients. Thus the lost facility revenues from Medicaid patients must be offset by expected or real gains from private-pay or Medicare revenues. Apparently, nursing home supply and demand are not in equilibrium because of reimbursement problems with Medicaid and the lack of price controls on private-pay rates.

Nursing home administrators continue to be concerned about policy effects on their facilities. Although a large percentage of respondents considered that the PPS had a direct effect on their facilities in terms of changes in residents, services, staffing, or other factors, other policies were also of concern to them. The stricter regulation of nursing homes, restrictions in Medicare and Medicaid eligibility and reimbursement policies, and other changes all were cited as important. While it may be difficult to distinguish the specific effects of policies on nursing homes, the findings from this study show that nursing homes are facing a changing and uncertain financial and regulatory environment. Changes will not necessarily have a positive effect on access to nursing homes, quality of care, or cost containment. Consideration of access to both nursing home and home health care is the topic of the next chapter.

CHAPTER **8**

Access to Nursing Home
and Home Health Services

*Fragmentation need not be a permanent feature of our health and social
service delivery system. It is possible to create systems that facilitate access
and that are caregiver/elder-centered.*

Austin, 1992, p. 82

▼

The Medicare diagnosis-related group (DRG) prospective payment
system (PPS), developed to limit hospital costs, has affected all
aspects of health care. Because Medicare covers the cost of care for
94% of older hospital patients, PPS effects on hospital length of stay
particularly affect usage of posthospital care (Hing, 1987b). The PPS is
credited with changing every part of the health care system (Guterman
et al., 1988). Rates of Medicare patient use of posthospital skilled
nursing facilities (SNFs) and home health care institutions rose from
12% in pre-PPS 1981 to close to 17% in post-PPS 1985 (Neu & Harrison,
1988). The average numbers of home health visits per user rose from
12.8 in 1981 to 14.1 in 1984, and the proportion of discharges involving home health services rose from 13.3% to 18.5% over the same
period (Neu & Harrison, 1988).

Access to care in the community is an issue of increasing concern
in the 1990s. Particularly for older persons, access to community
health care services—nursing homes and home health care, in particular—following hospitalization is a vital issue.

NOTE: The authors of this chapter are James H. Swan and Carroll L. Estes.

Access

Broadly speaking, the term *access* refers to the capacity to make use of or to get to something. According to a much-used framework, "access may be defined as those dimensions which describe the potential and actual entry of a given population group to the health care delivery system" (Aday, Fleming, & Andersen, 1984, p. 13). Among factors that might affect access, so defined, are distance to site of care, insurance coverage, income, and satisfaction with the care-seeking process (Aday et al., 1984).

Accessibility of care, Evans (1990) suggests, goes well beyond measurement and embodies implicit values and choices. "Accessibility per se is really a means to one or more ends, not an end in itself. The end that is sought through health care is health, and the accessibility of health care is valued principally on the belief that such care will contribute to someone's health" (Evans, 1990, pp. 10-11). This definition clearly goes beyond entry into the delivery system and incorporates the notion of the appropriateness and potential effect of the health care provided.

Wallace (1990a) points to the failure of long term care researchers to examine availability and acceptability of care along with studies on accessibility. Wallace suggests that accessibility is circumscribed by knowledge of available services and the economic means to make use of services. The availability and acceptability of services are thus considered distinct factors. In this discussion, however, availability and acceptability of services are treated as facets of accessibility and not separated from it. Although the availability, acceptability, and attainability of health care services can be defined and discussed separately, the concepts tend to meld and together constitute accessibility.

Nursing Homes

Institutionalization of the aged is a common occurrence. In the early 1980s, about 7% of elderly persons living in the community entered nursing homes over any 2-year period. While the rate of movement from community to nursing home was less than 2% of the population aged 65 to 69, almost one third of persons aged 90 or over moved from community to nursing home residence (Hanley, Alecxih, Weiner, & Kennell, 1989). Among the aged who are dependent in mobility or personal care, about one third require institutionalization—only about one sixth of those aged 65 to 69 years but as many as one half of those aged 85 or over (Weissert, 1985). Despite the high and continuing demand for care, however, the supply of needed services remains constrained.

Availability

Research findings continue to substantiate the perceived shortage of nursing homes. Swan and Harrington (1986) report widespread undersupply in 1982, identifying 20 states as severely undersupplied. More recent analysis suggests that there were as many states in short supply of nursing home beds in the late 1980s as there had been earlier in the decade (Swan, Harrington, & Miller, 1991). Although the number of nursing home beds increased in most states through the 1980s, the rate of increase was outstripped by the rate of growth in the elderly population in most states in most years (Harrington et al., 1988). Since the 1960s, nursing home occupancy rates nationwide have been high, ranging from about 85% to 95% (Hawes & Phillips, 1986). The national rate of occupancy during the 1980s hovered between 91% and 92%. The variation between states was pronounced, however, ranging from a low of 74% to a high of 98% in 1988.

One way to improve availability is to increase bed stock (Nyman, 1989). Nursing home bed stock has been kept artificially low, however, by certificate-of-need (CON) requirements, state-imposed moratoria, and other practices aimed at limiting growth. In the 1980s, state nursing home bed stocks tended to increase, but at rates slower than those of the aged population, so that bed capacity declined relative to need (Harrington et al., 1988; Strahan, 1987). Research provides evidence of the undersupply of beds, at least in the Medicaid market (Harrington & Swan, 1987; Scanlon, 1980b), and evidence that the undersupply is linked to state efforts to constrain growth through CON regulations (Swan & Harrington, 1990). It may be argued that, insofar as such policy or nonmarket forces lead to undersupply, easing these policies would result in greater bed supply and, in so doing, improve access for the elderly (Bishop, 1988).

A demand-side solution has also been proposed: Remedy the tight bed supply by reducing demand for institutional care. Noninstitutional care, thought to be a substitute for nursing home care, could reduce barriers to entry by reducing the excess demand for bed-scarce nursing homes. Noninstitutional care has not, however, been shown to reduce the demand for nursing home care (Weissert, Cready, & Pawelak, 1988). Other factors implicated in tight bed stock include high interest rates during the 1970s and 1980s, which slowed construction of new facilities. Recent acceleration in the growth of bed capacity has been credited to lowered interest rates and to the relaxation of CON requirements in many states.

Availability is not simply a matter of bed count or of current occupancy, however. A relatively high number of beds is irrelevant if beds never become free to accommodate new patients, and a mere bed without the offer of appropriate medical services for the potential patient negates the notion of availability. Rates of bed turnover and the provision or absence of ancillary services such as physical, respiratory, and speech therapy affect availability as much as does the presence of the bed itself.

Bed turnover—the rate at which people move in and out of an institution—bears heavily on bed availability in nursing homes. The more times per year a bed is emptied, the more times it may be filled. Turnover is determined by length of stay; the greater the number of short stays, the higher the turnover rate. Nursing home services are often differentiated into long-term stays and short-term stays, and bed availability may differ depending on the prospective resident's estimated length of stay. Kelman and Thomas (1990) found three types of nursing home patients: long-term (with stays averaging 2 years), short-term (with stays averaging 50 days), and those who died following nursing home admission (with stays averaging 53 days). These three groups of clients might be classified in terms of risk factors, with the long-term residents tending to be older and more impaired. Prospective nursing home residents in need of long-term stays (that is, averaging 2 years) tend to be distinguishable from prospective clients who are more likely to require shorter stays (50 days) on dimensions of age and impairment, and these very factors may pose barriers to entry. Moreover, long-stay residents are more likely to be covered by Medicaid and may thus face additional entry barriers, as discussed below.

Lack of ancillary services impinges on availability and, similarly, inadequate care may be equated with unavailability. Persons with acquired immunodeficiency syndrome (AIDS), for instance, often cannot find nursing home beds with the high level of care they need (Swan & Benjamin, 1990b; Swan, Benjamin, & Brown, in press).

Medicaid Limitations

The difficulty of limiting the notion of access to the knowledge of service provision and the economic means to obtain services is clearly illustrated in the case of Medicaid. Although Medicaid theoretically makes nursing home care attainable, its low reimbursement rates may at the same time depress the availability of services to the Medicaid-dependent population. These effects are sides of the same coin that, along with other factors, determine access to care.

The concern with access to long term care, especially in reaction to or fostered by state action, tends to focus on access to care by Medicaid-dependent clients. In 1987, Medicaid funded 44% of all nursing home care in the United States (Letsch, Levit, & Waldo, 1988). Although the Medicaid share of nursing home payments declined in the 1980s, the program remains by far the most important third-party payer for such care. Nursing home care is also an important, and costly, portion of the Medicaid budget, which increased rapidly in the 1970s (Levit, Lazenby, Waldo, & Davidoff, 1985; Rymer & Adler, 1984) but declined in the 1980s (Swan, 1990) from 34.8% in 1978 to 30.5% in 1986 (IHA, 1986, 1987).

Medicaid nursing home access tends to be a somewhat urban issue. Recent estimates of supply and demand equations (Miller et al., 1992) suggest that the larger the proportion of a state's population in metropolitan areas, the greater the Medicaid nursing home demand but the lower the supply of nursing home beds to Medicaid. Medicaid-eligible persons are thus caught in the middle. Medicaid patients average much longer stays than non-Medicaid patients (Shaughnessy et al., 1987), thus reducing the availability of beds to new patients. Hence it follows that, if Medicaid patients are allocated a fixed ration or quota of beds, the rate at which beds become available for new Medicaid patients will be lower than the rate at which beds become available for non-Medicaid patients. Generally, conditions that limit availability for clients needing long stays thereby limit Medicaid availability.

The Scanlon model (1980b) portrays nursing home beds as undersupplied to Medicaid recipients. All Medicaid recipients pay a single price, set by the state as the rate. States may set a rate for each specific facility or a flat rate for a class of facilities, but both are usually below the price for private-pay patients. Thus Medicaid recipients have access only to beds for which there are no higher-paying private patients, and they have access only as long as the Medicaid rate is above the nursing home marginal cost. Some, but far from all, Medicaid recipients will be served before the marginal cost of providing beds rises above the Medicaid rate.

An important corollary of the Scanlon model is that wider eligibility for Medicaid coverage (thus greater access to the program) does not expand access to nursing home beds but adds to the length of the queue of Medicaid eligibles seeking nursing home care. To increase access for Medicaid eligibles, the Medicaid rate would have to be increased, allowing access for additional Medicaid recipients until the marginal cost of providing beds again exceeded the Medicaid rate. The inadequacy of Medicaid payment rates creates an issue of availability of long term care for Medicaid-dependent persons. Observers have long argued that Medicaid rates are too low, perhaps below the cost of service provision (Grimaldi, 1982). Empirical evidence supports this contention with regard to high-cost nursing home residents (Murtaugh, Cooney, DerSimonian, Smits, & Fetter, 1988; Swan & Benjamin, 1990b). The debate regarding the adequacy of Medicaid payment rates has led to calls for special reimbursement for high-cost patients (Lewin et al., 1987) and has contributed to consideration by some states of such approaches as case-mix reimbursement. As valid as arguments for increasing Medicaid reimbursement rates for long term care may be, however, it is also arguable that rate hikes should not be encouraged as the major means of increasing access for Medicaid patients to nursing home beds.

Phillips and Hawes (1988) dispute contentions that higher payments will improve access for Medicaid-eligible persons to nursing homes. Especially because of the undersupply of nursing home beds, they argue, Medicaid rates serve as the base rates above which private-pay prices are set. When Medicaid rates increase, private-pay rates are raised in tandem, so that more private-pay patients rapidly deplete their resources, becoming Medicaid eligible. Examples are cited of states that raised their Medicaid rates without increasing access to services for persons dependent on Medicaid payments and of states that have generous Medicaid rates but continue to have access problems.

Recent estimates (Miller et al., 1992) suggest that Medicaid rates definitely affect supply of bed days to Medicaid patients. The issue is whether the effect is of sufficient magnitude to make accessibility a major justification for rate increases. Even if the effect were stronger, a rate increase would be a dangerous strategy in an era of severe budget limits when policymakers may choose cost containment over accessibility.

Kenney and Holahan (1990) report that Medicaid reimbursement policies affect nursing home access after hospital discharge. In particular, states with prospective reimbursement methods, which seek to keep reimbursement rate increases in check (Swan, Harrington, & Miller, 1991; Swan et al., 1988), are likely to have greater access problems. Because Kenney and Holahan (1990) do not include reimbursement rates in their analysis, it is not possible to assess the effects of payment methods, controlling for the effects of rate levels.

Nyman, Levey, and Rohrer (1987) present evidence that excess demand, rather than the low Medicaid reimbursement rate, explains the inaccessibility of nursing home beds to Medicaid-dependent patients. Medicaid reimbursement rates, themselves, though, may be the deciding factor in the case of high-need, high-cost patients (Murtaugh et al., 1988). For example, Swan and Benjamin (1990a) show that, with AIDS patients in a California SNF, the daily cost of providing nursing care alone (i.e., excluding all other costs of providing a bed and care) equaled or exceeded the Medicaid per diem rate.

Medicare Limitations

Medicare has been a minor payer for nursing home care, covering only 2% of nursing home cost in 1986 (Letsch et al., 1988). Medicare SNF coverage, however, became more important after the implementation of Medicare PPS hospital reimbursement (Lewis, Leake, Clark, & Leal-Sotelo, 1990; Neu & Harrison, 1988). In consequence, the numbers of SNFs certified for Medicare increased rapidly (Watkins & Kirby, 1987). The Medicare Catastrophic Coverage Act also greatly expanded the role of Medicare, but questions about the future of the provisions of this act make the significance of the change uncertain (Newman & Scanlon, 1989).

Because of its role in facilitating admissions, Medicare is more important in providing access to nursing homes than is suggested by its overall coverage of costs. Although Medicare coverage is restricted to rehabilitative and convalescent care and is most likely to be provided only at the time of hospital discharge, the rates are cost based and tend to be higher than Medicaid rates (Miller et al., 1992). Therefore nursing homes more readily admit Medicare than Medicaid patients. After Medicare benefits terminate, however, patients with continuing stays may spend down their resources and become eligible for Medicaid. In this way, Medicare may "shoehorn" Medicaid patients into nursing homes. Research (Liu et al., 1990) shows that Medicare-to-Medicaid crossovers may be less prevalent than often assumed, however. When Medicare nursing home stays became shorter following implementation of the PPS (Neu & Harrison, 1988), Medicare-to-Medicaid crossovers may have declined. At the same time, the increased rates of nursing home utilization by Medicare patients may have exacerbated the problem of access for Medicaid-dependent persons. Higher reimbursement rates for Medicare short-stay patients may displace Medicaid long-stay patients with lower reimbursement rates.

Until recently, variations in interpreting Medicare benefits meant that access to Medicare-covered nursing home care differed regionally (Smits, Feder, & Scanlon, 1982). Differences in interpretation by Medicare fiscal intermediaries (contract organizations responsible for determining which cases are paid and in what amounts) meant that cases acceptable for Medicare reimbursement in one region of the country would not be so accepted in another region. This problem was addressed in changes by the Health Care Financing Administration (HCFA) in 1988 (Newman & Scanlon, 1989).

Access Issues Outside Medicare and Medicaid

Not all access problems relate to Medicare and Medicaid. Nongovernmental nursing home access problems exist as well. Although private long term care insurance coverage is increasing (Wallack, 1989), a very small number of older persons (fewer than 500,000 nationwide) carry it.

Nursing home access is difficult for patients who require complex treatments (Hing, 1987b; Shaughnessy et al., 1987; U.S. GAO, 1983). Nursing homes have traditionally lacked both the capacity and the willingness to admit patients with high needs. This reluctance is related to payment. For example, if ancillary services are included in per diem rates instead of separately reimbursed when provided, facilities have little or no incentive to provide rehabilitative therapies (Swan et al., 1990).

Changes in the structure of health care industries, especially nursing homes, raise access issues. For-profit facilities are more likely than nonprofit facilities to accept Medicaid patients, but, when for-profit motivations predominate, issues of access and quality of care may be secondary concerns (Harrington, 1991a; Marmor et al., 1987; Schlesinger, Marmor, & Smithey, 1987). Thus the overwhelmingly for-profit cast of nursing home facilities suggests that issues other than quality and access are primary to the industry. Increased chain ownership of nursing homes also suggests possible access problems. At the very least, access problems caused by policies promulgated by chain ownership have the potential of being generalized to many nursing homes.

The implementation of the Medicare PPS in hospitals has changed some of the dynamics, however, as large numbers of severely ill patients are discharged to nursing homes after short hospital stays. As noted above, there has been an increase in shorter SNF stays paid for by Medicare (Guterman et al., 1988; Neu & Harrison, 1988). Gearing up to deal with high-need, short-stay clients requires SNFs to hire more skilled nursing staff. The nursing shortage, and the lower wages offered to nurses by SNFs in comparison to acute care hospitals, however, place nursing homes at a competitive disadvantage in attracting and hiring competent, skilled nursing staff. Thus the availability of short-term SNF care is by no means assured. Moreover, in the absence of an increase in bed capacity, shifts toward short-stay posthospital nursing home markets will mean limits of access to long-term nursing home care.

Discrimination and Acceptability

Differential access to care on the basis of ability to pay is not always considered to constitute discrimination. Providers are assumed to be within their rights and nondiscriminatory when they allot care on the basis of price paid. Social programs, such as Medicaid, may address issues of equity and need by enhancing the ability of the needy to pay. Lower than customary payment rates, however, have contributed to discriminatory practices against persons who must rely on Medicaid to reimburse providers for care. Insofar as beds are undersupplied to Medicaid-eligible persons, that population might be considered discriminated against. Certainly, multiple waiting lists, and especially separate Medicaid lists, raise the issue of discrimination (Ambrogi, Doctor, & Swan, 1988).

Low Medicaid reimbursement rates and the consequent discrimination against Medicaid patients (U.S. Senate, 1984) may have created a two-tiered or dual nursing home market, in which Medicaid patients are cared for by Medicaid-specialist homes with low costs based on less care, fewer amenities, and cheaper services (Phillips & Hawes, 1988). Paradoxically, although provision of care to private-pay patients is the most profitable, some homes specialize in Medicaid patients (Hawes & Phillips, 1986). These nursing homes tend to provide the lowest levels of care (Hawes & Phillips, 1986). In a dual market, minor increases in Medicaid rates may be insufficient to raise Medicaid patients above the market barrier. Medicaid rates may be so far below private-pay rates that states could not afford to raise them sufficiently to overcome market barriers. Medicaid rate increases may only increase prices in both tiers of a dual market, without improving access.

Discriminatory practices against Medicaid-eligible persons—differences in the attainability and acceptability of care—may not simply be attributed to low payment rates. Phillips and Hawes (1988) argue that Medicaid-reimbursed nursing home patients face systematic discrimination. Aside from the rate paid for their care, they are (by definition of their Medicaid eligibility) poor persons. Medicaid-dependent nursing home patients are, for the most part, from a different socioeconomic background than those who pay privately for their care. Access is not always based solely on the price one pays. Nursing home operators may prefer to admit non-Medicaid patients even at rates equal to those paid by Medicaid patients. Evidence of class-based discrimination may be found in the maintenance of separate waiting lists for Medicaid and non-Medicaid patients and the poorer care and fewer amenities provided to Medicaid-dependent patients than to private-pay patients (Phillips & Hawes, 1988). Differences in treatment may be linked to low Medicaid payment, and nursing home operators could suffer financially were Medicaid-dependent patients given equal access to admissions, care of high quality, and amenities, but Phillips and Hawes (1988) provide strong evidence from California that this is not so.

Phillips and Hawes (1988) report that, although the percentage of Medicaid-reimbursed patients in institutions is negatively related to financial indicators, the relationships are too weak to indicate financial hardship for homes admitting larger numbers of Medicaid patients. They also note that states with more generous Medicaid rates have not eradicated nursing home access problems for Medicaid-dependent patients. It may be that the figures reflect the ability of Medicaid specialists, whose clientele is largely or totally composed of Medicaid recipients, to profit from Medicaid patients in a way that private-pay facilities cannot. Phillips and Hawes (1988) show, however, that it is among homes with the highest proportion of Medicaid patients that the proportion of Medicaid to non-Medicaid patients is most strongly related to financial indicators. The researchers conclude that (a) discrimination against Medicaid recipients exists not based solely on Medicaid rates and (b) prohibitions on nursing home discrimination against Medicaid patients would not impose an overwhelming financial burden on facilities. In a single facility, differences in accessibility to care not based on price suggest discrimination, according to a U.S. district court in Tennessee (Saddler & Barrick, 1991). The problem is in determining to what degree differences in accessibility to care are based on price.

Medicaid payment is generally so far below private-pay prices that separating price-based differential barriers to access from other causes is difficult. Average Medicaid rates influence the supply of nursing home bed days to Medicaid-eligible persons, but the effect is fairly weak (Miller et al., 1992). Although Phillips and Hawes (1988) present data suggesting that there is more going on than simple price sensitivity, empirically it is difficult to separate price from other bases of unequal treatment. In the absence of strong research evidence, courts and policymakers may simply decide the issue on the basis of disparate impacts (Saddler & Barrick, 1991). In addition to the argument that care should be available to all who need it, the unequal treatment resulting from inadequate reimbursement by government programs poses another issue.

The Linton Plan (stemming from the district court case in Tennessee) imposed restrictions on how, and how rapidly, facilities may withdraw from the Medicaid program (Saddler & Barrick, 1991) but did not challenge the basic ability to withdraw and certainly did not address itself to facilities that did not already participate in the Medicaid program. This is a political issue. States could, if they wished, mandate Medicaid certification as a condition of licensure, as a condition of certificate-of-need (CON) approval, and/or as a prerequisite for nonprofit tax status. Such a mandate on a state's agenda might produce an interesting counterdemand that the state reimburse equitably under the Medicaid program.

Minorities use nursing homes at fairly low rates (Greene & Ondrich, 1990; Murtaugh, Kemper, & Spillman, 1990). This fact may be related to demand or to cultural or other differences that result in minority individuals being less likely than others to seek nursing home care (Morrison, 1983; Mutran, 1985). When the issue is supply, discrimination can arguably be charged (Wallace, 1990b). Discrimination against minorities is tied, in part, to the issue of Medicaid discrimination. Some persons argue that Medicaid discrimination is itself related to the class and ethnic makeup of Medicaid eligibles. In fact, the arguments in the Linton case relied on the 1964 Civil Rights Act, and the finding made specific reference to how Medicaid certification practices as well as practices regarding separate waiting lists disparately affected minorities (Saddler & Barrick, 1991). Aside from legal doctrines of disparate impact, however, it is difficult in research to differentiate Medicaid from minority access issues.

Miller and associates (1992) plan to attempt a partial test of this issue by including state population percentage of nonwhite persons in both the supply and the demand equations for Medicaid days of nursing home care. Despite problems with this approach, if the percentage of nonwhite persons shows a negative effect in the supply equation, the finding would suggest that states with higher percentages of nonwhite persons are less likely to supply nursing home bed days to Medicaid-eligible persons, controlling for all other supply factors.

Quite aside from and beyond discriminatory practices, nursing home care is generally considered unacceptable. The nursing home has a bad public image as the place where one goes, whether for days or for years, to die. Such reality or images aside, however, nursing homes differ in levels of acceptability. Today, the dominant policy is to enforce certain aspects of acceptability. Government payers and an increasingly important private sector now demand higher quality of care, instituting measures to assure it. The past history of increasing costs without assurance of quality has given way to the current policy of demanding quality without assurance of adequate payment. Undersupply means not only restricted access but quality problems as well (Nyman, 1989; Zinn, 1991). Nyman notes that "evidence is consistent with the hypothesis that the quality problems traditionally exhibited by nursing homes are linked to the absence of a need to compete for patients, created by the bed shortage conditions" (Nyman, 1989, p. 105).

Of central concern is Medicaid-covered care. As noted, low rates and discrimination against Medicaid patients may have created a two-tiered nursing home market. Insofar as Medicaid patients are cared for by Medicaid-specialist homes with low quality of care, the problem is not only availability of care to Medicaid-eligible persons but also the acceptability of care. Likewise, even in the same facility, Medicaid patients may receive less care, fewer amenities, and cheaper services. In general, Medicaid care is less acceptable than private-pay care.

Home Health Care

Researchers (Estes, Wood, et al., 1988; Neu & Harrison, 1988) find the effects of the PPS to extend beyond hospitals to other parts of the community-based delivery system. As one of the important bulwarks of postacute care for the elderly after implementation of DRG-based prospective payment, home health care availability and accessibility are increasingly salient topics to policymakers as well as to the elderly and their families. Guterman and associates (1988) report that percentages of Medicare beneficiaries using home health care following hospitalization rose for all age groups, across all states, in the PPS period. Home health utilization rose 55% between 1981 and 1985, and the percentage of patients receiving home health visits within 7 days of discharge increased by 14%.

Other researchers (DesHarnais et al., 1987; Van Gelder & Bernstein, 1986) report additional corroborative findings about PPS effects on home care. More than 80% of home health agencies reported serving more clients in need of high-tech care, multiple services, daily services, and higher volume of services immediately following the implementation of the PPS than before (Spohn et al., 1988).

Availability

The availability of home health care is not as constrained as for nursing home care. This is due in large part to the fact that home health care does not have the high capital investment barriers that impede entry into the institutional care market (Mundinger, 1983). Home health care grew tremendously in the 1980s, becoming a major mode of posthospital care (U.S. HCFA, 1987a). This expansion began prior to the implementation of the Medicare PPS for hospital reimbursement but received continued impetus from the effects of the new payment system.

The low barriers to entry of suppliers into the home health care market may lead to the assumption that home health care capacity is extremely elastic (Swan & Benjamin, 1990c). One constraint on the expansion of home health care, however, is the supply of staff. Staffing difficulties threaten to limit the availability of services or to diminish the acceptability of care when poorly qualified staff are hired (Canalis, 1987; Jones, 1988).

Accessibility

A majority of home health agencies (69%) reported that they could not serve certain clients for reasons relating to the inadequacy of Medicare reimbursement and client inability to pay for care or make copayments (Spohn et al., 1988). Reductions in hospital length of stay by more than 20% in just 5 years and a transfer of the site of much medical care from hospitals to ambulatory settings and to the home underscore the importance of access to home health care (Neu & Harrison, 1988). The limited scope of Medicare home health care coverage and the inability of many older persons to pay out of pocket for in-home care make the ability and willingness of agencies to provide care to uninsured and underinsured persons who are unable to pay out of pocket very important.

Massive entry of Medicare-certified, for-profit agencies has radically transformed the composition of the market. For-profit agencies have assumed primacy and are now the dominant organizational type in the home health care market for the first time in U.S. history. Between 1972 and 1986, the number of certified for-profit home health agencies mushroomed, growing by 4,251% (from 43 to 1,871) compared with a 105% growth (from 665 to 1,361) in the number of nonprofit agencies and a 7% decline in the number of public home health agencies (from 1,255 to 1,165) (Chapter 6; Estes et al., in press). As the single largest component of the home health industry, for-profit enterprises now constitute about one third (32%) of the certified market. The trend toward for-profit ownership is accompanied by a transformation in the structure of home health agencies of all types, signaled by growing numbers of chains and multifacility systems and complex organizational arrangements, some combining nonprofit and for-profit entities in mixed forms (Estes et al., in press). In fact,

> the most significant change in the home health industry has been the emergence of proprietary agencies, particularly chains, as the largest single form of organization. Studies indicate that home health agency (HHA) chains, perceiving home health to be a lucrative market, have been growing rapidly. (Waldo et al., 1986, p. 11)

There is a small but growing literature concerning the relationship of tax status to the propensity to limit or deny access and to practice "cream-skimming"—that is, selecting clients who can pay and who are profitable. Both for-profit and nonprofit providers have been charged with selecting the clients they treat in such a way as to avoid serving unprofitable clients and also with "dumping" patients, particularly hospital patients, on public sector hospitals and clinics.

Marmor and associates (1987) contend that differences between for-profits and nonprofits are reflected not in the presence but in the nature or extent of patient selection. Facilities may avoid unprofitable patients in many ways including locating facilities away from low-income areas, choosing not to provide services that are used disproportionately by the uninsured or underinsured, and actively screening for and discouraging admission (e.g., requiring a means test prior to admission or not offering sliding-scale fees) to those unable to pay for care.

Due to the limited ability to control for the many factors other than ownership that can affect institutional policies, Marmor and associates (1987) call for the cautious interpretation of the research and report that for-profit agencies are more likely to use the various methods of avoiding unprofitable clients. In particular, proprietary agencies may select clients according to their ability to pay and by so doing avoid the most costly types of clients.

Findings from past studies of ownership of and access to home health agencies suggest that for-profit agencies may skim patients and discontinue needed services (Nutter, 1984), are more likely to be located in high-income areas where most potential clients have private insurance coverage and are not covered by Medicaid (Bays, 1983; Homer et al., 1984; Marmor et al., 1987; Schlesinger, Marmor, & Smithey, 1987), are less likely to provide unprofitable services no matter how beneficial the service might be to the community being served (Arrington & Haddock, 1990; Cromwell & Kanak, 1982; Kaluzny, Gentry, Glasser, & Sprague, 1970; Renn, Schramm, Watt, & Derzon, 1985; Schlesinger & Dorwart, 1984; Schlesinger, Marmor, & Smithey, 1987; Shortell, Morrison, Hughes, Friedman, & Vitek, 1986), and are unlikely to determine fees by the use of sliding scales or to offer uncompensated care to low-income clients (Lewin, Eckles, & Miller, 1988; Schlesinger, 1985b; Schlesinger & Dorwart, 1984; Schlesinger, Marmor, & Smithey, 1987; Sloan, Valvona, & Mullner, 1986).

Increased competition among health care providers may influence accessibility. Various studies have uncovered the effects of market competition on home health care agencies. Lewin and Lewin (1984) suggest that competition among providers may reduce access to care by limiting an agency's ability to subsidize the cost of care provided to unprofitable patients with the profits earned through other patients. Schlesinger, Marmor, and Smithey (1987) report that the growing number of providers in the market makes it is easier for some agencies to become "free riders"—accepting only profitable cases and leaving other agencies to provide for the "public good." Weinstein (1984) suggests that the competitive ethos may reduce the responsiveness of community agencies.

The findings of the Institute for Health & Aging study on home health agency clientele (Swan & Estes, 1990a) and access limitations (Estes & Swan, 1989) generally support the contentions regarding differences between for-profit and nonprofit agencies when both agency types are independent and freestanding. Estes and Swan (1989) analyzed the limits on access to home health agencies and services between 1984 and 1987. Measures of access examined are (a) changes in hours of operation and in geographic areas served; (b) the tightening of eligibility criteria and increases in fees; and (c) home health agency reports of service refusal to clients of any type.

A strong finding is that, among independent, freestanding agencies, for-profit agencies were more likely than nonprofit agencies to refuse services to some types of clients. Within multifacility systems or chains, however, for-profit and nonprofit agencies were equally likely to refuse services to certain types of clients. The differences between nonprofit and for-profit agencies vanished when home health organizations were part of large rationalized systems.

Because the strongest findings in the analysis of access relate to service refusals and because service refusal is a direct means of limiting access, Swan and Estes (1990a) also examined how service refusals affect changes in clientele by age. The HHAs that report having to refuse access to certain clients are also less likely to increase services to either young-old or old-old clients. Thus the factors that lead to agency refusals result in fewer services for the aged. The increasing membership of home health agencies in chains and multifacility systems means that accessibility problems for the elderly are not limited to for-profit agencies. Access problems are also evident in nonprofit agencies.

Medicare Limitations

The major third-party payer for home health care is the Medicare program (Van Gelder & Bernstein, 1986). Policies are set nationally, without reference to state boundaries. To be eligible for Medicare coverage of home health care, Medicare-eligible patients must be homebound, need intermittent care (neither too frequent nor too infrequent visits), be able to show evidence of recovery, and need either skilled nursing care or physical therapy. These provisions have severe accessibility implications for the aged. Benjamin and associates (1989) studied 540 Medicare-covered discharged clients from two hospitals, 295 of whom were discharged with provision made for Medicare-reimbursed home health care; the remaining 245 patients (a comparison group) were discharged without being eligible for or receiving Medicare home health care benefits.

Benjamin and associates found that medical severity and functional debility were the major predictors of an elder's receiving Medicare home health care benefits at hospital discharge. Persons living alone were also more likely than others to receive home health care benefits at hospital discharge. Age, gender, and ethnicity were not predictors of being discharged from the hospital with the provision of Medicare home health care benefits. It is to be noted that "these statistically significant relationships do not mean that everyone in the non-home health group had no medical or functional needs" (Benjamin et al., 1989, p. ii). One fifth of the comparison group had major or severe medical problems at discharge, and one fourth required assistance in two or more activities of daily living (ADLs). Of persons provided with home health care benefits, three fourths had severe medical problems at discharge and two thirds required assistance in two or more ADLs. Although admission to home health care appears to be based on effective sorting out of the hospital discharges, many patients discharged without provision for home health care were in considerable need of such care.

Admission to Medicare home health care does not necessarily mean access to the specific in-home care needed. Not only are many in-home services not covered by Medicare, but Medicare-coverable services also must be authorized for Medicare users. Benjamin and associates (1989) found that, during the period of receiving home health services, more than half of the Medicare home health users received at least one of a list of in-home services not covered by Medicare (e.g., personal care attendant, homemaker/chore, home-delivered meals, medical transportation, escort to medical appointments, or in-home respite). Channels other than Medicare must be used to gain access to these services, often at considerable burden to patients and their families. Despite the high user rate of the uncovered services, Benjamin and associates (1989) report that the level of need is even greater than actual utilization. This suggests that lack of economic access, among other barriers, prevents persons from receiving services not covered by Medicare.

Patient discharge from home health care does not mean that all needs have been met. Benjamin and associates (1989) found that, at discharge from home health care, three fourths of Medicare home health users remained in need of assistance with activities of daily living (ADLs) or with instrumental activities of daily living (IADLs). One third remained in need of help with medically related tasks. Moreover, persons needing assistance with medically related tasks did not necessarily have stronger social support networks than persons without such needs. These high levels of need for care persisted at least through 6 months after hospital discharge, and levels of need were as high in the comparison group as among patients who had received Medicare-reimbursed home health care. There is considerable evidence, hence, that there are high levels of need to which Medicare home health benefits do not respond.

Benjamin and associates (1989) found that, although one fifth of the former Medicare home health beneficiaries remained in need of skilled nursing services 6 months after hospital discharge and one sixth remained in need of physical therapy, only 3 patient cases out of the 295 home health cases remained open at the end of 6 months. Failure to fulfill one or another of the qualifying criteria to receive Medicare home health benefits (e.g., being homebound, needing intermittent care, being able to show evidence of recovery, having care authorized by a physician) rather than illness itself led to the cessation of Medicare-covered benefits for many persons still in need of services. Unknown numbers of persons in need of home health care after discharge from hospitals never qualify for these benefits under Medicare.

High-Tech Care

With the expansion of home health care services has come a parallel development of highly technological care. The concurrent development of technology serves to adapt in-home services to the needs of early-discharge patients under the Medicare hospital PPS. In fact, trends include a return to physician house calls for diagnostic, therapeutic, and long term care purposes. "Home visits by the primary physician may be medically necessary and appropriate for patients with unstable medical conditions or technologically complex care" (CSA, 1990, p. 1243).

Data from the Institute for Health & Aging survey show increased provision of selected high-tech services over time (Binney et al., 1990). For example, increases between 1986 and 1987 in the provision of home health ventilator services tended to occur in agencies that also reported increases in fees and copayments. This suggests that the increased provision of high-tech care is accompanied by higher costs to the agency that are recovered, at least in part, by higher out-of-pocket payments by clients. Access to needed high-tech care may be impeded when payment for the additional charges must be made out of pocket.

There is much evidence for access limits for persons who could possibly benefit from home health care services. Some access barriers are imposed by the structure and operation of the home health care industry. Other barriers result from the lack of federal insurance protection or a national policy on long term care (Estes, 1984-1985) and from the provisions of Medicare, the major third-party payer of formal home health care. Access limits have also been attributed to the lack of adequate private long term care insurance, whether as a substitute for or as a complement to Medicare and other government program coverage (Wallack, 1989).

Acceptability of Services

Home health care has many quality problems (Grant & Harrington, 1989), exacerbated by the dispersed locus of the provision of care. To some degree, quality issues can be addressed by aggressive agency management (Peters, 1988). Further, geographic dispersion poses difficult problems for evaluating the process of caregiving in the home, but the outcomes of care can nevertheless be monitored (Lalonde, 1988). A number of studies have documented the poor quality of some home care services, including care resulting in physical suffering and death, intentional or accidental injury, failure to prevent or reduce decubitus ulcers, and improper use of medical equipment or intravenous lines. Other abuses involve unethical or illegal behavior, psychological abuse, theft, financial exploitation, and failure to provide services for which the client is billed (Grant & Harrington, 1989; U.S. GAO, 1987b; U.S. House of Representatives, 1986b, 1987a; U.S. Senate, 1986b). Many issues of quality in home care stem from irregular standards for professional or vocational training of staff and lack of ongoing supervision of caregivers except by the clients who are dependent on them. Legislation in 1987 was designed to make quality improvements through increased training and reporting, a toll-free hot line, and an investigative unit, among other changes. The major government funder of home health care is the Medicare program. Quality of care is more regulated and standards set higher for Medicare-reimbursed services than in the private-pay market (Grant & Harrington, 1989). The attention of policymakers has been focused on certified home health agencies with services paid for by Medicare or Medicaid. Little is known about uncertified and unlicensed providers of in-home services to the elderly and disabled (Grant & Harrington, 1989), although these providers are estimated to number 2 to 3 times the licensed and certified home health agencies and are considered increasingly important within the health care sector (Harrington & Grant, 1990).

Interaction Between Nursing Home and Home Health Care

Home health care has not reduced nursing home utilization. This does not mean, however, that home health care utilization fails to affect the demand for or access to nursing homes. Swan and Benjamin

(1990a) note that attention needs to be paid to the effects of the nursing home market on home health care (Benjamin, 1986b; U.S. GAO, 1982).

Swan and Benjamin (1990b) present a model for the effect of the length of nursing home queues on home health care utilization. According to the model, structural nursing home undersupply, at least to Medicaid recipients, means that there are semipermanent queues of individuals—not yet and perhaps never to be admitted—demanding nursing home care. Insofar as some of this demand for care could be met by home health agencies, it will be translated into demand for home health care. Because home health capacity is more elastic than is nursing home capacity (Mundinger, 1983), increases in the demand for home health care are more readily translated into actual home health care utilization.

The substitution model depends on overlap in nursing home and home health queues. For the model to be applicable, some patients must be able to receive either type of care—that is, care in one setting is substitutable for care in another. In spite of overall differences between nursing home and home health care users in terms of medical and functional status (Kramer, Shaughnessy, & Perrigrew, 1985; Sager et al., 1987), there is evidence for the substitutability of care. Nursing home patients vary greatly (Secord, 1986), and some elderly nursing home users are quite similar to home health care users (Sherwood, Morris, & Ruchin, 1986). Branch, Evans, Scherr, Smith, Taylor, and Wetle (1989) report that one difference between home health and nursing home clients is that the latter are more likely to have been living alone prior to admission to the nursing home and to differ in functional health as well. Clients of both types, however, are similar in age, gender, medical status, and mental function. Thus it is conceivable that part, but far from all, of the demand for nursing home care could be filled by home health care.

The model has profound implications for nursing home and home health access. A basic assumption of the Swan and Benjamin (1990c) model is that greater availability and use of home health care reduces the queue for nursing home care. Thus, even though home health care may not affect nursing home *utilization*, it may improve nursing home *access* by reducing the numbers of individuals competing for available beds. The degree to which this is true depends on the amount of overlap between the demand for nursing home care and the demand for home health care.

Home health care could alter the composition of nursing home queues by being a viable substitute for only select persons in the

queue. For example, Coughlin, McBride, and Lui (1989) report finding that home health aide visits negatively affect short-term nursing
home admissions but have a positive effect on long-term admissions.
In spite of evidence of an important degree of overlap, however, the
fact remains that much, if not most, of the demand for nursing home
care cannot be filled by home health or other in-home care.

Greater unfilled demand for nursing home care (or greater substitutability of home health care for nursing home care) will increase
the demand for home health care. Although home health capacity
can be more easily increased than can nursing home capacity, it is
neither infinitely nor spontaneously elastic. The nursing shortage
restricts home health capacity (Swan & Benjamin, 1990a). Likewise,
some states retain certificate-of-need (CON) controls on home health
agencies, which may restrict access to home health care (Estes &
Swan, 1989). Longer nursing home queues may mean unfilled home
health demand and signal greater access problems. Limited nursing
home bed capacity and nursing home access barriers may spill over
to create problems of access to home health care.

Conclusion

Access issues are salient for all kinds of posthospital care for the
elderly. These problems are most widespread with regard to nursing
home and home health care, however. As noted above, concepts of
availability, attainability, and acceptability of care help to define
accessibility.

Availability issues in nursing homes are many: undersupply of
beds, accompanying high occupancy rates and long waits for admission, increased demand for care by early-discharged hospital patients, variable lengths of stay for different types of patients, inadequate payment levels of government programs, difficulty of access
for and discrimination against Medicaid recipients, severe limitations on Medicare coverage of SNF care, and lack of private insurance for long term care. Of these, undersupply may be the most
serious issue. The effects of continuing supply restrictions by some
states need study, particularly as related to long term care patients
with special needs.

Attainability of long term care in the current health care market
centers on payer reimbursement policies, especially Medicaid policies. Medicaid reimbursement rates are generally so low that persons
eligible for Medicaid-reimbursed care find it difficult to secure beds

in nursing homes. Although there are strong arguments that across-the-board rate increases would not be an access panacea and could be a drain on already strapped public budgets, there are also strong arguments for more specific rate increases. For example, rate increases for specific types of high-need patients, by facility case mix, might be warranted. Discrimination, particularly against Medicaid recipients, must be eliminated. Government should address this problem directly and forthrightly, outlawing discrimination rather than merely providing incentives not to discriminate against particular types of patients.

Acceptability of nursing home care, at one time an issue for comment and lamentation only, has come to the fore as an area for government mandates. Under 1987 legislation, the quality of nursing home care is a major concern of government regulators. Regulation does not necessarily assure, however, that equally acceptable care will be available to Medicaid and non-Medicaid nursing home patients. Legal actions may reduce the Medicaid/non-Medicaid differences, but recent regulatory provisions may contribute to increased access barriers to nursing home care for Medicaid recipients.

Home health care provides a different set of access issues than does nursing home care. Organized care in the home grew at a rapid rate during the 1980s, greatly exceeding the rather slow growth of the nursing home industry. Although home health care is less subject to capacity constraints than the nursing home industry, there are severe constraints on this form of noninstitutional care.

Aside from the argument that home health is not merely (if at all) a cheap substitute for nursing home care, home health services are needed and justified in their own right. That persons who might otherwise have entered nursing home care are instead able to remain in their own homes with home health care and other assistance is in most cases to be commended. It is not likely, however, that such substitution will significantly alter nursing home utilization under current circumstances. How home health care can be a part of a reconstituted, community-based long term care system that achieves reduced nursing home usage is a question not answerable from currently available data.

Like nursing home care, home health care has experienced the effects of increased demand generated by early hospital discharges with the Medicare PPS. It also has been affected greatly by the general restructuring of the U.S. health care system and suffers from payment problems in terms of both restrictions under government programs and inadequate private long term care insurance coverage.

As a result, issues of accessibility to home health care are more salient than issues regarding the availability of such care. Although proposals for expanded government financing of services may be unpopular in today's resource-poor public policy context (Harrington, Cassel, Estes, Woolhandler, & Himmelstein, 1991), such consideration is unavoidable when policymakers face the existing long term care insurance crisis.

Thus far, the focus has been on the immediate posthospital system including discharge planners and nursing home and home health care. Subsequent chapters explore broader questions of community care for the elderly, beginning in the next chapter with the issue of informalization.

CHAPTER 9

Informalization and Community Care

The independence of family [caregiving] patterns from public policy is more impressive than the connections. While the demise of filial relations and responsibility has regularly been reported and their survival regularly rediscovered, parents and children have conducted their affairs with each other without attention to either kind of news. . . . Family life flows on, untroubled by scholars and columnists.

Schorr, 1980, p. 41

▼

The process of informalization provides a key to understanding the magnitude of the structural changes taking place in the community-based delivery of health and social services for the elderly and the effects of structural changes on the elderly and their families (Estes & Wood, 1986). *Informalization* is generally referred to as the process wherein selected services of hospitals and community agencies are transferred out of the formal delivery system into the informal provision arenas of home and community. Care that was once provided by paid professional providers is transferred to unpaid lay providers, and frequently with it the physical, intellectual, emotional, and economic responsibility for that care. A well-documented result of informalization is the transfer of a large portion of the long term care provision in this country to women.

A second dimension of informalization adds complexity to the concept. This aspect, which might be more properly termed a *transfer*

NOTE: The authors of this chapter are Elizabeth A. Binney, Carroll L. Estes, and Susan E. Humphers.

155

of care, involves a shift of high-tech and highly medical care from a hospital or other institutional setting to formal paid providers in the home and community. The shift in care responsibilities from a formal, institutional provider to a formal, community-based provider is usually accompanied by the second type of informalization. For example, an elderly patient who is discharged from a hospital to the home several days earlier than would have been the case prior to the implementation of the Medicare prospective payment system (PPS) will likely have a number of care tasks transferred to the home that would previously have been provided only in an acute care setting. Care may include chemotherapy, dialysis, intravenous therapies, or enteral/parenteral nutrition therapies. In most cases, these tasks will be, at minimum, supervised by a professional provider, such as a home health nurse, albeit in an informal setting. An informal caregiver or lay provider now, however, may be asked to perform the exact same tasks several times a day, providing care that trained paraprofessionals and even some categories of professionals would not be legally permitted to provide in an institutional setting. Thus there may be gradations in the care shifts that represent informalization from a formal, medically oriented site or provider to a formal, less medically oriented site, or, alternatively, from a formal site to an informal site or provider (i.e., the home). Coupled with this complex scenario, issues of staff training, supervision, and liability make the process of informalization—and its implications for policy—even more difficult and serious.

Background

During the 1980s and early 1990s, increasing attention was paid to the transfer of care from the formal to the informal sector as an essential part of the delivery of health and social services to all age groups. Informal or family caregiving to the elderly has received particular attention from policymakers, gerontologists, and others interested in health care policy issues (Abel, 1987a, 1987b, 1989; Albert, 1991; Barer & Johnson, 1990; Bass & Noelker, 1987; Baum & Page, 1991; Brody, 1981, 1985; Caserta, Lund, Wright, & Redburn, 1987; Christianson, 1986; Collins, Stommel, King, & Given, 1991; Corbin & Strauss, 1988; Doty, 1986; Frankfather, Smith, & Caro, 1981; Harel, Noelker, & Blake, 1985; Horowitz, 1985; Lawton, Brody, & Saperstein, 1989; Lawton, Kleban, Moss, Rovine, & Glicksman, 1989; Lerner, Somers, Reid, Chiriboga, & Tierney, 1991; Matthews, 1988;

Matthews, Werkner, & Delaney, 1989; Miller & McFall, 1991; Motenko, 1989; Novak & Guest, 1989; Perlin, Mullan, Semple, & Skaff, 1990; Scharlach & Boyd, 1991; Scharlach, Sobel, & Roberts, 1991; Sommers & Shields, 1987; Stephens & Christianson, 1985; Stone, 1991; Strawbridge & Wallhagen, 1991; U.S. House of Representatives, 1988b).

Informalization has particularly important consequences for women in their roles as both community service providers and family caregivers. Thus the discussion of the effects of informalization—both from institutional to home provision and from professional to lay provision—notes the differential (and often deleterious and long-term) effects on women.

The importance of informal caregiving—the unpaid care provided by family members or friends—is intensifying with efforts to contain rising health care costs and curtail formal care services (Stone, 1991; U.S. House of Representatives, 1988b). Various crises in the economy, including the unwillingness of policymakers to finance increasing demands for services, and concern about a nearly $800 billion annual health bill have generated pressure on the health care system. Programs for the elderly have become major targets for cost containment because the largest publicly financed health expenditure ($108.9 billion in 1990) is for the Medicare program (Estes, 1988; Levit, Lazenby, Cowan, & Letsch, 1991).

In the context of policy-making, which is increasingly framed in the language of economics and driven by concern for cost containment, the issue of informal caregiving has been conceptualized in terms of generational equity and intergenerational conflict (Binney & Estes, 1988; Binstock, 1983; Hewitt, 1986; Kingson, Hirshorn, & Cornman, 1986; Minkler, 1986; Preston, 1985; Taylor, 1986). Debates about family responsibility and caregiving deflect attention from broader structural problems and redirect attention toward the privatized, familial, and informal sectors. One line of argument used by those who would limit support to formal community-care provision (often even such support as tax advantages or respite vouchers for informal caregivers) contends that the formalization of caregiving is a source of disintegration of the modern family, which needs to be preserved, if not augmented, for the survival of society. Others believe that a move toward the informalization of caregiving has been supported by the ideologies of filial and familial obligation and responsibility. This responsibility for the elderly and their physical and social needs is supported and reinforced by the media and public policy based on notions of filial blood obligation and general familial obligation for care by individuals, kinship systems, and community rather than by impersonal institutions and a welfare state.

Because the home has traditionally been considered the "women's domain" and caring a "natural" female characteristic, caregiving is assumed to be women's responsibility (Sommers & Shields, 1987). Because informal caregiving is only minimally assisted by the State, either directly by economic support or indirectly through other public policies, the call for increased family responsibility is a call for increasing women's unpaid work and consequent hardship (Binney & Estes, 1988). For example, recent figures show that more than 75% of caregiving in the United States is performed by women, and 37% of female caregivers concurrently hold other jobs. In addition to paid employment averaging 31 hours per week, female caregivers provide an average of more than 20 hours of caregiving labor (U.S. House of Representatives, 1988b). Despite fears to the contrary, national poll data indicate that Americans remain committed to the familial care of dependent elders and supportive of increased programs to assist in that care, even if higher taxes are required (R. L. Associates, 1987).

The increase in the number of women in the labor market represents a major challenge to the preference of policymakers for hospital cost containment, which effectively increases women's work in the home through the informalization of care of the elderly. The constraints of the inflexible organization of formal jobs creates contradictions, which may be contrasted with the relative flexibility of casual jobs in the informal economy. Because society has not accepted the fact that women are in the labor force in massive numbers, "the domestic sphere, the world of work, [and] the welfare state are all organized as if women were continuing a traditional role" (Sassoon, 1987, p. 160). The constraints presented by labor force participation create great conflict for the largely female informal caregivers of the elderly.

In the patriarchal family, the primary role of women is caregiving and their primary status, dependency. Because a substantial amount of women's work is rendered invisible through lack of pay and lack of benefits, social policy continues to reflect the conception of women as dependents residing in the stereotypical nuclear family, primarily filling domestic and reproductive roles and only secondarily participating in the paid labor force. The magnitude of the sacrifices entailed by women's caregiving is unrecognized because family labor tends to be viewed as free labor, if it is recognized as "labor" at all. Yet, "over 40 percent of adult offspring participating in one survey reported that the time spent on caregiving tasks was equivalent to the time required by a full-time job" (Feldblum, 1985, p. 220). For the women who are caregivers for disabled spouses, there is a drain on savings and assets acquired in the marriage, particularly for those who must "spend down" to receive necessary medical care and, eventually, public assistance. For caregivers of elderly parents, siblings, or spouses, there are also the direct financial costs often required to supplement the inadequate resources of an older family member and the "opportunity cost" to the caregiver—forsaking employment altogether, significantly altering one's work schedule, or taking early retirement to become a caregiver (Arendell & Estes, 1987; Brody, 1985).

The National Long Term Care Survey shows that a majority of women who give care experienced these and/or other serious conflicts between caregiving and employment (Stone & Kemper, 1989; U.S. House of Representatives, 1988b). Each of these opportunity losses is likely to affect health and disability insurance as well as retirement income adversely. Thus caregivers of the elderly find themselves particularly disadvantaged because of the refusal of both employers and federal policy to make accommodations (e.g., day-care centers or leave of absence benefits) to the caregiving work that must be rendered. Additional costs are the high physical health risks of caregiving (Bader, 1985; Brody, 1985) and the fact that many caregivers are themselves old or approaching old age (Stone, Cafferata, & Sangl, 1986), when their strength and health may be easily compromised.

The irony is that the transfer of responsibility from the hospital to the home and women through the PPS has not resulted in significant overall Medicare cost savings. Hospitals, in particular, reported unprecedented profits in the year following the implementation of prospective payment (U.S. GAO, 1987b). Additionally, Medicare cost sharing has increased so that the elderly absorbed more than a 155% increase in their Part A hospital deductible between 1981 and 1987 and also paid dramatically increased costs for physician services under Part B of Medicare. While these rising costs affect all elderly, they hit older women hardest because of their lower incomes, higher health service utilization rates, and higher out-of-pocket health costs than older men. Further, because women are much more likely than men to outlive their spouses, women are also more likely to reach old age in need of caregiving but without a caregiver available, increasing their likelihood of institutionalization.

Private citizens, especially women, continue to be the cornerstone of the provision of long term care through the contribution of informal caregiving. Three fourths of severely disabled elders receiving long term care in the community rely solely on family or other unpaid providers. Two thirds of people who need assistance in all activities of daily living receive no paid assistance at all, and only 3% use paid care alone, illustrating the importance of informal care to the noninstitutionalized disabled elderly (Pepper Commission, 1990a; U.S. Senate, 1991).

Despite overwhelming evidence to the contrary, the myth of family abandonment of sick and infirm elders persists and has contributed to the reticence of policymakers to address the very real economic, social, physical, and psychological needs of informal caregivers for fear that the provision of public aid will reduce family commitment to the responsibility of caregiving and contribute to spiraling health care costs (U.S. House of Representatives, 1988b).

Prospective Payment and Informal Care

The Medicare prospective payment system (PPS), implemented in 1983, sets hospital payment amounts in advance for particular conditions or diagnosis-related groups (DRGs) and pays the hospital a fixed cost before the care is given and regardless of actual cost. This policy provides a financial incentive for hospitals to provide care that costs less than the payment received. A result of this policy was a drop in hospital length of stay for the elderly and an increase in the number of early discharges of elderly patients. As discussed in Chapter 1, admissions for persons over 65 declined unexpectedly (an average of 2.2% per year) between 1984 and 1987 (ProPAC, 1988). Due to decreasing lengths of stay and fewer admissions, occupancy rates for community hospitals declined from 76% in 1981 to less than 64% during the first 8 months of 1986 (ProPAC, 1987a). Numerous studies have focused on the short-term impacts of the PPS, particularly in terms of the use and cost of hospital services (Guterman et al., 1988).

When elders are released from the hospital "sicker and quicker"— earlier and in a considerably more ill and frail condition—they encounter a community service delivery system transformed by a series of federal budget cuts and limited by increasingly stringent Medicare and Medicaid reimbursement policies (Chapter 12; Estes, 1987a). The creation of this "no-care zone" has left millions of elders dependent on the informal provision of care, overwhelmingly secured from women, when formal care is not available or cannot be purchased. The result in the first year of the PPS alone was an annual transfer of 21 million days of care previously rendered in the hospital and financed by the government to the home and community, adding to the already heavy burden of unpaid caregiving (Stark, 1987a). Providers, both informal and formal, of community-based long term care are increasingly relied upon to care for the elderly, a process both encouraged by technological advances and necessitated by cost-containment policies.

Informalization has been defined in various ways, but in general has been expressed as a shift toward "ways of working outside the statistically defined labor force" (Redclift & Mingione, 1985). Less often considered are attributes of informalization. "Far from being marginal or residual, . . . [it is] connected by myriad strands to the [formal] economy proper, recycling its products, provisioning its workers, supplying elements of its production process and reproducing its labor force" (Redclift & Mingione, 1985, p. 2). This definition has important implications for caregivers of the disabled elderly. The extensive and growing literature on caregivers and social support is addressed here because of the importance of the caregiving role in labor force issues.

Both the unpaid labor of caregivers and the paid labor of formal providers in the community setting in many ways represent all of the elements cited above. This labor is certainly connected to the formal economy in myriad ways. Both types of caregiving support an $800 billion health industry (Francis, 1991). Further, they recycle both the material and the nonmaterial products of the health industry. The production and use of material products, such as drugs and durable medical equipment, are supported by the informal and formal community-based economies; nonmaterial products are reproduced in the form of services, such as providing support to patients who have undergone treatment. Both informal and formal community-based labor allow for the production and the reproduction of the labor force to support the formal, institutional health industry by facilitating and enabling the treatment and care provided by professionals. The unpaid labor of caregivers and the paid labor of community-based providers, then, support the medical-industrial complex by allowing the community residence of disabled elders to remain viable and their consumption of both community and institutional care to continue. Ironically, the extent to which the process of informalization is occurring, coupled with the dearth of public financing for long term care, threatens the ability of many informal caregivers to provide long term care to community-resident elders.

Micro Versus Macro Perspectives

Informal caregiving can be a private phenomenon, occurring on a microsociological level, yet it influences and is influenced by macrosociological phenomena. Much of the recent literature and the majority of currently funded research related to informal caregiving are concerned with enhancing the coping capacity and ability of the family to provide care (Barer & Johnson, 1990; Cavanaugh, Dunn, Mowery, et al., 1989; Gratton & Wilson, 1988; Lawton, Brody, & Saperstein, 1989; Lawton, Kleban, et al., 1989; Matthews, 1988; Matthews et al., 1989; Moritz, Kasl, & Berkman, 1989; Motenko, 1989; Novak & Guest, 1989; Parsons, Cox, & Kimboko, 1989; Quayhagen & Quayhagen, 1989; Rubenstein, 1989; Spitze & Logan, 1989). Relatively few studies acknowledge or examine the economic, political, and social forces that shape informal caregiving and render it a social problem. Instead, most research on caregiving employs the assumption that informal care of the elderly is a familial responsibility. The construction of informal caregiving as a problem often defines the deficiency as the coping capacity of caregivers rather than as the societal forces that render caregiving an increasingly significant social problem.

The conceptualization of the issues of informal caregiving as "the personal troubles of the milieu" rather than the "public issues of social structure" (Mills, 1959, p. 8) supports the status quo. First, the problem devolves to the individual rather than to the broader society. This shift has the advantage of allowing individual circumstances rather than cross-societal interests to take precedence in discussions of "solutions." Second, structural and ideological causes of the process of informalization are much easier to ignore, as are the more complex and complicated policy changes required to ameliorate them. In reality, the creation of a dichotomy between micro and macro perspectives on informal care and informalization is in itself a political act. The conception that these issues are either mere private troubles or amorphous problems of the economy deflects attention from meaningful policy interventions. Rather, both perspectives of the process of informalization and the experience of informal caregivers must be integrated into the analysis to grasp the profound impact of informalization on U.S. society.

Studies that fail to place the problem of informal caregiving of the elderly in its social and historical context, without surprise, often locate the problem of caregiving as a deficiency in the coping capacity of the caregiver. For example, Lawton, Brody, & Saperstein (1989) and Lawton, Kleban, et al. (1989) measure caregivers' subjective appraisal of the caregiving process. They typify caregiver burden as an externally manifested demand or threat but conceptualize the problem of caregiving as a subjective, or internally manifested, phenomenon. Caregiving is seen as stressful only if coping capabilities are insufficient to adapt to the demands of caregiving. Similarly, Rubenstein (1989) examines caregiving from the perspective of the narratives of individuals and the meanings they attribute to caregiving. Again, both the problem and the solution are perceived as resting with individual caregivers rather than as connected to broader societal conditions. In addition, recent research compares the burden of caring for elderly Alzheimer's disease patients in the home and in institutions and reports that social support had little effect on the experience of burden for caregivers (AARP, 1989).

Another indicator of the tendency to view caregiving as a micro-level phenomenon is evident in a review of federally funded research grants (National Institute on Aging, 1988). Studies that deal with informal caregivers tend to be concerned primarily with the microsociological and psychological aspects of informal caregiving. For example, studies of the effects of psychoeducational interventions on the well-being of caregivers and care recipients predict that caregiver coping capacity will increase with skill training classes and information/support classes. Other research examines the burdens to the adult children of parents with Alzheimer's disease, factors that mediate the stressful effects of caregiving, and ways in which adult children and their parents cope with these problems. Researchers look for indicators of whether family members assume, continue, or reject their roles as primary caregivers for elderly relatives. Caregivers and care recipients are queried regarding their morale, attitudes of affection and obligation, and expectations for assistance, but less attention is given to extra-individual factors that might affect the level of acceptance of the caregiver role.

Research on health service utilization (Caserta et al., 1987; Collins et al., 1991; Zev, Noelker, & Blake, 1985) considers formal, community-based services and their use by familial caregivers. The research by Caserta and associates (1987) documents a shift in the responsibility for care to informal provision in the home setting. They report a significant need for respite services among 597 caregivers to noninstitutionalized elderly patients. The increased burden of care experienced by formal community-based providers following the implementation of the PPS is not, however, considered.

Parsons and associates (1989) examine informal caregiving from the perspective of elderly recipients of care to determine what factors influence their satisfaction with the care they receive. They, like Motenko (1989), argue that the quality of the relationship between caregiver and elderly recipient of care, rather than the functional level of the care recipient, is a primary determinant of family ability to cope with the stress of caregiving. The researchers offer suggestions for enhancing satisfaction with caregiving, such as the need for families to develop meaningful late-life roles for elders and for families and elders to engage in problem solving on a mutual basis. Novak and Guest (1989) also suggest interventions for reducing caregiver burden, such as increasing knowledge of the care recipient's condition, increasing social support, and providing day hospital and respite programs.

Several studies argue for the enhancement of services for familial caregivers. For example, Lawton, Brody, and Saperstein (1989) argue that respite care should be made more readily available as a preventive service for caregivers. Moritz and associates (1989) examine the social and psychological consequences of elderly individuals living with cognitively impaired spouses. Although studies such as these make an important connection between the health policy goal of increasing the caring capacity of informal caregivers and the need to understand the social and psychological impact of informal caregiving, the increased demand for services provided by the formal community-based sector is often neglected.

Dual Processes of Informalization

The two processes of informalization identified above are related. The transfer of care from formal to informal providers tends to accompany the transfer from formal to informal sites of care provision. Both types of informalization are marked by a shift away from institutional services and toward the purchase of goods to assist in the informal provision of services. For example, informalization is reflected in the purchase of durable medical goods so that the individual or informal caregiver can provide care him- or herself instead of using a formal service such as that of a home health nurse. Medicare patients receiving fewer days of hospital care need to buy medical equipment and minimal skills or training from a provider. This self-servicing enables Medicare and other resources to be redirected away from payment for the provision of labor. Although the rationale is that costs are reduced, actually both costs and work are being transferred elsewhere.

The modes of provision of acute care and, increasingly, long term care are profoundly influenced (i.e., driven) by technological advances. Technical innovations have been aggressively developed in health care institutions, and a number of policy, managerial, economic, and organizational strategies have resulted. For example, technological progress has affected the division of labor in health care as evidenced by the increased specialization of the professions. Certain kinds of work have been relinquished by professionals in favor of more technological imperatives, a process that ultimately fosters informalization. Without the lessening of professional control over tasks such as injections, catheterization, and tube feeding, informalization at the noninstitutional and nonprofessional levels could not have taken place.

This trend is a form of *de-skilling*, a term that usually refers to the attempt to rationalize and control labor by breaking down tasks into simpler steps carried out by workers with lower skills. It is important to differentiate between at least two levels of de-skilling. On the first level, heavier and more highly technical care moves from the hospital to the home, rendering formal home health providers responsible for care that was once provided only in a hospital setting, often exclusively by physicians. This level of de-skilling increases pressure on agencies to provide personnel capable of delivering highly technical care while also responding to cost-containment and reimbursement-driven pressures. One response to such pressure is to attempt to institute "skill-mix" strategies that substitute lower-skilled, lower-paid employees to perform jobs currently done by higher-skilled, better-paid workers. Another strategy is new hiring to increase the proportion of lower-paid employees, who are also lower-skilled.

Szasz (1990) reports that individual home health agencies were only moderately successful in instituting skill-mix strategies but that the overall effect of skill-mix strategies on the home health market has been significant, especially among non-Medicare-certified agencies. Coupled with pressures originating from the shortage of nurses, these adaptation strategies have resulted in attempts to increase the productivity of all workers, particularly registered nurses involved in the delivery of reimbursable services and not working on a contract basis. The second level of de-skilling results from the transfer of tasks previously performed in the hospital by supervised trained professionals to lay people (e.g., family) in the home, who perform them with a minimum of training and supervision. In addition, the informal sector's lack of legitimating credentials prevents their capitalizing on these often complex and technical skills.

Informalization of both kinds is particularly disadvantageous to women. Women make up the majority of the lower-skilled and lower-paid workers hired in the informal sector on a part-time basis without benefits such as health insurance and Social Security coverage. Informalized care also usurps women's time. When women are not reimbursed for their caregiving work, their labor time is essentially being donated, often at the expense of paid employment. As a result, many women lose the opportunity to secure, through paid employment, health care and retirement benefits for their own old age.

One of the important indicators of the process of informalization involves the type and direction of care shifted. If there are differences in such patterns, they represent important indicators of the differential effects of these processes. Two emerging trends support the concept that informalization is occurring on multiple levels and in multiple sites (IHA, 1986, 1987). The majority of all provider types in the IHA study reported observing a shift in responsibility for the care of the elderly after 1984, and the most immediate postacute providers (home health, discharge planning, and hospice) were most likely to observe a shift in responsibility for the care of the elderly to the informal sector. Nursing homes, probably due to their institutional nature, were less likely than other providers to note such a shift, yet a clear majority of nursing homes reported the same trend. The majority of respondents in all provider types (except adult day care and senior centers) reported a shift in direction away from formal service provision and toward the informal provision of care. It is important to note, however, that, in addition, a substantial number of respondents also described a shift toward the formal provision of care in the community. Well over a third of nursing homes, discharge planning, adult day centers, and home health agencies described a shift toward the formal provision of high-tech and skilled care in the community. This shift in care cited by a majority of respondents of all provider types was linked to adverse effects of caregiving on families.

Due to its complexity, the process of informalization could have a number of causes and sources but of particular interest is the degree to which agencies that reported a shift attribute that shift to the Medicare hospital prospective payment system. The overwhelming majority of agencies in the IHA study that observed a shift in types of care attributed the change either moderately or solely to the PPS. Very few agencies reported shifts in care not attributed to the PPS (Table 9.1).

Provider Effects

The availability of adult children, particularly daughters, to provide care is the significant factor in keeping frail and disabled elders out of residential care (Feldblum, 1985; Vladeck, 1980). Indeed, researchers have repeatedly found that the major factor in keeping the

TABLE 9.1   Care Shifting by Agency Type, 1987

Agency Type	Types of Care Shifted[a]	Not at All (percentage)	Moderately (percentage)	Solely (percentage)
		Attribution to DRGs		
Home health	Informal (158)	2.5	74.0	23.4
	Formal (36)	19.4	69.4	11.1
Nursing homes	Informal (85)	20.0	55.3	24.7
	Formal (58)	10.3	75.9	13.8
Discharge planners	Informal (141)	9.2	71.6	19.2
	Formal (81)	17.3	70.4	12.4
Adult day centers	Informal (19)	10.5	63.2	26.3
	Formal (21)	19.0	71.4	9.5
Hospices	Informal (34)	3.0	64.7	32.4
	Formal (6)	33.3	66.7	0.0
Senior centers	Informal (33)	6.1	72.7	21.2
	Formal (34)	38.2	61.8	0.0
Community mental health centers	Informal (34)	20.6	73.5	5.9
	Formal (37)	35.1	59.5	5.4

SOURCE: Data from Institute for Health & Aging DRG study, provider instrument (1987).
NOTE: Question on instrument: "Since 1984, have you observed any shift in responsibility for care of the elderly? That is, a shift between care provided by formal service providers and care provided by family and friends?" (*Formal* means paid providers.)
a. Up to two responses recorded.

elderly in the community is not the degree of functional impairment but the level of access to family care and social support (Feldblum, 1985). More than 1.6 million elders, three fourths of whom are women, reside in institutions. Marital status, as previously mentioned, is a major determinant of the likelihood that one will be institutionalized. The majority of older men have living spouses and usually receive informal care from their wives. In contrast, older women must depend on care from offspring, relatives, and friends (Manton & Soldo, 1985). The importance of family support in preventing institutionalization is reflected in the fact that single, divorced, or separated persons living alone have a tenfold greater possibility of being institutionalized than do married persons (Butler & Newacheck, 1981).

These findings provide important evidence for the "ripple effects" that major policy changes in one sector of the system (in this case, hospitals) have on other providers, even those not engaged in the direct provision of acute medical care. The majority of respondents from all agency types studied report taking at least one step to adapt to the shifts in caregiving responsibility, and many report several such steps (Table 9.2). Patient education programs are the most commonly

TABLE 9.2 Percentage of Agencies Responding to Caregiving Shifts, 1987

Agency Type	Patient Education (Percentage)	Family Member Training (Percentage)	Family Support Group (Percentage)	Other (Percentage)
Home health	93.5	92.8	40.6	39.9
(N = 139)				
Nursing homes	68.0	70.5	68.0	31.4
(N = 105)				
Discharge planners	87.4	85.3	54.9	38.4
(N = 143)				
Adult day centers	88.9	66.7	59.3	40.7
(N = 27)				
Hospices	100.0	100.0	51.9	40.7
(N = 27)				
Senior centers	61.8	26.7	47.4	40.5
(N = 76)				
CMHCs	70.4	68.5	63.0	46.3
(N = 54)				

SOURCE: Data from Institute for Health & Aging DRG study, provider instrument (1987).
NOTE: Question on instrument: "Is your agency doing any of the following in response to this shift in caregiving responsibility?"

mentioned activity, particularly by home health, discharge planning, adult day-care, and senior center providers. Training programs for family members are also a common response of all agency types except senior centers, and the organization of family support groups is a strategy reported by about half of all agencies. In addition, approximately one third of the agencies reporting a response cited other programs or services they had instituted. These include transitional care programs, increased social support and social service programs, respite care services, education programs for communities and staff, and information and referral services. As long as the problems of rising health care costs and long term care remain unsolved, the problems of informalization and informal caregiving can only grow. A recent poll (R. L. Associates, 1987) demonstrates the pervasiveness of the caregiving problem: The majority of registered voters (more than 60%) in a nationally representative sample personally experienced the need for long term care by elderly family or friends and another 20% expected to experience such a need in the next 5 years.

There are certainly some positive aspects to the informal provision of care: keeping individuals as independent as possible in their homes and communities, having care provided by familiar and devoted providers, and avoiding unnecessary institutionalization. Unfortunately, there are also a number of potentially negative risks to an uncontrolled informalization of care for the elderly. Risks include, but are not limited to, the financial, emotional, and physical burdens placed especially on female caregivers, their lost opportunity to pursue paid work, the lack of standards of quality of care in the informal sector, and the dearth of financial support by the state for informal caregiving. The de-skilling practiced by formal providers in an attempt to garner low-paid workers presents obvious compromises to the quality of care delivered. Further, community-based organizations may increasingly find the need to provide training in the use of medical technologies not only to their own employees but to informal caregivers as well. Currently, however, there are no regulations governing training of informal caregivers, much less regulations specifying the quality and duration of informal caregiver training.

Conclusion

Findings from research provide evidence of the intensification of the informalization process on two dimensions since the implementation of the PPS. The majority of respondents in each of the seven provider types observed a shift in the responsibility for care of the elderly. The dual dimensions on which this shift is occurring are also reflected by IHA data. Care for the elderly is being shifted both to paid (formal) and to unpaid (informal) community providers as efforts are being made on the federal policy level to curtail costs in the acute care (hospital) setting. The trickle-down effect of cost-containment policies is evidenced by the greater likelihood of the most immediate postacute care providers to report a shift in responsibility for the provision of skilled care. Agencies providing more custodial, social, and long term care services were more likely to report a shift in responsibility for the provision of these types of services. Thus overwhelming evidence is provided for the far-reaching structural and service effects, in particular the informalization of many types of care, that have occurred as a result of federal cost-containment policies, especially prospective payment to hospitals.

Additional research is needed to determine the appropriateness of the identified shifts in responsibility for the care of the elderly.

Studies must address the effects of these shifts on both formal providers and informal caregivers as well as on elderly recipients of care. Policy solutions must be developed both to move toward the achievement of cost-containment goals and to support the positive effects of caring for family and friends without jeopardizing either the quality of care or the caregivers. An unchecked informalization of both highly skilled and long-term social supportive care for the elderly will adversely affect caregivers, many of whom already find themselves undersupported and overwhelmed by the magnitude of demand. Without a thoughtful public policy, the process of informalization not only will fail to save real costs but also promises to have serious unintended effects. Only through recognition of the increasing demand that cost-containment policies place on both formal and informal caregivers in the community can humane policy solutions to the problem of informal caregiving be found. The next chapter considers implications for formal community-based providers of care.

CHAPTER 10

Access in Peril

Allowing these health and long-term care problems to persist not only deprives millions of Americans of what they ought to be able to have . . . it diminishes our economy . . . [and] the United States of America. I don't think it's possible to say . . . that we are a civilized nation when so many of our people . . . do not have long-term care, do not have health insurance.

John D. Rockefeller (in the Pepper Commission, 1990b, p. 1)

▼

Community-based delivery systems have been changing apace with major shifts in the health care industry, especially in relation to governmental policy changes. In particular, the incentives for acute care services were reversed under the Medicare prospective payment system (PPS), so that it is now in a hospital's best interest, in terms of diagnosis-related group (DRG) payment, to move patients out of the facility as quickly as medically possible. Consequently, nearly a decade after implementation of the PPS, a large portion of the provision of care has shifted from the hospital to the community-based delivery system (DesHarnais et al., 1987; Easton, Cogen, & Fulcomer, 1991; Goldberg & Estes, 1990; Guterman et al., 1988; Harlow & Wilson, 1985; McCreary, 1986; U.S. GAO, 1986; U.S. Senate, 1985; Van Gelder & Bernstein, 1986; Wood et al., 1986). As a result, access is in peril.

Community-based care is sometimes expected to act as a substitute for institutional, particularly nursing home, care (Braun, Rose, &

NOTE: The authors of this chapter are Sheryl C. Goldberg, Carol C. McKetty, James H. Swan, Juanita B. Wood, Stanley R. Ingman, Augusta M. Villanueva, and Patrick J. Fox.

Finch, 1991). Better access to community-based care should enhance care options for individuals who would otherwise seek institutional care. It may also contribute to improving access for individuals who continue to seek institutional care. Improved access has not been shown to be the case, however, because (a) in general, community-based care does not sufficiently reduce the risk of nursing home use to make an overall difference in nursing home utilization; (b) there has been inadequate targeting of community-based care to those in risk of nursing home care; and (c) many modes of community-based care have not been shown to be effective, beneficial, or even harmless (Braun et al., 1991; Wan & Ferraro, 1991; Weissert et al., 1988). Further, many forms of community-based care have not been shown to be cost effective as measured by their ability to reduce overall demand for institutional care (Weissert et al., 1988), although they could potentially do so (Weissert, 1988). Perhaps more importantly, however, it has been demonstrated that community-based care can reduce hospitalization (Weissert et al., 1988). This research suggests a role for community care in serving recipients of early hospital discharge.

Another important mission of organizations that constitute the community-based delivery system is to maximize the independence and dignity of older persons living at home by providing supportive health and social services, to prevent premature or inappropriate institutionalization (Wallace, 1990a), and to provide respite for informal caregivers (Weissert et al., 1989). In many communities, such services are unavailable, substandard, or strained (U.S. Senate, 1985). Because the adequacy of these organizations to respond to the new care demands for the elderly in this PPS era remains questionable (Wood & Estes, 1990), concerns about access to needed services are raised.

Chapter 4 reveals that increased numbers of older clients who are more acutely ill are seeking posthospital care (Goldberg & Estes, 1990) and that the majority of providers link the increase in client demand and declining health status to the PPS reimbursement system. Using the same data base, Goldberg and Estes (1988) and Estes and Swan (1989) explored community variations in reported access measures (e.g., refusing services, initiating waiting lists), demonstrating that the PPS interacts with state and local factors (including demographics, resource supply, policies, and funding practices) to influence access to care at the community level.

Organizational Access Issues

The organizational providers studied in the IHA research report access limitations affecting the elderly. The study model, in fact, examines the domino effects occurring from one posthospital service mode to another, as the effects of the Medicare hospital PPS and other changes in health care systems ripple from hospitals to nursing homes and home health agencies and on to other services in the community-based delivery system, namely, hospices, adult day-care centers, senior centers, and community mental health centers.

Hospices

Hospice has recently become an acceptable referral for the posthospital care of elderly patients. Reporting on hospice data from the IHA study, Wong and associates (1988) conclude that, in an era of cost containment, hospice has evolved from an alternative form of care to an integral component of the long term care system. Congress enacted legislation that included hospice as a Medicare-reimbursable benefit effective November 1983. Medicare-certified hospices increased by 367% between 1983 and 1986 (Guterman et al., 1988).

Hospices in the IHA study report that, in 1986, more than half (59%) of their budgets derived from Medicare. This percentage dropped in 1987 (to 48%). In both years of the study, Medicaid and out-of-pocket payments constituted about one fourth of the funding for these agencies. Wong and associates (1988) write that many hospice services are not reimbursable (e.g., bereavement counseling), which "exacerbates what hospice administrators already believe to be inadequate reimbursement levels" (Wong et al., 1988, p. 159).

Based on interviews with 24 hospice administrators, Wong and associates (1988) found that the number of clients served by the majority of these organizations increased between 1984 and 1987. The "quicker and sicker" discharges of hospitalized elderly patients under the Medicare PPS served to increase the demand for hospice care. Hospice administrators believed overwhelmingly that the PPS had important indirect effects on their programs. More than 80% reported that the PPS changed the types of clients served. Under the Medicare PPS, patients referred to hospice were more frail and acutely ill and had greater formal and informal care needs. The IHA researchers found that hospices have been using more medical-technical interventions and have shifted their services to provide higher levels of care. The most frequently reported shifts in service are toward more acute high-tech care, more skilled nursing care, and more antibiotic intravenous therapy. Wong and associates (1988) raise questions about these service changes, observing that, "with the increased disability levels of the patients being referred and the increasing medicalization of services to meet the patients' needs, hospices may be pushed toward the medical model of care they once sought to replace" (Wong et al., 1988, p. 163).

The IHA research uncovered community variations in access to hospice care. Several illustrations follow. In 1986, the percentage of hospices that reported tightening eligibility by restricting access to certain clients ranged from zero in the Miami SMSA to three fourths of the hospices in the Philadelphia area. Variations existed within states as well. In 1987, hospice directors in the Dallas/Ft. Worth area reported increasing fees or copayments for services whereas there were no such reports in the Houston SMSA. The majority of hospice administrators in all of the communities studied reported service refusals for clients with physical and mental health problems and/or needs beyond the scope of the agency. The reasons clients could not be served related to client condition, reimbursement/funding and cost issues, and eligibility limitations.

Adult Day-Care Centers

Adult day care has grown rapidly in the past two decades (Luken & Vaughan, 1990; Mehta & Mack, 1987; Von Behren, 1986) as an important alternative to institutional care (Spiegel, 1987). It differs from other forms of care in being neither institutional nor in-home care (Weissert et al., 1989). Wood and Ingman (1988) explain that as the demand for posthospital care has increased, so too have the numbers of adult day-care centers (ADCCs) and their importance in the continuum of long term care. Some researchers debate the sagacity of using these programs, citing the increased cost of ADCC service over customary care even though medical efficacy outcomes were equal for both (Hedrick, 1991). Nonetheless, the number of ADCCs increased from 300 in 1978 to more than 2,000 in 1989 (Von Behren, 1989).

Adult day-care centers are not a primary posthospital referral but have experienced the secondary wave of effects of the earlier and sicker discharges of elderly patients from hospitals into the community-based delivery system (Estes, Wood, et al., 1988). Since implementation of the PPS, adult day-care centers have increasingly become "the recipients of the clientele to whom nursing homes deny entry and whom home health agencies release before their needs are satisfied" (Wood & Ingman, 1988, p. 154). ADCCs are the next agency in the continuum of services for the many people who require fairly constant care when their Medicare home health care coverage expires. The likelihood that an ADCC will receive such posthospital clients depends, however, on the model the ADCC follows. While research to identify and classify distinct forms of ADCCs continues (Conrad, Hughes, Hanrahan, & Wang, 1991), two commonly accepted subgroupings of ADCCs are the medical- or health-oriented model and the social service-oriented model (Weissert, 1976, 1977). More recently, Weissert and associates (1989) have developed a different schema to subdivide ADCCs into three types: (a) high-staffed health and social service ADCCs providing care to an older, physically dependent clientele, with little public reimbursement; (b) publicly funded ADCCs that largely provide social services and health assessment to younger-old clients who often suffer mental disorders but are seldom physically dependent; and (c) special-purpose ADCCs that differ widely in center purposes and clientele but serve clientele who are fairly homogenous within each center. The second type of ADCC tended to increase its health focus in the 1980s (Weissert et al., 1989), and the varied types of ADCCs came to fit the service profile demanded by various types of older clients discharged from the hospital.

Data from the IHA survey (1986, 1987) and others show that most adult day-care funding comes from Medicaid and from client fees (Von Behren, 1986; Zelman et al., 1991), both of which are increasing as a funding source, introducing the issue of cost as an access limit. ADCCs are not large entities, most having budgets less than a half million dollars in 1987 (Wood, 1989). Although Medicaid covers care for poor elderly who are eligible, meeting Medicaid certification requirements regarding staffing and service levels is costly for ADCCs, meaning higher overhead costs for all clients, including those paying out of pocket. Medicaid payment levels may also be inadequate to cover the cost of client care provided by ADCCs, highlighting the need for alternative sources such as Medicare (Wood, 1989).

Many private-pay clients were delaying use of adult day care until they were more debilitated because they could not afford to pay the costs on a long-term basis (IHA, 1986, 1987). Some state Medicaid requirements also restrict services to those who are severely debilitated. Such factors increase the needs of the average ADCC client.

These mechanisms drive up per client costs of providing adult day care, exacerbating access problems. Many of the 39 adult day-care center directors in the study reported that, as a result of the PPS, there have been increases in the number of clients and those in more disabled conditions. Higher care needs also create other access problems. For example, many high-need clients require longer hours of care.

In both 1986 and 1987, the most frequently requested service that ADCCs reportedly could not provide was extended hours, including hours for respite care. The combination of lengthening care demands and a lack of financial assistance to help with the cost of extended care results in the unavailability of these services for the length of time they are needed by many individuals and their families. Furthermore, the ADCC population is expected to grow as a result of state changes relative to level of care criteria in nursing homes, which eliminate many intermediate care beds and necessitate the early release of clients from both hospitals and home health agencies (Wood & Ingman, 1988). Concern about the increasing need for this type of care and the current access restrictions has led ADCCs to seek Medicare coverage for services rendered. Moreover, increased demand derives from persons not eligible for Medicaid (Wood, 1989). If Medicare begins to fund this service, subsequent growth will be evidenced (Wood, 1989).

Similar to hospices, adult day-care centers reported slanting their services toward medical care needs (Weissert et al., 1989). This was true for both the medical and the social model agencies included in the study. In 1986, the majority of center directors reported an increase in health monitoring services. The movement toward additional medical services in adult day care is related both to the changing characteristics of the clientele, with growing client needs overwhelming even increased center capabilities, and to strict funding and reimbursement criteria (Wood, 1989). The increasing emphasis on medical services carries higher costs. Thus adult day care may show not only the indirect effects of quicker hospital discharges under the PPS but also the domino effects through other posthospital services, creating a variety of types of demand on access to care, most of them requiring greater emphasis on medical services.

Community variations were evidenced for ADCCs as well. In 1986, reports of tightening eligibility in adult day-care centers ranged from zero in the Houston and Philadelphia SMSAs to three fourths of centers in the San Diego area. Access restrictions in the form of increased fees and copayments varied by community. In 1986, more than three fourths of Seattle ADCCs reported increasing fees and copayments while not one center in either the Houston or the Pittsburgh SMSA reported taking this action.

In 1987, none of the centers in the Houston area reported having a waiting list for adult day-care services; this was in marked contrast to reports that all of the centers in the Tampa/St. Petersburg SMSA had waiting lists. The fact that Medicaid funding has become more available for adult day care in Florida may help explain why there is a waiting list for the service there. In addition, Older Americans Act funds were cut for adult day-care centers in Florida, which forced centers to reach out to more rehabilitation clients covered under Medicaid. All of the adult day-care centers in the Miami, Tampa/St.Petersburg, and San Diego SMSAs reported refusing services to certain clients in 1986; not one center in the Philadelphia area indicated doing the same. In all of the sites studied, clients most often denied entry into adult day-care centers were those with certain physical and mental health problems (e.g., totally incontinent).

Senior Centers

Because senior centers play a valuable role in community service networks for the elderly (Krout, 1991; Ralston, 1991b), they, like other services, have been affected by PPS shifts (Goldberg, 1988). The senior center is another form of community-based service that has grown rapidly and assumed greater importance to acutely and chronically ill persons living in the community, in the process increasingly adopting medically related services (NCOA, 1984; Ralston, 1991a; Wood, 1985). By 1990, there were approximately 10,000 to 12,000 senior centers in this country serving 5 to 8 million aged participants (Krout et al., 1990).

Most of the 104 senior center directors interviewed in the IHA study reported PPS-related effects similar to those of other community-based service providers (IHA, 1986, 1987). Clients were generally sicker and more frail and consequently in need of more care. Almost three fourths of the centers reported that the number of elderly participants (including those over the age of 75) increased between 1984 and 1986. In both years of the survey, about half of the directors stated that participants attending the centers required more staff supervision than before.

Access was a concern of senior centers. In the 1986 and 1987 surveys, senior center respondents were asked a series of questions about access issues and restrictions. In 1986, increased revenues were of concern: 63% of the centers reported they had increased their suggested contributions (mandatory copayments are not allowed for those receiving Older Americans Act funds), while 21% reported tightening eligibility. Only 25% reported refusals of access to potential participants.

The focus changed by 1987, however, when 48% reported service refusals. Reports of service denials for potential participants doubled (from one fourth to one half of the centers) between the years of data collection. Senior center directors indicated refusing access to elderly persons with physical health care needs beyond the scope of their services, such as those with Alzheimer's disease, physical disabilities, or urinary incontinence. The majority of directors attributed service refusals to staff shortages and inadequate staff training. In 1987, only 36% of centers reported increases in suggested contributions (only 12% reported tightening eligibility). Thus, in the 1-year period, the focus shifted from efforts to increase revenues toward actual denial of access. In fact, centers that suggested increased contributions in 1986 were significantly more likely than other centers to move toward refusing services by 1987. Although higher contributions and access refusal were not associated in 1986, higher contributions and service refusal were associated in 1987, signaling that a subset of centers with revenue problems were likely to be forced to begin refusing services.

To survive under competitive market conditions, senior centers have initiated structural changes that include an emphasis on medically oriented services (Wood, 1985). Research (Krout, 1989; NCOA, 1984; Wood, 1985) highlights the fact that health-related services provided by senior centers are on the rise. A 1983 survey of 728 centers conducted by the National Institute of Senior Centers (NCOA, 1984) reported that an array of health services were being provided by most centers. The majority of the centers screened participants for high blood pressure and diabetes, conducted individual health counseling, and provided transportation to medical appointments. Almost all of the centers in the IHA study reported increasing health monitoring and mental health services. This medicalization of senior center programs has been further encouraged by the implementation of the Medicare PPS.

Measures taken to restrict access to senior centers varied by community as well. The percentage of centers reporting an increase in the suggested client contribution in 1986 ranged from about 40% in the Pittsburgh area to twice that amount in the Dallas/Ft. Worth SMSA. This donation was most often for congregate meals served on the premises of the center. These meal programs are of great importance to the elderly (Goldberg, 1988). Variations also existed within states. In 1986, client refusals were reported by only about 10% of the directors in the Dallas/Ft. Worth area while close to two thirds of centers in the Houston SMSA reported refusals.

Community Mental Health Centers

Roughly 15% to 25% of the U.S. elderly population suffers from significant mental health problems (U.S. House of Representatives, 1989), but the effect of the Medicare hospital PPS on outpatient mental health providers is not often discussed. Community mental health centers (CMHCs) are not usually perceived as providing posthospital care. Moreover, the aged population to which the PPS is usually applied is not the primary user of community mental health services (Flemming et al., 1986). Despite perceptions to the contrary, clients discharged from the hospital constitute a portion of the CMHC caseload, and the great need elders have for community mental health services is belied by their low rates of use (Fox, Swan, & Estes, 1986). Furthermore, the PPS may augment demand for posthospital mental health services.

The PPS may affect community mental health centers in a variety of ways. The PPS incentive for early discharge of patients from hospitals may mean that psychiatric patients are released while they are more acutely ill. Patients with coexisting physical and mental illnesses also may be released while they are still quite physically ill, complicating treatment for their mental disorders. Moreover, early hospital discharge, itself, may result in the development of mental disorders or need for counseling and support for elders or their caregivers. These scenarios alter not only the level of patient demand for CMHC services but the profiles of persons needing care and the nature of service needs as well.

Almost half of the CMHCs in the IHA survey reported feeling the repercussions of the hospital prospective payment system. The centers reported having to cope with more acutely ill, physically ill, and terminally ill persons. One third of the CMHCs reported making shifts in the services they offer as a result of the PPS. At the same time that centers were seeing more acutely ill patients, many (40%) were finding it more difficult to refer clients to hospitals.

The rate of elderly use of community mental health centers does not accurately reflect their need for mental health services (Swan, Fox, & Estes, 1986). CMHCs generally underserve the elderly (Flemming et al., 1986). The prevalence of many psychiatric disorders is lower in the aged than in the younger population (Bliwise et al., 1987), but conditions such as organic brain syndrome, depression, and paranoia are more common in old age (Harper, 1992). The rate of use of community mental health services by the elderly relative to that of the younger population is not explained by the difference in prevalence rates but is in large part attributable to access problems (Swan & McCall, 1987). As Harper (1992) notes, community-based mental health services for the elderly are inadequate, fragmented, and unaffordable (Ray et al., 1987). Medicare funding, for example, excludes all freestanding CMHC services (Flemming, Buchanon, Santos, & Rickards, 1984).

Evidence from the IHA study indicates that community mental health centers are not easily accessible. More than half of the directors interviewed reported that persons seeking service had been turned away due to drug- or alcohol-related problems or to reimbursement and cost issues. The existing reimbursement systems were seen by CMHC directors as inadequate and as providing disincentives for CMHCs to provide services to elderly persons. The budgetary climate for the mental health centers has become more restrictive; only a small number of centers in the IHA study reported recent budget increases. More than 60% of responding CMHCs reported raising their eligibility requirements between 1984 and 1987, and more than two thirds reported establishing waiting lists during the same period.

Swan and associates (1989) found service budgets of CMHCs to be positively affected when the number of aged clients either increased or decreased, with a stronger positive change in the case of the latter. Thus CMHCs have an incentive to specialize in one population or the other. In light of the already low representation of the elderly in CMHC populations, decisions to specialize would likely be heavily weighted on the side of the younger population, further exacerbating the difficulties in access already faced by elders.

The Mental Health Systems Act of 1980, which had the goal of helping assure that persons in need of mental health care gained access to that care, was repealed in 1981, and funding for community mental health services was combined with that for drug and alcohol abuse treatment (U.S. House of Representatives, 1991). The block grant was initially distributed equally between the two sets of services—drug and alcohol abuse treatment and community mental health care—but, by 1991, only 20% of the funding was designated for mental health services (U.S. House of Representatives, 1991). Original funding for CMHCs was distributed as seed money that was withdrawn over time. Such a funding strategy required the centers to find other funding sources and has made serving all population groups increasingly difficult. The predominant source of funds for community mental health care is now state revenues.

One result of the shifting of responsibility for mental health services from federal seed grants to state and local funding is a wide variation in the scope and type of care offered across geographic areas (Fox & Swan, 1988). In 1986, the percentage of CMHC directors reporting tightening eligibility ranged from one sixth of centers in the Tampa/St. Petersburg SMSA to two thirds in the Seattle area. More centers in Seattle than anywhere else reported having increased fees and copayments and having refused access to potential clients. All communities in the survey reported establishing waiting lists for clients, but centers in the Tampa/St. Petersburg area were the most likely to do so.

Trends and Issues

The following general trends and issues emerge from the research findings. Since the implementation of the Medicare PPS in 1984, community-based service organizations have overwhelmingly experienced an increase in the number of elderly clients needing higher levels of care. Study data suggest that various organizations that constitute the community-based delivery system, such as hospices, adult day-care centers, senior centers, and community mental health centers, have been saturated with physically sicker clients needing heavier care. The growing number of elderly clients who are more acutely ill has placed increasing pressure on the system.

The predominant strategy used by organizations to confront this increased demand for care is the initiation or expansion of measures to restrict access by tightening eligibility, increasing fees and copayments, initiating waiting lists, and ultimately refusing service. In this era of fiscal constraint, the access-restricting measures being taken by many organizations in the community-based delivery system have created unmet needs for the elderly. Care gaps and no-care zones have developed in communities because of the inability to meet the demands of sicker patients after hospital discharge (Sankar et al., 1986). In addition, Medicare coverage for services outside of the hospital remains extremely limited. An increased need for these services has been shown to raise the already high out-of-pocket expenses of health care for the elderly, exacerbating the problems of access for older persons with low incomes (Wood & Estes, 1990).

New concerns arise from Medicare policy changes such as the recent implementation of physician reimbursement under Medicare using the resource-based relative value scale (RBRVS). The RBRVS payment is based on estimates of the time and intensity of physician work (Ginsburg, LeRoy, & Hammons, 1990). One effect is a shift of resources among specialties, particularly away from surgery (Ginsburg et al., 1990). Such changes will not necessarily hurt the aged; geriatrics should gain under the RBRVS (Hammons & Pawlson, 1989). Beneficial provisions include strong incentives to accept Medicare assignment, which should reduce some charges to patients (Lee, LeRoy, Ginsburg, & Hammons, 1990; Mitchell & Menke, 1990). Nevertheless, insofar as Medicare payment is reduced for some types of physicians, Medicare user access to such physicians is likely to suffer. Further, early initiatives have included levels of funding that might severely cut Medicare physician payment in general, offsetting even positive shifts toward certain specialties. Thus, to a greater or lesser degree, Medicare health care users, whose hospital care has already been squeezed by Medicare PPS limits, may experience a squeeze as well on ambulatory care. The shocks to the community-based care system for the elderly continue. Hospitals moved toward joint ventures with physicians, in anticipation of RBRVS (Anderson, 1991). The implications for posthospital community-based care of the types considered here will be profound.

Another trend expressed by community organization directors is a shift toward the medicalization of services. Service packages are changing, not only to meet the increasingly medical needs of clients but, more importantly, for reasons related to funding and reimbursement. Medicare policy has fostered an increasing medicalization of services over the years, and DRGs have exacerbated the trend (Binney et al., 1990; Estes, 1979; Estes & Binney, 1989; Wood & Estes, 1988). Wood and Estes (1988) describe the process of medicalization as it affects community-based services: "Community-based services are being reconstituted to provide medical or medically related support services to the older population. This process of 'making things medical' accords legitimacy to acute care needs while denying the legitimacy of social supportive needs of the elderly" (Wood & Estes, 1988, p. 36).

Wong and associates (1988) claim that hospice is moving toward the medical model it sought to replace. Wood and Ingman (1988) conclude that both the social and the medical models of adult day care are shifting toward a more medical perspective. Furthermore, the numbers of hospices and adult day-care centers continue to grow as they are increasingly recognized as significant parts of the continuum of medical care services.

Concurrently, questions remain about the legitimacy of the social and mental health models of care being provided by senior centers and by community mental health centers. As reported by various researchers (Goldberg, 1988; Wood, 1985), senior centers are being faced with the choice of providing increasingly health-related services or going out of business. Fox and Swan (1988) report that CMHCs have also increased the medically oriented services they provide. By rendering services that meet the medical care needs of the elderly, these agencies are better repositioned to receive funding. The medical needs met by these agencies are real, and capacity to meet even medical needs alone is inadequate. Older persons, however, have many additional needs that the social and mental health models were originally developed to address. Consequently, in this era of cost containment, illogical trade-offs benefit the medical model of service delivery to the detriment of the holistic functioning of the elderly person.

Access-restricting practices are generally consistent across organizations in the community-based delivery system reviewed above. Moreover, attempts to justify community-based services as "cost effective" or "cost beneficial" necessarily entail further access restrictions under the rubric of "more effective targeting" (Weissert, 1988). Community variations exist, and, within each community, different organizational types are using diverse strategies concerning access. For example, three fourths of the hospices in the Philadelphia SMSA tightened eligibility, while none of the adult day-care centers in the area reported the same action. Organizational and community-level findings make it obvious that the environment of health care and social services is undergoing much turbulence and change. As a consequence, considerable inconsistency and confusion exist in the current community-based delivery system and the inevitability of unmet needs remains.

Conclusion

As evidenced by the discussion above, the PPS expanded the importance of the concept of the continuum of care. The full spectrum of health care and social service organizations must now be taken into account when considering the appropriate package of care for an elderly patient. In addition, the PPS served to magnify many of the shortcomings of the community-based delivery system and the consequences of severely restricted community resources. Shifting elderly patients out of acute care settings has placed both the social and the health care sectors under intense scrutiny.

With the advent of the Medicare PPS, attention turned to posthospital care and the adequacy of the community-based delivery system. The burden of care has continued to shift from the acute care hospital to the home and to community-based services. Many older patients being discharged from the hospital with lower levels of functioning and greater needs for ongoing care are finding inadequate and strained community resources. Now, Medicare physician payment under the RBRVS has begun to shift the basis of physician payment for the aged in the community. While difficulties have plagued providers and communities in the past, the critical nature of the problem today is both unprecedented and unlikely to be remedied without significant policy change. Yet there are difficulties in monitoring and evaluating posthospital care, as well, given that it comprises multiple organizational entities, most of which have few linkages with one another. In particular, there is no assurance that an older person who is denied access to one type of service will necessarily be referred to, and served by, another.

The most important conclusion about community-based care is that access has become an issue for all elements of the delivery system. Each has experienced the ripple or domino effects of the Medicare hospital PPS and other policy changes, and each has been influenced by the restructuring of the U.S. health care system. The more "social," more so than health or medical, forms of care have also experienced the greatest effects of spending constraints in U.S. domestic expenditures. The findings of IHA research underscore the need for more community-based noninstitutional services and the creation of adequate funding and reimbursement mechanisms to support the total package of care for elders and all other age groups. The way in which these dynamics play themselves out differently in various environments is described in detail for three communities in the next chapter.

CHAPTER 11

Community Variation
in Policy Implementation

The financing and delivery of long term care services for the elderly is one of the most pressing issues facing states today. For the past two decades state governments have made major commitments to expand these services. Those commitments are reflected in the expenditure of state matching funds to long term support services through Medicaid, in the establishment of long term care programs financed totally with state general revenues, and in the development of detailed policies governing the provision of long term care services.

Justice, 1988, p. i

▼

One unexamined consequence of the implementation of the prospective payment system (PPS) is its impact on state long term care policy formation and subsequent effects on networks of community-based organizations that serve elders. Several issues are raised in the course of the discussion: Which funding mechanisms (Medicaid state plan benefits, Medicaid waivers, Social Services Block Grant funds, Older Americans Act funds, or state general funds) have states used in developing their long term care services? What is the relative level of expenditure of federal versus state dollars for long term care service development in each state? Do states supplement the federally established SSI (Supplemental Security Income) payment level? If so, by how much, and what, if any, is the relationship between SSI

NOTE: The authors of this chapter are Pamela Hanes Spohn, Sheryl C. Goldberg, Ellen M. Morrison, Lorraine M. Kramek, Susan E. Humphers, and Carroll L. Estes.

supplementation and the commitment of other state funds to aging services? What reported impact has the implementation of DRGs had on the network of community-based agencies serving the elderly? What state and community characteristics may explain variation in effects of the PPS reported by community-based agencies?

Descriptions of state and local policy environments before and after the implementation of the PPS focus on three states—California, Pennsylvania, and Washington—included in the DRG Impact Study conducted by the Institute for Health & Aging (IHA, 1986, 1987; Introduction). Community variations in policy effects were examined through case studies of San Francisco, Philadelphia, and Seattle. Organizational and key informant survey data were used to supplement the data collected from case study respondents.

Representative organizations that provide the health and social services most frequently used by older persons were selected for inclusion in the study. Among these were acute care hospitals, postacute care services to which elders are referred at hospital discharge when a need for skilled care exists (nursing homes and home health agencies), and community-based long term care services. Examination of various dimensions of the community networks represented in the IHA study highlights the complexities involved in attempting to untangle specific policy effects and illustrates the relationship between public policy and its intended and unintended consequences for organizational behavior.

The organization and financing of agencies that serve elders have been significantly affected by numerous policy changes occurring in tandem with the implementation of the PPS. Because the IHA study focused on organizations, *communities* were defined as the networks of organizations serving elders in the metropolitan areas included in the study. *Community*, for the purpose of this chapter, is defined as organization-centric in Mulford's sense of the term: "If transactions between organizations are repeated and relationships persist, we speak in terms of the emergence of 'community structure' " (Mulford, 1984, p. 4).

Organizations and Their Environments

The guiding questions of the research reported in this chapter are drawn from the literature on organizational behavior. The framework suggests that, following the implementation of the PPS, the increasingly turbulent organizational environment will lead to increased manipulation and use of hierarchical authority by dominant funding agencies. As a consequence, it is expected that certain clients within the community care system will encounter access barriers to community-based care.

Emery and Trist (1965) classify organizational environments into four ideal types: (a) *placid, randomized* environments; (b) *placid, clustered* environments; (c) *disturbed, reactive* environments; and (d) *turbulent* environments. Turbulent organizational environments are characterized by high uncertainty, rapid change, and increasing levels of interdependency among organizations as they struggle to survive within a given environmental context. The environments in which health and social service organizations operated during the 1980s can be characterized as turbulent, or extremely dynamic and unstable. This is especially true for the home health industry, which, in recent years, has "expanded, diversified, and died at rates that delight any organizational sociologist" (Estes et al., in press).

Benson (1975) takes the classification further in specifying four basic strategies available to organizations for altering the conditions and structures of interorganizational networks. These options include (a) *cooperation*, in which change occurs through joint planning and cooperative agreements; (b) *disruption*, in which purposive activities that "threaten the resource generating capacities of a target agency" are undertaken to destabilize one agency within a network to the advantage of the instigating agency; (c) *manipulation*, in which the "purposive alteration" of environmental factors affects the flow of resources to organizations within a particular network (i.e., changing governmental mandates intended to modify the ways in which certain targeted organizations conduct their business); and (d) *authority*, in which relationships between organizations are precisely specified by a hierarchical authority capable of controlling the flow of resources to a particular network of organizations. Each of these strategies involves a force that operates external to individual organizations within a circumscribed network. In the case of *cooperation*, power is evenly distributed among the organizations that compose the network. Conversely, in the case of *authority*, power is exercised by a dominant organization over the less powerful organizations within the network.

Benson's "processes" are particularly useful for examining the role played by federal and state policies in the reported changes in community-based organizations that serve older clients. Organizational respondents and key informants interviewed in the IHA study suggest that the majority of changes that took place following implementation of the PPS, at both the intra- and the interorganizational levels, were in direct response to the environmental uncertainty caused by shifting public policy mandates (IHA, 1986, 1987).

Table 11.1 presents dominant policy arenas (i.e., Medicare, Medicaid, and other state and local programs) by organizational type and level of governmental authority. It is clear that Medicare and Medicaid policies are the dominant authorities that significantly affect the network of organizations in the IHA study. Using the information garnered through the interviews, IHA researchers argue that the combined influence of the federal Health Care Financing Administration (HCFA) and state Medicaid agencies (including licensing and certification activities) represent the most powerful extraorganizational force in the network of community-based organizations studied.

Sociodemographic Characteristics of the Aging Population

The ability of community-based long term care organizations to meet the needs of their elderly clients adequately is not only a function of changing federal and state policies and funding mechanisms but is also contingent on demand factors such as the size and characteristics of the population to be served. Age, economic status, and prevalence of functional limitations are the strongest predictors of need for long term care services. The states included in the IHA study are quite similar to one another along each of these dimensions. Although there was significant disparity among the states in terms of the absolute numbers of elderly persons in their populations, the three states are comparable when persons aged 65 and older are viewed as a percentage of their total populations (Table 11.2). This same comparability holds constant when projections of the "old-old" (85 years and older) into the year 2000 are examined.

The prevalence of functional limitation in activities of daily living (ADL) for the population as a whole is projected to grow significantly between 1980 and 2000. In Washington, a 50% to 183% increase in the incidence of persons with ADL limitation is projected; in California, it is a 31% to 49% increase; and, in Pennsylvania, a 7% to 12% increase (Rice & Wick, 1985). Because the incidence of ADL limitation is projected to increase and because ADL limitation is the single most important criterion for determining eligibility for publicly financed long term care services, this demographic variable

TABLE 11.1   Policy Effects by Organizational Type

Organization Type	Level of Governmental Authority		
	Federal	*State*	*Local*

Hospitals	Medicare[a]
	Medicaid[a]
		Medicaid
		Licensing/certification
		Certificate of
		  need (CON)[b]
			Zoning
			  ordinances

Home health
  agencies
	Medicare[a]
	Medicaid
		Medicaid
		Licensing/certification
		Certificate of
		  need (CON)	

Nursing homes	Medicare
	Medicaid[a]
		Medicaid
		Licensing/certification
		Certificate of
		  need (CON)
			Zoning
			  ordinances

Hospice programs	Medicare[b] Medicaid	Medicaid Licensing	
Adult day health	Medicaid[b]	Medicaid Licensing	County/city funding

Community
  mental health
  centers
	Mental health
	  block grants[b]
		State mental
		  health policies
			County/city
			  funding

Senior centers	Older Americans
	  Act
		State units on aging	County/city
			  funding[a]

a. Denotes a policy/program/agency that is highly significant in terms of authority vis-à-vis this agency.
b. Denotes a moderately significant policy/program/agency.

may be the most significant indicator of the growing need for community-based services.

The other area of similarity among the states in the study has to do with the number of Supplemental Security Income (SSI) recipients (i.e., low-income elders) in the state. With the exception of Washington, the other states were among the top 10% of states in number of persons on SSI. California ranked 1st with more than 700,000 persons; Pennsylvania ranked 6th; and Washington, 27th in the country with almost 50,000 SSI recipients.

TABLE 11.2   Three-State Comparison of Population Aged 65 and Older

State	Population 65+	Rank	Percentage Total Population	Percentage Change 1980-1985	Percentage Change, 65+ 1980-1984
California	2,848	38	10.6	+14.6	11.6
Pennsylvania	1,736	2	14.6	+17.7	17.7
Washington	520	32	11.7	+29.5	29.5

SOURCES: Data from U.S. Bureau of the Census (1990a) and U.S. HCFA (1986).

State Long Term Care Policy

The long term care system is composed of health and social services designed to maintain chronically ill and/or functionally impaired persons at an optimal level of functioning. These services range from "most" to "least" restrictive based on whether they are provided in an institutional setting or in the client's home (Spohn, Holstein, & Estes, 1986). To put the long term care (LTC) spending experience of the sample states into broader perspective, it is instructive to note national LTC spending trends at two points in time during the 1980s. In fiscal year 1980, national expenditures on long term care totaled $10.1 billion, with nursing home expenditures accounting for 77% of total spending and community-based services accounting for the remaining 23% (Cohen, 1983). Using comparable program categories, the Intergovernmental Health Policy Project identified $13.9 billion in public spending in 1986, representing an increase of 38% since 1980. Institutional spending increased to 81% of total expenditures for long term care (Lipson, Donohoe, & Thomas, 1988).

Tables 11.3 and 11.4 show the major categories of LTC expenditures and sources of funding for the three states in the IHA study for which detailed case studies were conducted. These state expenditures are compared with national averages. There is significant variation among the states in both source of funds and expenditure categories for long term care.

California

As illustrated in Tables 11.3 and 11.4, California used the majority of its federal Social Services Block Grant (SSBG) allocation ($195 million) to fund the in-home supportive services (IHSS) program—a social model homemaker and personal care program for disabled

TABLE 11.3   Federal and State Spending on LTC for the Elderly by Service Setting and Source of Funds[a] for Select States, 1986

State	Medicaid Institutional	Medicaid Waiver	Other Federal HCBS	Other State HCBS & SSP	Total
California	$761	$15	$206	$170	$1,152
	(66%)	(1%)	(18%)	(15%)	
Pennsylvania	$583	$1	$18	$37	$640
	(91%)	(0%)	(3%)	(6%)	
Washington	$159	$16	$18	$24	$217
	(73%)	(7%)	(8%)	(11%)	
Mean (all states)	(81%)	(9%)	(4%)	(6%)	

SOURCE: Data from Lipson and Donohoe (1988, pp. 12-15).
NOTE: HCBS = home and community-based LTC services, SSP = state supplemental payment (state supplement to federal SSI payment).
a. Amounts are millions of dollars.

and elderly persons with low incomes. In fact, much of the $88.4 million in state home and community-based service (HCBS) funds in California ($64.5 million) was used to match federal SSBG dollars for the IHSS program in 1986. The primary LTC funding strategy of populous California, with its large LTC population, was to fund generously IHSS and provide a large supplement to SSI. California is the most generous state in terms of state supplementation of the federal Supplemental Security Income (SSI) program. California's SSI supplementation level of $82 million compares with $26 million in New York, the next most generous state. Among the states studied by IHA, California had the smallest percentage (67%) of its overall LTC program funded by Medicaid despite the fact that California includes adult day health care as a Medicaid benefit and has a much larger ratio of skilled nursing facilities (SNFs) to intermediate care facilities (ICFs) than the other states in the study.

The California strategy is unique among states in that it provides substantially increased purchasing power through the SSI program and couples this income supplement with generous funding for the LTC service most needed by persons with disability and functional limitation, that is, personal care and homemaker/chore services. This two-pronged strategy appears to reflect a policy agenda of maximizing personal autonomy and choice through a basic income guarantee (SSI) and funding the core service needed by persons with disability to maintain their maximum functional capacity and independence. California has made a relatively small and restrictive

TABLE 11.4 Select Federal and State LTC Program Expenditures by State, 1986[a]

State	Other Federal		Other State			State Spending		
	OAA	SSBG	SSP	HCBS	Pharmcare	Total	Per Capita	Rank
California	$11	$195	$82	$88	0	$1,153	$60	6
Pennsylvania	$18	0	$2	$35	$150	$640	$21	18
Washington	$6	$12	$1	$23	0	$217	$46	8

SOURCE: Data from Lipson and Donohoe (1988, pp. 12-15).
NOTE: OAA = Older Americans Act; SSBG = Social Services Block Grant; SSP = state supplemental payment (state supplement to federal SSI payment); HCBS = home and community-based LTC services; Pharmcare = Pennsylvania's pharmaceutical assistance program.
a. Amounts are millions of dollars.

state-only dollar commitment to long term care system development. The two programs established with state-only funds—Linkages (a pseudo-case management program) and Alzheimer's Day Care Centers—are not evenly distributed or equally accessible across the state.

IHA researchers used telephone surveys to interview key informants in state units on aging (SUAs), area agencies on aging (AAAs), and Social Service Block Grant (SSBG) agencies in each of the communities in the study. Respondents were the agency director, deputy director, or a program planner, who, in all but one case, had been affiliated with the agency for more than 5 years. These key informants were asked for their perceptions on the most pressing problems and unmet needs for services among the elderly and also about which policies had the greatest impact on the delivery of health and social services in the state since 1984.

Key informant interviews in California support the finding of a generally adequate LTC system, characterized by growth and an overall commitment to meeting the needs of elderly citizens in the state. The "aging network" agencies (i.e., the SUA and AAAs) identified affordable housing as the most pressing problem facing the elderly in California, followed closely by escalating health care costs. The Department of Social Services (DSS), which administers the SSBG funds, also identified health care costs as a pressing issue facing the elderly. Given the general costs of housing and the ever-deepening health insurance crisis in the state, these are not surprising revelations. Key informants also spoke of housing options for elders who need some level of supportive care.

All respondents were in agreement that availability of and access to LTC services in California were increasing and that the state had made a significant commitment to program expansion. In fact, the DSS informant discussed the passage of recent legislation that made the IHSS program an entitlement for low-income elders in the SSI program.

Reported state and community-level PPS-related impacts were identified as related primarily to increased service demands. Spokespersons from the SUA, the DSS, and the AAAs reported that agencies were overwhelmed by an increased demand for services from elders with increasingly severe impairments. California has used a variety of federal and state funding sources to piece together a fairly well-developed long term care system relative to other states. It is well below the national average for Medicaid-funded institutional care (66% to 81%), well above the average for both federally and state-funded home and community-based services (16.5% to 5%), and ranks sixth in the country for total per capita state dollars spent on LTC programs for the elderly (Table 11.3).

Pennsylvania

Pennsylvania had the second highest percentage of persons over the age of 65 among the 50 states. In terms of targeted dollars for the elderly, it has a minimal state supplemental income program ($2 million) and has instead put a significant commitment of state dollars ($150 million) into a pharmacy assistance program. Additionally, the state moderately funds a range of home and community-based services (HCBS), primarily with its federal OAA allocation and state matching funds. Major programs funded under the OAA umbrella include personal care, home-delivered meals, case management, adult day care, and home health care. In terms of per capita spending for LTC (both federal and state funds, excluding Medicare) in 1986, Pennsylvania ranked 31st among the 50 states.

Pennsylvania, one of the oldest states in the country, has historically been represented by an industry-based economy. The profound changes that have occurred in all Eastern cities relative to the serious decline of the industrial sector and often less-than-successful shift to an information- and/or service-based economy, have had a devastating effect on the economy and fiscal integrity of states like Pennsylvania. With a weakened economic base, Pennsylvania ranked 6th in the country in percentage of total state spending on welfare programs, and, in an effort to meet the heavy needs created by the slow economy, 10th in welfare spending per capita (Table 11.5).

Pennsylvania ranked 43rd in per capita spending for overall health expenditures while still ranking 13th for Medicaid spending on SSI recipients. These data point to the complexities involved in state spending patterns. For example, although constrained by a diminishing tax base caused by the out-migration of jobs and high levels of poverty, Pennsylvania is still a big Medicaid spender largely because of the significant number of poor elderly in its SSI population. Unfortunately, these Medicaid dollars are used almost exclusively to pay for institutional care. Specifically, Pennsylvania spent 91% of its federal and state LTC funds on institutional care in contrast to the national average of 81%.

The state has instituted an aggressive preadmission screening and case management demonstration program known as LAMP (long term care assessment and management project) in seven counties, which represent 40% of the state population over age 65. LAMP was

TABLE 11.5 State and Local Per Capita Spending on Select Health and Welfare Programs, 1985

State	Welfare Spending as Percentage of Total	Rank	Welfare Spending	Rank	Health Spending	Rank	Medicaid Spending on SSI Recipients	Rank
California	16.2	8	$428	6	$228	14	$951	46
Pennsylvania	16.3	6	$332	10	$130	43	$2,772	13
Washington	10.8	23	$272	19	$194	24	$5,703	3

SOURCE: Data from Brizius and Foster (1987, tables H-1, H-3, I-22, I-28).

established with state funds and is jointly administered by Public Welfare and the Department of Aging. The purpose of LAMP is to divert individuals who would otherwise enter nursing homes to community care based on level of care needs and availability of community resources.

The vast majority of capacity-building activities in the Pennsylvania LTC system occurred within the "aging network" agencies of the State Department of Aging and the AAAs. As noted above, all HCBS are administered through these agencies because the state Medicaid plan supports virtually no community-based care and the state has not initiated any Medicaid home and community-based waiver programs. Clearly, the most significant commitment of state funds for the elderly has been made to the pharmaceutical assistance program. It is the largest of its kind in the country, serving 440,000 elders in 1986 at a cost of $150 million (Lipson et al., 1988).

Unlike California, Pennsylvania has made a minimal commitment to income support and the supportive community-based services (such as adult day care, home-delivered meals, or homemaker/chore services). Instead, Pennsylvania has focused on assisting elders with their drug bills—an in-kind medical benefit. This strategy is of particular interest because more than 20% of persons over the age of 60 in the state are poor, and, in Philadelphia, the major population center in the state, the elderly are at higher risk of poverty than are older Americans in general. Census data from 1980 revealed that 17% of elders in Philadelphia fell below the poverty level and another 25,000 were at or near the poverty line (Spohn et al., 1988). According to a study conducted by the Philadelphia Health Management Corporation in 1986, the city's elderly also had significantly higher rates of functional limitation than elders nationally (PHMC, 1985). Moreover, approximately one third of the city's elderly lived alone, suggesting that the need for both income supplements and supportive services was great.

Key informants in Pennsylvania confirmed the prevalence of poverty among the state's elderly population. The informant from the State Department on Aging identified lack of income as the most pressing problem facing the elderly. The AAA respondent in Pittsburgh noted the lack of adequate financial resources to pay for health care as one of the most pressing problems facing elderly people in that city. The unavailability of health and social services was noted by AAA respondents from both Philadelphia and Pittsburgh. As in California, key informants in Pennsylvania expressed optimism at the increased access and availability of LTC services since 1984.

Area agency on aging informants noted significant PPS effects among agency clients, who required more intensive services, and among contracting agencies that were having a difficult time responding to increased service needs. The SUA reported that the increased demand for services following the implementation of the prospective payment system resulted in an additional $24 million in state funds for in-home services in fiscal year 1986-1987.

Pennsylvania continues to have a strong institutional bias in terms of the state funds made available for long term care. The state's Medicaid institutional budget was well above the national average (91% to 81%), and its Medicaid waivers well below (0 to 9%). In terms of other state and federal dollars allocated to long term care services for the elderly, Pennsylvania ranked lowest among the states in the IHA study (4% to 8.4%) in federal spending and second from the bottom in state spending (6% to 9%).

As noted above, the major state expenditure for the elderly was for pharmaceuticals and, because of this program, Pennsylvania ranked 18th among all states for state spending per capita on the elderly. The net effect of its spending decisions is that the state has made a very modest commitment to LTC system development (i.e., a client-centered, community-based system) and instead continues to meet its Title 19 (Medicaid) obligation for funding institutional care while additionally funding a generous in-kind drug assistance program based on a medical model. As discussed in Chapter 13, recent interviews with decision makers in the state highlight growing concern over the rapidly increasing cost of the drug program and the inadequacy of the state lottery program to meet the rising demand for services.

Washington

Washington can be characterized as a relatively generous state in terms of the percentage of its budget that supports both health and welfare programs (Table 11.2). On the measure of total federal and state per capita funding for LTC programs for the elderly, Washington ranked first among the states in the IHA study: $417 per capita as compared with $405 per capita in California and $369 per capita in Pennsylvania. Additionally, Washington ranked second among the three in per capita state funds expended on LTC services for the elderly. Washington's LTC funding strategy is unique among the states in that it supports a fairly broad range of HCBS with state-only funds and combines these expenditures with a significant expansion of its Medicaid state plan in the areas of home health care services and adult day-care programs. Like California, Washington has made a major commitment to funding homemaker/chore services through combining state dollars and SSBG funds. Also similar to California, Washington provides an SSI supplement to persons living independently as well as in the household of another, although the level of this supplementation is significantly less than in California.

The uniqueness of Washington's system development strategy is reflected in its two-pronged approach: (a) the development of a large Medicaid waiver program—COPES (community options program entry system), which covers residential and personal care—with a modestly funded OAA aging network, which supports primarily congregate and home-delivered meals, and (b) the combined commitment of SSBG and state-only funds for enhancing service capacity. Washington policymakers have pursued a wide-ranging assortment of financing strategies to facilitate the development of a fairly comprehensive state HCBS long term care system.

A proportionately higher percentage of state and federal funding was allocated to noninstitutional care in Washington. Nursing homes, however, are protected by a fairly strict certificate-of-need program that discourages new entrants into the market, leaving occupancy rates high. Nursing homes are also more adequately reimbursed for their services than in many other states, being paid on a cost-plus system (cost of care plus depreciation and inflation, tied to the consumer price index). State-funded programs for the elderly include personal care/homemaker, adult day health care, respite, adult foster care, and congregate housing. These programs, authorized under the state Senior Citizen's Service Act, are available only to persons 65 or older with low incomes (Lipson & Donohoe, 1988).

Key state informants interviewed in 1987 reported that the most pressing problems facing the elderly in Washington included access to community-based long term care, especially in-home services, homemaker/chore workers, personal care, and respite care. The state unit on aging representative raised the issue of how institutional and community-based long term care services were financed. The informant noted that the state had a generous transfer of assets law so that a person did not have to become pauperized if his or her spouse needed nursing home care. He further stated that the legislature was looking for ways to save money and had been considering limiting the transfer of assets provision in current law. Because of the financial condition of the state, the legislature is increasingly challenged to find new sources of funds to support growth in community-based care. Regarding the effects of DRGs, there are increased pressures for community agencies outside of the hospital, especially nursing homes, to serve elders who are more frail and have more medical complications than before the implementation of prospective payment. Service needs are greater than the available funding.

In sum, even with a comprehensive and well-funded community-based delivery system for the elderly, key informants interviewed in Washington State reported significant changes in the demand for posthospital care since the implementation of the PPS and questioned the ability of organizational providers to adequately meet these increased demands.

Community Variation

Researchers conducted community case studies in one metropolitan area in each of the three states in the IHA study. The goal of the community case studies was to examine in detail the interactions of federal and state policy with the history, politics, and people of a community. It was hypothesized that these interactions would result in community-specific variations in the organization and delivery of long term care services available to older persons in these communities. Incorporated in the case study discussion are secondary data from the broader IHA study (i.e., sociodemographic data and telephone survey data). San Francisco, Philadelphia, and Seattle provide interesting comparisons and contrasts in local political environments, the structure of long term care services developed, and implications for the elderly population.

San Francisco

The city and county of San Francisco is central to the Bay Area, a large metropolitan five-county region. The telephone survey data are representative of the larger San Francisco/Oakland SMSA. Although geographically the smallest county in the state, San Francisco is recognized as the financial and cultural center of Northern California. San Francisco is also a major point of entry for large numbers of immigrants from countries all over the world (Castells, 1983).

The San Francisco Commission on the Aging (COA), a city/county department, is the designated AAA in San Francisco. The COA acts as a contracting agency, having formal arrangements with community-based nonprofit and public agencies to provide direct services to San Francisco residents over the age of 60. The COA operates the

Senior Information and Referral Program, which provides 24-hour telephone information on all senior resources, and offers educational, consumer, and health promotion services. In San Francisco, the Department of Social Services is the administrative agent for in-home supportive services (IHSS). Currently, the department contracts with independent providers, a private for-profit organization, and a coalition of seven minority-run community-based nonprofit organizations (i.e., the IHSS Consortium) to provide in-home supportive services to frail elders and functionally impaired individuals. These services include homemaker/chore and personal care services (e.g., meal preparation, cleaning, personal grooming). In fiscal year 1991-1992, the COA also granted a small contract to supplement the work of the IHSS Consortium.

San Francisco stands out as a county that is extremely generous in the provision of local funding for community-based aging services (Goldberg, 1990). A 1978 ordinance of the San Francisco Board of Supervisors committed one third of the local off-street parking fees and annual interest to aging service programs in the city. Almost half of the total commission budget now comes from this source. Many case study respondents mentioned that this local funding source insulated San Francisco from budgetary cuts exercised at the state and federal levels.

The majority of dollars COA contracted out to community-based agencies supported congregate meal programs and senior center activities. Respondents from both public and nonprofit agencies suggested that the time was long overdue for the COA to change its funding priorities to make better use of its resources. A number of respondents questioned the continuing preference of the COA to fund existing services to the exclusion of long term care planning and program development activities. Critics argued that not being more attentive to long term care system development conflicted with a major client shift affecting the system, namely, the rise in the number and needs of frail elders.

San Francisco is regarded as a resource-rich service community for elders. In spite of resource richness, access to care can be a confusing and frustrating process. Some providers commented that politics in San Francisco have created a "patchwork quilt" of aging services rather than a planned system. For example, there are 17 case management programs to facilitate access to care and the coordination of services for frail elders in San Francisco. Unlike the planned network developed in Philadelphia, each case management program in San Francisco has its own eligibility criteria and service package.

San Francisco is also the home of a number of model programs that provide care to at-risk elders. The On Lok Risk-Based Community Care Organization for Dependent Adults (CCODA) began in 1972 and became the prototype for the California adult day health care legislation passed in 1977. On Lok is a comprehensive long term care system designed with financial incentives to keep people in their homes and communities as long as medically, socially, and economically possible (Zawadski & Ansak, 1983). Seven adult day health care (ADHC) centers are strategically located throughout the city, making San Francisco the first in the country to have a citywide ADHC network. This well-planned ADHC system is comparable to that developed for case management services via the senior center network in Philadelphia. The Adult Day Health Network, created in 1983, represents a unique approach to service delivery. The network functions as a joint fund-raising and advocacy body by providing technical assistance, staff training, transportation, marketing, and outreach for the seven ADHC centers in the city.

Despite the plethora of agencies in San Francisco, study respondents reported that the needs of the large and growing elderly population were not being adequately met. Many community-based organizations were unable to respond to the increasing demand for care. State-level informants noted that the increasing demand for posthospital care was a direct result of the implementation of the Medicare PPS. Several respondents suggested that San Francisco should be considered underserved because the waiting lists for so many services are so long.

In the San Francisco Bay Area, numerous coalitions and consortiums function to bring service providers together for the purpose of program planning and advocacy. Included among them are the Consortium for Elder Abuse Prevention, Home-Delivered Meals Clearinghouse, IHSS Consortium, and the Geriatric Mental Health Coordinating Committee. It has been suggested that, because San Francisco is a small geographic area, service providers are able to see each other more often than might be possible in a geographically dispersed community. Additionally, since 1982, the Commission on Aging has been renegotiating individual service contracts on a yearly basis, a mechanism that has served to lessen direct competition among community-based providers. Some service providers perceived that the trend toward cooperation and coordination was a result of the Medicare PPS. Specifically, they believe that DRGs started a chain of events that required discharge planners and community agency providers to talk to one another more often. In direct contrast, others report that competition is the dominant mode of interaction among agencies in the city and that a strong feeling of territoriality exists among agencies.

In 1986, close to three fourths of the hospital discharge planners interviewed in the telephone survey said that referrals to nursing homes and homemaker/chore agencies were more difficult to negotiate after 1984 (78% and 72%, respectively). Discharge planners in the San Francisco Bay Area described an increasing demand for home-delivered meals and a subsequent growth in waiting lists. Even though there is a relatively large number of hospices in the San Francisco Bay Area, it was reported that hospice care is significantly more difficult to secure in this community than in the other study sites. This finding may be influenced by the large number of persons with AIDS who are using hospice services.

In 1987, essentially all of the nursing home directors surveyed in the San Francisco/Oakland SMSA (95%) reported having to refuse service to some patients. The San Francisco Bay Area has a relatively small number of nursing homes and there has therefore been a historic tendency to refer patients (particularly those requiring heavy care) to surrounding communities. A study conducted by the San Francisco Ombudsman Program revealed that 30% of Medicaid patients had to leave the city for institutional care and 80% of these were patients who required heavy care (Doherty & Kaufman, 1988).

In the first year of the telephone survey (1986), Bay Area home health directors were significantly more likely than those in the other study communities to report service refusals to persons not having adequate insurance coverage (64% to 52%). Persons refused service included elders with health care problems not covered by Medicare and without private resources to pay for the uncovered care. The irony of the federal government's forcing patients out of the hospital sooner, while at the same time cutting back coverage of home health care, was noted by at least one home care agency administrator.

The unmet needs described by agency providers expose many of the current gaps in service experienced by older persons in the San Francisco Bay Area. Even though the state generously funds IHSS, these services (which include homemaker/chore services and companion/custodial care) are reported to be sorely needed to address adequately the needs of the elderly in San Francisco and the larger Bay Area. Furthermore, many study respondents observed that one of the scarcest resources for elders in San Francisco is nursing home care (especially for those who are Medicaid eligible). Respondents associated barriers to service delivery with the larger environmental context and conditions (i.e., diversity of regulations, reimbursement gaps) as well as the antiquated funding priorities of the COA.

Philadelphia

Philadelphia is a city in which privately organized charity and philanthropy have been institutionalized into the fabric of community life. The degree of penetration of the nonprofit sector in human services sets Philadelphia apart from other communities in the IHA study. By way of illustration, 96% of the IHA hospital sample in the Philadelphia SMSA consisted of nonprofit facilities compared with an average of 53% in the other eight SMSAs in the study. Another case in point is that 65% of all home health agencies in Philadelphia were nonprofit at the time of sample selection (1986), the highest rate of nonprofit agencies among all the communities in the study and almost double the rate of the other SMSAs (38%).

The area agency on aging (AAA) in Philadelphia—the Philadelphia Corporation on Aging (PCA)—is a nonprofit organization with an elected board of directors and an advisory committee of predominantly elderly members. The PCA is the hub of the aging services network in Philadelphia. As the most powerful single organizational entity responsible for planning and coordinating all but institutional services for the elderly, its actions define the successes and failures of the system of care for the city's elderly population. The decision to incorporate the Philadelphia AAA as a nonprofit agency was a deliberate one so as to avoid any possibility of political patronage that might occur if the agency were part of city government. The reason the issue of auspice was a particularly important one in Philadelphia is that all the dedicated lottery dollars, state and federal funds, and many private foundation funds for services to the city's elders were administered through the PCA (more than $43 million in 1988). Consequently, the tensions between the city and the PCA arise when Philadelphia leadership tries to find new ways to stretch its limited human services budget. At the time of the case study, the mayor's office and city hall were relatively minor players in the elderly service agency arena.

The PCA instituted several demonstration projects in Philadelphia targeted at posthospital elderly patients and other at-risk elders. The state-funded LAMP program of preadmission screening and care management operates in Philadelphia. A project that was highly acclaimed by case study respondents was the Post-Hospital Care Project administered by the Philadelphia Center for Older People (an inner-city senior center). This program was developed in direct response to the PPS and had as its goals to establish a cost-effective model of nonmedical support to promote health recovery and independence and to develop a new system of payment for services, the cost of which would be shared by patient, hospital, and third-party payers. A unique aspect of the project is that it has been a partnership between PCA, a senior center, and several hospitals. A similar project, the Emergency Room/Aging Connection Project, was also being administered by the PCA in collaboration with a university hospital and a senior center. Although this project has a slightly different target population, the goal of increasing access to community-based care was the same. In each case, the PCA attempted to test alternative strategies for building a coordinated system of long term care in Philadelphia.

Table 11.6 shows that, in 1987, hospital discharge planners in Philadelphia reported significantly more difficulty in securing posthospital care for their patients in nursing homes and home health care agencies than that reported in the other communities in the study. Also, in the discharge planner survey, IHA researchers found high levels of concern about the lack of homemaker/chore services in Philadelphia and particularly about the issue of the waiting lists for care that developed after the implementation of the PPS. The greatest impact of the PPS reported by discharge planners was the increased pressure to provide services to an ever-larger population of at-risk elders.

There is general agreement among the respondents that Philadelphia has an undersupply of nursing home beds relative to demand. This demand has been steadily increasing because of the growing elderly population and the earlier discharge of patients from hospitals. Relative to SMSAs in other states, however, Philadelphia nursing homes reported fewer negative effects resulting from the PPS. Reduced access to care, particularly related to reimbursement, was significantly less severe among Philadelphia's home health care agencies than in the other communities studied. This is of particular interest because, at the time of the study, the Philadelphia SMSA had the largest proportion of Medicare-certified home health agencies in the sample (96% in the Philadelphia SMSA as compared with 82% in the other communities) and a much higher proportion of hospital-based home health agencies. The access crisis for home health care in Philadelphia may have been less severe than that of other communities because of the historically favorable reimbursement policies for hospital-based home health agencies, which then were much more prevalent in the Pennsylvania community than in others studied.

TABLE 11.6 Difficulty of Discharge Planners in Securing Posthospital Referrals in Philadelphia and Selected Other Communities, 1986 and 1987

| | Nursing Home | | Home Health Care | | Homemaker/Chore | |
| | Philadelphia | Other | Philadelphia | Other | Philadelphia | Other |
Year	(percentage)	(percentage)	(percentage)	(percentage)	(percentage)	(percentage)
1986	76	68	36	28	68	70
1987	76	58	46	25	52	59

SOURCE: Data from Institute for Health & Aging DRG study (1986, 1987).

Reports of specific PPS impacts among the home health agencies in the Philadelphia sample were unique for several reasons. Philadelphia home health agency (HHA) informants were significantly less likely to report increases in sicker clients with greater care needs but were more likely to report an increase in premature discharges from hospitals. Likewise, Philadelphia home health agency informants were significantly less likely than those in the other communities to report shifts to a higher intensity of service provision or more high-tech types of care.

A major building block in the community-based system of long term care in Philadelphia has been the network of 31 senior centers and their 33 satellites throughout the city. Philadelphia is somewhat unique among communities in that it has carved out a major role for senior centers in the development of its community-based long term care system. In 1977, the state mandated that 20% of all dollars for the aging go to in-home services. With this incentive, senior centers entered the business of providing in-home care, becoming the designated sites for management of the in-home service program. Each senior center has a catchment area to which outreach and case management services are offered. The PCA splits the funding for senior centers between center clients (congregate meals and center services) and service management for frail elders (home-delivered meals, case management, counseling, protective services, homemakers, home health aides, chore workers, day-care placement, ombudsmen, and attendant care). In interviews with service providers, it was clear that, because of the tremendous increase in demand for services for frail elders, the PCA was targeting this population for homemaker/chore services.

Adult day care (ADC), as a component of the community-based long term care system, is still in its infancy in Philadelphia. The lack of funding and support for ADC is a result of Pennsylvania's not including the service in its Medicaid state plan or as an allowable service under a Medicaid waiver program (Pennsylvania has no Medicaid waivers for institutionally at-risk elders).

Philadelphia policymakers maintain a profound commitment to the private provision of social goods and services not found to the same extent in the other sample communities. Even though Pennsylvania ranks low in per capita long term care funding, the data indicate that, during the 1986-1987 study period, Philadelphia was somewhat better off on a number of organizational access measures relative to other communities studied. The data suggest that the community is attempting to maintain a viable system of health and social services with significantly fewer resources.

Seattle

Seattle is the largest city in Washington, yet the smallest of the SMSAs in the IHA study. Compared with the rest of the state, Seattle is "highly urbanized and ethnically diverse" (Bureau of Aging and Adult Services, 1984). Seattle is also home to a strong and vocal consumer movement and has been quite successful in conflict resolution in its political structure. Cooperatives are organizations that promote choice in the marketing of commercial goods as well as in the provision of health care. Group Health of Puget Sound, founded in 1945, is one of the oldest and most enduring health maintenance organizations (HMOs) in the country.

One example of Seattle's ability to work through its problems is the negotiation of control over the local area agency on aging. In the late 1970s, the county attempted to "secede" from the city-operated Division on Aging and form its own AAA. Through negotiation, an interlocal agreement was established, which created a tripartite system. Although still operated by the executive branch of the city of Seattle, the Seattle-King County Division on Aging (DOA) is now governed by three equally represented "sponsors": the city, King County, and the United Way Agency of Seattle. Under this arrangement, power and authority are shared, and opportunities for multiple sources of input, negotiation, and compromise are enhanced.

The Division on Aging contracts with local providers for home and community-based services. Key informants reported that the DOA has been focusing an increasing share of its resources on the growing frail elderly population. The coordination and quality of services provided through the DOA received unqualified praise from nearly all respondents. Seattle's aging service network was characterized as informal and involved a high degree of communication and cooperation among all parties.

In Seattle, in sharp contrast to Philadelphia, 72% of nursing homes, 56% of home health agencies, and 32% of senior centers were operating under for-profit auspices. Seattle respondents reported two trends in the structure of the community-based long term care delivery system. The trend of for-profit nursing homes converting to nonprofits was said to be due to the favorable Medicaid reimbursement and property tax advantages of nonprofit status. Respondents also reported witnessing an "explosion" of growth in the nonregulated arenas of long term care, particularly in case management services.

In spite of relatively high funding from federal and state sources for homemaker/chore services in Seattle, these services were still cited as one of the most pressing problems by key informants at the SMSA and state levels. In 1987, more hospital discharge planners in Seattle (80%) than in all other study SMSAs (59%) reported difficulty in placing patients into homemaker/chore programs. At the time of the IHA interviews, the Community Options Program Entry System (COPES), a Medicaid-funded home and community-based care program, had recently cut back its homemaker/chore service program, requiring that elders have personal care needs in addition to homemaker needs to qualify. In response to these cuts, Catholic Community Services implemented a sliding-scale homemaker/chore service and was pursuing block grants and political negotiation to increase resources in this area.

Seattle nursing home survey respondents differed from those in all other SMSAs in 1987 in their consistent reports of changes in the types of patients served and the level and types of services provided as a result of the prospective payment system. Their responses were considerably higher than the average in reports of changing patient illness acuity levels and needs after the implementation of the PPS.

In 1986, more Seattle home health agencies than in the other sites perceived that they had increased their intensity of services and provided a higher level of care than in 1984. By 1987, home health agencies in all study sites reported that their intensity of services and levels of care had increased considerably since 1986, but in Seattle even more than in the other sites. Also in 1987, a substantially higher percentage of home health agency respondents in Seattle than in other areas reported that patients were sicker, had more serious problems, were more likely to have been discharged from the hospital prematurely, and were more likely to have been readmitted within the past service year.

The provision of mental health services was a topic of great interest in the Seattle interviews. A higher percentage of Seattle community mental health centers (CMHCs) than in other sites reported
tightening eligibility (64% in 1986), increasing fees (82% in 1986), and
refusing services (82% in 1987). Interview data suggest that, as resources become tighter, mission-oriented nonprofit CMHCs must
avoid providing services to clients who, because they will not sign a
release for treatment, will not meet eligibility requirements.

Seattle, with its well-developed cooperative network of long term
care providers and supporters, was perhaps better prepared for the
PPS than even Philadelphia or San Francisco. One Seattle-based
respondent summed up the interview and survey findings quite well
by explaining that, in general, Seattle provides a wide range of
well-coordinated home and community-based services to the elderly. The problem is that there are just not enough services to meet
the needs of the population. Similar sentiments were expressed by
respondents in the other communities studied. Even an innovative,
well-organized community such as Seattle, perhaps the most progressive community in our sample, is now approaching "crisis" in
terms of the capacity of the social and medical system to adequately
support its elders, particularly with the provision of low-tech home
care such as homemaker/chore services.

Conclusion

Reviewing the effects of the Medicare PPS on long term care policy
formation in California, Pennsylvania, and Washington and on elder
service organizations at the community level contributes to an understanding of the relationship between public policy and its intended and unintended consequences for organizational behavior.
As evidenced in this book, community and organizational variations
in the impact of the PPS and other state and local policy initiatives
on access to long term care services for the elderly are significant.

The implications of public policy for organizational structure and
outcomes are profound. In all three study sites, key informants and
agency providers described an increasing demand for services for
the elderly as a result of the PPS. That they also reported diminishing
resources to respond to the needs of the population illustrates the
fact that organizational and community environments are dynamic
and complex.

The policy implications of the IHA study are numerous. The PPS has produced systemic changes in the mode of, location of, and delivery of care for the elderly. Spillover effects and unintended consequences have produced problem shifting instead of problem solving. The DRG-based prospective payment policy served to magnify some of the shortcomings of the community-based long term care system in the ability to meet the needs of the elderly. Although many problems had plagued organizations prior to the PPS, the critical nature of the problems is unprecedented. Respondents from the states and communities targeted in this study confirmed the need for more community-based noninstitutional services as an important and complementary part of the long term care system.

It is clear that careful consideration must be given to cost-effective financing in creating an adequate infrastructure for community-based long term care services for the chronically ill and disabled elderly. Although such a planned approach runs contrary to the current contemporary health policy emphasis on competition and the role of the market in resolving the problems of cost and access, the myriad difficulties that confront the elderly who need community-based long term care justify a new approach. The next chapter considers how change has occurred under the old approach.

CHAPTER 12

Waves of Change

We live in a turbulent and exhilarating age of change, an age which reflects the potential for liberation and self-determination. The so-called "problems of age" in this new age are indeed the problems of society: they reflect its malaise and also the distribution of power in American society. Yet every discipline, every institution, every nation-state, every human group cannot fail to be challenged by the profound issues of age.

Kuhn, 1984, p. 7

An overriding issue throughout this volume is the effect of policy changes during the 1980s on the providers of community-based care for the elderly. An important underlying theme concerns how private nonprofit providers have been affected by the increasingly austere conditions of the 1980s and early 1990s. This period was marked by a significant change in political sentiment and explicit White House actions in the form of policies designed to reduce federal and increase local responsibility for the provision and funding of human services. The era has been characterized by reduced federal spending on community services (Abramson & Salamon, 1986; Estes, Wood, et al., 1988) and significant increases in federal expenditures for medical services funded under Medicare and Medicaid (Chapter 1). Medicare expenditures, in particular, have grown

---

NOTE: The authors of this chapter are Carroll L. Estes and Juanita B. Wood (parts of this chapter are revisions of the authors' article, The Impact of DRGs on Community-Based Service Providers: Implications for the Elderly, *American Journal of Public Health, 80,* 1990, 840-843).

much faster than the rate of inflation, even though the rate of hospital expenditure growth has slowed. Despite the implementation of cost-containment policies, the overall rate of increase in health care expenditures well exceeds the general rate of inflation throughout the period. Policy changes during this time have been accompanied by a worsening of problems of access to health care, an escalation in beneficiary cost sharing, a decline in benefit coverage, and an increase in the proportion of the population that is uninsured.

A series of studies conducted at the Institute for Health & Aging (IHA) between 1978 and 1990 shows that these and other shifts in the nation's economic picture and public policy have significantly challenged community-based service providers, particularly nonprofit health and social service agencies that serve older persons. Community-based providers have been pressed to adopt strategies long used in the proprietary sector, such as engaging in the highly competitive search for ways to increase market share and revenue. The changes that occurred during the 1980s raise important questions concerning (a) the capacity of communities to serve the elderly who need community care but are unable to pay privately for services, (b) the respective roles of the public and private sectors, and (c) the special status and tax subsidies accorded to nonprofit service entities.

Waves of Response

A number of changes have occurred in community-based services as a result of fiscal conditions and policies implemented between 1978 and 1984 (Estes & Wood, 1986; Swan, Estes, & Wood, 1982; Wood, Estes, Lee, & Fox, 1983; Wood et al., 1986). Three major waves of service provider response to policy changes in the early 1980s have been identified (Wood & Estes, 1988). The first of these was the period of cutback management (1978-1981) following taxpayer revolts and federal budget cuts incorporated into the 1981 Omnibus Reconciliation Act (OBRA). The second wave (1982-1983) was one of reorganization, in which service providers began to respond to the growing competition initiated by policy changes during the first 2 years of the Reagan administration. The third wave (1984 to the current time) is characterized by full-fledged provider participation in the competitive service delivery system.

An overall trend during the entire period was the medicalization of community services for the elderly. Community-based services were increasingly required to respond to the needs of medically ill elders who were being discharged from hospitals earlier than ever before (Binney et al., 1990; Wood & Estes, 1988). The newly narrowed focus of community-based services targets an especially needy population but leaves the multiple other nonmedical service needs of elders largely unaddressed. The ability of community agencies to assist older persons with nonmedical needs such as housing, transportation, social support, and assistance with personal care is compromised by the increased emphasis placed on attending to the medical posthospital care needs of older patients. The social service orientation of many community agencies has been diluted by the infusion of large numbers of clients with serious medical care needs. This reflects an extension of the influence of medical decisions on community-care provision that is consistent with a cultural acceptance of aging as a medical problem (Estes, 1979; Estes & Binney, 1989).

Wave 1: Cutback Management

In the period of cutback management (1978-1981), funding reductions occurred in many cases not only at the federal level but also at the state and local levels. Strains were felt at every level following the tax revolt and fiscal crisis in the wake of Proposition 13 in California, Proposition 2½ in Massachusetts, and a host of other taxpayer initiatives. By 1981, the dominant response of public officials at all levels of government was to reduce expenditures rather than to increase taxes or to contemplate new revenue sources (Swan et al., 1983). Within human services, social services suffered larger cutbacks than medical services, led by the decline of 22% in social service funding at the federal level with the initiation of the Social Services Block Grant (Lindeman & Pardini, 1983).

Wave 1 was a period in which a provider's skill in cutback management was at a premium. As states struggled with the consequences of federal cuts, state taxpayer revolt, and inflation in their Medicaid programs, they were in no position to significantly augment their investment in human services (Estes, 1986). Community-based service agencies generally responded by initiating across-the-board cuts. During this period of initial Reagan-led cutbacks in domestic programs, local providers were resolute in attempting to preserve their existing organizational infrastructure. Cuts were spread across all elements of the provider system. Provider agencies also attempted to survive by making across-the-board cuts in virtually all major operations.

Wave 2: Structural Shifts

The second period (1982-1983) was characterized by shifts in the nature and structure of the community-based delivery system. Because of reductions in social service funding, providers began to emphasize medically oriented and medically linked services to attract the frail and homebound Medicare-eligible elderly. Although the effects of federal cutbacks were more severe in 1982 than in 1983, provider interviews drawn from 32 urban communities in eight geographically diverse states demonstrate the broad reach of the cuts contained in the 1981 OBRA. Nearly one half (44%) of all providers reported cutting services in 1983. Of the six types of providers studied (home health, nutrition programs, adult day care, community health centers, senior centers, and information and referral agencies), the programs most negatively affected by funding cuts were those most involved in providing social services and those serving low-income clients. Medicaid eligibility was narrowed and the growth in Medicaid spending virtually halted between 1981 and 1984 (Holahan & Cohen, 1986).

The majority of community-based providers of all types studied by IHA reported that demand for service had grown, but only home health providers were able to increase their staffs commensurate with the increased patient demand (Wood & Estes, 1988). Competition for patients able to pay for services became the preoccupation of providers. Organizations made changes in service offerings to increase the number of Medicaid- and Medicare-reimbursable services on their lists and the likelihood of attracting clients eligible for reimbursement. Priority was given to services that could be reimbursed under a government program or paid for privately. Social support services were generally devalued unless they filled immediate posthospital care needs and could thus contribute to hospital cost savings (and profit) and/or be reimbursed under the increasingly stringent federal programs.

These findings were consistent across geographic locations, indicating the influence of federal policy such as the PPS on community agencies. Agency services became directed (and reconstituted) to provide medical or medically related support services to the elderly. This process of medicalization, or "making things medical" (as in the case of the "medical social service" designation for Medicare home health reimbursement), lends legitimacy to acute care needs, displacing the value of social support needs (Estes & Binney, 1989; Wood & Estes, 1988).

Wave 3: Competition

By 1984, the period of full-fledged competition was under way. Wave 3 was characterized by greater acceptance of private sector goals by nonprofit agencies. Providers no longer sought to regain their lost or altered staff, organizational functions, services, or clients. Instead, they worked to make their respective organizations more viable in the market. In this ideological shift, the harsh discipline of the market was accepted by nonprofits as the law by which they would live or die. It was clear that social services would not generate the profits that provision of medical care services promised. Commitment to full participation in the competitive community service delivery system required providers to engage in a series of organizational changes that previously would have been unthinkable. Mergers, vertical and horizontal integration, tax status changes, and the establishment of subsidiaries became commonplace.

The waves of organizational change within nonprofit community health care agencies mirrored the dramatic and swift changes taking place throughout the medical care delivery system. The changes occurred in the context of increased interagency competition and economically based decision making and contributed to what IHA researchers identify as a transformation of the community-care system (Estes, 1984-1985, 1986; Estes & Wood, 1986; Wood & Estes, 1988). In this context, the Medicare hospital PPS, which gives hospitals the financial incentive to discharge patients as early as possible, was implemented in 1983. Hospitals accomplish early discharge by leaving patients and their families to substitute informal and other home and community-based care for hospital care, whether or not such services are available or reimbursable. The overall changes were tantamount to a cultural revolution in the behavior of nonprofits, as shown in Figure 12.1.

Federal Funding of Social Services

Social services often provide the glue that holds together the array of federal, state, and local programs as well as the lives of older individuals and their caregivers. These services may provide the means by which an individual can remain independent in the community without total reliance on family. Client advocacy may also be provided, especially for clients unable or insufficiently informed to advocate for themselves (Gutowski & Koshel, 1982). Federal support

---

- Winning in Price Competition

- Quick Turnover of Clientele

- Providing Maximum Service Units for Minimum Cost

- Unbundling Services

- Elimination of Unprofitable Services
  (regardless of need)

- Attracting Paying Clients
  (avoid adverse selection)

- Avoiding "No-Pay" & "Low-Pay" Clients

Figure 12.1. The Cultural Revolution in Nonprofits

has long represented the lifeblood of social service providers. Federal commitment to social services remains an essential element in social service availability and access. Providers must rely on sources other than Medicare and Medicaid, however. Social services are not generally funded under Medicare and are therefore not universally available to elderly and disabled persons who may need such services (Lindeman & Pardini, 1983). An exception is the very limited "medical social service" benefit in home health under Medicare. In-home care and other services are funded under the federal/state Medicaid program, which is highly variable from state to state. Given that the Medicare and Medicaid contributions to the funding of social services are severely circumscribed, other federal sources of funding such as the Social Services Block Grant (SSBG) and Older Americans Act programs must also be relied upon.

The federal nurturing of social services for the aging and disadvantaged took off in 1965 and peaked in 1978. Between 1978 and 1981, there was a modest decline in federal support for social services, which weakened the foundation of community-based services and set the stage for future cuts to be imposed by the Reagan administration (Estes, 1991). Social services were cut more than 20%

during the first 2 years of the Reagan presidency under a policy designed to promote cuts in domestic programs, reduce federal responsibility, and increase family responsibility. The SSBG program, enacted as part of the 1981 Omnibus Budget Reconciliation Act, reduced funding levels in the former Social Security Title XX program and eliminated state matching and key reporting requirements. Funding under the Older Americans Act, initiated in 1965, also declined slightly in the early 1980s and has been held in check despite the growth of the older population and the demand on community service providers funded by federal programs (U.S. Senate, 1986a). Federal discretion for targeting social service funding was transferred to the state and local levels under the block grants. States that had previously assumed the greatest responsibility for federally aided entitlement programs were particularly hard hit, with combined cuts ranging from 10% to 50% (Chubb, 1985; Nathan, Doolittle, et al., 1984).

Between 1982 and 1987, cuts in federal aid to states in the health and human services (excluding Social Security) exceeded $530 million. The overall budget for social services between 1981 and 1987 rose by only 8.1%, well below the inflation rate. This situation compromised the ability of states and localities to maintain even the existing level of service available prior to 1981.

Effects of the Medicare PPS

As noted in Chapter 1, a number of studies focus on the short-term effects of the Medicare PPS, particularly in terms of the utilization and cost of hospital services (ASIM, 1985; Crane, 1986; DesHarnais et al., 1987; Eggers, 1987; Guterman et al., 1988; Heinz, 1986; Manard et al., 1988; ProPac, 1987b, 1988; Schramm & Gabel, 1988; Stark, 1987a; U.S. Senate, 1985). Few studies focus on the effects of the PPS on posthospital care, and they are generally limited to studies of Medicare-reimbursed services such as home health (Benjamin, 1986a; Bergthold, 1987; Chelimsky, 1985, 1987; Feder, Scanlon, & Hoffman, 1988; Kane, 1987; Kenney, 1991; Neu & Harrison, 1988; U.S. GAO, 1986; Van Gelder & Bernstein, 1986; Wood, 1984). Aside from the authors' investigations, there has been little documentation of the effect of the PPS on noninstitutional community-based service providers and, by extension, its impact on the elderly population needing or using those services.

Research on the effects of the PPS on posthospital care has consistently credited this Medicare policy with increasing the demand for postacute care. Neu and Harrison (1988) document the rise in the percentage of Medicare patients using the posthospital care services of nursing homes (SNFs) and home health care agencies as well as a small rise in the average number of home health visits following the implementation of the PPS (DesHarnais et al., 1987; Morrisey, Sloan, & Valvona, 1988; Van Gelder & Bernstein, 1986; Chapters 1, 6, and 8). Kenney (1991) reports that the PPS increased Medicare outlays for home health by approximately 25%, although the increase in the proportion of Medicare beneficiaries using home health services and in their average number of visits was relatively small. Growth in the proportion of home health care service users occurred primarily before and in the early implementation phase (1980 to 1984) of the PPS (Bishop & Karon, 1988; U.S. HCFA, 1987b). The average number of visits per user increased slightly between 1980 and 1983 (from 23 to 27) but declined (to 25) in 1985 (Kenney, 1991). As noted in Chapters 6 and 8, these trends no doubt reflect the imposition of stricter eligibility and reimbursement requirements on Medicare home health benefits as well as an increase in the number of claims denied reimbursement.

Five major findings emerged from the IHA study (1986, 1987; Introduction to this volume). The new DRG payment scheme, although aimed at acute care providers, had far-reaching effects. These effects were not, however, immediate nor were they experienced similarly or simultaneously by all community-based providers. The types of clients served, services offered, and ability to refer patients to appropriate providers all changed as a result of the new payment scheme.

Far-Reaching PPS Effects

The effects of the PPS were pervasive in that they were experienced by all posthospital providers between 1984 and 1986 (Figure 12.2). More than half of all seven provider types studied reported one or more effect, with almost all hospital discharge planners, nursing homes, and home health agencies affected. The repercussions of the PPS spread well beyond hospitals, for which the policy was intended, being experienced by both social and medical nonhospital service providers.

First and Second Generation Impacts

In response to an open-ended question asking respondents to name the policy that had most affected their organization between 1984 and 1987, the policies identified most frequently were the PPS and other Medicare policies (Table 12.1). Predictably, the effects of the policies included increased patient demand resulting from the earlier discharge from hospitals of elderly patients still needing some form of care. Increased difficulty in procuring Medicare reimbursement for services was another frequently cited effect of the new policies.

The force of the PPS was, however, neither immediately nor uniformly felt by all provider types (Table 12.1). The effects of the new hospital payment system were first experienced (1984-1986) by hospital discharge planners, nursing homes, home health agencies, and, to a much lesser degree, community mental health centers. The second generation of effects occurred a year later (between 1986 and 1987) for adult day care and hospice programs.

Adult day-care agencies reported receiving referrals from home health agencies for posthospital patients whose health care needs had not yet been met but whose Medicare benefits had been exhausted. Adult day-care agencies are not reimbursed by Medicare. Services provided by these agencies must be paid for privately or by Medicaid or limited state social service funds. Although the percentage of adult day-care centers reporting PPS effects is not large, there is an easily traceable line from the PPS to changes in referrals to services ranging from adult day care through home health care.

Types of Clients Served

Organizations most likely to receive patients immediately following hospital discharge (home health agencies, hospices, and nursing homes) more frequently reported, as expected, a change in their clientele than did other sample agencies (Chapter 4). The agency type most oriented toward the provision of social services—senior centers—however, also experienced changes in clientele, which they explicitly linked to the PPS. The majority of agencies reporting clientele changes noted that their clients were more frail, sicker, or in need of more acute care services (Chapter 3).

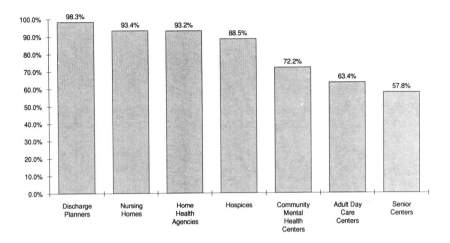

Figure 12.2. Reports of Any DRG Effect by Agency Type: Types Sorted by Proportions of Reports, 1986

SOURCE: Institute for Health & Aging DRG study, provider instruments (1986, 1987).

Services Offered

Changes in patient case mix due to the earlier discharge of older patients from hospitals were reflected in the service changes. For home health agencies, hospices, and nursing homes, the most frequently reported shifts were toward more acute high-tech care, skilled nursing or subacute nursing care, and antibiotic intravenous therapy. Senior centers were more frequently called upon for provision of information and referrals. Adult day-care centers were pressed to provide more direct supervision and rehabilitation therapy, and community mental health centers shifted toward more case management and services for the chronically mentally ill. In addition, a majority of providers reported changes in the units of service required by their clientele in response to the PPS.

Referral Ability

It was anticipated that providers would experience an increase in referrals from hospitals under the PPS (Table 12.2). It was not anticipated, however, that community providers would experience

TABLE 12.1   Providers Reporting DRGs and Medicare Policies as the Most
Important Policies Affecting Their Agencies, 1986 and 1987

	1986[a]		1987[b]	
Agency Provider Type	DRG (percentage)	Medicare (percentage)	DRG (percentage)	Medicare (percentage)
Discharge planners	90	11	62	12
Nursing homes	28	12	24	13
Home health agencies	37	41	13	34
Community mental health	6	0	0	0
Adult day care	0	0	13	26
Hospice programs	0	67	25	79
Senior centers	0	0	0	0

SOURCE: Data from Institute for Health & Aging DRG study, provider instruments (1986, 1987).
NOTE: Question on instrument: "Please tell me what policies, or interpretations of policy, have had the greatest impact on your agency in the past twelve months, and what that impact has been."
a. Data are for the 1984-1986 time period.
b. Data are for the 1986-1987 time period.

increased need to refer clients to hospitals and other community-care providers and difficulty in doing so. The majority of hospices, home health agencies, adult day-care centers, and nursing homes reported changes in their ability to refer patients. The increased difficulty in referring clients from community service providers to hospitals due to stricter hospital admission policies was the most frequently reported problem. New hospital policies made both admission and readmission more difficult.

About one third of the discharge planners noted the increased difficulty in successfully referring patients to posthospital care services after implementation of the PPS. Referral problems, in rank order, include greater difficulty in obtaining chore services, fewer resources available in general, and longer agency waiting lists. Of all the provider types studied, only nursing homes noted a positive change in referral ability. On the other hand, the home health agencies, hospices, adult day care, and community mental health and senior centers reporting negative changes or difficulty in referring clients to other services often also noted difficulty in securing places for their clients in nursing homes.

Conclusion

The research reported above documents several major trends, including the pervasive reach or trickle down of the Medicare hospital PPS on virtually all aspects of the community-based delivery system (Table 12.2). The effects of the PPS touched not only the hospitals but also senior centers, home health agencies, nursing homes, hospices, community mental health centers, and adult day-care centers. Although there was a lag in the effects on certain types of providers, all were affected. The pressures created by the PPS have contributed serious impediments to the ability of community providers to refer clients to each other and to and from hospitals. The increasing difficulty providers have in referring clients to services in the community raises questions of access to care.

Related to these problems is concern about the increasing attention given to informal caregiving as a means to control costs (Chapter 9). Barring a major federal initiative in long term care, the informal sector will be the next to feel the ripple in the shifting wave of responsibility for care of an increasingly large number of disabled and chronically ill older adults.

The data suggest that the community-based service system has been saturated with clients with heavy care needs who have filtered down from the hospital to home health agencies, nursing homes, hospices (where appropriate), and adult day-care centers. If patients continue to exit from hospitals with heavier care demands, the ability of the community to meet their needs is questionable. Service providers that receive posthospital clients have altered their service mix to reflect a population with heavier care needs. This shift causes concern about the ultimate effect of system changes on the future of care for the chronically ill in the community. The current situation suggests that difficult trade-offs are likely in trying to meet the acute care versus the chronic care needs of the elderly in the society.

Research to date has answered some questions raised about the effects of the PPS, DRGs, and cost containment on communities, agencies, and clients, but it has simultaneously raised questions about the long-term effects of current health care policy. Important issues include the way the changes identified in public policy and service demand will affect the capacity of nonprofit health and social

TABLE 12.2 Pecentage of Agencies Reporting DRG Effects, 1986 and 1987

| | Agency Type and Year | | | | | | | |
| | Discharge Planners | | Nursing Homes | | Hospices | | Community Mental Health Centers | |
Reported Effects	1986	1987	1986	1987	1986	1987	1986	1987
Changes in types of clients served	71.3	70.9	84.3	87.2	87.5	60.9	30.8	40.7
Shifts in types of service provided	68.9	a	55.2	55.2	75.0	56.5	33.3	27.5
Changes in units of service required	78.5	a	c	74.8	c	69.6	55.7	29.9
Changes in ability to refer to hospitals	b	b	30.5	25.9	58.3	40.0	43.3	38.6
Changes in referrals to other agencies	70.1	48.0	c	18.0	c	22.7	c	21.8
Changes in number of referrals from hospitals	b	b	c	52.2	81.8	82.6	d	d

SOURCE: Data from Institute for Health & Aging DRG study (1986, 1987).
a. Question not asked in 1987.
b. Question not asked of discharge planners.
c. Question not asked in 1986.
d. Question not asked of community mental health centers.

service agencies to provide needed services as well as the way the services ultimately available to older persons in the community and in the home will be structured.

Nonprofit health and social services grew dramatically between 1965 and 1980 with the help of federal funding. Tax status provisions shielded nonprofit providers from competition in the marketplace until the 1980s. As nonprofit health and social service agencies attempt to survive in the competitive mode, their traditional goals are influenced and shaped by considerations of price competition, profit making, market share, and averting adverse consequences to the bottom line. The current dilemma is that as nonprofit agencies are pressed to operate and to target and sell their services on the basis of market principles, they unintentionally contribute to their own legitimacy problems as institutions designed for charitable purposes (Chapter 2). Further, these changes affecting community service agencies are likely to be especially significant for low-income individuals, a large proportion of whom are old.

Eli Ginzberg's assessment of the health care field as "destabilized" (Ginzberg, 1986) is equally valid for long term care services. A serious question is whether the incentives to discharge the elderly from the hospital in the shortest possible period of time have inadvertently worsened access to care for elders who have not been hospitalized and who have a variety of nonmedical care needs. The issue is whether the changes in the delivery system reported throughout this volume have placed marginal (but mobile and ambulatory) older persons at a disadvantage in obtaining services important to their ability to remain in the community. Because of the lack of augmented federal funding for social services following the PPS, there has not been a shift in financing from costly hospital to community-care services. If the appropriate service delivery system for elders is redirected to serving the interests of hospital cost containment alone (i.e., early hospital discharge), elders may find themselves without access to necessary community services unless they can privately pay for them. Such trade-offs between social and medical services inevitably generate other costs such as the added cost of personal and informal care when formal service provision is not available. They may also generate added acute care costs when delay in receiving necessary care occurs and preventive or rehabilitative strategies are not available during a course of chronic illness. Attention to the supportive care of older individuals is requisite to the appropriate use of medical systems and institutions. Attempts to control expenditures must account for the total cost, including the cost of nonmedical services and particularly the cost of informal care necessitated by cost-containment policies.

What will the future bring? Judging by the past, the no-care zone will likely widen. Subsequent chapters consider this possibility along with alternatives. The next chapter describes the response of state and local policy elites to fiscal crisis.

CHAPTER 13

Policy Elites and Fiscal Crisis

In 1987 we had some ability to cope with fiscal constraints through cost containment and program restructuring. . . . [Now] we've done all the restructuring we can do and we still have shortfalls.
State Medicaid Director (in Estes, Binney, & Carrell, 1992, p. 13)

With the devolution of federal responsibility for social and health policy to state and local governments, policy efforts have become more consequential at these levels for older persons who need community-based services (Estes, 1991; Estes & Gerard, 1983; Estes et al., 1983). An exploration of changes and conditions in state and local community-based long term care systems from the perspective of "elite" actors—key administrators of public programs and charitable organizations, policy analysts, and provider trade association executives—is instructive. State and local elites surveyed in 1987 and 1991 reported substantial levels of unmet long term care need, particularly in the areas of home and community-based services. Providers and policymakers expressed a general sense of weariness and pessimism regarding the ability of public programs to keep pace with growing demands. Persisting fiscal and budgetary constraints, exhaustion of available streamlining measures, and the need to address other important social problems are major factors contributing to the difficulties being faced by state and local long term care programs.

NOTE: The authors of this chapter are David S. Carrell and Carroll L. Estes (with Carolinda Douglass).

In 1983, 22.7 million people had chronic conditions that limited their ability to carry out major daily activities. Of these, 6.6 million (29%) were 65 years of age or over. The risk of having such disabilities is 1 in 4 for an older person compared with less than 1 in 12 for the population under age 65 (National Center for Health Statistics [NCHS], 1986). Evidence suggests that, as people live longer, they will do so with more disability (Rice & LaPlante, 1988), creating greater demand for home and community-based care. Even under the most optimistic assumptions, the size of the disabled population over age 65 will increase significantly in the future (Manton, 1989). By one estimate, the number of persons over age 85, those most likely to need long term care for chronic disability, will more than double in the next 30 years, reaching 7.2 million in 2020 (Rivlin & Wiener, 1988). Although there has been progress in recent years in reducing premature death, there has been no corresponding progress in the prevention or control of the chronic diseases or disorders that cause disability (Guralnik & Schneider, 1990). Considering recent projections that 43% of persons who turned 65 in 1990 will enter a nursing home at some time before they die (Kemper & Murtaugh, 1991), the need for better alternatives to institutional care is substantial.

Socioeconomic correlates of disability among older persons underscore the importance of public policy in long term care. The prevalence of disability within the older population is substantially higher among the poor and minorities (Rowland & Lyons, 1991). For persons aged 65 and over, the probability of having limitations in major daily activities is inversely related to family income. Of persons with family incomes above $35,000, 18% report such disability; the proportion increases for successively lower income categories, reaching nearly one third (31%) among those with family incomes below $10,000 (NCHS, 1986). The significance of this association for policy is underscored by the distribution of disability in absolute terms. More older persons with disability are in the lowest income category (below $10,000) than in all higher income categories combined (NCHS, 1986).

As the number of persons with chronic disability grows, individual preferences for home and community-based care remains high. Older persons strongly prefer in-home care to all other alternatives when they are unable to care for themselves (Cetron, 1985; McAuley & Blieszner, 1985). It is not surprising, as the U.S. Department of Health and Human Services found in the 1982 National Long-Term Care Survey, that 95% of chronically disabled older persons living in the community express the desire to stay out of a nursing home as long as possible (Rivlin & Wiener, 1988). This strong preference for in-home care is attributable to its positive impact on quality of life. Home care by formal service providers preserves independence and reduces the sense of being a burden to one's family (Doty, 1986).

Public demand for an expanded government role in providing home and community-based services is likely to grow as the overall need for care increases. Chronically disabled persons as well as their family members strongly favor expanded public financing of in-home care services. Nationally, 87% of people polled in 1988 expressed support for a federal long-term home care program for chronically ill and disabled older persons (Louis Harris & Associates, 1988). Popular support for public programs that enable the chronically ill to avoid institutionalization is strong even if it means higher costs (R. L. Associates, 1987).

The needs and preferences for home and community-based care expressed by U.S. residents are not unique. Comparable demographic and disability patterns in Britain have generated similar needs and preferences. Older persons in the United Kingdom express strong desires to avoid dependence on children for care needs resulting from chronic disabilities. They also believe responsibility for their care in later life should shift toward the public sector (Chapter 14; Daatland, 1990; Phillipson, 1992; Salvage, Vetter, & Jones, 1989; Waerness, 1990; West, Illsley, & Kelman, 1984).

Elite Survey

By virtue of their unique positions in government and the health industry, respondents interviewed in the Institute for Health & Aging (IHA) elite surveys reported here (IHA, 1981, 1986, 1987, 1991) provide valuable and otherwise unobtainable insights into the issues confronting existing care systems. In fulfilling their day-to-day obligations, state and local elites possess an intimate familiarity with the environment—historical, current, and emergent—in which long term care services are delivered. This context includes state and federal fiscal, social, and health policies; conditions and changes in the provider industry; and the nature and extent of individual needs within the community. As several chapters in this volume demonstrate, the broader context in which providers of care operate can have profound consequences for quality and cost of, and access to aging services (Chapter 10). Key informants are the most accessible and often the only available source of evidence regarding the causal connections between this context and the provision of care services.

The Institute for Health & Aging (IHA) study in California, Florida, Pennsylvania, Texas, and Washington provides insights into the functioning of long term care systems within the boundaries of five states and their respective regions and, to a lesser extent, the country as a whole. In 1990, 31% of the nation's older population—nearly 10 million persons aged 65 or over—lived in these five states, and this proportion will increase during the 1990s (U.S. Bureau of the Census, 1990c). These states also have been identified as pacesetters in their respective regions (Harrington, Estes, Lee, & Newcomer, 1985; Newcomer, Benjamin, & Estes, 1983). Substantial variations across the five states with respect to demographic characteristics, health and welfare expenditures, and government approaches to addressing long term care needs (Newcomer, Estes, Benjamin, Swan, & Peguillan, 1981; Swan et al., 1982; Chapters 10 and 11) enhance the generalizability of the findings beyond the sample states.

Key informant data were collected in two studies conducted by the IHA in 1987 (Estes, Wood, et al., 1988) and 1991. Within each state, a purposive key informant sample was drawn from both the public and the private sectors. In the earlier survey, a sample of advocacy groups in aging was also interviewed. The professional and institutional affiliations of the informants in both surveys are reported in Table 13.1. Difference in the number and types of informants contacted and in some of the questions posed in the two studies are attributable to differences in the primary research questions they address. As described in the Introduction, response rates for the elite survey are exceptionally high (96% for the 1987 survey and 94% for the 1991 survey). Survey data are examined regarding the effects on long term care services of fiscal constraints, the supply of and access to aging services, and structural changes in local and state policy.

Data are analyzed with comparisons across time periods, states, and informant types. Because the number of each type is relatively small (Table 13.1), informants are aggregated for comparative purposes by their affiliation with the private or public sectors. This dichotomy is meaningful both theoretically, given the differing aims and interests of the two sectors, and empirically, as indicated in previous IHA studies (Estes, Wood, et al., 1988; Swan et al., 1982). Private sector informants include long term care provider or trade associations and United Way representatives. Public sector informants include representatives of area agencies and state units on aging (AAAs and SUAs), state legislative staff, and state and local health and social service program administrators. Advocacy groups surveyed in 1987 are examined separately as the third type of informant. Fiscal intermediaries were not included

TABLE 13.1   Key Informant Survey Sample Characteristics by Survey Year

	Number of Respondents	
Key Informant Type	*1987*	*1991*
Public sector:		
area agencies on aging	22	11
state units on aging	5	5
legislative staff/policy analysts	10	4
Social Service Block Grant administrators	5	2
state Medicaid offices	—	5
mayors' offices	8	—
legislative budget analysts	3	—
Private sector:		
nursing home trade associations	3	10
home health trade associations	4	5
hospital trade associations	—	5
adult day-center trade associations	—	5
nurse associations	—	5
United Way foundations	—	9
aging interest/advocacy groups	23	—
fiscal intermediaries	—	3
Total	83	69
(response rate)	(96%)	(94%)

SOURCE: Data from Institute for Health & Aging DRG study (1987) and Community-Based Long Term Care study (1991).

in either the public or the private sector groupings because of their unique relationship to both sectors.

Fiscal Constraints and Long Term Care

The implications of governmental budgetary constraints for long term care services are of widespread interest and concern (Estes et al., 1983; Harrington, Newcomer, et al., 1985; Weissert et al., 1988). State and local fiscal and budgetary problems are a product of political and economic trends spanning more than a decade. Most states, which have inherited progressively greater responsibility for health and social services since the beginning of the Reagan administration's new federalism campaign in the early 1980s (Estes et al., 1983), are struggling to meet expanding health and social service needs at a time when the lackluster national economy and fiscal conservatism have diminished available tax revenues. Between 1980 and 1990, state Medicaid outlays as a proportion of total state expenditures increased more than 50% and continued to grow in the 1990s at a 10% annual rate of increase. In 1991, 32 states spent more than anticipated on these programs (NGA & NASBO, 1991). A widespread sense that Medicaid budgets are out of control and that growth has been driven largely by long term care expenditures for older persons raises serious questions about the impact of continuing fiscal constraints on the LTC system (Estes, Binney, & Correll, 1992).

To assess the fiscal context of state and local long term care policy, key informants were queried regarding the fiscal and budgetary outlook in the states examined. Substantial constraints were reported by state and local elites in both 1987 and 1991 (Figure 13.1), and the fiscal situation appears to have worsened during this 4-year period. In 1987, nearly half of all informants (46%) reported poor or very poor fiscal conditions. Fully two thirds reported fiscal conditions to be either quite or extremely limiting by 1991. One informant observed that since 1987 fiscal conditions have worsened each year at both the state and the federal levels. Another notable difference between the two periods is the near disappearance of the view that fiscal conditions were moderate, a view held by 29% of respondents in 1987 but only 2% in 1991. One trade association executive summed up the situation succinctly, observing that most states are simply broke.

State-level rankings on perceived fiscal constraint were similar for 1987 and 1991 with the exception of Texas. Ranked first in terms of perceived constraints in 1987, Texas fell to the midpoint among the five states 4 years later. Although Texas has begun a mild recovery from the earlier recession associated with slumping oil prices, the state's fiscal problems persist, and its health and welfare spending remains generally low. In 1991, respondents from California, one of the few states in which welfare benefits are indexed to inflation, reported considerably higher levels of constraints than other states. The extremely limiting fiscal condition cited by respondents is not surprising, considering the strict limits imposed on county budgets by the taxpayers' revolt of the 1980s. Proposition 13 forced California to absorb many of the financial burdens that depleted county treasuries can no longer meet. In 1991, the state withheld the cost-of-living adjustment for welfare benefits and seriously contemplated reducing welfare expenditures for the first time in recent history. Washington and Pennsylvania reported the lowest levels of constraint in 1991; Florida and Texas ranked in the middle. That Wash-

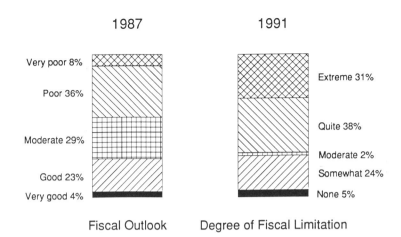

Fiscal Outlook   Degree of Fiscal Limitation

Figure 13.1. Fiscal Constraints for Aging Services by Survey Year

SOURCE: Institute for Health & Aging DRG study (1987) and Community-Based Long Term Care study (1991).

NOTE: Question on 1987 instrument: "In your opinion what is the fiscal outlook for your state for the coming year? Would you say it is (1) very good, (2) good, (3) moderate, (4) poor, or (5) very poor?" Question on 1991 instrument: "Thinking about current fiscal and budgetary constraints at the state level as they relate to community-based services for the elderly, would you say these constraints are (1) not very limiting at all, (2) somewhat limiting, (3) moderately limiting, (4) quite limiting, or (5) extremely limiting?"

ington and Pennsylvania report lesser fiscal strain is not surprising. Washington enjoys a comparatively robust economy and a tradition of commitment to health and welfare programs (Chapter 11). In Pennsylvania, a state lottery provides a dedicated source of funding for aging services. Nevertheless, even in these two states, fiscal constraints are moderately limiting.

Key informants from the private sector report slightly higher levels of fiscal constraint than their public sector counterparts, a pattern consistent in both 1987 and 1991. Although not statistically significant, the difference in perceptions between these two sectors is likely to be attributable to their respective positions within the long term care delivery system. Public sector officials represent mainly the supply end of the public financing chain, where fiscal constraints are reflected in overall budgetary targets and anticipated aggregate caseload. Private sector informants, on the other hand, represent mainly the providers of services, which in some senses more directly experience the effects of fiscal austerity. To the extent that fiscal constraints translate into potential or actual threats to the viability of agencies or into unmet needs within the community, those working in the private sector may be more sensitive to economic barriers to service delivery. Consistent with this interpretation is the finding that in 1987 interest group respondents (including advocates for the aged), who are most knowledgeable about services from the consumer or demand side, reported the highest levels of perceived fiscal constraint.

State and local outlooks for aging services, another topic addressed in the IHA surveys, reflect a general sense of pessimism and weariness brought on by years of persistent budgetary constraint, the absence of fiscal relief in the foreseeable future, and competing obligations to address the health and social service needs of other deserving groups in society. One public sector respondent explained that in 1987 there was some ability to cope with fiscal constraints through cost containment and program restructuring but that, after all the restructuring possible, there were still shortfalls. For these and related reasons, most elites (nearly two out of three) characterized the future outlook for aging services as moderate or very unfavorable in both 1987 and 1991. During this 4-year period, there was a doubling of the proportion of elites reporting a very unfavorable outlook in terms of capacity of funding levels to keep pace with growing demands, the prospects for program development, and other challenges (Figure 13.2).

According to the 1987 survey, the outlook for aging services was similar across both states and key informant types. Between 1987 and 1991, the outlook for aging services worsened in two of the states and remained about the same in the three others. The greatest decline in outlook occurred in California, where one respondent characterized the picture as bleak, observing that health and human services are "sliding down hill." The future appeared similarly dismal in Florida, which, along with California, reported the least favorable outlook among the five states studied in 1991. Paralleling the pattern described above, private sector informants held somewhat more negative outlooks for aging services than their public sector counterparts in 1991. One representative of the nursing home industry conveyed the exasperation felt by many elites in noting that in his state the dismal outlook for aging services resulted not from a shortage of innovative thinking but simply from an absence of money.

In both surveys, higher levels of perceived fiscal constraint were positively associated with less optimistic outlooks for aging services. Although this relationship was not statistically significant in 1987, it had become so by 1991. From the perspective of knowledgeable infor-

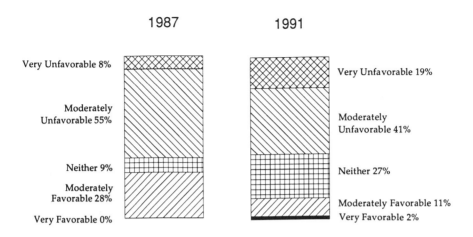

Figure 13.2. Outlook for Aging Services by Survey Year

SOURCE: Institute for Health & Aging DRG study (1987) and Community-Based Long Term Care study (1991).
NOTE: Question on 1987 and 1991 instruments: "Given current fiscal conditions, how would you assess the general outlook for health and social services for the elderly? Would you say the outlook is (1) very favorable, (2) favorable, (3) neither favorable nor unfavorable, (4) unfavorable, or (5) very unfavorable?" (Note: The response "neither favorable nor unfavorable" was a write-in category in the 1987 survey.)

mants, persistent budgetary austerity appears to present a greater threat to aging services in the 1990s than it did in the late 1980s.

Issues of intergenerational equity emerge whenever an attempt is made to meet growing needs for health and social services under conditions of severe fiscal constraint. To address these issues, key informants were asked to assess the vulnerability of aging services to cutbacks compared with programs for other groups in society (e.g., education, welfare, and other health services). Aging programs were perceived to be about as vulnerable to cutbacks as programs for other groups in both 1987 and 1991. Differences are observed between public and private sector informants, with those in the private sector reporting greater vulnerability for aging services than those in the public sector. Interest groups in aging (surveyed in 1987 only) reported the highest levels of vulnerability for aging programs of all respondent types that year. On average, interest groups considered aging services to be more vulnerable to cutbacks than other groups.

The most striking change regarding program vulnerability observed in the two surveys is Pennsylvania's shift from an extremely

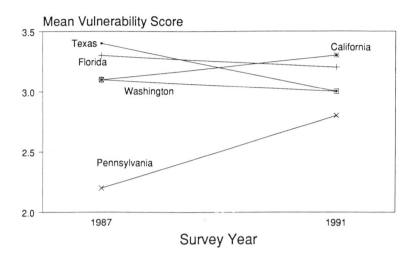

Survey Year

Figure 13.3. Vulnerability of Aging Programs to Cuts by State and Survey Year

SOURCE: Institute for Health & Aging DRG study (1987) and Community-Based Long Term Care study (1991).
NOTE: Question on 1991 instrument: "Considering current fiscal and budgetary realities at the state level, in your view how vulnerable to cutbacks are health and human services for the elderly compared to these services for other groups in your community? Would you say they are (1) much less, (2) less, (3) about the same, (4) more, or (5) much more vulnerable?" (Note: The wording on the 1981 and 1987 instruments is substantially the same as on the 1991 instrument.) Overall vulnerability scores for each state were computed as the mean of responses from each state using the numeric codes shown above.

supportive environment vis-à-vis aging services to one on a par with the vulnerability reported in other states (Figure 13.3). Pennsylvania's outlier status in 1987 is attributable to its strong commitment to aging services (Spohn et al., 1988) and the presence of a large and dedicated source of revenue to finance them—state lottery proceeds. Although the funding stream still exists, several factors may account for weakened support for aging services in Pennsylvania. One is the growing sense that health care expenditures, including state-funded coverage of prescription drugs for older persons, are out of control. Between 1987 and 1991, Pennsylvania's Medicaid expenditures nearly doubled. Compounding these budgetary concerns is the impact of congressionally mandated expansion of Medicaid eligibility criteria in 1989. Though the mandate largely has been ignored in Pennsylvania and some other states, it enlarges the state liability to provide free unlimited health care services for certain categories of low-income pregnant women and children who were previously ineligible for Medicaid coverage. In 1991, child health advocates in Pennsylvania brought the first lawsuit against any state to seek enforcement of "every dimension of the children's health care system as Congress mandated it" (Hinds, 1991, p. A20). The dreary backdrop to these spending issues in Pennsylvania is the 8.2% revenue shortfall for fiscal year 1991, the fourth largest state budget deficit in the country (National Conference of State Legislatures [NCSL], 1990). Despite aggressive efforts to avoid cutbacks and preserve essential program funding, fiscal realities in Pennsylvania have resulted in increased program vulnerability as reported by key informants.

The vulnerability of aging programs in 1987 and 1991 occurs within a broader historical setting. This context is examined across three different periods, the 1987 and 1991 surveys already described and a much earlier 1981 survey conducted by IHA in 10 states and 32 communities (Swan et al., 1982). As shown in Table 13.2, the perceptions of provider trade associations concerning the vulnerability of aging services in 1991 are nearly identical to those held a decade before, in the early years of the nation's fiscal crisis. Area agencies on aging (AAAs) demonstrate a growing sense of the vulnerability of aging programs over the same 10-year period. While three fourths of AAAs in 1981 considered aging programs to be relatively less vulnerable to cutbacks than other programs, this proportion declined steadily over the three time points, reaching a low of 27% in 1991. Conversely, the proportion of AAAs reporting greater vulnerability for aging programs increased between the earlier surveys (1981 and 1987) and the 1991 survey. Paralleling these changes, an increasing vulnerability of aging programs to cutbacks between 1981 and 1987 was reported by interest groups.

In general, elites surveyed in 1991 reported aging programs to be receiving slightly less than their "fair share" of public resources compared with programs for other groups in society. A solid plurality (45%) views the current distribution as fair. Several respondents, however, qualified this assessment by noting that it was *fairness of equal deprivation*. Among remaining respondents, those reporting aging programs to be receiving less than their fair share outnumbered those holding the opposite view by a 2-to-1 margin. This pattern of opinions was observed in both the public and the private sectors and across states, with one notable exception. Pennsylvanians reported that, on average, older persons were receiving more than their fair share of state resources in 1991. While this should not be interpreted as evidence of greed or insensitivity toward the needs of others (indeed, advocates for aging

TABLE 13.2   Relative Vulnerability of Aging Programs by Survey Year and Key Informant type

| | Survey Year | N | Relative Vulnerability of Aging Programs | |
			Less or Much Less (percentage)	More or Much More (percentage)
Trade associations	1981	45	27	38
	1987	—	—	—
	1991	30	24	38
Area agencies on aging	1981	32	72	19
	1987	22	55	14
	1991	11	27	36
Aging interest groups	1981	84	24	44
	1987	23	14	77
	1991	—	—	—

SOURCE: Institute for Health & Aging Fiscal Crisis study (1982; 1981 data), DRG study (1987), and Community-Based Long Term Care study (1991).
NOTE: Question on 1991 instrument: "Considering current fiscal and budgetary realities at the state level, in your view how vulnerable to cutbacks are health and human services for the elderly compared to these services for other groups in your community? Would you say they are (1) much less, (2) less, (3) about the same, (4) more, or (5) much more vulnerable?" (Note: The wording of this question on the 1981 and 1987 instruments is substantially the same as on the 1991 instrument.)

services cooperated with state policy makers in determining where $50 million in aging service cuts should be made), it suggests that levels of relative deprivation among other deserving groups in Pennsylvania are more pressing. Elite responses regarding fair share reflect the need to make difficult choices in the allocation of resources as the pie of Pennsylvania resources for human services is shrinking and recent Medicaid mandates for inclusion of all the poor (a surviving provision of the Medicare Catastrophic Health Care bill) stretch state dollars to the limit. Pennsylvania aside, 1991 views on questions of fair share are comparable to those from the 1981 IHA survey (Swan et al., 1982), indicating little change over the decade in perceived fairness of allocation patterns among aging and other public programs.

Unmet Needs and Underserved Clients

A frequently proclaimed advantage of the new federalism is its potential to allow state and local governments to concentrate their attention and energies on matters of local need and concern. Nowhere has this promise been more elusive than in the area of home and community-based aging services. While public opinion consistently and overwhelmingly supports the expansion of government-financed long term care (Louis Harris & Associates, 1988; R. L. Associates, 1987), the record of states and localities in meeting these needs continues to fall short.

Home and community-based long term care services are consistently identified by state and local elites as the most important area of unmet need. For example, shortages in in-home services, such as in personal care and homemaker/chore services, were identified by 43% of respondents in 1987 and 38% in 1991 (Table 13.3). Transportation services, which are instrumental to obtaining access to many other services, were the next most significant area of need in both periods. The unmet needs reported in these surveys are consistent with findings of the 1984 National Long Term Care Survey indicating that more than one third of disabled older persons living in the community have unmet daily needs (Manton, 1989).

Deficiencies in aging services were further assessed with regard to current supplies of specific types of long term care services. Fully 60% of state and local elites reported a service undersupply in 5 or more service areas from a list of 11 (Figure 13.4). The most common areas of service shortage were caregiver support services, transportation, adult day centers, and community mental health services. Thus, even in supporting the informal care system, widely considered a smart investment, state and local governments encounter great difficulty meeting the needs of their older populations.

A cruel but increasingly familiar feature of state and local long term care programs is their inability to respond adequately to the needs of the poor. When asked to identify the type of older persons with unmet needs within their respective states and communities, more than 60% of elite informants identified those with limited economic resources. The prevalence of service deficiencies for low-income persons reveals serious gaps in the implementation of the safety-net principle and also calls into question the workability of solutions heavily reliant on the private sector. The increasing proportion of providers operating as for-profit enterprises (Chapters 2 and 6) will reinforce the natural tendencies of these businesses to concentrate on the types of services and clients that offer the greatest financial return, doing little to alleviate the care needs of the poor. Other types of older persons reported to have significant unmet needs include those with special needs, such as the frail, minorities,

TABLE 13.3   Most Significant Unmet Needs in Aging Services by Survey
Year

Most Significant Unmet Need in Aging Services	1987		1991	
	Percentage	Rank	Percentage	Rank
In-home services	43	1	38	1
Transportation	25	4	22	2
Affordable care	37	3	19	5
Housing	37	3	19	5
General care services	9	6	19	5
Respite care	6	7	13	6
Adult day care	5	10	11	7
Nutrition/meals	5	10	8	9
Case management	5	10	8	9
Institutional care	9	6	5	10
Mental health services	1	11	5	10

SOURCE: Institute for Health & Aging DRG study (1987) and Community-Based Long Term Care study (1991).
NOTE: Question on 1987 and 1991 instruments: "In your opinion, what are the most significant unmet needs, if any, for services among the elderly in your state?" (Up to three open-ended responses were recorded.)

women, those living outside metropolitan areas, and those with emotional or cognitive problems.

Conclusion

The survey results reported above indicate that, despite the efforts of many states and localities to improve their long term care programs over the past decade, little progress has been made. Severe fiscal constraints have collided with growing demands from a variety of population groups for health and social services to create a situation that can only be characterized as bleak. In many instances, programs currently in place are not keeping pace with current levels of demand.

Under such conditions, improvements in service offerings and expansion of eligibility criteria are simply out of the question. Evidence of the increasing vulnerability of aging services to serious cutbacks, even in Pennsylvania, a longstanding leader in this area of public policy, is disquieting. While many states and localities have, over the past decade and a half, attempted to cope with budgetary constraints through efficiency-oriented restructuring of programs and

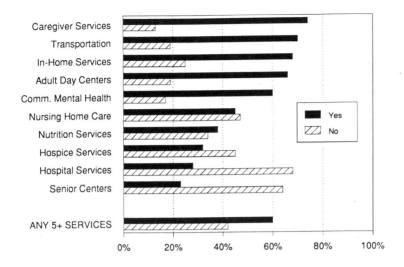

Figure 13.4. Aging Services in Short Supply, 1991

SOURCE: Institute for Health & Aging DRG study (1987) and Community-Based Long Term Care study (1991).

NOTE: Question on instrument: "From your perspective, are any of the following services for the elderly in short supply in your state? Please try to answer yes or no for each of the following: (a) nursing home care, (b) home health services, (c) hospice services, (d) adult day care, (e) senior centers, (f) community mental health centers, (g) hospital services, (h) homemaker/chore services, (i) meals programs, (j) transportation, (k) caregiver services, and (l) other." Note: The percentages for "yes" and "no" for the category "Any 5+ Services" indicate the percentage of respondents recording 5 or more "yes" responses and 5 or more "no" responses. Because this question addresses 11 types of services, some respondents contributed to both columns, yielding a combined percentage that exceeds 100%.

cost-containment measures, there is an emerging sense that a period that can only be described as grave is imminent. After 15 years of fiscal austerity, the current era of advanced retrenchment is characterized by a situation in which virtually all opportunities for program restructuring and budgetary containment have been exploited, yet care needs continue to grow.

As these conditions persist, the suffering of the poor will be perpetuated. In the absence of fundamental change in the current long term care system, those most vulnerable are not only the poor but the middle class as well. That most people will be asked to bear the cost of securing long term care services without government assistance is daunting, particularly in view of the potential $30,000 to $50,000 annual price tag that will surely bankrupt the average family.

Given this outlook, it is understandable that grantmakers and experts in a recent national survey identified the most pressing issues of the 1990s as (a) the financing of long term care, (b) access to and quality of health care, and (c) allocating resources to meet the needs of all generations (Greenberg, Gutheil, Parker, & Chernesky, 1991). The grantmakers' conclusion that the funding of community-based support services and health programs needs to be the highest priority in the next 5 years is consistent with the elite views of unmet needs and underserved older persons described above. The next chapter concerns how persons receiving services may, or may not, be empowered by the priorities of the elites.

CHAPTER **14**

Empowerment Imperative

The independence and control sought by the elderly individual . . . conflicts with the creation of dependency by all those offering care and support. . . . Will community care become a euphemism for a somewhat more benign but still dependency-creating paternalism?

Lloyd, 1991, p. 130

Social policy and community care will be shaped from now into the 21st century by sociodemographic changes, unresolved problems concerning health care access and costs, the biomedicalization of aging, and the social creation of dependency. The magnitude of these forces presents a major challenge to policymakers, philanthropy, and society to address these issues in new and strategic ways most beneficial to older persons.

Sociodemographics

Population dynamics constitute a significant element in the politics and economics of aging. Statistics underscore the well-documented demographic shift in U.S. society—the graying of the United States. The over-65 population will double in the next 40 years. With the population 85 years and older as the fastest growing age group, the number of oldest-old will increase more than threefold (Guralnik, Yanagishita, & Schneider, 1988). By 2050, older persons will constitute nearly one

---

NOTE: The authors of this chapter are Carroll L. Estes, Monica J. Casper, and Elizabeth A. Binney.

241

fourth of the population. The need for long term care will have tripled, and associated costs will have increased tenfold (Rice, 1986).

Population demographics will continue to be shaped by three scenarios occurring simultaneously (Verbrugge, 1989). In the scenario of tertiary prevention, costly and heroic medical measures save many persons from the brink of death, prolonging their lives without influencing their principal illnesses. In the scenario of secondary prevention, fatal chronic diseases are controlled (i.e., there is lower per case fatality), with the result that more people have disease for more years of their lives. This second is the scenario of longer life but worsening health. The scenario of primary prevention is typified by life-style changes that diminish comorbidity and the chances of acquiring disease.

The cumulative result of these three scenarios is an increase in "population frailty" as "death becomes less selective . . . [and] intrinsically non-robust people stay in the living population" (Verbrugge, 1989, p. 30). Significantly, from a policy viewpoint, none of these scenarios deals with nonfatal chronic conditions, conditions that are not likely to be as amenable to medical cure and life-style intervention as fatal diseases are. The profound societal issues raised have provided the basis for the social construction of a crisis mentality concerning old age. The 1980s have witnessed the social production and political usage of the demographics of aging, more appropriately described as "apocalyptic demography" (Robertson, 1991), to promote the idea that there is an "intergenerational war" (Binney & Estes, 1988). The conflict imagery thus evoked has been exploited by political interests and the media to drive a wedge between the generations and to effect domestic program cutbacks. A regrettable result is that elders have been falsely labeled by some as selfish "greedy geezers" who are compromising the future of all generations.

Unresolved Health Care Problems

The second force affecting the future of aging and community care is health care. Problems of health care access have risen significantly during the 1980s and 1990s, growing almost in geometric proportion to dramatic increases in the cost of medical care. Dimensions of the problem include escalating costs, declining coverage and access to care, gaping holes in private health insurance protection, and negligible long term care coverage. The relevance and importance of each of these problems to older persons is clear. If the issues of access and cost are not dealt with, they will eclipse the nation's chances of providing decent and humane community care for all U.S. residents, young and old.

The cost of health care in the United States exceeded $738 billion and was more than 13% of the nation's gross national product (GNP) in 1991. In spite of policies designed to promote competition and cost containment, costs continue to rise at several times the inflation rate. Commerce Department projections are for a cost jump of almost $100 billion between 1991 and 1992 alone, elevating health spending to 14% of the GNP. At the current rate, medical costs will exceed an astounding 30% of the nation's GNP by 2020.

In addition to dramatic cost increases, there has been a staggering rise of 24% in the total number of U.S. citizens uninsured for health care as well as a 40% increase in the number of uninsured children (Blendon & Edwards, 1991; U.S. Congressional Research Service, 1988). Serious problems of access to care touch the almost 16% of the U.S. population (35 to 37 million people) uninsured for health care and not covered by other programs. Another 50 to 60 million persons are seriously underinsured. When examined longitudinally over a 28-month time period, the number of people without a regular source of health insurance (i.e., without health insurance for at least one month) is much higher; it exceeds 60 million (28% of the population) and includes more than half of U.S. Hispanics and more than half of all young adults between 18 and 23 years of age (U.S. Bureau of the Census, 1990b).

On average, elders pay more than 18% of their health costs out of pocket, consuming 4.5 months of their entire annual Social Security income (U.S. House of Representatives, 1990). Projected to rise to 20% by 2000, out-of-pocket costs for elders rose more than twice as fast as the average monthly Social Security payment between 1983 and 1989. These out-of-pocket costs now exceed the amount ($2,394) paid by Medicare (U.S. House of Representatives, 1990). Direct personal payments by older persons are high because Medicare covers less than half of the costs of their health care, and these costs are inversely related to income and ability to pay.

For older women, out-of-pocket health costs exceed $1,800 a year, representing a particular burden. Medicare covers only an average of 33% of the health care costs of single older women living alone. It is estimated that these women pay as much as 42% of their income out of pocket for health care annually (ICF, 1985). Out-of-pocket medical costs for elders will continue to increase throughout the 1990s because congressional budget agreements increased out-of-pocket Medicare beneficiary costs by $350 million in 1991 alone and more than $10 billion over the subsequent 5 years (U.S. Senate, 1991).

The life chances of elders (longevity, health, and well-being) are strongly influenced by gender, race, ethnic status, and income (Estes & Rundall, 1992). Although life expectancy is higher for women, older persons who are women, minorities, and/or with low incomes tend to have more health problems and higher health care costs than those who are men, white, and/or with higher incomes. It is not surprising that problems of rising costs and difficulties in access to care are compounded for the poor, minorities, and women.

Biomedicalization of Aging

The biomedicalization of aging is the third force affecting the future of aging and community care. It is reflected in the tendency to think of old age as a disease and aging as a medical problem that can be alleviated, if not eradicated, through the "magic bullets" of medical science. This view places medicine, with its focus on individual organic pathology and medical interventions, in charge of old age and associated policies. With physicians in control of the definition and treatment of old age, aging is socially constructed as a process of decremental physical decline, and the needs of the elderly are defined largely in terms of acute care services. This biomedicalization has affected all facets of the aging field and its development, including scientific research and the knowledge base, the status and work of the professions in the field, and public policy and opinion (Estes, 1979; Estes & Binney, 1989). The biomedicalization of aging contributes to the current surfeit of high-tech and high-cost illness care, while essential attention and resources are often diverted from more appropriate and efficacious solutions to the problems of aging. With this view, not only are the chronic illness and long term care needs of the population given short shrift but so also are significant aspects of the broader social dimensions of aging, including housing, income, and support for personal care and other assistance that would enable older persons to live out their lives with dignity.

Social Creation of Dependency

As a result of changes occurring during the prior decade, the 1990s began with a challenged, weakened, and transformed system of community care. The apparent inadequacy of the existing system has created problems for elders living in the community and their families as well as for the public, for employers, and for government. These problems are made more serious by the approaches that have characterized public policy and philanthropy and that have dominated care of the elderly—approaches that have simultaneously financed and institutionalized the medicalization of care, challenged the charitable impulse in nonprofit service delivery, and fostered the dependency of elders.

The problem of dependency among the elderly needs to be understood in terms of its origins. Dependency as an inherently social product (Estes, 1979; Townsend, 1981; Walker, 1980) can easily be understood in terms of the effects of public policy. For example, without Social Security, older persons as a group would be impoverished—not because of lack of foresight but because the economy is organized according to differential rewards for productive labor, from which elders are generally and systematically excluded via retirement (Estes et al., 1984, p. 71).

As a social product, dependency is constructed by a multitude of social forces: (a) social policies and practices that have permitted age discrimination and, until recently, mandatory retirement; (b) the lower incomes of persons in retirement; (c) the declining income of persons with increasing age; and (d) the treatment of functional debility and illness in old age as acute medical care problems rather than in terms of providing social and personal support in the home and community; and (e) the discrimination and exclusion of elders from multiple arenas of social life accompanying the losses of retirement, widowhood, and the death of age peers. Dependency is also produced by (f) low self-esteem and lack of confidence resulting from the stigmatized status of older persons (Rodin, 1989) and (g) asymmetrical power relations between older persons and the professional caregivers who provide services to them (Estes, 1979; Phillipson & Walker, 1986). In these and other ways, professionals and service providers have functioned as moral overseers (Zola, 1975) who shape and manipulate the behavior of elderly people (and others). This process is seen at its worst in the authoritarian regimes that operate inside nursing homes and in some hospital wards, residential care homes, and wherever there is belittling and demeaning behavior of caregivers to elders.

There is a long and venerable literature on medicine as a form of social control that underscores the role of physicians as gatekeepers who have immense power to certify illness and eligibility for valued services and benefits (Ehrenreich & Ehrenreich, 1978; Friedson, 1970; Parsons, 1964). The dilemmas of the power and dependency of doctor-patient relationships are nowhere more evident than in the field of aging. Social policy and professional practice in aging may combine to produce an analogue to the notion of iatrogenesis (Illich, 1976), or doctor-induced illness. Socially induced dependency is fostered through unequal professional practitioner-client relationships between elderly persons and their caregivers, particularly where the emphasis is on social management or control of the older person rather than on opportunities for rehabilitation and empowerment.

Community long term care services are thus more than systems for distributing services; they are systems of social relationships that reflect and bolster the power inequity between experts and lay persons and between providers and recipients of services. Because service strategies foster the stigmatization of elderly clients as recipients in need, older persons may be blamed and treated as having failed to assume responsibility for their health and lives (Estes, 1979).

The combination of these four trends means that a significant and growing financial burden falls on an increasing number of elders and their families, particularly those who are chronically ill and in need of long term care. The empowerment imperative stems from the knowledge that the acute care model currently incorporated into health policy is woefully inadequate to deal with the largely social and personal care needs of millions of elders. An equally important objection to the medical model is that it simultaneously fosters the domination of care by professional experts and promotes the dependency of elders (Estes & Binney, 1989). The social and economic costs of an extravagant, depersonalized, and technologically and medically driven system of care are unaffordable. Instead, explicit attention must be given to interventions designed to promote the fullest feasible capacity of elders for self-esteem, personal control, and action. The current design of health policy manufactures dependency of elders through iatrogenesis and unequal power relations between patients and care providers.

Community Care

Serious considerations of public policy and community care must take into account the state of the existing system of service provision in view of the dramatic and rapid changes of the 1980s and 1990s. Policy changes, budget cuts, cost containment, and deepening fiscal austerity in the states and localities have challenged and compromised the capacity of both formal and informal caregivers to address the community-care needs of elders.

In community studies examining the effects of public policy on local service delivery for the elderly during the 1981-1987 period (IHA, 1986, 1987), several major waves of change have been identified (Chapter 12). First, a period of state and local fiscal crisis and taxpayer revolt occurred in the late 1970s and early 1980s, including the initial Reagan years, 1981-1982. During this period, the primary response of community agencies was to manage the budget cutbacks by uniformly applying cuts across the system and across all elements within their own individual agencies. The second period was one of cost containment coinciding with the implementation of the PPS. Occurring between 1983 and 1984, market competition and privatization became paramount. This period also marked the initiation of a cultural revolution in the service provision of nonprofits (Chapters 2 and 12). Provider response at the community level was dramatic, as reflected in the major restructuring and transformation of community care during the 1982-1984 period (Estes, 1986; Estes & Wood, 1986). In the third wave of change, a period continuing from 1984 to the current time, providers are fully participating in a rapidly changing and highly competitive service market. Provider decisions are dominated by the realities and discipline of the market, and the weakness of social services is measured in terms of market profitability and reimbursability in the delivery system regardless of evidence of a growing unmet need for personal care and other social support services.

Overall changes in local service delivery include weeding out weaker, less competitive nonprofit community-based agencies; consolidation and concentration within and across provider industries, with freestanding independent agencies facing especially tough survival questions; dramatic growth in the number and influence of for-profit providers; and blurred boundaries between nonprofit and proprietary service organizations (Chapters 2 and 12).

The cultural revolution in nonprofit service delivery has imposed a new set of values on community services: winning in price competition, quick turnover of clientele, policies and strategies to provide the greatest number of service units at the lowest cost, the unbundling of services, eliminating unprofitable services regardless of need, attracting clients who can pay for services, and avoiding the "adverse selection" of no-pay and low-pay clients (Figure 12.1). These values are more familiar to the medical care industry than to the traditional local voluntary social service provider. The resulting behavioral changes have occurred in an environment replete with ideological and political attacks on nonprofits (Estes, Binney, & Bergthold, 1988).

As detailed in Chapter 2, these attacks have been advanced on several fronts. There are an increasing number of (a) questions concerning the right of nonprofit organizations to their special tax status and tax subsidies from government, (b) accusations that nonprofits are not meeting their obligations to fulfill a charitable mission, and (c) contentions about the unfairness of the competition from nonprofit organizations. Nonprofits have even been characterized as illegitimate in a capitalist system. Political attacks have been manifested in challenges to the right of particular entities to tax-exempt status, to charitable deductions, to the property tax exemption, to unrelated business income, and to postal subsidies. There have also been efforts to impose severe restrictions on lobbying, educational activities, and other advantages of nonprofits. The unfortunate predicament of nonprofit providers reflects an interesting contradiction during a period in which the ideology and rhetoric of the Reagan and Bush administrations argue that the private and voluntary sector must assume more responsibility while the government assumes less.

The majority of community-care workers (paid and unpaid) who provide long term care are in the voluntary sector. As noted in Chapter 2, nonprofits constitute more than half of all social services delivered and almost half of all community health services (Hodgkinson & Weitzman, 1989; Salamon, 1987b). As a consequence, the difficulties currently confronting the nonprofit sector vitally affect services used and needed by the elderly. The problems faced by the voluntary sector spill over in important ways into the provision of long term care. The serious and looming economic problems of the 1990s, the federal deficit, extremely high interest payments on the debt, and the unabated and alarming escalation of health care costs assure that pressures on limited government resources will remain intense. Because the service sector that provides assistance to elders is largely nonprofit in nature, an important question concerns the commitment of private philanthropy to aging services.

The Role of Philanthropy

Foundations and corporations are more active in the field of aging than they were 10 years ago (Schreter, 1990). Nevertheless, Ginzberg

(1987) argues that foundations have been displaced by health care lobbyists, legislators, and the National Institutes of Health and that leaders of private philanthropy have been "minor actors" in "leveraging and transforming the extant health care system" (Ginzberg, 1987, p. 134). Several factors account for this apparent paradox with respect to the role of philanthropy in aging.

In the years from 1978 to 1982, foundation spending for the elderly approximated $115 million, less than $1/2$ of $1/10$ of 1% of government expenditure (Burden Foundation, 1986). Between 1983 and 1987, nonprofit funding for aging increased by 75%, from $39 million to $68 million, and the total number of aging grants increased 44% from 762 to 1,096 (Greenberg et al., 1991). A portion of this increase may be explained by the 26% growth in the number of grantmakers in the field of aging between 1983 and 1987, from 209 to 263 (Greenberg et al., 1991). Overall philanthropic support for aging rose 10% between 1983 and 1987 (Greenberg et al., 1991), precisely during the period of implementation of the prospective payment system in hospitals.

Despite what appears to be philanthropy's growing role in aging, these statistics do not tell the whole story. As Schreter and Brummel (1988) point out, "Between 1978 and 1985, foundations and corporate contributor programs directed less than 3% of their funds to services for the elderly, and two-thirds of the foundation money came from just 32 major grantmakers" (Schreter & Brummel, 1988, p. 538). Further, only 10% of the larger philanthropies have been involved in aging. Although an increasing number of foundations is involved in the field of aging, they represent a small percentage of total foundations and foundation dollars and an even smaller proportion compared with public funding for aging.

Significantly, foundations have traditionally directed their resources toward three major areas: health, long term care, and community support services. Health programs account for about 55% of all aging funds, with medical care and treatment receiving the largest share (61%) of health funding (Greenberg et al., 1991). Further, resources have been targeted to program development and research; in fact, funding for research tripled from 1983 to 1987 (Greenberg et al., 1991). Historically, foundations have focused on specific programs such as medical research and care rather than on influencing policy on a broad scale. In terms of solving the nation's health care problems and addressing the needs of the elderly, the success of philanthropy in the aging domain is unclear.

For thorough understanding, the complex and contradictory role of philanthropy in aging must be examined in the current context of shifting public policy. A fiscally conservative environment of cuts and reductions in public funding over the last decade has been accompanied by an increasing emphasis on the private sector. The policies of the Reagan administration consistently promoted private sector responsibility for social needs (Estes, 1991). Schreter and Brummel (1988) suggest that the funding climate was transformed from government and public resources (e.g., the Older Americans Act of 1965) to private sources when Reagan "vowed to tap the resources of the private sector with the same energy that Franklin Roosevelt sought government resolutions to problems" (Schreter & Brummel, 1988, p. 530). This shift, however, presents a deep cultural contradiction with respect to the traditional nonprofit sector ideology of innovation, pluralism, and participation. Nonprofit sector rhetoric has historically stressed that its role is to do what government and the market are unable to do rather than what they are unwilling to do.

As the third sector of society and an alternative to the government and corporate sectors, philanthropy has traditionally argued that it should not be responsible for picking up the slack from government, such as filling in the gaps from government cutbacks in the Reagan years. Pleas to foundations to fill in for government shortfalls challenge the historically self-defined role perception of philanthropies as innovators for unmet needs. Yet this self-image may be illusory. Although ostensibly serving as the innovative sphere with a mission to fulfill needs unmet by the public sector, private philanthropy has become devoted to funding projects that address cost containment, particularly in health care. A study of foundation responses to the early budget cuts of the Reagan administration finds that funders say their role is to do what government cannot do (innovation), yet they are pressed into providing gap-filling funding when federal dollars are cut (doing what government will not do). In spite of their responsiveness to government, foundations described their practices as "business as usual" (Mahoney & Estes, 1986). The reactions of philanthropy to both social needs and Reagan's invitation to increase the involvement of the private sector reflect a divergence between their symbolic and material responses. Insofar as foundations merely reflect government and business concerns rather than addressing social needs from an independent perspective, philanthropy may become part of the broader problem rather than the solution.

When philanthropy fills government's role, as promoted by the Reagan and Bush administrations, serious questions are raised for multiple segments of society. The shift from public to private sector funding also transfers responsibility for society's problems. Further, this shift creates a dilemma in light of the philanthropic philosophy that prescribes its role as promoter of social and cultural innovation, in which ideas are introduced and tested with the support of "philanthropic capital," after which the successful innovations may make a claim on public funds (Payton, 1984). What underlying factors might account for the contradictions presented by a shift to the private sector? A review of philanthropic responses to health care in a climate of fiscal austerity illuminates elements of the contradiction and illustrates what may be called the *illusion of innovation* in philanthropy.

Mahoney (1988) researched the relationship between grantmaking for aging and U.S. health policy in the cost-containment era of the mid-1980s. Analyzing Foundation Center data bases, she demonstrates that the national health policy goal of cost containment is adopted as the highest priority of private philanthropy in health and aging. Mahoney (1988) shows that the nonprofit and public sectors are linked; yet she argues that public policy is influencing foundations rather than philanthropy affecting policy. "In 1985, foundations in the field of aging allocated grantmaking resources in ways that supported a national health policy agenda that benefits the interests of both government and business" (Mahoney, 1988, p. vii). The agenda of foundations is predominantly one of cost containment, with little attention to access to care. This research suggests that foundations support the status quo with respect to a national health policy agenda, also suggesting that the self-image of foundations as innovators may be misleading.

To assert, as Ginzberg (1987) has, that one sign of philanthropic neglect of social needs is the failure to address and/or influence policy is to contend that philanthropy should engage in the policy process so as to be effective. This position itself is the focus of a complex debate being waged in the public, private, and academic sectors (Ginzberg, 1987; Maloney, 1988) among grantmakers who want to support demonstration projects, those who want to shape policy, and those who want to effect social change. This debate has intensified recently as a number of philanthropies, including the Robert Wood Johnson Foundation, the Kaiser Family Foundation, and Families USA Foundation, have joined the fray. Far removed from the stance of doing what government cannot do, some foundations even claim a programmatic mission of government reform, as exemplified by the Kaiser Family Foundation's (1991) priority in government and health and its goal of revitalizing the public sector. In addition, the findings of the most recent Burden Foundation report (Greenberg et al., 1991) suggest that the impact of public policy is one of the top 10 concerns for grantmakers. Philanthropy in aging, however, has had limited success in engaging either policy or the national health care agenda, instead focusing on more specific service programs such as long term care. An important question, then, concerns the nature of philanthropy's role in the policy process.

Ginzberg (1987) contends that, in the 1970s and 1980s, most foundation support in health was targeted at health services research. While some foundations addressed issues on the nation's health care agenda, few focused on the overall agenda. Ginzberg recommends that future foundation support in health be reallocated to planning and policy initiatives to assess "the strengths and weaknesses of different dimensions of the existing system and determining how weak links could be strengthened and new links put in place" (Ginzberg, 1987, p. 138). He calls for an active role by foundations in policy formulation to improve the health care system and the establishment of selected policy centers to address critical questions.

The philanthropy/policy debate lacks consensus, however. Maloney (1988) offers five major reasons to explain why more foundations are not involved in policy issues: (a) There are other worthwhile projects; (b) influencing national policy conflicts with beliefs about popular democracy; (c) foundations do not have the necessary resources; (d) the role of policy studies in shaping health care has not been sufficiently demonstrated; and (e) there is too little evidence that engaging in the policy process is effective. He asserts that, rather than expanding the role of philanthropy in policy, "the success or failure of foundations' efforts to inform public policy will depend most on the quality of projects sponsored by that small group of foundations already committed to engaging in public policy formation" (Maloney, 1988, p. 212).

Maloney's reasoning for limited philanthropic involvement in policy may conserve the illusion of innovation at the expense of effecting social change. Six reasons may be advanced to support a broader policy role for philanthropy: (a) Policy is a worthwhile project that has not been accorded priority status by foundations in general; (b) if the goals of influencing policy are to enhance access to health care, expand needed social and personal care services, improve the lives of older persons, and increase services to those traditionally underrepresented, then they certainly appear to be democratic; (c) foundations have the necessary resources available to effect change if a commitment is made to distribute them differently (i.e., strategically); (d) what has been demonstrated is that supporting health care services directly has not necessarily shaped the overall system or the nation's health care agenda in the direction of the problem solving or system restructuring currently needed; (e) because deliberately avoiding engagement in the policy process has been ineffective, the alternative should be pursued; and (f) by not overtly engaging in policy, foundations covertly support the status quo—this is not a truly apolitical or neutral stance. This position challenges philanthropy to be part of a broader effort to make the nonprofit sector more effective in helping the public sector meet its responsibilities.

The nature of the economic, cultural, and structural problems facing society today, including the trends affecting aging, are more complex than at any time in our history (Figure 14.1). Popular issues can command the attention and resources of a harried, financially stressed, and only partially informed public. Likewise, well-organized and well-financed political groups can influence policy to such an extent that grantmakers are in the unenviable position of having to respond not only to their constituencies but to a larger policy environment in which, regardless of foundation size, they are only small, individual actors. Philanthropy faces important challenges on several fronts, including "changes in social, economic, and political conditions; a more dynamic competitive environment; and a declining level of donor support" (Harvey & McCrohan, 1990, pp. 40-41). More specifically, Gutheil and Chernesky (1991) portray the funding climate in the 1990s as one in which support for aging will be increasingly challenged by the growing social problems of other populations.

The 1990s have presented both philanthropy and the public with a challenge unprecedented in our time. The ways in which both sectors rise to meet this challenge will in part determine the future of old age in the United States. Achenbaum (1991) is correct in asserting that the time is right "for foundations to respond to the federal government's spending cutbacks and flagging commitment by filling the void with fresh ideas and daring alternatives to the status quo" (Achenbaum, 1991, p. 27).

Conclusion

Social policy interventions supported by all levels of government and the private and nonprofit sectors are a major factor in determining "whether old age is a time of dependency or freedom . . . from the threat or reality of financial [or other] hardship" (Phillipson &

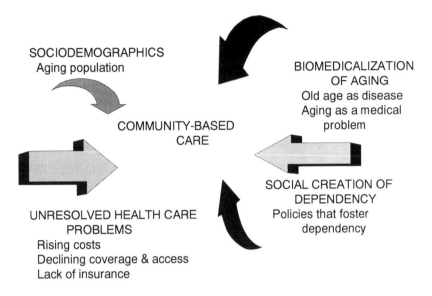

SOCIODEMOGRAPHICS
Aging population

BIOMEDICALIZATION
OF AGING
Old age as disease
Aging as a medical
problem

COMMUNITY-BASED
CARE

SOCIAL CREATION OF
DEPENDENCY
Policies that foster
dependency

UNRESOLVED HEALTH CARE
PROBLEMS
Rising costs
Declining coverage & access
Lack of insurance

Figure 14.1. Problems Faced by Public Policy in Ameliorating Dependency

Walker, 1986). Thus the design of public policy and intervention strategies, including those supported by the philanthropic sector, must attend fully to the possibility that these interventions may generate more rather than less dependency. Multiple levels of intervention are needed to promote empowerment, including interventions that address everyday life, professional practice and service delivery, and social structure (Riley & Riley, 1989). Priority must be given to maximizing self-efficacy and competence as well as enhancing control of the personal environment (Rodin, 1989) for all older persons. The challenge on all three levels is to break the link between aging and dependency (Phillipson & Walker, 1986).

Everyday Life

Interventions designed to improve the personal control of the elderly in everyday life situations are needed. Such interventions have been shown to have positive effects on self-esteem and functioning (including memory, health status, and criteria for institutionalization) (Rodin, 1989). Examples of community care interventions designed to enhance older persons' control include programs to (a) increase the degree of choice and self-control that older persons have with respect to their care planning and management; (b) correct the belief of older persons that decline is inevitable; (c) provide explicit training to develop skills for coping with daily stress; and (d) reduce the dependency of older persons on medical caregivers (Rodin, 1989). Interventions include the creation of alternative care services, establishment of self-help support systems, and formation of organizations and advocacy groups that serve the self-defined needs of elders (Bernard & Phillipson, 1991). In this context, empowerment and self-care are adjuncts to, rather than replacements for, professional services and community care.

Another area of intervention to empower older persons is rehabilitation (Ory & Williams, 1989). The neglect of rehabilitation reflects the emphasis of the field of gerontology on accommodative rather than restorative approaches (Estes, 1980). The dominant accommodative approach views improvement as unlikely, indirectly discouraging elders from becoming independent. The alternative restorative approach builds on the excellent potential of well-designed interventions to improve functioning in old age (e.g., for stroke, hip fracture, and urinary incontinence) (Ory & Williams, 1989). The requisite interaction of biomedical, behavioral, and social factors in recovery necessitates setting small attainable goals that will foster motivation and success; addressing the life course timing of disability and the impact of the age at which disability is experienced; dealing with the definition of disability and coping patterns of those involved (negative definitions diminish coping ability); social support systems to facilitate rehabilitation including families, hospital staff, other caregivers, and community support; and acknowledging the length of rehabilitation processes by incorporating sustained interventions into daily routines and life-styles (Ory & Williams, 1989).

Included in everyday life interventions are self-care strategies, but ones that are not "narrowly defined in terms of *more* individual and family activity and *less* support" for publicly financed social and health services (Phillipson & Walker, 1986, p. 283). "Self-care could actually entail both more support from formal caregivers (as people become more conscious of their rights) and greater control by older people of skills and knowledge to assist them" in old age (Phillipson & Walker, 1986, p. 283).

Professional Practice and Organization

Interventions are needed to promote the ability of institutions and professionals to enhance the personal control of older persons. The most immediate tasks are (a) to expand access to needed community-based care that meets nonmedical needs and (b) to renegotiate the boundaries that separate the expert from the elder (Glendenning, 1985; Phillipson & Walker, 1986; Savo, 1984) by qualitatively changing the relationship between elders and professionals.

Community gerontology teams, working on a neighborhood or block basis, are a potential vehicle for reshaping the power imbalance between elders and professionals who try to help them (Phillipson & Walker, 1986). Such teams might consist of formal and informal caregivers, together with representatives from senior citizen's, children's, and other social action groups who meet regularly to discuss, from an intergenerational perspective, issues that affect older people. These teams could advise caregivers working with older people, stimulate efforts to influence local and national planning affecting older persons, and develop experimental projects and initiatives designed to give power to older persons with regard to the health and social issues that concern them (Phillipson & Walker, 1986). To promote the empowerment of older persons, explicit programs are needed for professional caregivers (and the resocialization of those who are already trained) to counter the dependency-generating approaches that result from their professional training and the medicalization of aging (Estes & Binney, 1989; Phillipson & Walker, 1986).

Social Structure

Interventions are needed to address the deep structural conditions that generate and institutionalize discriminatory and deleterious practices toward the old in society. A policy of universal life course entitlement (Estes & Binney, 1988) to health care and social services is an example of a major type of social structural change that could reduce inequities based on age, gender, race, class, and other factors. Such entitlement could address the problem of "imbalance . . . —the mismatch—between the strengths and capacities of the mounting numbers of long-lived people and the lack of . . . opportunities in society to utilize and reward these strengths" (Riley & Riley, 1989, p. 14). This is a problem of structural lag that necessitates "interventions in the social matrix in which [elders'] lives are embedded" (Riley & Riley, 1989, p. 15). A universal entitlement would also be consistent with the lead of several private foundations (e.g., the

Kaiser Family Foundation and the Robert Wood Johnson Foundation) that are explicitly committed to working on problems of the uninsured and access to care.

Structural change in the direction of universal life course entitlement could also promote gender justice by reducing the exploitation of caregiving women, whose activities enable the nation to avoid formally paying the cost of long term care (Baldock & Ungerson, 1991; England, Keigher, Miller, & Linsk, 1990; Leat & Gay, 1987). In conjunction with strategically designed empowerment initiatives, structural change would foster and shape both the new politics of aging (Phillipson & Walker, 1986, p. 289) and a reinvigorated system of community care. Such changes will, however, necessitate a new vision—the topic of the final chapter.

CHAPTER 15

No-Care Zone and Social Policy

Much of the immediate concern must be how we develop a new vision for community care with older people in the 1990s. Any reassessment of community care will need to have at least three key elements: first, a redefinition of the nature of dependency; secondly, a new approach to family care; thirdly, a major injection of resources to underpin community care provision.

Phillipson, 1992, p. 5

▼

The 1990s opened with serious unresolved issues on the domestic agenda and a Congress concerned about the growing exposure of U.S. citizens to the financial burden of inadequate health care coverage. With the surprise 1991 election of a Democratic U.S. Senator in Pennsylvania on a platform of universal national health care and a torrent of national opinion polls indicating remarkable consistency in U.S. views of the dismal state of health care coverage (Taylor, 1992), the 103rd Congress introduced 30 bills aimed at health care reform, with many including long term care.

Although the no-care zone in community care is an increasingly salient concern for the public and policymakers, little effort has been devoted to developing policy models from a critical perspective. The critical approach largely emanates from feminist perspectives on caregiving and European scholarship on the welfare state. For more than a decade, Walker (1982, 1983, 1985) and Phillipson (1982, 1992; Walker & Phillipson, 1986), and, more recently, Lloyd (1990, 1991), Collins (1991), and Thornton (1991), have explored the role of the

---

NOTE: The authors of this chapter are Carroll L. Estes and James H. Swan.

State and social policy in community care. The exploitation of women and their disproportionate share of unpaid caregiving has also been examined by Finch and Groves (1980, 1983), Finch (1989), Okin (1989), Leat and Gay (1987), Ungerson (1987), Baldock and Ungerson (1991), Sassoon (1987), Lewis and Meredith (1988), and others (e.g., Simonen, 1990). Related work on the dependency-producing elements of public policy in North America has been contributed by scholars from the political economy perspective (Estes, 1979; Olson, 1982) and includes recent work on the welfare state (Binney & Estes, 1988; Estes, 1991; Quadagno, 1990) and on gender justice (Arendell & Estes, 1991; Dickinson & Russell, 1986; Kirp, Yudof, & Franks, 1986; Osterbush, Keigher, Miller, & Linsk, 1987).

Notes Toward an Agenda
on Community Care

Research indicates substantial skepticism about the cost effectiveness of community-based care (Weissert et al., 1988), even though enhancement of quality of life may result. Research also documents the significant sacrifices that caregivers, particularly women, make in providing the majority of the nation's long term care without remuneration (Stone et al., 1987; U.S. House of Representatives, 1988b). With rising numbers in the dependent population, the high labor force participation of women, and the desire of elders to remain in their own homes as long as possible, pressures for community-care solutions are mounting. These pressures will accelerate in light of three trends: (a) Many future family caregivers will have caregiving responsibilities for not just one, but two, disabled parents; (b) low birthrates will result in a smaller number of adult children being available to care for their elderly parents (Stone & Kemper, 1989); and (c) the number of adults sandwiched between caring for parents, children, and, increasingly, even grandchildren is growing.

The nation's economic problems cast a long shadow over the policy debate and constrain the framing of options. The call for more community care is heralded by both progressive and conservative forces, but for different reasons, as reflected in the conservative and liberal discourse on community care (Lloyd, 1991). For conservatives, community care (particularly in the form of women's free labor) is a mechanism to reduce the publicly financed cost of care and to restore the patriarchal family and women's traditional role in it. It is a means of shrinking the welfare state by shifting care responsibility from the public to the private arena (Lloyd, 1991). A major assumption is that there is a potential caregiving population (an informal sector of family, friends, and neighbors) that can, and should, be exploited to provide more support to community-resident elders (Lloyd, 1991; Thornton, 1991). This discourse and the call for increased family responsibility, when it is well known that women and other informal caregivers already provide more than 80% of long term care, may be understood in terms of the larger economic, political, and ideological stakes (Estes, 1991). For progressives, social policy to provide community care offers the possibility of (a) entitlement to much needed long term care, (b) augmented public (State) responsibility, (c) a means to redress the unequal burden of responsibility currently carried by women, and (d) empowerment of care receiver and caregiver.

Lloyd characterizes the two major positions on community care in terms of conflict and consensus discourse. The consensus discourse represents gatekeeping and the distribution of community-care resources as benign and unproblematic. The community-care gatekeepers and managers who administer the assessment processes are assumed to be people of goodwill who are acting in the best interests of their clients. In contrast, the conflict discourse emphasizes the "structural contradictions and conflicts of individual interest, oppositions" inherent in social situations (Lloyd, 1991, p. 129). The conflict discourse attends to the participation and power concerns of older persons faced with the increasingly bureaucratized and rationalized structures of service delivery and the professionalization of geriatric assessment and case management.

Contradictions and Problems

Community care presents multiple fundamental dilemmas. Instead of forcing older people into institutions or forcing informal caregivers to provide care, dependency can theoretically be ameliorated and independence maximized through the provision of community-care alternatives. Community care is also advanced as a means of facilitating choice within free market economies, in spite of the implicit rationing of care related to ability to pay and the absence of countervailing power by care recipients (C. Phillipson, personal communication, January 25, 1992). Significant conflicts of interest are inherent in the provision of human services because "the independence and control sought by the elderly individual . . . conflicts with the creation of dependency" (Lloyd, 1991, p. 130) fostered by care providers. "Unilateral dependency" is produced subsequent to the establishment of bureaucratic

structures to provide services to disadvantaged and dependent populations (Estes, 1979, p. 24). These client populations are generally compromised in their ability to "work the system" in the face of complicated
formal rules and regulations and the tendency of bureaucrats to maintain social distance from their clients. Bureaucracies thus reinforce the
class structure (Sjoberg, Rymer, & Farris, 1966).

Reciprocity is a crucial element of the social relationship between
older persons and their care providers (Finch, 1989). "The help rendered may be given from the purest and most benevolent of motives,
yet the very fact of being helped degrades" (Coser, 1963, p. 145).
Because the client and the professional "belong to two basically different worlds . . . the asymmetry is not only of feelings and attitudes, it is
also an asymmetry of power" (Coser, 1963, pp. 146-147). The deleterious effect of such power inequities on the weaker party is well documented (Blau, 1964; Collins, 1991). The fact that "power resides implic-
itly in the other's dependency" (Emerson, 1962, p. 32) explains research
findings that older persons resent unpaid charitable help and that those
"who are unable to reciprocate may themselves avoid establishing
relations with others" (Collins, 1991, p. 215) even to the point of consent-
ing to become destitute, if that is the price. Older persons are like younger
persons in their willingness to endure great hardship to avoid becoming
dependent. "Nowhere is this negotiation of role and expectations more
poignant than within the family" (Lloyd, 1991, p. 131; Francis, 1984).

Thus social policy reaches inside the life experiences of older
persons and may severely limit their potential for self-sufficiency
(Estes, 1979). Low self-esteem and learned helplessness are produced
through the internalization by older persons of negative labels of
incompetency and stigmatization as dependents (Estes, 1980; Rodin
& Langer, 1980). "Stereotypes of old persons as senile . . . may teach
older persons that they are becoming senile . . . so that they act the
part, irrespective of their competence" (Estes, 1979, p. 13). Alex
Comfort defines this as "sociogenic aging" to call attention to "the
role which society imposes on people as they reach a certain chron-
ological age" (Comfort, 1976, p. 9).

These social difficulties are compounded by the control exerted
over the definitions of social problems and policy implementation
by agency managers, who are strongly positioned to influence policymakers to protect and expand their domains. A core attribute of
professionalization is the ability of the professional to maximize
autonomy and discretion over key aspects of his or her work (Friedson,
1970). Professional autonomy supports the tendency of gerontological
specialists to control the flow of information to clients. It also limits

public accountability inasmuch as fellow professionals are the only ones judged competent to evaluate their work. Professional autonomy is an important, generally laudable, ever-present reality of health care provision, but it carries this tension within it. It is clear that augmented community-based service systems are needed. Nevertheless, it is essential to recognize that negative consequences of community care result from policies that assign (a) a dependent status to the aged offering them little opportunity to reciprocate for services received and (b) a special status to service providers and managers (Estes, 1979). Such policies unwittingly permit providers to become agents of their clients' degradation.

Although "dependency is . . . unavoidable" at some time and at some level during the life course of many persons, the inescapable conclusion is that

> the degree to which elderly people are enabled to feel in control of their lives, solving their own problems, making choices for themselves, seems likely to promote happiness and a feeling of well-being which is reflected in both health and longevity (Buie, 1988). Much depends . . . on the way in which elderly people actually experience the provision of services and care. (Lloyd, 1991, p. 133)

The previous chapter on the empowerment imperative points out that, in the future, effective strategies require the prevention and amelioration of dependency in old age to the fullest extent possible. Without explicit attention to the effects of policy interventions on dependency, the existing structure of medical service provision and professionalization can be expected to contribute to the production of more, rather than less, dependency in the population. The essential contradiction is that, to foster independence in a dependent population, a high level of support is needed; yet that very support has the strong potential to undermine independence.

The central question with regard to community-care policies is whether they will become a vehicle for the production of more, rather than less, dependency. Lloyd suggests that, without elder empowerment, community care may simply foster and legitimate an extended form of dependency and paternalism (Lloyd, 1991).

Managed Care Revolution

The 1990s are the age of the managed care revolution, as the truly remarkable market penetration of managed care illustrates. Austin and O'Connor (1989) note that there are different models of case management: gatekeeper and advocate. Indeed, managed care has come to mean so many things that its precise definition is highly questionable (Hunter, 1991). In the current policy context, however, the popularity of case management is motivated more by cost containment than by client advocacy goals. Thus the predominant meaning of case management is that there is a gatekeeper who manages, controls, and limits referrals and care received. Geriatric assessment and case management are both mechanisms to aid in controlling costs and utilization. To the extent that consumer choice is involved, the legacy of the 1980s is that the consumer has been reconstituted as an actor capable of rational choice (Enthoven, 1990). How to resolve the tensions between consumer choices (rational or not, voiced or not) and the rational choices of the gatekeepers remains unclear.

Case management is a mixed bag of organizations, procedures, and goals that promises an easy solution to the multitude of problems plaguing health care: inadequate access, skyrocketing costs, service fragmentation, and the lack of a long term care policy. Nevertheless, "15 years of research on community-based care management fails to support most of the claims of its effectiveness in solving the problems for which it was intended" (Callahan, 1989, p. 181). By definition, managed care requires professionals to coordinate efforts in the provision of care. The daily lives of persons needing assistance require continual negotiation with others—family members, voluntary workers, and formal care providers—all of which involves struggles and conflicting interests, but with the greatest personal stakes and consequences for care recipients. Elders strive, often in vain, "to express a somewhat different set of needs and expectations and . . . [their] obvious failure[s] lead to verbal stumbling, answers which are 'irrelevant' . . . [with these] respondents [being] . . . characterized as senile and therefore incapable of sharing in decisions about their future" (Lloyd, 1991, p. 132; Vesperi, 1985).

Phillipson (1992) identifies a key issue in managed care that applies to the United States—that there are virtually no provisions or mechanisms for elders or their informal caregivers to participate in or challenge the decisions of case managers, should clients disagree with the assessments and decisions made. This is a crucial point given that the decisions of the case manager are loaded with major consequences for an elder's access to care and quality of life. Insofar as financing, organization, and delivery issues overrun concerns about caring, the attitudes and experiences of community-care recipients, as well as the role of consumer decision making, are relegated to minor concerns, if considered at all.

An additional difficulty is that formal care workers and managers, most of whom work in nonprofit sector organizations, are stretched between their altruism and desire for client-centered representation and the managerially imposed cost-control policies fostered by the corporatized and rationalized bureaucratic systems of which they are a part. These services are increasingly provided in a "contract culture" (Thornton, 1991). Cost control, the dominant theme of the 1990s, has strengthened the power of the formal caregiver in the gatekeeper role to constrain the utilization of valuable and necessary benefits. There are contradictions between the rewards experienced by service providers and managers (e.g., autonomy or meeting the needs of individual clients) and their mandates to deliver targeted services to clients who are eligible for payment or reimbursement for particular services under the myriad varying insurance programs. The issues raised include quality, quantity, targeting, and service guarantees (Thornton, 1991).

These problems are compounded by the fact that nonprofits, the major providers of health and social services, have been under attack (Estes et al., 1989). A cultural revolution is developing in the altruistic behavior of voluntary organizations, because charity is no longer rewarded by public policies that now promote competition, the cheapest service units, and profits in care delivery (Chapters 2 and 13). This important development has dramatically affected the normative environment in which social work and other services are offered as well as the personal lives and rewards of service workers.

In the context of this sociocultural sea change and current concerns about the U.S. economy, managed care has the potential of becoming the blunt instrument of rationing. It may institutionalize mechanisms that deprive the disabled and dependent of the last remnants of their personal control. The insured majority also has reason for concern in this respect because of the narrowing of choice in employer-sponsored insurance plans. The pervasive loss of a client's actual, as well as perceived, control through the imposition of depersonalized and highly professionalized case management and assessment processes may have extremely deleterious effects.

On the caregiver side, payment of home and community-based service workers is often low, and many positions have meager or no benefits. Workers find themselves exploited and burned out (Dressel, 1984). Further, much of this work is performed on a part-time basis, often under contract with pay per day or per service unit. Although, in the past, contracting was valued by many formal caregivers as enhancing caregiver autonomy, even this benefit has been threatened by the routinization and increased control of in-home work. The organizations that employ these workers are taking measures to achieve productivity increases, including work speedups and restructuring of the division of labor (Szasz, 1990).

Despite the current affinity of policymakers for managed care and geriatric assessment, there is no actual "right" to assessment, although the Omnibus Budget Reconciliation Act of 1987 expanded the requirement for patient assessment in nursing homes (Morris, Hawes, Fries, et al., 1990). As is the case in England, U.S. public policy is "silent on redress for consumers in the form of requests for second opinions or appeals of decisions of the 'care manager' " (Lloyd, 1991, p. 128).

Medical-Industrial Complex

Additional difficulties result from the dominant view of old age as portrayed in the media and understood by the public. It is conceptualized as a problem requiring medical technology and services as the primary, if not the only, treatment. As discussed extensively elsewhere (Estes, 1979; Estes & Binney, 1989; Estes et al., 1984), this problem definition, described as the biomedicalization of aging, contributes to the commodification of the needs of the elderly. The biomedical construction of aging (Estes & Binney, 1989) and attendant policy solutions provide the underlying rationale for a very expensive and profitable medical-industrial complex (Estes et al., 1992). It is noteworthy that the medical-industrial complex prospers from the iatrogenic consequences of a technologically and medically oriented approach to the largely social problems of old age as well as from the dependency it promotes.

Entitlement to Community Care

Under conservative regimes, the "ethos of community care" will likely reinforce, but only minimally supplement, the already existing networks of family, friends, and neighbors. Policies to promote care *by* the community rather than care *in* the community (Phillipson, 1992) require an ever widening circle of willing and largely unpaid members of the personal network or social world of the person needing help. As Collins notes, however, these policies are predicated on assumptions that overstate the forms of and the extent to which personal networks exist, and the policies ignore how the networks operate. People have "supportive strands" but these are not interrelated, coherent, or "predisposed to being interwoven. . . . Personal networks operate on lines of idiosyncrasy and personal preference . . . which makes them . . . unpredictable, unstable and inherently incomplete" (Collins, 1991, p. 210).

Government long term care policy is built on the foundation of informal care and assumes that personal care networks are both secure and available strands of assistance. This assumption contradicts the research, which demonstrates the fragility and uncertainty of care networks. The vulnerability of these relationships poses major problems for the design and implementation of realistic and effective policies for community care (Phillipson, 1992). In addition, recent opinion studies and attitude surveys challenge the rhetoric of informal care and necessitate a reassessment of the nature (and certainty) of family obligation for the future in light of recent and provocative findings on the caregiving preferences of elders (Daatland, 1990; Phillipson, 1992; Salvage et al., 1989; Waerness, 1990; West et al., 1984).

Research conducted in several European countries indicates that older persons increasingly prefer "the support of public as opposed to family care, especially where they have extensive care needs, such as those arising from long standing illness" (Phillipson, 1992). Findings that family and informal care are one of "the least preferred options" and that care by providers in the formal sector is strongly preferred are understandable in view of expressed public unwillingness "to place the major burden of care on informal carers . . . the family and women in particular. They are especially unwilling to allocate the major responsibility for care to close kin; the children or siblings of dependent persons" (West et al., 1984, p. 294). Finch's (1989) persuasive research shows that the "sense of obligation" that characterizes kin relations is unreliable, inconsistent, and highly variable. These data render problematic the continuing and unswerving commitment of policymakers to informal care as the primary solution to the growing demand for community care. Studies are needed on the preferences of older Americans for their care and on the sense of obligation and operation of kin networks in the context of profound and dynamic changes occurring in the structure of the family.

Older persons prefer to "rely on paid agents of the State rather than on volunteers, even kin . . . [in part] because the recipients of care are then exonerated from liability for direct and personal reciprocation" (Collins, 1991, p. 216). A major problem with the current policy of informal care as the major source of long term care service provision is that elders must depend on the goodwill of caregivers, for whom this is one of several competing responsibilities (Collins, 1991; Phillipson & Walker, 1986). Research on how older persons have been shown to perceive and experience the giving and receiving of help suggests that informal care policies are likely to create particular reciprocity and dependency problems for older persons who choose to remain in their own homes (Collins, 1991). Finally, as already acknowledged, policies of informal care ignore core values of care recipients such as privacy, independence, and control.

The ultimate dilemma and contradiction is that the volatile and sensitive nature of personal relationships "undermines another cornerstone argument advanced in support of community care . . . that it will enable people in need to exercise power in their own affairs to a greater extent than previously" (Collins, 1991, p. 210). The actual and perceived control experienced by an older person will be enhanced to the extent to which there is entitlement to services rather than their provision as a gift or charity (Figure 15.1). Lloyd notes that "the experience of control" flows from the "belief that the statutory [government-funded] services are received as a right (and therefore to be demanded) rather than as a 'charity' and by the introduction of reciprocity into informal caring relationships" (Lloyd, 1991, p. 134). Social policies that provide the right (entitlement) to both payment and choice are requisite to the preservation of personal control (Collins, 1991).

Universal entitlement offers the further advantage of assured predictability in the supply of, and equity in access to, the community-based services it provides (Estes et al., 1983; Phillipson, 1992). Variations in resources and access to care across the states under state and/or local programs that allow discretion (e.g., Medicaid) are well documented in terms of both eligibility and benefits (Holahan & Cohen, 1986). Without the uniform provisions assured by entitlement, it is likely that the no-care zone and wide disparities in the availability of and access to community care will remain. Further, the life chances of similarly disabled people, including access to formal services, will continue to vary from community to community, and the results will predictably discriminate against the most disadvantaged.

Framework for Policymaking

In matters of access to posthospital and other community-based care, the stakes are high. This volume raises many questions and

- Reciprocity is essential to self-esteem

- Elders prefer services to which they are entitled

- Entitlement to services enhances personal control

- Entitlement accords the right to demand services

- Autonomy and equity are maximized by entitlement

Figure 15.1. Elders and Community Care

suggests some answers. Some of the coauthors advance definitive recommendations (Harrington et al., 1991), but the purpose at this point is to propose a framework within which policymakers, administrators, academicians, and advocates may consider the issues and devise solutions.

The matrix of policy choices concerning health financing and community care found in Table 15.1 represents a continuum of policy change (Binstock, 1985; Estes & Binney, 1988; Zones, Estes, & Binney, 1987). *Modification,* describing various forms of small-scale change or incrementalism, has been a recurrent experience in the health care arena. *Alteration,* representing more thoroughgoing, innovative, and institutional reforms, is not only on the national horizon but also the subject of state-level experimentation. *Transformation,* or change in entire societal sectors, may be on the national agenda in the foreseeable future. *Revolution,* a fundamental change in the social and economic structure, represents the most far-reaching policy alternative. Whatever one's evaluation of the choices, health policy changes entailing small-scale increments will not provide adequate long-term remedies for problems historically rooted in the dominant values and political-economic structures of the social order. On the other hand, far-reaching structural change may be more likely than generally thought. Times change and society, economics, and politics change with the times.

As this volume goes to press, the California Medical Association has announced its intent to seek a referendum mandating employers to provide health insurance to all full-time workers. Should such an

TABLE 15.1 Policy Choices for Intervention

Choices	Health Financing	Community Care
Modification	Copayment levels Deductible levels Premiums Prospective payment of providers Tax law changes	Family responsibility Health promotion and education Incentives for increasing nursing homes beds Public subsidy of private long term care (LTC) insurance Respite care
Alteration	Rationing medical care by condition Redefining age of eligibility Vouchers Means testing Compensation for informal care	Medicare enhancement Medicaid enhancement Life care Community housing
Transformation	National health insurance Federally insured continuum of LTC by entitlement Universal single-payer public insurance	Empowerment of care recipients Gender justice
Revolution	No profit in health care delivery	Public provision of LTC to all citizens through insurance Nationalization of all health and social services Community control of public caregiving system

SOURCE: Adapted from Zones, Estes, and Binney (1987, p. 293) and Estes and Binney (1988, p. 78).

alteration be successfully initiated, it would likely have momentous societal and economic impact: changes to the insurance industry to reverse structural impediments that have arisen to the provision of group health insurance policies by small employers, major economic boosts to health care providers, alterations in management-labor relations, and general changes in social expectations of large sectors of the populace. Changes on a smaller scale should not be eschewed. Many health care modifications and alterations are needed immediately, but such changes seldom touch the root of the problem. For example, rapidly rising health care costs threaten most sectors of the society and economy and have proven intractable in the face of even the most far-reaching policy initiatives chronicled in this volume. As calls for a solution become more widespread, a transformation of health care in one form or other, for better or worse, is already being debated as part of the national agenda.

This volume asserts that alterations are on the horizon. Widespread discussion about health care rationing is typified by a recent debate at the 1991 American Public Health Association meetings, but there is little agreement on what rationing means (Morreale, 1991). Yet the state of Oregon has gone forward with a controversial rationing plan applied only to Medicaid (Block, 1991) although originally intended by some to apply far more widely (Garland, 1991). In the context of such debates, consideration of the pros and cons of a universal single-payer public insurance plan is introduced (Simpson, 1991).

Whether for modification, alteration, transformation, or revolution, parties on all sides are vigorously contesting every initiative. At issue is how well the voices of older persons, the chronically ill, the uninsured, and the poor will be heard. The chronically ill and disabled, old and young, and especially the disadvantaged, including female caregivers, make up the front line that will experience the effects of policy decisions (Zones et al., 1987).

Conclusion

Social policy both shapes and mirrors the structural arrangements of age, race, gender, and social class divisions in society (Estes, 1979). Differences in the political, economic, and ideological resources on which different segments of the social order can call are inscribed upon the society's public policy. Although social policy can either modify or reinforce and reproduce existing arrangements, it is usually responsive to the most powerful structural interests (Estes, 1979). Thus policy on aging tends to reproduce social inequalities that are the product of a lifelong position in the social structure. Because this is so, social policy for community care will require explicit and conscious attention to designing interventions to counteract and compensate for the inequalities and disempowerment that the current system will continue to produce unless otherwise modified.

The 1960s were characterized by collective social change, in which bold and sweeping structural alterations related to civil rights and racial and gender inequality were a priority. In the period following the enactment of Medicare and Medicaid in the mid-1960s, the medical-industrial complex mushroomed (Estes et al., 1992). The 1970s were devoted to planning and coordination with policymakers attempting to shift gears and to devolve federal responsibility to lower levels of government through the first wave of new federalism (Estes et al., 1983). The 1980s were marked by the use of public policy to transfer responsibility from government to the private sector and to promote a return to the patriarchal family. The Reagan era initiated a resurgence of the ideologies of individualism and the market (Estes, 1991). In this period of increased privatization and corporatization of human services, the standard of living of children, the poor, women, minorities, and even the middle class declined.

In the 1990s, renewed economic crisis is accompanied by the dominant ideology of austerity. In the health and human services, this is the decade of managed care in which considerations of cost are likely to eclipse all else. Phillipson and Walker are correct in observing that

> the task over the next ten years is to break the link between growing old and becoming dependent. This will involve action on both political and economic fronts, but it will also involve . . . a challenge to our work as carers—in both formal and informal settings. Crucially, it will demand that older people become centrally involved. (Phillipson & Walker, 1986, p. 290)

The 21st century is a potential turning point—the point at which the common stake may be realized and visionary sociostructural change and improvement may again be achievable through social policy. In this period, the dream of life course entitlement (Binney & Estes, 1988) could be realized and the health and well-being of all American people throughout their life spans become a national priority.

Appendix:
Policy Changes Affecting
Home Health Care, 1961 to 1990

1961—The Community Health Services and Facilities Act authorized the Surgeon General to make project grants from 1962 to 1967 to public or nonprofit agencies for the development of home health services outside the hospital.

1965—Medicare, Title XVIII of the Social Security Act, authorized home health and required agencies to provide nursing service and at least one additional service.

Medicaid, Title XIX of the Social Security Act, authorized home health as an optional state service.

1971—Home health benefits were mandated under Medicaid.

1972—Medicare eligibility and benefits were extended to disabled persons receiving Social Security benefits for 2 or more years.

The copayment of 20% for Medicare Part B home health services was eliminated. Social Security Amendments modified the formula for increasing Medicare Part B premium amounts to the percentage increase that Social Security beneficiaries received in their cost of living adjustment (COLA). (As a result, the proportion of the Part B premium that covers program costs declined from 50% to less than 25% by 1982.)

The waiver of liability clause was introduced.

1973—Older Americans Act Amendments created state and area agencies on aging and provided limited funding for community-based social services, including in-home services.

1974—Title XX of the Social Security Act established federal-state social services, including in-home personal care and social services for the aged, disabled, and children.

1976—Hearings were held on home health service expansion and quality.

1977—Two bills (HR 9829 and HR 12676) introduced, but not passed, set the stage for later home health liberalization (see 1980).

Medicare-Medicaid Anti-Fraud and Abuse Amendments addressed claims for care not meeting conditions of participation in terms of need for skilled care, inadequate record keeping, and agencies accepting only Medicare clients, thus receiving reimbursement based on excessive and inflationary costs.

The Rural Health Clinics Services Act authorized home health services through clinics (in addition to certified home health agencies).

1978—End-stage renal disease patients came under Title XVIII with home dialysis.

1980—The Omnibus Reconciliation Act liberalized home health by eliminating prior hospitalization requirement for Part A and 100-visit limit for home health under Parts A and B of Medicare, eliminating restrictions on Medicare certification of proprietary home health agencies in states without licensure, and eliminating Part B deductible.

1981—The Omnibus Budget Reconciliation Act mandated studies of prospective payment and converted the Title XX Social Services Program into the Social Services Block Grant, with a 20% reduction in federal funding.

Title XX reporting requirements were eliminated.

1982—The Tax Equity and Fiscal Responsibility Act set the Part B premium at the level necessary to cover 25% of program costs, and this level has been extended by Congress each year since.

1983—The Medicare prospective payment system based on diagnosis-related groups (DRGs) was implemented for hospitals.

1984—To address inconsistencies in Medicare fiscal intermediary interpretations of coverage and to reduce overhead costs, HCFA reduced the number of fiscal intermediaries from 157 to 47 regional intermediaries.

Home health claims denials averaged 2.5% under Medicare Part A.

1985—Plan of Treatment and Documentation Guideline Forms (485-488) were revised, creating confusion and claims denials. Fiscal intermediaries imposed billing barriers to coordination of benefits under Medicare and Medicaid.

1986—Health Care Financing Administration (HCFA) and fiscal intermediaries were implicated in a home health claims denial crisis by eliminating waiver of liability, tightening guidelines, complicating reporting forms, increasing claims review, and revising home health cost limits.

Denials resulted in the Secretary of Health and Human Services Commission formed to investigate the denials; the *Duggan v. Bowen* (USDC, D.C., Aug. 1, 1988) suit filed in 1987 against HCFA resulted in liberalization of coverage and a revised and clarified manual; and Congress extended the Medicare Quality Protection Act, which required hospital discharge planning, extended waiver of liability provisions, and favorable presumption.

Omnibus Budget Reconciliation Act of 1986 included several reforms aimed at addressing quality of care concerns, including discharge planning rights.

Public Law 99-509 established current methodology for determining home health care limits. Limits are set at 112% of the mean of the labor-related and nonlabor per unit costs for each type of service provided by freestanding home health agencies; adjustments are made for hospital-based agencies.

The number of Medicare fiscal intermediaries was reduced again, from 47 to 10.

1987—The Omnibus Budget Reconciliation Act redefined the "homebound" eligibility requirement, required fiscal intermediaries to furnish provider and beneficiary a written explanation of denial and added steps to strengthen the regulation of home care, and required home health and nursing home quality improvements.

Demonstration and study on prospective payment of home health care was mandated.

The Older Americans Act added separate authorization of funds for nonmedical in-home services for frail elderly.

Home health claims denials averaged 8.2% (almost 4 times the 1984 average) under Medicare Part A.

Medicare Part B monthly premium increased 38.5% in 1988 from $17.90 to $24.80.

Medicare and Medicaid Patient and Program Protection Act mandatorily excluded from participation in Medicare, Medicaid, Maternal and Child Health Block Grant, and the Social Services Block Grant any medical practitioner (including organizations) convicted of a criminal offense for patient neglect or abuse. It also strengthened requirements regarding the publication of HCFA policies and established a home health hot line and investigative unit.

1988—The Medicare Catastrophic Coverage Act expanded the "intermittent" skilled nursing care definition with "daily" care defined as up to 7 days a week; increased the number of days of coverage for home health services to 38; initiated a limited respite care benefit (effective January 1, 1990); and limited out-of-pocket medical expenditures for the elderly.

Five long term care bills were introduced in the U.S. Congress, each with implications for the expansion of in-home care.

1989—The Medicare Catastrophic Coverage Act was repealed, including its home health provisions.

Medicare Part B premium increased 12.5% to $27.90—963% higher than the premium cost in 1966 ($382.80 per year, compared with $36 per year, respectively).

The Omnibus Budget Reconciliation Act of 1989 established a new payment system for physician services with payments based on a relative value scale (RVS), a method of valuing individual services in relationship to each other. Beginning in January 1992, payments to physicians were based on a fee schedule incorporating the RVS for the services, a conversion factor for the year, and a geographic adjustment factor.

1990—The Omnibus Budget Reconciliation Act (OBRA) extended waiver of liability for home health agencies until December 31, 1995. Compensation requires that a provider have Medicare claims denial rates of less than 2.5%

OBRA also increased the Medicare payroll tax of 1.45% on income from a maximum level of $51,300 to $125,000 to increase revenues in the Medicare Hospital Insurance Trust Fund but especially to reduce the federal deficit.

OBRA also incorporated a 5-year federal deficit reduction plan designed to reduce Medicare outlays by $3.6 billion in fiscal year 1991 and by $44.1 billion over 5 years through cuts in payments to hospitals under Part A, physicians under Part B, and increased out-of-pocket costs to beneficiaries of $10.1 billion over the next 5-year period.

OBRA added controls aimed at curtailing growth in Medicare spending for durable medical equipment (DME).

Home Health Care and Alzheimer's Disease Amendments to the Public Health Services Act were revised and extended for 3 years. Demonstration programs for health care services in the home are to include skilled nursing care, homemaker/home health aides, or personal care services for low-income individuals and for persons with Alzheimer's disease.

Part B premium was increased more than 4%, to $29 per month. Part B premiums are to increase to $46.10 per month by 1995 to cover 25% of program costs.

The first $55 of a biennial mammogram was covered for female Medicare beneficiaries.

The 210-day Medicare limit on hospice care was eliminated.

The cost of injectable drugs for the treatment of osteoporosis was covered.

Partial hospitalization in community mental health centers was covered.

References

Abel, E. K. 1987a. *Informal Care for the Frail Elderly: Policy Options.* Unpublished manuscript, University of California, Los Angeles.

Abel, E. K. 1987b. *Love Is Not Enough: Family Care of the Frail Elderly.* Washington, DC: American Public Health Association.

Abel, E. K. 1989. The Ambiguities of Social Support: Adult Daughters Caring for Frail Elderly Parents. *Journal of Aging Studies, 3,* 211-230.

Abramson, A. J., & L. M. Salamon. 1986. *The Nonprofit Sector and the New Federal Budget.* Washington, DC: Urban Institute.

Achenbaum, W. A. 1991. A Brief History of Foundation Funding in Aging. In B. R. Greenberg, I. A. Gutheil, L. M. Parker, & R. H. Chernesky (Eds.), *Aging: The Burden Study of Foundation Grantmaking Trends,* pp. 17-29. New York: Foundation Center.

Aday, L., G. V. Fleming, & R. Andersen. 1984. *Access to Medical Care in the United States: Who Has It, Who Doesn't.* Center for Health Administration Studies Research Series No. 32. Chicago: University of Chicago.

Albert, S. M. 1991. Cognition of Caregiving Tasks: Multidimensional Scaling of the Caregiver Task Domain. *The Gerontologist, 31,* 726-735.

Alexander, J. A., L. L. Morlock, & B. D. Gifford. 1988. The Effects of Corporate Restructuring on Hospital Policy Making. *Health Services Research, 23,* 311-337.

Alford, R. R., & C. L. Estes. 1987. *Theorizing the Nonprofit Sector.* Unpublished manuscript, University of California, San Francisco, Institute for Health & Aging.

Ambrogi, D. M., D. Doctor, & J. H. Swan. 1988. *The Admission Process in California Nursing Homes and Its Impact on Resident Autonomy.* Final Report to the Retirement Research Foundation. San Francisco: California Law Center on Long Term Care.

American Association of Retired Persons (AARP), Andrus Foundation. 1989, June 5. *Recent Research on Caregiving.* Memorandum. Washington, DC: Author.

American Hospital Association (AHA). 1987. *Discharging Hospital Patients: Legal Implications for Institutional Providers and Health Care Professionals.* Chicago: American Hospital Association.

American Society of Internal Medicine (ASIM). 1985. [The Impact of DRGs on Patient Care: A Survey, March 1984-October 1985]. Washington, DC: Author.

American Society of Internal Medicine (ASIM). 1988, February. [The Impact of Prospective Payment on Patient Care: A Survey of Internists' Experiences Under DRGs]. Washington, DC: American Society of Internal Medicine.

Anderson, H. J. 1991. RBRVS Creates Incentives for Hospital-Physician Joint Ventures. *Hospitals*, 65(4), 31.

Arendell, T., & C. L. Estes. 1987. Unsettled Future: Older Women, Economics and Health. *Feminist Issues*, 7(1), 3-24.

Arendell, T., & C. L. Estes. 1991. Older Women in the Post-Reagan Era. In M. Minkler & C. L. Estes (Eds.), *Critical Perspectives on Aging: The Political & Moral Economy of Growing Old*, pp. 209-226. Amityville, NY: Baywood.

Arrington, B., & C. C. Haddock. 1990. Who Really Profits from Not-for-Profits? *Health Services Research*, 25, 291-304.

Austin, C. D. 1992. Resources for Caregivers: Ohio's Options for Elders Program. In *Resourceful Aging: Today & Tomorrow, Conference Proceedings: Vol. 3. Family/Caregiving*, pp. 79-83. Washington, DC: American Association of Retired Persons.

Austin, C., & M. O'Connor. 1989. Case Management: Components and Program Contexts. In M. Petersen & D. White (Eds.), *Health Care of the Elderly*. London: Sage.

Auten, G. E., & G. Rudney. 1985. Tax Policy and Its Impact on the High Income Giver. In Independent Sector, *Giving and Volunteering: New Frontiers of Knowledge*, pp. 525-545. Spring Research Forum Working Papers. Washington, DC: Independent Sector.

Bader, J. 1985. Respite Care: Temporary Relief for Caregivers. *Women and Health*, 10(2/3), 39-52.

Baldock, J., & C. Ungerson. 1991. What D'Ya Want If You Don' Want Money? A Feminist Critique of "Paid Volunteering." In M. McLean & D. Groves (Eds.), *Women's Issues in Social Policy*, pp. 136-158. London: Routledge & Kegan Paul.

Balinsky, W., & J. N. Shames. 1985. Proprietary and Voluntary Home Care Agency Evolution: The Emergence of a New Entity. *Home Health Care Services Quarterly*, 6(2), 5-17.

Barer, B. M., & C. L. Johnson. 1990. A Critique of the Caregiving Literature. *The Gerontologist*, 30, 26-29.

Bass, D., & L. Noelker. 1987. The Influence of Family Caregivers on Elders' Use of In-Home Services: An Expanded Conceptual Framework. *Journal of Health and Social Behavior*, 28, 184-196.

Baum, M., & M. Page. 1991. Caregiving and Multigenerational Families. *The Gerontologist*, 31, 762-769.

Bays, C. W. 1979. Case Mix Differences Between Nonprofit and For-Profit Hospitals. *Inquiry*, 14, 17-21.

Bays, C. W. 1983. Patterns of Hospital Growth: The Case of Profit Hospitals. *Medical Care*, 21, 950-957.

Beale, P., & M. Gulley. 1981. Discharge Planning Process: An Interdisciplinary Approach. *Military Medicine*, 146, 713-716.

Becker, E., & F. Sloan. 1985. Hospital Ownership and Economic Performance. *Economic Inquiry*, 23(1), 21-36.

Benjamin, A. E. 1985. Community-Based Long Term Care. In C. Harrington, R. J. Newcomer, C. L. Estes, et al., *Long Term Care of the Elderly: Public Policy Issues*, pp. 197-212. Beverly Hills, CA: Sage.

Benjamin, A. E. 1986a. [Medicare Post-Hospital Study]. Proposal funded by the Commonwealth Fund Commission on the Elderly Living Alone, University of California, San Francisco, Institute for Health & Aging.

Benjamin, A. E. 1986b. State Variations in Home Health Expenditures and Utilization Under Medicare and Medicaid. *Home Health Care Services Quarterly*, 7(1), 5-28.

Benjamin, A. E. 1986c. Trends and Issues in the Provision of Home Health Care: Local Governments in a Competitive Environment. *Health*, 7(4), 480-494.

Benjamin, A. E. 1992. An Overview of In-Home Health and Supportive Services for Older Persons. In M. G. Ory & A. P. Duncker (Eds.), *In-Home Care for Older People: Health and Supportive Services*, pp. 9-52. Newbury Park, CA: Sage.

Benjamin, A. E., P. J. Fox, J. H. Swan, et al. 1989. *Medicare Posthospital Study*. Final Report to the Commonwealth Fund Commission on Elderly People Living Alone. San Francisco: Center for Aging Services Research and University of California, Institute for Health & Aging, and San Francisco Institute on Aging, Mount Zion Hospital and Medical Center.

Benson, J. K. 1975. The Interorganizational Network as a Political Economy. *Administrative Sciences Quarterly*, 20, 229-249.

Berger, P., & T. Luckmann. 1966. *The Social Construction of Reality*. Garden City, NY: Doubleday.

Bergthold, L. A. 1987. The Impact of Public Policy on Home Health Services for the Elderly. *Pride Institute Journal of Long Term Home Health Care*, 6, 12-21.

Bergthold, L. A., C. L. Estes, & A. M. Villanueva. 1990. Public Light and Private Dark: The Privatization of Home Health Services for the Elderly in the U.S. *Home Health Care Services Quarterly*, 11(3/4), 7-33.

Berliner, H. S. 1987. Walk-In Chains: The Proprietarization of Ambulatory Care. *International Journal of Health Services*, 17, 585-594.

Berliner, H. S., & R. K. Burlage. 1987. Proprietary Hospital Chains and Academic Medical Centers. *International Journal of Health Services*, 17, 27-46.

Berliner, H. S., & C. Regan. 1987. Multinational Operations of U.S. For-Profit Hospital Chains: Trends and Implications. *American Journal of Public Health*, 77, 1280-1284.

Berliner, H. S., & C. Regan. 1990. Multi-National Operations of U.S. For-Profit Hospital Chains: Trends and Implications. In J. W. Salmon (Ed.), *The Corporate Transformation of Health Care: Issues and Directions*, pp. 155-165. Amityville, NY: Baywood.

Bernard, M., & C. Phillipson. 1991. Self-Care and Health in Old Age. In S. Redfern, *Nursing Elderly People* (2nd ed.), pp. 405-415. Edinburgh: Churchill Livingstone.

Biggs, E. L., J. Kralewski, & G. Brown. 1980. Contract-Managed and Traditionally Managed Nonprofits. *Medical Care*, 18, 585-596.

Binney, E. A., & C. L. Estes. 1988. The Retreat of the State and Its Transfer of Responsibility: The Intergenerational War. *International Journal of Health Services*, 18, 83-96.

Binney, E. A., & C. L. Estes. 1990. Setting the Wrong Limits: Class Biases and the Biographical Standard. In P. Homer & M. Holstein (Eds.), *A Good Old Age? The Paradox of Setting Limits*, pp. 240-257. New York: Simon & Schuster.

Binney, E. A., C. L. Estes, & S. E. Humphers. 1989. Informalization and Community Care for the Elderly. In C. L. Estes, J. B. Wood, et al., *Organizational and Community Responses to Medicare Policy: Consequences for Health and Social Services for the Elderly*, Vol. 1, pp. 204-229. Final Report. San Francisco: University of California, Institute for Health & Aging.

Binney, E. A., C. L. Estes, & S. R. Ingman. 1990. Medicalization, Public Policy, and the Elderly: Social Service in Jeopardy? *Social Science and Medicine*, 30, 761-771.

Binstock, R. H. 1983. The Aged as Scapegoat. *The Gerontologist*, 23, 136-143.

Binstock, R. H. 1985. The Oldest Old: A Fresh Perspective or Compassionate Ageism Revisited? *Milbank Memorial Fund Quarterly/Health and Society*, 63, 420-451.

Bishop, C. E. 1988. Competition in the Market for Nursing Home Care. *Journal of Health Politics, Policy and Law*, 13, 341-360.

Bishop, C. E., & S. L. Karon. 1988. *The Composition of Home Health Expenditure Growth*. Waltham, MA: Bigel Institute for Health Policy.

Blau, P. M. 1964. *Exchange and Power in Social Life*. New York: John Wiley.

Blendon, R. J., & J. N Edwards. 1991. Caring for the Uninsured: Choices for Reform. *Journal of the American Medical Association*, 265, 2563-2565.

Bliwise, N. G., M. E. McCall, & S. J. Swan. 1987. The Epidemiology of Mental Illness in Late Life. In E. E. Lurie, J. H. Swan, et al., *Serving the Mentally Ill Elderly: Problems and Perspectives*, pp. 1-38. Lexington, MA: Lexington/Heath.

Block, L. E. 1991. *Health Care Rationing: Is It Discriminatory?* Paper presented at the American Public Health Association Annual Meeting, Atlanta.

Bly, J. L. 1981. Measuring Productivity for Home Health Nurses. *Home Health Care Services Quarterly*, 2(3), 23-40.

Boone, C. R., C. Coulton, & S. Keller. 1987. The Impact of Early and Comprehensive Social Work Services on Length of Stay. *Social Work in Health Care*, 7(1), 1-9.

Branch, L. G., D. A. Evans, P. A. Scherr, L. Smith, J. O. Taylor, & T. Wetle. 1989. *A Prospective Study Differentiating the Baseline Characteristics of Future Elderly Users of Medical Home Care and Nursing Home Care*. Paper presented at the American Public Health Association Annual Meeting, Chicago.

Branch, L. G., & A. M. Jette. 1983. Elders' Use of Informal Long-Term Care Assistance. *The Gerontologist*, 23, 51-56.

Braun, K. L., C. L. Rose, & M. D. Finch. 1991. Patient Characteristics and Outcomes in Institutional and Community Long-Term Care. *The Gerontologist*, 31, 648-656.

Brizius & Foster. 1987. *State Policy Data Book, 1987*. Alexandria, VA: State Policy Research.

Broaddus, W. 1987. Toe to Toe with IRS. *Foundation News*, 28(1), 60-62.

Brody, E. M. 1981. Women in the Middle and Family Help to Older People. *The Gerontologist*, 32, 471-480.

Brody, E. M. 1985. Parent Care as a Normative Family Stress. *The Gerontologist*, 25, 19-29.

Brody, E. M., & S. J. Brody. 1989. The Informal System of Health Care. In C. Eisdorfer, D. A. Kessler, & A. N. Spector (Eds.), *Caring for the Elderly*, pp. 259-290. Baltimore, MD: Johns Hopkins University Press.

Brody, S. J., & J. S. Magel. 1984. DRG: The Second Revolution in Health Care for the Elderly. *Journal of the American Geriatrics Society*, 32, 676-679.

Brody, S. J., & J. S. Magel. 1989. Long-Term Care: The Long and Short of It. In C. Eisdorfer, D. A. Kessler, & A. N. Spector (Eds.), *Caring for the Elderly*, pp. 235-258. Baltimore, MD: Johns Hopkins University Press.

Brody, S. J., & N. Persily. 1984. *Hospitals and the Aged: The New Old Market*. Rockville, MD: Aspen.

Buie, J. 1988, July. Control Studies Bode Better Health in Aging. *APA Monitor*, p. 20.

Burden Foundation. 1986. *Grantmaking for the Elderly: An Analysis of Foundation Expenditures, 1978-1982*. New York: Florence V. Burden Foundation.

Bureau of Aging and Adult Services. 1984. *1983 Annual Report*. Seattle: State of Washington, Department of Social and Health Services.

Butler, L. H., & P. W. Newacheck. 1981. Health and Social Factors Affecting Long Term Care Policy. In J. Meltzer, F. Farrow, & H. Richman (Eds.), *Policy Options in Long Term Care*, pp. 38-77. Chicago: University of Chicago Press.

California Hospital Association (CHA). 1986. *Continuity of Care/Discharge Planning in California Hospitals*. Unpublished manuscript, California Hospital Association, Subcommittee, Sacramento.

Callahan, D. 1987. *Setting Limits: Medical Goals in an Aging Society.* New York: Touch-stone.

Callahan, J. J. 1989. Case Management for the Elderly: A Panacea? *Journal of Aging & Social Policy,* 1(1/2), 181-195.

Canalis, D. M. 1987. Homemaker-Home Health Aide Attrition: Methods of Prevention. *Caring,* 6(4), 84-89.

Caro, F. G. 1989. Alternatives to Institutionalization: Community Long-Term Care. In C. Eisdorfer, D. A. Kessler, & A. N. Spector (Eds.), *Caring for the Elderly,* pp. 50-70. Baltimore, MD: Johns Hopkins University Press.

Caserta, M., D. Lund, S. Wright, & P. Redburn. 1987. Caregivers to Dementia Patients: Use of Community Services. *The Gerontologist,* 27, 209-213.

Castells, M. 1983. City and Culture: The San Francisco Experience. In *The City and the Grassroots.* Berkeley: University of California Press.

Cavanaugh, J. C., N. J. Dunn, D. Mowery, et al. 1989. Problem-Solving Strategies in Dementia Patient-Caregiver Dyads. *The Gerontologist,* 29(2), 156-158.

Cetron, M. 1985. The Public Opinion of Home Care: A Survey Report Executive Summary. *Caring,* 4(10), 12-15.

Chelimsky, E. 1985. *Information Requirements for Evaluating the Impacts of Medicare Prospective Payment on Post-Hospital Long-Term Care Services.* Preliminary Report to U.S. Senate Special Committee on Aging. Washington, DC: U.S. General Accounting Office.

Chelimsky, E. 1986, June. *Post-Hospital Care: Efforts to Evaluate Medicare's Prospective Payment Effects Are Insufficient.* Report to Chairman, U.S. Senate Special Committee on Aging. Washington, DC: U. S. General Accounting Office.

Chelimsky, E. 1987. [Access to Post-Hospital Care for Medicare Beneficiaries]. Testimony before the U.S. House of Representatives Select Committee on Aging, Subcommittee on Health and Long-Term Care. Washington, DC: U.S. General Accounting Office.

Christianson, J. B. 1986. *Channeling Effects of Informal Care.* Princeton, NJ: Mathematica Policy Research.

Chubb, J. E. 1985. Federalism and the Bias for Centralization. In J. E. Chubb & P. E. Peterson (Eds.), *New Directions in American Politics,* pp. 277-281. Washington, DC: Brookings Institution.

Clarke, L., & C. L. Estes. 1992. Sociological and Economic Theories of Markets and Nonprofits: Evidence from Home Health Organizations. *American Journal of Sociology,* 97, 945-969.

Clarke, N. M., & M. Pinkett-Heller. 1979. The Institution of Administrative Change in the Home Health Service Industry. *Home Health Care Services Quarterly,* 1(1), 7-17.

Clotfelter, C. T. 1985. Tax Reform Proposals and Charitable Giving in 1985. In Independent Sector, *Giving and Volunteering: New Frontiers of Knowledge,* pp. 447-488. Spring Research Forum Working Papers. Washington, DC: Independent Sector.

Clotfelter, C. T. 1989. Federal Tax Policy and Charitable Giving. In R. Magat (Ed.), *Philanthropic Giving,* pp. 105-127. New York: Oxford University Press.

Coe, M., A. Wilkinson, & P. Patterson. 1986. *Preliminary Evidence on the Impact of DRGs: Dependency at Discharge Study.* Beaverton: Northwest Oregon Health Systems.

Cohen, J. 1983. Publicly Financed Long Term Care. In *Project to Analyze Existing Long-Term Care Data.* Washington, DC: Urban Institute.

Collins, C., M. Stommel, S. King, & C. W. Given. 1991. Assessment of the Attitudes of Family Caregivers Toward Community Services. *The Gerontologist,* 31, 756-761.

Collins, J. 1991. Power and Local Community Activity. *Journal of Aging Studies,* 5, 209-218.

Comfort, A. 1976. *A Good Age*. New York: Crown.

Conrad, K. J., P. Hanrahan, & S. L. Hughes. 1990. Survey of Adult Day Care in the United States: National and Regional Findings. *Research on Aging*, 12(1), 36-56.

Conrad, K. J., S. L. Hughes, P. F. Campione, & R. S. Goldberg. 1987. Shedding New Light on Adult Day Care. *Perspectives on Aging*, 16(6), 18-21.

Conrad, K. J., S. L. Hughes, P. Hanrahan, & S. Wang. 1991. *Classification of Adult Day Care: A Cluster of Analysis of Services and Activities*. Unpublished manuscript, Northwestern University, Center for Health Services and Policy Research, Evanston, IL.

Conrad, P., & J. W. Schneider. 1980. *Deviance and Medicalization: From Badness to Sickness*. St. Louis, MO: C. V. Mosby.

Consumer Price Index. 1989. *Statistical Abstract of the United States: 1988*. Washington, DC: Government Printing Office.

Corbin, J. M., & A. Strauss. 1988. *Unending Work and Care: Managing Chronic Illness at Home*. San Francisco: Jossey-Bass.

Coser, L. 1963. The Sociology of Poverty. *Social Problems*, 13, 140-148.

Coughlin, T. A., T. D. McBride, & K. Liu. 1989. *Determinants of Transitory and Permanent Nursing Home Admissions*. Paper presented at the American Public Health Association Annual Meeting, Chicago.

Coulton, C. 1988. Prospective Payment Requires Increased Attention to Quality of Post Hospital Care. *Social Work in Health Care*, 13(4), 19-30.

Coulton, C., R. Dunkle, J. Chow, M. Haug, & D. Vielhaber. 1988. Dimensions of Post-Hospital Care Decisionmaking: A Factor Analysis. *The Gerontologist*, 28, 218-223.

Coulton, C., N. Paschall, D. Foster, A. Bohnengel, & L. Slivinske. 1979. *Social Work Quality Assurance Programs: A Comparative Analysis*. Washington, DC: National Association of Social Workers.

Council on Scientific Affairs (CSA), American Medical Association. 1990. Home Care in the 1990s. *Journal of the American Medical Association*, 263, 1241-1244.

Crane, M. 1986. How Badly Are Cost Controls Hurting Patients? *Medical Economics*, 63(8), 61-64.

Crawford, R. 1980. Healthism and the Medicalization of Everyday Life. *International Journal of Health Services*, 10, 365-388.

Cromwell, J., & J. R. Kanak. 1982. The Effects of Prospective Reimbursement Programs on Hospital Adoption and Service Sharing. *Health Care Financing Review*, 4(2), 67-88.

Daatland, S. 1990. What Are Families for? On Family Solidarity and Preference for Help. *Ageing and Society*, 10, 1-17.

Davidson, K. W. 1978. Evolving Social Work Roles in Health Care: The Case of Discharge Planning. *Social Work in Health Care*, 4(1), 228-234.

Davis, K., & D. Rowland. 1986. *Medicare Policy*. Baltimore, MD: Johns Hopkins University Press.

DesHarnais, S. I., E. J. Kobrinski, J. D. Chesney, M. J. Long, R. P. Ament, & S. T. Fleming. 1987. The Early Effects of the Prospective Payment System on Inpatient Utilization and the Quality of Care. *Inquiry*, 24, 7-16.

DeVita, C. J., & L. M. Salamon. 1987. Commercial Activities in Human Service Organizations. In Independent Sector, *The Constitution and the Independent Sector*, pp. 403-415. Spring Research Forum Working Papers. Washington, DC: Independent Sector.

Dickinson, J., & B. Russell. (Eds.). 1986. *Family Economy and State: The Social Reproduction Process Under Capitalism*. Toronto: Garamond.

DiMaggio, P. 1982. Structural Analysis of Organizational Fields. In B. Staw & L. L. Cummings (Eds.), *Annual Review of Research on Organizations*, Vol. 8. Greenwich, CT: JAI Press.

DiMaggio, P. J., & W. W. Powell. 1983. The Iron Cage Revisited: Institutional Isomorphism and Collective Rationality in Organization Fields. *American Sociological Review*, 82, 147-160.

Division of National Cost Estimates (DNCE), Office of the Actuary, U.S. Health Care Financing Administration. 1987. National Health Expenditures, 1986-2000. *Health Care Financing Review*, 8(4), 1-36.

Dobson, A., & R. Bialek. 1985. Shaping Public Policy from the Perspective of a Data Builder. *Health Care Financing Review*, 6(6), 117-134.

Doherty, M., & D. Kaufman. 1988. *Elderly Medi-Cal Patients as Second Class Citizens: A Study of Discriminatory Admissions Practices in San Francisco Nursing Homes*. Unpublished manuscript, Family Service Agency of San Francisco, Long Term Care Ombudsman Program.

Doty, P. 1986. Family Care of the Elderly: The Role of Public Policy. *Milbank Memorial Fund Quarterly/Health and Society*, 64, 34-75.

Doty, P., K. Liu, & J. Wiener. 1985. An Overview of Long-Term Care. *Health Care Financing Review*, 6(3), 69-78.

Douglas, J. 1983. *Why Charity?* Beverly Hills, CA: Sage.

Dressel, P. 1984. *The Service Trap: From Altruism to Dirty Work*. Springfield, IL: Charles C Thomas.

Eastaugh, S. R. 1981. *Medical Economics and Health Finance*. Boston: Auburn.

Easton, L. S., R. Cogen, & M. Fulcomer. 1991. Effect of Medicare Prospective Payment System on a Home Health Agency: Changes in Patient Population and Services Provided. *Applied Nursing Research*, 4, 107-112.

Eggers, P. 1987. Prospective Payment System and Quality Early Results and Research Strategy. *MCFR Annual Supplement*, 2, 9-37.

Ehrenreich, J., & B. Ehrenreich. 1978. Medicalization and Social Control. In J. Ehrenreich (Ed.), *The Cultural Crisis of Modern Medicine*, pp. 39-79. New York: Monthly Review Press.

Eisenberg, P. 1987. In Search of More Responsible Philanthropy. *Foundation News*, 28(1), 51-53.

Emerson, R. M. 1962. Power Dependence Relations. *American Sociological Review*, 27, 31-41.

Emery, F., & E. Trist. 1965. The Causal Texture of Organizational Environments. *Human Relations*, 18(1), 21-32.

Enders, A. 1986. Issues and Options in Technology for Disability and Aging. In C. W. Mahoney, C. L. Estes, & J. E. Heumann (Eds.), *Toward a Unified Agenda: Proceedings of a National Conference on Disability and Aging*, pp. 64-89. San Francisco: University of California, Institute for Health & Aging.

England, S. E., S. M. Keigher, B. Miller, & N. L. Linsk. 1990. Community Care Policies and Gender Justice. In M. Minkler & C. L. Estes (Eds.), *Critical Perspectives on Aging: The Political and Moral Economy of Growing Old*, pp. 227-244. Amityville, NY: Baywood.

Enthoven, A. C. 1990. Health Care Costs: Why Regulation Fails, Why Competition Works, How to Get There from Here. In P. R. Lee & C. L. Estes (Eds.), *The Nation's Health*, pp. 286-293. Boston: Jones & Bartlett.

Ermann, D., & J. Gabel. 1984. Multihospital Systems: Issues and Empirical Findings. *Health Affairs*, 3(1), 50-64.

Estes, C. L. 1979. *The Aging Enterprise*. San Francisco: Jossey-Bass.

Estes, C. L. 1980. Construction of Reality: Problems of Aging. *Journal of Social Issues*, 39(2), 117-132.

Estes, C. L. 1984-1985. The United States: Long Term Care and Federal Policy. *Home Health Care Services Quarterly*, 5(3/4), 315-328.

Estes, C. L. 1986. The Politics of Ageing in America. *Ageing and Society*, 6, 121-134.

Estes, C. L. 1987a. [Medicare Hospital DRG Margins]. Unpublished statement before the U.S. House of Representatives Committee on Ways and Means, Subcommittee on Health.

Estes, C. L. 1987b, February 26. Testimony. In *Medicare Hospital Diagnosis-Related Group (DRG) Margins*. Hearing before the U.S. House of Representatives Committee on Ways and Means, Subcommittee on Health. Washington, DC: Government Printing Office.

Estes, C. L. 1987c, February 14. Testimony. In *The President's FY 1988 Budget Proposals*. Hearing before the U.S. House of Representatives Committee on the Budget. Washington, DC: Government Printing Office.

Estes, C. L. 1988. Cost Containment and the Elderly: Conflict or Challenge? *Journal of the American Geriatrics Society*, 36, 68-72.

Estes, C. L. 1991. The Reagan Legacy: Privatization, the Welfare State, and Aging in the 1990s. In J. Myles & J. Quadagno (Eds.), *States, Labor Markets, and the Future of Old Age Policy*, pp. 59-83. Philadelphia: Temple University Press.

Estes, C. L., & R. Alford. 1990. Systemic Crisis and the Nonprofit Sector: Toward a Political Economy of the Non-Profit Health and Social Services Sector. *Theory and Society*, 19, 173-198.

Estes, C. L., & L. Bergthold. 1989. The Unravelling of the Nonprofit Sector in the U.S. *International Journal of Sociology and Social Policy*, 9(2/3), 18-33.

Estes, C. L., & E. A. Binney. 1988. Toward a Transformation of Health and Aging Policy. *International Journal of Health Services*, 18, 69-82.

Estes, C. L., & E. A. Binney. 1989. The Biomedicalization of Aging: Dangers and Dilemmas. *The Gerontologist*, 29, 587-596.

Estes, C. L., E. A. Binney, & L. A. Bergthold. 1988. The Delegitimation of the Nonprofit Sector: The Role of Ideology and Public Policy. In Independent Sector, *Looking Forward to the Year 2000: Public Policy and Philanthropy*, pp. 498-514. Spring Research Forum Working Papers. Washington, DC: Independent Sector & United Way Institute.

Estes, C. L., E. A. Binney, & L. A. Bergthold. 1989. How the Legitimacy of the Sector Has Eroded. In V. A. Hodgkinson, R. W. Lyman, et al., *The Future of the Nonprofit Sector*, pp. 21-40. San Francisco: Jossey-Bass.

Estes, C. L., E. A. Binney, & D. S. Carrell. 1992. *Fiscal Austerity and Intergenerational Tradeoffs in Community-Based Long Term Care*. Paper presented at the American Society on Aging Annual Meeting, San Diego, CA.

Estes, C. L., & L. E. Gerard. 1983. Governmental Responsibility: Issues of Reform and Federalism. In C. L. Estes, R. J. Newcomer, et al., *Fiscal Austerity and Aging: Shifting Government Responsibility for the Elderly*, pp. 41-58. Beverly Hills, CA: Sage.

Estes, C. L., L. E. Gerard, J. S. Zones, & J. H. Swan. 1984. *Political Economy, Health, and Aging*. Boston: Little, Brown.

Estes, C. L., C. Harrington, & S. Davis. 1992. Medical-Industrial Complex. In E. F. Borgatta & M. L. Borgatta (Eds.), *The Encyclopedia of Sociology*, Vol. 3, pp. 1243-1254. New York: Macmillan.

Estes, C. L., & P. R. Lee. 1986. Health Problems and Policy Issues of Old Age. In L. Aiken & D. Mechanic (Eds.), *Applications of Social Science to Clinical Medicine and*

Health Policy, pp. 335-355. New Brunswick, NJ: Rutgers University Press (Reprinted in P. Brown, Ed. (1989). *Perspectives in Medical Sociology*. Homewood, IL: Dorsey)

Estes, C. L., R. J. Newcomer, & Associates. 1983. *Fiscal Austerity and Aging: Shifting Governmental Responsibility for the Elderly*. Beverly Hills, CA: Sage.

Estes, C. L., & T. G. Rundall. 1992. Social Characteristics, Social Structure, and Health in the Aging Population. In M. G. Ory, R. P. Ables, & P. D. Lipman (Eds.), *Aging, Health, and Behavior*, pp. 299-326. Newbury Park, CA: Sage.

Estes, C. L., & J. H. Swan. 1988. Privatization and Access to Home Health Care for the Elderly. In *Organizational and Community Responses to Medicare Policy: Consequences for Health and Social Services for the Elderly*, Vol. 3, pp. 175-226. Final Report. San Francisco: University of California, Institute for Health & Aging.

Estes, C. L., & J. H. Swan. 1989. *Privatization, System Membership, and Access to Home Health Care for the Elderly*. Paper presented at the Society for the Study of Social Problems Annual Meeting, Berkeley.

Estes, C. L., J. H. Swan, L. A. Bergthold, & P. H. Spohn. In press. Running as Fast as They Can: Organizational Changes in Home Health Care. *Home Health Care Services Quarterly*.

Estes, C. L., & J. B. Wood. 1986. The Non-Profit Sector and Community-Based Care for the Elderly in the U.S.: A Disappearing Resource? *Social Science and Medicine*, 23, 1261-1266.

Estes, C. L., J. B. Wood, et al. 1988. *Organizational and Community Responses to Medicare Policy: Consequences for Health and Social Services for the Elderly*, 3 Vols. Final Report. San Francisco: University of California, Institute for Health & Aging.

Evans, R. G. 1990. Accessible, Acceptable, and Affordable: Financing Health Care in Canada. In *Improving Access to Affordable Health Care: The Richard and Hinda Rosenthal Lectures, 1990*, pp. 7-47. Washington, DC: Institute of Medicine.

Evanswick, C. J. 1985. Home Health Care: Current Trends and Future Opportunities. *Journal of Ambulatory Care Management*, 8(4), 4-17.

Evanswick, C. J., T. Rundall, & B. Goldiamond. 1985. Hospital Services for Older Adults. *The Gerontologist*, 25, 631-636.

Fackelmann, K. A. (Ed.). 1987. Discharge Planning Comes of Age. *Medicine and Health Perspectives*, 41(6), 4.

Feather, J., & L. Nichols. 1985. Hospital Discharge Planning for Continuity of Care: The National Perspective. In E. Harigan & D. J. Brown (Eds.), *Discharge Planning for Continuity of Care*, rev. ed., pp. 71-77. New York: National League for Nursing.

Feder, J., J. Hadley, & S. Zuckerman. 1987. How Did Medicare's Prospective Payment System Affect Hospitals? *New England Journal of Medicine*, 317, 867-872.

Feder, J., & W. J. Scanlon. 1980. Regulating the Bed Supply in Nursing Homes. *Milbank Memorial Fund Quarterly/Health and Society*, 58(1), 54-58.

Feder, J., W. Scanlon, & J. Hoffman. 1988. *PPS and Post-Hospital Care: Facts and Questions*. Paper presented at the Health Services Research Association Annual Meeting, San Francisco.

Feldblum, C. R. 1985. Home Health Care for the Elderly: Programs, Problems and Potentials. *Harvard Journal of Legislation*, 22(1), 193-254.

Ferris, J., & E. Graddy. 1988. Fading Distinctions Among the Three Sectors: Implications for Public Policy. In Independent Sector, *Looking Forward to the Year 2000: Public Policy and Philanthropy*, pp. 41-56. Spring Research Forum Working Papers. Washington, DC: Independent Sector.

Finch, J. 1989. *Family Obligations and Social Change*. London: Polity Press & Basil Blackwell.

Finch, J., & D. Groves. 1980. Community Care and the Family: A Case for Equal Opportunities? *Journal of Social Policy*, 9, 487-511.

Finch, J., & D. Groves. (Eds.). 1983. *A Labour of Love: Women, Work and Caring*. London: Routledge & Kegan Paul.

Fischer, L. R., & N. N. Eustis. 1988. DRGs and Family Care for the Elderly: A Case Study. *The Gerontologist*, 28, 383-389.

Flemming, A. S., J. G. Buchanon, J. F. Santos, & L. D. Rickards. 1984. *Mental Health Services for the Elderly: Report on a Survey of Community Mental Health Centers*, Vol. 1. Washington, DC: Action Committee to Implement the Mental Health Recommendations of the 1981 White House Conference on Aging.

Flemming, A. S., J. G. Buchanon, J. F. Santos, & L. D. Rickards. 1986. *Mental Health Services for the Elderly: Report on a Survey of Community Mental Health Centers*, Vol. 3. Washington, DC: Action Committee to Implement the Mental Health Recommendations of the 1981 White House Conference on Aging.

Foucault, M. 1975. *The Birth of the Clinic*. New York: Vintage.

Fox, D. M., K. S. Andersen, A. E. Benjamin, & L. J. Dunatov. 1987. Intensive Home Health Care in the United States: Financing as Technology. *International Journal of Technology Assessment in Health Care*, 3(4), 561-573.

Fox, P. J., & J. H. Swan. 1988. Community Mental Health Centers: A Report of 1986 and 1987 Survey Findings. In C. L. Estes, J. B. Wood, et al., *Organizational and Community Responses to Medicare Policy: Consequences for Health and Social Services for the Elderly*, Vol. 1, pp. 166-177. Final Report. San Francisco: University of California, Institute for Health & Aging.

Fox, P. J., J. H. Swan, & C. L. Estes. 1986. Community Mental Health Centers and Their Response to Public Policy Changes: Effects on the Elderly. *Hospital and Community Psychiatry*, 37, 937-939.

Francis, D. 1984. *Will You Still Need Me, Will You Still Feed Me, When I'm 84?* Bloomington: Indiana University Press.

Francis, S. 1991. U.S. Industrial Outlook 1991: Health and Medical Services. *Medical Benefits*, 8(4), 1-2.

Frankfather, D. L., M. J. Smith, & F. G. Caro. 1981. *Family Care of the Elderly: Public Initiatives and Private Obligations*. Lexington, MA: Lexington/Heath.

Freedman, S. A. 1985. Megacorporate Health Care: Choice for the Future. *New England Journal of Medicine*, 312, 579-582.

Friedman, B., & S. Shortell. 1988. The Financial Performance of Selected Investor-Owned and Not-For-Profit System Hospitals Before and After Medicare Prospective Payment. *Health Services Research*, 23, 237-267.

Friedman, E. 1988, January 20. Interview: Taylor: Tax Exemptions v. Charitable Spirit. *Hospitals*, pp. 58-60.

Friedson, E. 1970. *Profession of Medicine*. New York: Dodd/Mead.

Fritz, M. 1990, January 8. Health. *Forbes*, pp. 180-182.

Fuchs, V. R. 1990. The Health Sector's Share of the Gross National Product. *Science*, 247, 534-538.

Garland, M. J. 1991. *In Praise of Rationing: Reflections on Oregon's Experience*. Paper presented at the American Public Health Association Annual Meeting, Atlanta.

Ginsburg, P. B., L. B. LeRoy, & G. T. Hammons. 1990. Medicare Physician Payment Reform. *Health Affairs*, 9(1), 178-188.

Ginzberg, E. 1986. The Destabilization of Health Care. *New England Journal of Medicine*, 315, 757-871.

Ginzberg, E. 1987. Foundations and the Nation's Health Agenda. *Health Affairs*, 6(4), 128-140.

Glassman-Feibusch, B. 1981. The Socially Isolated Elderly. *Geriatric Nursing,* 2, 28-31.
Glendenning, F. (Ed.). 1985. *Educational Gerontology: International Perspectives.* London: Croom Helm.
Goldberg, S. C. 1987. *Field Research: Discharge Planning for Elderly Patients in a Cost Containment Environment.* Unpublished manuscript, University of California, San Francisco, Institute for Health & Aging.
Goldberg, S. C. 1988. Senior Centers and Their Nutrition Services in an Era of Cost Containment. In C. L. Estes, J. B. Wood, et al., *Organizational and Community Responses to Medicare Policy: Consequences for Health and Social Services for the Elderly,* Vol. 1, pp. 178-189. San Francisco: University of California, Institute for Health & Aging.
Goldberg, S. C. 1990. Changes in Access in an Era of Cost Containment: Organizations Serving the Elderly in the San Francisco Bay Area (Doctoral dissertation, University of California, San Francisco). *Dissertation Abstracts International,* 51/08-A, 2890.
Goldberg, S. C., & C. L. Estes. 1988. Community Variations in Access to Care. In C. L. Estes, J. B. Wood, et al., *Organizational and Community Responses to Medicare Policy: Consequences for Health and Social Services for the Elderly,* Vol. 2, pp. 62-100. Final Report. San Francisco: University of California, Institute for Health & Aging.
Goldberg, S. C., & C. L. Estes. 1990. Medicare DRGs and Post-Hospital Care for the Elderly: Does Out of the Hospital Mean Out of Luck? *Journal of Applied Gerontology,* 9, 20-35.
Goldsmith, J. 1984. Death of a Paradigm: The Challenge of Competition. *Health Affairs,* 3(3), 5-19.
Goldsmith, J. 1989, February. Chronic Illness and the Technologic Transformation of American Health Care. *Decisions in Technology Economics,* pp. 4-13.
Gornick, M., & M. J. Hall. 1988. Trends in Medicare Use of Post-Hospital Care. *Health Care Financing Review* (Annual Supplement), pp. 27-38.
Grant, L. A., & C. Harrington. 1989. Quality of Care in Licensed and Unlicensed Home Care Agencies: A California Case Study. *Home Health Care Services Quarterly,* 10(1/2), 115-138.
Gratton, B., & V. Wilson. 1988. Family Support Systems and the Minority Elderly: A Cautionary Analysis. *Journal of Gerontological Social Work,* 13(1/2), 81-93.
Grazier, K. L. 1986. The Impact of Reimbursement Policy on Home Health Care. *Pride Institute Journal of Long Term Home Health Care,* 5(1), 12-16.
Greenberg, B. R., I. A. Gutheil, L. M. Parker, & R. H. Chernesky. 1991. *Aging: The Burden Study of Foundation Grantmaking Trends.* New York: Foundation Center.
Greene, E. 1990. IRS Makes a $1.2 Billion Error, Skewing a Report on Corporate Giving to Philanthropy. *Chronicle of Philanthropy,* 2(22), 5, 8.
Greene, V. L., & J. I. Ondrich. 1990. Risk Factors for Nursing Home Admissions and Exits: A Discrete-Time Hazard Approach. *Journal of Gerontology,* 45, S250-S258.
Grimaldi, P. L. 1982. *Medicaid Reimbursement of Nursing Home Care.* Washington, DC: American Enterprise Institute.
Guralnik, J. M., & E. L. Schneider. 1990. The Compression of Morbidity: A Dream Which May Come True, Someday! In P. R. Lee & C. L. Estes (Eds.), *The Nation's Health,* 3rd ed., pp. 42-53. Boston: Jones & Bartlett.
Guralnik, J. M., M. Y. Yanagishita, & E. L. Schneider. 1988. Projecting the Older Population of the U.S.: Lessons from the Past and Prospects for the Future. *Milbank Memorial Fund Quarterly/Health and Society,* 66, 283-308.
Guterman, S., & A. Dobson. 1986. Impact of the Medicare Prospective Payment for Hospitals. *Health Care Financing Review,* 7(3), 97-114.

Guterman, S., P. W. Eggers, G. Riley, T. F. Greene, & S. A. Terrell. 1988. The First 3 Years of Medicare Prospective Payment: An Overview. *Health Care Financing Review*, 9(3), 67-77.

Gutheil, I. A., & R. H. Chernesky. 1991. Foundation Support for Aging in the 1990s: The Emerging Picture. *Journal of Applied Gerontology*, 10(1), 117-130.

Gutowski, M. F., & J. F. Koshel. 1982. Social Services. In J. F Palmer & I. Sawhill (Eds.), *The Reagan Experiment*, pp. 307-308. Washington, DC: Urban Institute.

Habermas, J. 1975. *Legitimation Crisis*. Boston: Beacon.

Hall, P. D. 1987. Abandoning the Rhetoric of Independence: Reflections on the Non-profit Sector in the Post-Liberal Era. In S. A. Ostrander, S. Langton, & J. Van Til (Eds.), *Shifting the Debate: Public/Private Sector Relations in the Modern Welfare State*, pp. 11-28. New Brunswick, NJ: Transaction Books.

Ham, R. J. 1985. Home and Nursing Home Care of the Dependent Elderly Patient. *American Family Practitioner*, 31, 163-169.

Hammons, G. T., & L. G. Pawlson. 1989. Physician Payment Reform: Implications for Geriatrics. *Journal of the American Geriatrics Society*, 37, 1084-1091.

Hanaway, P. 1986. *The Corporation of American Medicine: The Report of the AMSA Study Group on For-Profit Health Care*. Reston, VA: AMSA Publications.

Hanley, R. J., L. B. Alecxih, J. M. Weiner, & D. L. Kennell. 1989. *Predicting Elderly Nursing Home Admissions: Results from the 1982-84 National Long-Term Care Survey*. Paper presented at the American Public Health Association Annual Meeting, Chicago.

Hansmann, H. 1980. The Role of Nonprofit Enterprise. *Yale Law Journal*, 89, 835-901.

Hansmann, H. 1987a. Economic Theories of Nonprofit Organizations. In W. W. Powell (Ed.), *The Nonprofit Sector: A Research Handbook*, pp. 27-42. New Haven, CT: Yale University Press.

Hansmann, H. 1987b. The Evolution of the Law of Nonprofit Organizations. In Independent Sector, *The Constitution and the Independent Sector*, pp. 17-26. Spring Research Forum Working Papers. Washington, DC: Independent Sector.

Hansmann, H. 1988. The Two Independent Sectors. In Independent Sector, *Looking Forward to the Year 2000: Public Policy and Philanthropy*, pp. 15-24. Spring Research Forum Working Papers. Washington, DC: Independent Sector.

Hanson, P. 1986. Discharge Planning: Whose Responsibility. *Discharge Planning Update*, 7(1), 1-24.

Harder, W. P., J. C. Gornick, & M. R. Burt. 1986. Adult Day Care: Substitute or Supplement? *Milbank Memorial Fund Quarterly/Health and Society*, 64, 414-441.

Harel, Z., L. Noelker, & B. Blake. 1985. Comprehensive Services for the Aged: Theoretical and Empirical Perspectives. *The Gerontologist*, 25, 644-649.

Harlow, K., & L. Wilson. 1985. *DRGs and the Community-Based Long Term Care System*. Presentation for the U.S. House of Representatives Committee on Education and Labor, Subcommittee on Human Resources, Washington, DC. Dallas: Southwest Long Term Care Gerontology Center, University of Texas Health Science Center.

Harper, M. S. 1992. Home and Community-Based Mental Health Services for the Elderly. In M. G. Ory & A. P. Duncker (Eds.), *In-Home Care for Older People: Health and Supportive Services*, pp. 126-135. Newbury Park, CA: Sage.

Harrington, C. 1988. Hospital-Based HHA's Continue to Increase. *Home Health Line*, 12, 186.

Harrington, C. 1989. The Structured Approaches. In C. Eisdorfer, D. A. Kessler, & A. N. Spector (Eds.), *Caring for the Elderly*, pp. 31-49. Baltimore, MD: Johns Hopkins University Press.

Harrington, C. 1991a. The Nursing Home Industry: A Structural Analysis. In M. Minkler & C. L. Estes (Eds.), *Critical Perspectives on Aging: The Political and Moral Economy of Growing Old*, pp. 153-164. Amityville, NY: Baywood.

Harrington, C. 1991b. The Organization and Financing of Long Term Care. In L. H. Aiken & C. M. Fagin (Eds.), *Charting Nursing's Future: Agenda for the 1990's*, pp. 181-197. Philadelphia: J. B. Lippincott.

Harrington, C., C. Cassel, C. L. Estes, S. Woolhandler, D. U. Himmelstein, & the Working Group on Long-Term Care Program Design, Physicians for a National Health Program. 1991. A National Long-Term Care Program for the United States: A Caring Vision. *Journal of the American Medical Association*, 266, 3023-3029.

Harrington, C., & C. L. Estes. 1989. *Trends in Nursing Homes in the Post Medicare Prospective Payment Period*. Unpublished manuscript, University of California, San Francisco, Institute for Health & Aging.

Harrington, C., C. L. Estes, P. R. Lee, & R. J. Newcomer. 1985. State Policies on Long Term Care. In C. Harrington, R. J. Newcomer, C. L. Estes, et al., *Long Term Care of the Elderly: Public Policy Issues*, pp. 67-88. Beverly Hills, CA: Sage.

Harrington, C., & L. A. Grant. 1990. The Delivery, Regulation, and Politics of Home Care: A California Case Study. *The Gerontologist*, 30, 451-461.

Harrington, C., R. J. Newcomer, C. L. Estes, & Associates. 1985. *Long Term Care of the Elderly: Public Policy Issues*. Beverly Hills, CA: Sage.

Harrington, C., S. D. Preston, L. A. Grant, & J. H. Swan. 1990. *Trends in State Nursing Home Bed Capacity and Occupancy in the 1978-1989 Period*. Paper presented at the American Public Health Association Annual Meeting, New York.

Harrington, C., & J. H. Swan. 1985. Institutional Long-Term Care Services. In C. Harrington, R. J. Newcomer, C. L. Estes, et al., *Long-Term Care of the Elderly: Public Policy Issues*, pp. 153-176. Beverly Hills, CA: Sage.

Harrington, C., & J. H. Swan. 1987. The Impact of State Medicaid Nursing Home Policies on Utilization and Expenditures. *Inquiry*, 24, 157-172.

Harrington, C., J. H. Swan, & L. A. Grant. 1988. Nursing Home Bed Capacity in the States, 1978-86. *Health Care Financing Review*, 9(4), 81-97.

Harvey, J. W., & K. F. McCrohan. 1990. Changing Conditions for Fund Raising and Philanthropy. In J. Van Til et al. (Eds.), *Critical Issues in American Philanthropy: Strengthening Theory and Practice*, pp. 39-64. San Francisco: Jossey-Bass.

Hatten, J., & D. Gibson. 1987. Medicare Discharges by the Facility Status Under the Prospective Payment System, 1984-86. *Health Care Financing Review*, 9(1), 97-101.

Havir, L. 1991. Senior Centers in Rural Communities: Potentials for Serving. *Journal of Aging Studies*, 5, 359-374.

Hawes, C., & C. D. Phillips. 1986. The Changing Structure of the Nursing Home Industry and the Impact of Ownership on Quality, Cost, and Access. In B. H. Gray (Ed.), *For-Profit Enterprise in Health Care*, pp. 492-538. Washington, DC: National Academy Press.

Hawley, A. H. 1968. *Human Ecology: A Theoretical Synthesis*. Chicago: University of Chicago Press.

Hedrick, S. C. 1991. *Evaluation of Effectiveness and Costs of Adult Day Health Care* (Research supported by Health Services Research & Development Service, Department of Veterans Affairs). Seattle, WA: Northwest HSR&D Field Program, Seattle VA Medical Center.

Heinz, J. 1986. The Effects of DRGs on Patients. *Business and Health*, 20, 17-20.

Hewitt, P. 1986. *A Broken Promise*. Washington, DC: Americans for Generational Equity.

Higgins, J. 1988. *The Business of Medicine: Private Health Care in Britain.* London: Macmillan Education.

Himmelstein, D., & S. Woolhandler. 1986. Cost Without Benefit: Administrative Waste in U.S. Health Care. *New England Journal of Medicine,* 314, 441-445.

Hinds, M. D. 1991, November 14. Suit Says Pennsylvania Has Failed to Carry out U.S. Health Plan for Poor Children. *The New York Times,* p. A20.

Hing, E. 1987a. *Impact of the Prospective Payment System on Nursing Home Care: Evidence from the 1985 National Nursing Home Survey.* Paper presented at the American Public Health Association Annual Meeting, New Orleans.

Hing, E. 1987b. Use of Nursing Homes by the Elderly: Preliminary Data from the 1985 National Nursing Home Survey. *NCHS Advancedata,* 135, 1-11.

Hodgkinson, V. A., R. W. Lyman, et al. 1989. *The Future of the Nonprofit Sector: Challenges, Changes and Policy Considerations.* San Francisco: Jossey-Bass.

Hodgkinson, V. A., & M. S. Weitzman. 1984. *Dimensions of the Independent Sector.* Washington, DC: Independent Sector.

Hodgkinson, V. A., & M. S. Weitzman. 1986. *Dimensions of the Independent Sector,* 2nd ed. Washington, DC: Independent Sector.

Hodgkinson, V. A., & M. S. Weitzman. 1988. *Dimensions of the Independent Sector* (Interim Update). Washington, DC: Independent Sector.

Hodgkinson, V. A., & M. S. Weitzman. 1989. *Dimensions of the Independent Sector,* 3rd ed. Washington, DC: Independent Sector.

Holahan, J., & J. W. Cohen. 1986. *Medicaid: The Trade-Off Between Cost Containment and Access.* Washington, DC: Urban Institute.

Hollingsworth, C. E., & B. Sokol. 1978. Predischarge Family Conference. *Journal of the American Medical Association,* 239, 740-741.

Homer, C. G., D. D. Bradham, & M. Rushefsky. 1984. Investor-Owned and Not-for-Profit Hospitals: Beyond the Cost and Revenue Debate. *Health Affairs,* 3(1), 133-136.

Homer, P., & M. Holstein (Eds.). 1990. *A Good Old Age? The Paradox of Setting Limits.* New York: Simon & Schuster.

Hopkins, B. R. 1987. Legal Issues Involving Competition by Nonprofits with Small Business. In Independent Sector, *The Constitution and the Independent Sector,* pp. 309-324. Spring Research Forum Working Papers. Washington, DC: Independent Sector.

Horowitz, A. 1985. Family Caregiving to the Frail Elderly. In C. Eisdorfer, M. P. Lawton, & G. L. Maddox (Eds.), *Annual Review of Gerontology and Geriatrics,* Vol. 5, pp. 194-246. New York: Springer.

Hoyer, R. G. 1990. Public Policy and the American Hospice Movement: The Tie That Binds. *Caring,* 9(3), 30-35.

Hughes, S. 1986. *Long-Term Care: Options in an Expanding Market.* Homewood, IL: Dow Jones-Irwin.

Hunter, H. 1991. *Managed Care: Is It Losing Its Competitive Edge?* Unpublished manuscript, California State University, Long Beach, Health Care Administration Program.

ICF, Inc. 1985. *Medicare's Role in Financing the Health Care of Older Women.* Paper submitted to the American Association of Retired Persons (AARP). Washington, DC.

Iglehart, J. K. 1986. Early Experience with Prospective Payment for Hospitals. *New England Journal of Medicine,* 314, 1460-1464.

Illich, I. 1976. *Medical Nemesis.* New York: Pantheon.

Independent Sector. 1991. 1991 Legislative Wrap-Up. *State Tax Trends for Nonprofits, 7*, 2-3.

Institute for Health & Aging (IHA). 1981. [Fiscal Crisis: Impact on Aging Services Study]. San Francisco: Author.

Institute for Health & Aging (IHA). 1986. [DRG Study]. San Francisco: Author.

Institute for Health & Aging (IHA). 1987. [DRG Study]. San Francisco: Author.

Institute for Health & Aging (IHA). 1991. [Community-Based Long Term Care for the Post-Acute and Chronically Ill Elderly Study]. San Francisco: Author.

Institute of Medicine (IOM). (B. H. Gray, Ed.). 1986a. *For-Profit Enterprise in Health Care.* Washington, DC: National Academy Press.

Institute of Medicine (IOM). (Staff and National Research Council Staff). 1986b. *Improving the Quality of Care in Nursing Homes.* Washington, DC: National Academy Press.

Institute of Medicine (IOM). (K. Lohr, Ed.). 1990. *Medicare: A Strategy for Quality Assurance*, Vol. 1. Washington, DC: National Academy Press.

Irwin, T. 1978. *Home Health Care: When a Patient Leaves the Hospital.* New York: Public Affairs Commission.

Joe, T. 1989. Policies for People: A Proposal for Redirection of Long-Term Care for the Elderly. In C. Eisdorfer, D. A. Kessler, & A. N. Spector (Eds.), *Caring for the Elderly*, pp. 507-520. Baltimore, MD: Johns Hopkins University Press.

Johnson, D. E. L. 1985a. Chains Integrate Healthcare Services into Local Networks. *Modern Healthcare*, 15(12), 2.

Johnson, D. E. L. 1985b. Investor-Owned Chains Continue Expansion, 1985 Survey Shows. *Modern Healthcare*, 15(12), 75-90.

Jones, P. A. 1988. The Home Care Personnel Shortage Crisis: Preliminary Results of a NAHC Survey. *Caring*, 7(5), 6-9.

Justice, D. 1988. *State Long Term Care Reform: Development of Community Care Systems in Six States.* Washington, DC: Center for Health Policy Research, National Governor's Association.

Kafka, F. 1961. The Metamorphosis. In *The Penal Colony*, pp. 67-132. New York: Schocken.

Kahl, A., & D. E. Clark. 1986. Employment in Health Services: Long-Term Trends and Projections. *Monthly Labor Review*, 109(8), 17-36.

Kahn, K. K., D. Draper, E. B. Keeler, et al. 1992. *The Effects of the DRG-Based Prospective Payment System on Quality of Care for Hospitalized Medicare Patients.* Santa Monica, CA: Rand.

Kaiser Family Foundation. 1991. *Annual Report.* Menlo Park, CA: Author.

Kaluzny, A. D., J. T. Gentry, J. H. Glasser, & J. B. Sprague. 1970. Diffusion of Innovative Health Care Services in the United States: A Study of Hospitals. *Medical Care, 8*, 474-487.

Kane, R. A. 1980. Discharge Planning: An Undischarged Responsibility. *Health and Social Work, 5*, 2-3.

Kane, R. A., & R. L. Kane. 1982. *Values and Long Term Care.* Lexington, MA: Lexington.

Kane, R. A., & R. L. Kane. 1987. *Long-Term Care: Principles, Programs and Policies.* New York: Springer.

Kane, R. A., & R. L. Kane. 1989. Vacating the Premises: A Reevaluation of First Principles. In C. Eisdorfer, D. A. Kessler, & A. N. Spector (Eds.), *Caring for the Elderly*, pp. 490-506. Baltimore, MD: Johns Hopkins University Press.

Kane, R. L. 1987. *PAC: A National Study of Post-Acute Care.* Funded by the Office of the Assistant Secretary for Planning and Evaluation and the Health Care Financing Administration, University of Minnesota, Minneapolis.

Kelman, H. R., & C. Thomas. 1990. Transitions Between Community and Nursing Home Residence in an Urban Elderly Population. *Journal of Community Health*, 15, 105-122.

Kemper, P., & C. M. Murtaugh. 1991. Lifetime Use of Nursing Home Care. *New England Journal of Medicine*, 324, 595-600.

Kenney, G. M. 1991. Understanding the Effects of PPS on Medicare Home Health Use. *Inquiry*, 28, 129-139.

Kenney, G. M., & J. Holahan. 1990. The Nursing Home Market and Hospital Discharge Delays. *Inquiry*, 27, 73-85.

Kidder, D., & D. Sullivan. 1982. Hospital Payroll Costs, Productivity, and Employment Under Prospective Reimbursement. *Health Care Financing Review*, 4(2), 89-100.

Kingson, E. R., B. A. Hirshorn, & J. M. Cornman. 1986. *Ties That Bind*. Washington, DC: Seven Locks.

Kinoy, S. K., M. Adamson, & S. Sherry. 1988. *The ABCs of DRGs: How to Protect and Expand Patients' Rights*. Washington, DC: Villers Foundation.

Kirby, W., V. Latta, & C. Helbing. 1986. Medicare Use and Cost of Home Health Agency Services, 1983-84. *Health Care Financing Review*, 8(1), 93-100.

Kirp, D. L., M. G. Yudof, & M. S. Franks. 1986. *Gender Justice*. Chicago: University of Chicago Press.

Kirwin, P. M., & L. W. Kaye. 1991. Service Consumption Patterns over Time Among Adult Day Care Program Participants. *Home Health Care Services Quarterly*, 12(4), 45-58.

Kotelchuck, R. 1986. And What About the Patients? Prospective Payment's Impact on Quality of Care. *Health/Pac Bulletin*, 17(2), 13-17.

Kramer, A. M., P. W. Shaughnessy, & M. L. Perrigrew. 1985. Cost-Effectiveness Implications Based on a Comparison of Nursing Home and Home Health Case Mix. *Health Services Research*, 20, 387-405.

Kronefeld, J. J., & M. L. Whicker. 1984. *U.S. National Health Policy*. New York: Praeger.

Krout, J. A. 1989. *Senior Centers in America*. Westport, CT: Greenwood Press.

Krout, J. A. 1991. Senior Center Participation: Findings from a Multidimensional Analysis. *Journal of Applied Gerontology*, 10, 244-257.

Krout, J. A., S. J. Cutler, & R. T. Coward. 1990. Correlates of Senior Center Participation: A National Analysis. *The Gerontologist*, 30, 72-79.

Kuhn, M. 1984. Challenge to a New Age. In M. Minkler & C. L. Estes (Eds.), *Readings in the Political Economy of Aging*, pp. 7-9. Farmingdale, NY: Baywood.

Kulys, R. 1983. Future Crises and the Very Old: Implications for Discharge Planning. *Health and Social Work*, 8, 182-195.

Kusserow, R. 1986. *Inspections of Inappropriate Discharges and Transfers*. Chicago: Office of Analysis and Inspections, Office of the Inspector General.

Lalonde, B. 1988. Assuring the Quality of Home Care via the Assessment of Client Outcomes. *Caring*, 7(1), 20-24.

Lane, L. F. 1984. *Developments in Facility-Based Services*. Paper prepared for the National Institute of Medicine, Nursing Home Study Committee.

LaViolette, S. 1983. Nursing Home Chains Scramble for More Private-Paying Patients. *Modern Healthcare*, 13(5), 130-138.

Lawton, M. P., E. M. Brody, & A. R. Saperstein. 1989. A Controlled Study of Respite Service for Caregivers of Alzheimer's Patients. *The Gerontologist*, 29, 8-16.

Lawton, M. P., M. H. Kleban, M. Moss, M. Rovine, & A. Glicksman. 1989. Measuring Caregiving Appraisal. *Journal of Gerontology*, 44, P61-P71.

Lazenby, H. C., & S. W. Letsch. 1990. National Health Expenditures, 1989. *Health Care Financing Review*, 12(2), 1-26.

Leat, D., & P. Gay. 1987. *Paying for Care: A Study of Policy and Practice in Paid Care Schemes.* London: Policy Studies Institute.

LeBrun, P. 1986. Payers Step up Roles in Discharge Planning. *Hospitals,* 59(12), 98-102.

Lee, P. R., & P. B. Ginsburg. 1988. Building a Consensus for Physician Payment Reform in Medicare. *Western Journal of Medicine,* 149, 352-358.

Lee, P. R., L. B. LeRoy, P. B. Ginsburg, & G. T. Hammons. 1990. Physician Payment Reform: An Idea Whose Time Has Come. *Medical Care Review,* 47, 137-163.

LeGrand, J., & R. Robinson. 1984. *Privatization and the Welfare State.* London: Allen & Unwin.

Lerman, D. (Ed.). 1987. *Home Care: Positioning the Hospital for the Future.* Chicago: American Hospital Publishing.

Lerner, M. J., D. G. Somers, D. Reid, D. Chiriboga, & M. Tierney. 1991. Adult Children as Caregivers: Egocentric Biases in Judgements of Sibling Contribution. *The Gerontologist,* 31, 746-755.

Letsch, S. W., K. R. Levit, & D. R. Waldo. 1988. National Health Expenditures, 1987. *Health Care Financing Review,* 10(2), 109-122.

Levit, K. R., H. C. Lazenby, C. A. Cowan, & S. W. Letsch. 1991. National Health Expenditures, 1990. *Health Care Financing Review,* 13(1), 29-54.

Levit, K. R., H. C. Lazenby, D. R. Waldo, & L. M. Davidoff. 1985. National Health Expenditures, 1984. *Health Care Financing Review,* 7(1), 1-35.

Lewin & Associates. 1976. *Investor-Owned Hospitals: An Examination of Performance.* Chicago: Health Services Foundation.

Lewin & Associates. 1987. *An Evaluation of the Medi-Cal Program's System for Establishing Reimbursement Rates for Nursing Homes.* Report by the Auditor General of California. Sacramento: Office of the Auditor General.

Lewin, L. S., T. J. Eckles, & L. B. Miller. 1988. Setting the Record Straight: The Provision of Uncompensated Care by Not for Profit Hospitals. *New England Journal of Medicine,* 318, 1212-1215.

Lewin, L. S., & M. E. Lewin. 1987. Financing Charity Care in an Era of Competition. *Health Affairs,* 6(1), 47-60.

Lewin, M. E., & L. S. Lewin. 1984. Health Care for the Uninsured. *Business and Health,* 1(9), 9-14.

Lewis, J., & B. Meredith. 1988. *Daughters Who Care: Daughters Caring for Mothers at Home.* London: Routledge & Kegan Paul.

Lewis, M. A., B. Leake, V. Clark, & M. Leal-Sotelo. 1990. Changes in Case Mix and Outcomes of Readmissions to Nursing Homes Between 1980 and 1984. *Health Services Research,* 24, 713-728.

Lewis, M. A., B. Leake, M. Leal-Sotelo, & V. Clark. 1987. The Initial Effects of the Prospective Payment System on Nursing Home Patients. *American Journal of Public Health,* 77, 819-821.

Light, D. 1986. Corporate Medicine for Profit. *Scientific American,* 255(6), 38-45.

Lindeman, D. A., & A. Pardini. 1983. Social Services: The Impact of Fiscal Austerity. In C. L. Estes, R. J. Newcomer, et al., *Fiscal Austerity and Aging: Shifting Government Responsibility for the Elderly,* pp. 133-155. Beverly Hills, CA: Sage.

Lindsey, L. B. 1987. Individual Giving Under the Tax Reform Act of 1986. In Independent Sector, *The Constitution and the Independent Sector,* pp. 133-146. Spring Research Forum Working Papers. Washington, DC: Independent Sector.

Lipson, D. J., & E. Donohoe. 1988. *State Financing of Long-Term Care Services for the Elderly: Vol. 1. Executive Report.* Washington, DC: Intergovernmental Health Policy Project, George Washington University.

Lipson, D. J., E. Donohoe, & C. Thomas. 1988. *State Financing of Long-Term Care Services for the Elderly: Vol. 2. State Profiles*. Washington, DC: Intergovernmental Health Policy Project, George Washington University.

Liu, K., P. Doty, & Manton, K. 1990. Medicaid Spenddown in Nursing Homes. *The Gerontologist*, 30, 7-15.

Lloyd, P. C. 1990. The Relationship Between Voluntary Associations and State Agencies in the Provision of Social Services at the Local Level. In H. K. Anheier & W. Siebel (Eds.), *The Third Sector: Comparative Studies of Nonprofit Organizations*, pp. 241-253. Berlin: Walter DeGruyter.

Lloyd, P. C. 1991. The Empowerment of Elderly People. *Journal of Aging Studies*, 5, 125-135.

Longo, D. R., B. A. McCann, & L. A. Ahlgren. 1987. *The Nature, Process, and Modes of Hospice Care Delivery: Final Report*. Chicago: Joint Commission on Accreditation of Hospitals.

Loth, R. 1987, May 31. The No-Care Zone: Abandoning the Sick. *The Boston Globe Magazine*, p. 15.

Louis Harris & Associates. 1988. *Majorities Favor Passage of Long Term Health Care Legislation*. New York: Author.

Luken, P. C., & S. Vaughan. 1990. Organizational Factors Affecting Growth and Decline in Adult Day-Care Programs: A Comparative Study. *Journal of Applied Gerontology*, 9, 363-374.

Lurie, E., B. Robinson, & J. Barbaccia. 1984. Helping Hospitalized Elderly: Discharge Planning and Informal Support. *Home Health Care Services Quarterly*, 5(2), 25-42.

Lyles, Y. 1986. Impact of Medicare DRGs on Nursing Homes in the Portland, Oregon Metropolitan Area. *Journal of the American Geriatrics Society*, 34, 573-578.

Mahoney, C. W. 1988. The Role of Foundations in Aging: Grantmaking in an Era of Cost-Containment Health Policy (Doctoral dissertation, University of California, San Francisco). *Dissertation Abstracts International*, 50/03-A, 803.

Mahoney, C. W., & C. L. Estes. 1986. The Changing Role of Private Foundations. In D. Hyman & K. Parkum (Eds.), *Models of Health and Human Services in the Nonprofit Sector*. University Park, PA: Association of Voluntary Action Scholars.

Mahoney, C. W., C. L. Estes, & J. E. Heumann (Eds.). 1986. *Toward a Unified Agenda: Proceedings of a National Conference on Disability and Aging*. San Francisco: University of California, Institute for Health & Aging.

Maloney, T. W. 1988. The Commonwealth Fund Responds. *Health Affairs*, 7(3), 209-212.

Manard, B., J. Gong, J. Meicel, & M. Kupperman. 1988. *The Provision of Subacute Care in Hospitals: Variations Among Five Case Study States and the United States*. Paper presented at the Health Services Research Association Annual Meeting, San Francisco.

Manley, M. 1987. *Medicare's Prospective Payment System and the Long Term Care System in Snohomish County*. Everett, WA: Snohomish County Division on Aging.

Manton, K. G. 1989. Epidemiological, Demographic, and Social Correlates of Disability Among the Elderly. *Milbank Memorial Fund Quarterly*, 67(Suppl. 2, Pt. 1), 13-58.

Manton, K. G., & B. J. Soldo. 1985. Dynamics of Health Changes in the Oldest-Old: New Perspectives and Evidence. *Milbank Memorial Fund Quarterly/Health and Society*, 63, 206-285.

Manton, K. G., & R. Suzman. 1992. Forecasting Health and Functioning in Aging Societies: Implications for Health Care and Staffing Needs. In M. G. Ory, R. P. Ables, & P. D. Lipman (Eds.), *Aging, Health, and Behavior*, pp. 299-326. Newbury Park, CA: Sage.

Margolis, R. J. 1990. *Risking Old Age in America.* Boulder, CO: Westview.

Marmor, T. R., M. Schlesinger, & R. W. Smithey. 1987. Nonprofit Organizations and Health Care. In W. W. Powell (Ed.), *The Nonprofit Sector: A Research Handbook,* pp. 221-239. New Haven, CT: Yale University Press.

Matthews, S. H. 1988. The Burdens of Parent Care: A Critical Evaluation of Recent Findings. *Journal of Aging Studies,* 2, 157-165.

Matthews, S. H., J. E. Werkner, & P. J. Delaney. 1989. Relative Contributions of Help by Employed and Nonemployed Sisters to Their Elderly Parents. *Journal of Gerontology,* 44, S36-S44.

McAuley, W. J., & R. Blieszner. 1985. Selection of Long Term Care Arrangements by Older Community Residents. *The Gerontologist,* 25, 188-193.

McCreary, K. 1986, January. The Utilization of Alternative Health Care Services Immediately Following Acute Hospital Discharges: A Study. *Health Care Strategic Management,* pp. 10-13.

Mehta, N. H., & C. M. Mack. 1987. Day Care Services: An Alternative to Institutional Care. *Journal of the American Geriatrics Society,* 13, 281.

Meiners, M. R., & R. M. Coffey. 1985. Hospital DRGs and the Need for Long-Term Care Services: An Empirical Analysis. *Health Services Research,* 20, 359-382.

Miller, B., & S. McFall. 1991. Stability and Change in the Informal Task Support Network of Frail Older Persons. *The Gerontologist,* 31, 735-746.

Miller, L., J. H. Swan, & C. Harrington. 1992. *The Annual per Capita Demand and Supply of Medicaid-Financed Nursing Home Bed Days in the States.* Unpublished manuscript, University of California, San Francisco, Institute for Health & Aging.

Mills, C. W. 1959. *The Sociological Imagination.* New York: Oxford University Press.

Minkler, M. 1986. "Generational Equity" and the New Victim Blaming: An Emerging Public Policy Issue. *International Journal of Health Services,* 16, 539-551.

Mitchell, J. B., & T. Menke. 1990. How the Physician Fee Schedule Affects Medicare Patients' Out-of-Pocket Spending. *Inquiry,* 27, 108-113.

Mor, V. 1987. *Hospice Care Systems: Structure, Process, Costs, and Outcomes.* New York: Springer.

Mor, V., G. Hendershot, & C. Cryan. 1989. Awareness of Hospice Services: Results of a National Survey. *Public Health Reports,* 104, 178-183.

Moritz, D. J., S. V. Kasl, & L. F. Berkman. 1989. The Health Impact of Living with a Cognitively Impaired Elderly Spouse: Depressive Symptoms and Social Functioning. *Journal of Gerontology,* 44, S17-S27.

Morreale, J. C. 1991. *Budgetary Retrenchment in New York State: Effects on Health Care Programs and Equity.* Paper presented at the American Public Health Association Annual Meeting, Atlanta.

Morris, J. N., C. Hawes, B. E. Fries, et al. 1990. Designing the National Resident Assessment Instrument for Nursing Homes. *The Gerontologist,* 30, 293-307.

Morrisey, M. A., F. A. Sloan, & J. Valvona. 1988. Medicare Prospective Payment and Posthospital Transfers to Subacute Care. *Medical Care,* 26, 685-698.

Morrison, B. J. 1983. Sociocultural Dimensions: Nursing Homes and the Minority Aged. In G. Getzel & M. J. Mellor (Eds.), *Gerontological Social Work Practice in Long-Term Care,* pp. 127-145. New York: Haworth.

Moskowitz, M. 1983, March 28. The Health Care Business is Healthy. *San Francisco Chronicle,* p. 50.

Motenko, A. K. 1989. The Frustrations, Gratifications, and Well-Being of Dementia Caregivers. *The Gerontologist,* 29, 166-172.

Mulford, C. 1984. *Interorganizational Relations: Implications for Community Development.* New York: Human Sciences Press.

Mundinger, M. O. 1983. *Home Care Controversy: Too Little, Too Late.* Rockville, MD: Aspen.

Murtaugh, C. M., L. M. Cooney, R. R. DerSimonian, H. L. Smits, & R. B. Fetter. 1988. Nursing Home Reimbursement and the Allocation of Rehabilitation Therapy Resources. *Health Services Research,* 23, 467-493.

Murtaugh, C. M., P. Kemper, & B. Spillman. 1990. The Risk of Nursing Home Use in Later Life. *Medical Care,* 28, 952-962.

Mutran, E. 1985. Intergenerational Family Support Among Blacks and Whites: Response to Culture or to Socioeconomic Differences? *Journal of Gerontology,* 40, 382-389.

Nathan, R. P., F. C. Doolittle, et al. 1984. *Overview: Effects of the Reagan Domestic Program on States and Localities.* Working Paper. Princeton, NJ: Princeton University, Urban and Regional Center.

National Center for Health Statistics (NCHS). 1986. Current Estimates from the National Health Interview Survey, United States, 1983. *Vital and Health Statistics,* Ser. 10, No. 154.

National Conference of State Legislatures (NCSL). 1990. *The President's 1991 Budget: Impact on the State.* Washington, DC: National Conference of State Legislatures.

National Council on the Aging (NCOA), National Institute of Senior Centers (NISC). 1984. Health Services in Senior Centers on the Rise. *Senior Center Report,* 7(2), 1-2.

National Governors Association (NGA) and National Association of State Budget Officers (NASBO). 1991. *Fiscal Survey of the States.* Washington, DC: National Governors Association.

National Hospice Organization (NHO). 1987. NHO Reports Seven Percent Growth in Hospice Programs. *Hospice News,* 6(2), 1, 3.

National Institute on Aging (NIA). (1988). *Behavioral and Social Science Research Program: Currently Active Grants.* Baltimore, MD: National Institute on Aging.

Nelson, D. W. 1986. A State Perspective: The False Promise of New Federalism for the Elderly and Disabled. In C. W. Mahoney, C. L. Estes, & J. E. Heumann (Eds.), *Toward a Unified Agenda: Proceedings of a National Conference on Disability and Aging,* pp. 105-109. San Francisco: University of California, Institute for Health & Aging.

Neu, C. R., & S. C. Harrison. 1988. *Posthospital Care Before and After the Medicare Prospective Payment System.* Santa Monica, CA: Rand.

Newcomer, R. J., A. E. Benjamin, & C. L. Estes. 1983. The Older Americans Act. In C. L. Estes, R. J. Newcomer, et al., *Fiscal Austerity and Aging: Shifting Government Responsibility for the Elderly,* pp. 187-205. Beverly Hills, CA: Sage.

Newcomer, R. J., C. L. Estes, A. E. Benjamin, J. H. Swan, & V. Peguillan. 1981. *Funding Practices, Policies, and Performance of State and Area Agencies on Aging,* 2 Vols. Final Report. San Francisco: University of California, Institute for Health & Aging.

Newman, S., & W. J. Scanlon. 1989. *Delivery of Long-Term Care Services: New Developments in Nursing Homes and Housing.* Paper presented at the conference, "The Economics and Politics of Long-Term Care," Irvine, CA.

Novak, M., & C. Guest. 1989. Caregiver Response to Alzheimer's Disease. *International Journal of Aging and Human Development,* 28, 67-79.

Nutter, D. 1984. Access to Care and the Evolution of Corporate, For-Profit Medicine. *New England Journal of Medicine,* 31, 917-919.

Nyman, J. A. 1989. Excess Demand, Consumer Rationality, and the Quality of Care in Regulated Nursing Homes. *Health Services Research,* 24, 105-127.

Nyman, J. A., S. Levey, & J. E. Rohrer. 1987. RUGs and Equity of Access to Nursing Home Care. *Medical Care,* 25, 361-372.

O'Connell, B. 1983. *America's Voluntary Spirit*. New York: Foundation Center.

O'Connor, J. 1973. *The Fiscal Crisis of the State*. New York: St. Martin's.

O'Connor, J. 1984. *Accumulation Crisis*. New York: Basic Blackwell.

O'Connor, B. 1987. *The Meaning of Crisis*. Oxford: Basil Blackwell.

Offe, C. 1984. *Contradictions of the Welfare State*. Cambridge: MIT Press.

Okin, S. M. 1989. *Justice, Gender and the Family*. New York: Basic Books.

Olsen, J. K., & B. Cahn. 1980. Helping Families Cope with Elderly Patients. *Journal of Gerontological Nursing*, 6, 152-154.

Olson, L. 1982. *The Political Economy of Aging*. New York: Columbia University Press.

Ory, M. G., & T. F. Williams. 1989. Rehabilitation: Small Goals, Sustained Interventions. *Annals of the American Academy of Political and Social Science*, 503, 60-71.

Osterbush, S. E., S. M. Keigher, B. Miller, & N. L. Linsk. 1987. Community Care Policies and Gender Justice. *International Journal of Health Services*, 17, 217-232.

Ostrander, S. A., S. Langton, & J. Van Til (Eds.). 1987. *Shifting the Debate: Public/Private Sector Relations in the Modern Welfare State*. New Brunswick, NJ: Transaction Books.

Parsons, R. J., E. O. Cox, & P. J. Kimboko. 1989. Satisfaction, Communication and Affection in Caregiving: A View from the Elder's Perspective. *Journal of Gerontological Social Work*, 13(3/4), 9-20.

Parsons, T. 1964. *The Social System*. New York: Free Press.

Pattison, R., & H. Katz. 1983. Investor-Owned and Not-for-Profit Hospitals. *New England Journal of Medicine*, 309, 347-353.

Payton, R. 1984. *Major Challenges to Philanthropy*. Washington, DC: Independent Sector.

Pepper Commission (U.S. Bipartisan Commission on Comprehensive Health Care). 1990a. *A Call for Action*. Washington, DC: Government Printing Office.

Pepper Commission (U.S. Bipartisan Commission on Comprehensive Health Care). 1990b. *A Call for Action: Executive Summary*. Washington, DC: Government Printing Office.

Perlin, L. I., J. T. Mullan, S. J. Semple, & M. M. Skaff. 1990. Caregiving and the Stress Process: An Overview of Concepts and Their Measures. *The Gerontologist*, 30, 583-594.

Peters, D. A. 1988. Quality Documentation: Quality Care. *Caring*, 7(10), 30-34.

Philadelphia Health Management Corporation (PHMC). 1985. *An Analysis of the Impact of Federal Health Policy Changes on Selected Health Services in Philadelphia: 1981-1984*. Philadelphia: Philadelphia Health Management Corporation.

Phillips, C. D., & C. Hawes. 1988. *Discrimination by Nursing Homes Against Medicaid Recipients: The Potential Impact of Equal Access on the Industry's Profitability*. Research Triangle Park, NC: Research Triangle Institute.

Phillipson, C. 1982. *Capitalism and the Construction of Old Age*. London: Macmillan.

Phillipson, C. 1992. Challenging "the Spectre of Old Age": Community Care for Older People in the 1990s. In W. Manning & R. Page (Eds.), *Social Policy Yearbook*, pp. 1-22. London: Social Policy Association.

Phillipson, C., & A. Walker. 1986. Conclusion: Alternative Forms of Policy and Practice. In A. Walker & C. Phillipson (Eds.), *Ageing and Social Policy: A Critical Assessment*, pp. 280-281. London: Gower.

Powell, W. W. 1987. Institutional Effects on Organizational Structure and Performance. In L. Zucker (Ed.), *Institutional Patterns and Organizations: Culture and Environment*. Boston: Pitman.

Powell, W. W., & R. Freidkin. 1987. Organizational Change in Nonprofit Organizations. In W. W. Powell (Ed.), *The Nonprofit Sector: A Research Handbook*, pp. 180-194. New Haven, CT: Yale University Press.

Preston, S. H. 1985. Children and the Elderly in the U.S. *Scientific American*, 251(6), 44-49.

Prigerson, H. G. 1991. Determinants of Hospice Utilization Among Terminally Ill Geriatric Patients. *Home Health Care Services Quarterly*, 12(4), 81-111.

Prospective Payment Assessment Commission (ProPAC). 1986. *Medicare Prospective Payment and the American Health Care System*. Report to Congress. Washington, DC: Author.

Prospective Payment Assessment Commission (ProPAC). 1987a. [Medicare Hospital DRG Margins]. Testimony by Stuart Altman before the U.S. House of Representatives Ways and Means Committee, Subcommittee on Health. Washington, DC: Author.

Prospective Payment Assessment Commission (ProPAC). 1987b. *Medicare Prospective Payment and the American Health Care System*. Report to Congress. Washington, DC: Author.

Prospective Payment Assessment Commission (ProPAC). 1988. *Medicare Prospective Payment and the American Health Care System*. Report to Congress. Washington, DC: Author.

Prospective Payment Assessment Commission (ProPAC). 1990. *Medicare Prospective Payment and the American Health Care System*. Report to Congress. Washington, DC: Author.

Quadagno, J. 1990. Race, Class and Gender in the U.S. Welfare State: Nixon's Failed Family Assistance Plan. *American Sociological Review*, 55, 11-28.

Quayhagen, M. P., & M. Quayhagen. 1989. Differential Effects of Family-Based Strategies on Alzheimer's Disease. *The Gerontologist*, 29, 150-155.

Ralston, P. A. 1987. Senior Center Research: Policy from Knowledge? In E. F. Borgatta & R. J. Montgomery (Eds.), *Critical Issues in Aging Policy: Linking Research and Values*, pp. 201-135. Beverly Hills, CA: Sage.

Ralston, P. A. 1991a. Determinants of Senior Center Attendance and Participation. *Journal of Applied Gerontology*, 10, 258-273.

Ralston, P. A. 1991b. Senior Centers and Minority Elders: A Critical Review. *The Gerontologist*, 31, 325-331.

Rappaport, M., & C. L. Estes. 1991. *Impact of DRGs on Certified and Uncertified Home Health Agencies*. Paper presented at the Gerontological Society of America Annual Meeting, New Orleans, LA.

Rappaport, M., & J. B. Wood. 1989. Financing and Home Health Agencies. *Home Health Care Services Quarterly*, 10(3/4), 131-147.

Ray, S. S., N. List, R. M. Clinkscale, B. C. Duggar, & J. S. Pollatsek. 1987. *Assessment of the Current Utilization of C/MHCs by the Elderly and an Assessment of the Capability of C/MHCs to Develop Comprehensive Community-Based Primary Care Health Service Systems for the Elderly*. Final Report to Health Resources and Services Administration. Columbia, MD: La Jolla Management Corporation.

Redclift, N., & E. Mingione. (Eds.). 1985. *Beyond Employment: Household, Gender and Subsistence*. New York: Basil Blackwell.

Rehr, H. 1985. Medical Care Organization and the Social Services Connection. *Health and Social Work*, 10, 245-257.

Rehr, H. 1986. Discharge Planning: An On-Going Function of Quality of Care. *Quality Review Bulletin*, 12(2), 47-50.

Relman, A. S. 1980. The New Medical-Industrial Complex. *New England Journal of Medicine*, 303, 963-970.

Renn, S., C. Schramm, J. Watt, & R. Derzon. 1985. The Effects of Ownership and System Affiliation on the Economic Performance of Hospitals. *Inquiry*, 22, 219-236.

Rice, D. P. 1986. Living Longer in the U.S.: Social and Economic Implications. *Journal of Medical Practice Management,* 1(3), 162-169.

Rice, D. P., & M. P. LaPlante. 1988. Chronic Illness, Disability, and Increasing Longevity. In S. Sullivan & M. E. Lewin (Eds.), *The Economics and Ethics of Long Term Care and Disability,* pp. 9-55. Washington, DC: American Enterprise Institute.

Rice, D., & A. Wick. 1985. *Impact of an Aging Population: State Projections.* Final Report. San Francisco: University of California, Institute for Health & Aging.

Riley, M. W., & J. W. Riley. 1989. The Lives of Older People and Changing Social Roles. *Annals of the American Academy of Political and Social Science,* 503, 14-28.

Rivlin, A. M., & J. M. Wiener. 1988. *Caring for the Disabled Elderly: Who Will Pay?* Washington, DC: Brookings Institution.

R. L. Associates. 1987. *The American Public Views Long-Term Care.* Washington, DC: American Association of Retired Persons and Villers Foundation.

Robertson, A. 1991. The Politics of Alzheimer's Disease: A Case Study in Apocalyptic Demography. In M. Minkler & C. L. Estes (Eds.), *Critical Perspectives on Aging: The Political and Moral Economy of Growing Old,* pp. 135-152. Amityville, NY: Baywood.

Rock, B. 1987. Beyond Discharge Planning. *Hospital and Community Psychiatry,* 38, 529-530.

Rodin, J. 1989. Sense of Control: Potentials for Intervention. *Annals of the American Academy of Political and Social Science,* 503, 29-42.

Rodin, J., & E. Langer. 1980. Aging Labels: The Decline of Control and the Fall of Self-Esteem. *Journal of Social Issues,* 36(2), 12-29.

Rodwin, V. G. 1986. *The Public Private Mix in the American Health Sector: A Misleading Dichotomy.* Paper presented at the conference sponsored by Fondazione Smith Klein, Riva Del Garda, Italy.

Rose-Ackerman, S. 1986. *The Economics of Nonprofit Sector Institutions.* New York: Oxford University Press.

Rosenbach, M., & J. Cromwell. 1985. *Physician's Perceptions About the Short Run Impact of Medicare's Prospective Payment System.* Chestnut Hill, MA: Health Economics Research.

Rowland, D., & B. Lyons. 1991. The Elderly Population in Need of Long Term Care. In D. Rowland & B. Lyons (Eds.), *Financing Home Care: Improving Protection for Disabled Elderly People,* pp. 3-26. Baltimore, MD: Johns Hopkins University Press.

Rubenstein, R. L. 1989. Themes in the Meaning of Caregiving. *Journal of Aging Studies,* 3, 119-138.

Ruchlin, H., D. Pointer, & L. Cannedy. 1973. Comparison of For-Profit Investor-Owned Chain and Non-Profit Hospitals. *Inquiry,* 10, 13-23.

Rymer, M., & G. Adler. 1984. *Short-Term Evaluation of Medicaid: Issues.* Cambridge, MA: Urban Systems Research & Engineering.

Saddler, R. T., & W. M. Barrick. 1991. Distinct Parts Lawsuit May Restrict Access to Care. *Provider,* 17(1), 36-39.

Sager, M. A., E. A. Leventhal, & D. V. Easterling. 1987. The Impact of Medicare's Prospective Payment System on Wisconsin Nursing Homes. *Journal of the American Medical Association,* 257, 1762-1766.

Salamon, L. M. 1983. *Nonprofit Organizations and the Rise of Third Party Government: The Scope, Character and Consequences of Government Support of Nonprofit Organizations.* Paper presented at the Independent Sector Research Forum, New York.

Salamon, L. M. 1987a. Of Market Failure, Voluntary Failure, and Third-Party Government: Toward a Theory of Government-Nonprofit Relations in the Modern

Welfare State. In S. A. Ostrander, S. Langton, & J. Van Til (Eds.), *The Shifting Debate: Public/Private Sector Relations in the Modern Welfare State*, pp. 29-49. New Brunswick, NJ: Transaction Books.

Salamon, L. M. 1987b. Partners in Public Service: The Scope and Theory of Government-Nonprofit Relations. In W. W. Powell (Ed.), *The Nonprofit Sector: A Research Handbook*, pp. 99-117. New Haven, CT: Yale University Press.

Salamon, L. M. 1988. *The Voluntary Sector and the Future of the Welfare State: Some Initial Thoughts*. Paper presented at the Spring Research Forum, Independent Sector, San Francisco.

Salmon, J. W. 1987. The Medical Profession and the Corporatization of the Health Sector. *Theoretical Medicine*, 8, 19-29.

Salvage, A. V., N. J. Vetter, & D. A. Jones. 1989. Opinions Concerning Residential Care. *Age and Ageing*, 18, 380-386.

Salvatore, T. 1985. Organizational Adaptation in the VNA: Paradigm Change in the Voluntary Sector. *Home Health Care Services Quarterly*, 6(2), 19-31.

Sankar, A., R. J. Newcomer, & J. B. Wood. 1986. Prospective Payment: Systemic Effects on the Provision of Community Care for the Elderly. *Home Health Care Services Quarterly*, 7(2), 93-113.

Sassoon, A. S. (Ed.). 1987. *Women and the State: The Shifting Boundaries of Public and Private*. London: Hutchinson.

Savo, C. 1984. *Self-Care and Self-Help Programmes for Older Adults in the U.S.* Working Papers on the Health of Older People, No. 1. Keele, England, UK: Health Education Council and Department of Adult Education, University of Keele.

Scalzi, C. C., & M. Meyer. 1991. Closures and Mergers of VNA Home Care Agencies: A Model for the Study of Causal Factors. *Home Health Care Services Quarterly*, 12(4), 113-125.

Scanlon, W. J. 1980a. Nursing Home Utilization Patterns: Implications for Policy. *Journal of Health Politics, Policy and Law*, 4, 619-641.

Scanlon, W. J. 1980b. A Theory of the Nursing Home Market. *Inquiry*, 17, 25-41.

Scharlach, A. E., & S. L. Boyd. 1991. Caregiving and Employment: Results of an Employee Survey. *The Gerontologist*, 29, 382-387.

Scharlach, A. E., E. Sobel, & R. E. L. Roberts. 1991. Employment and Caregiver Strain: A Conceptual Model. *The Gerontologist*, 31, 778-787.

Schiff, J. A. 1987. Tax Reform and Volunteering. In Independent Sector, *The Constitution and the Independent Sector*, pp. 147-156. Spring Research Forum Working Papers. Washington, DC: Independent Sector.

Schiff, J. A., & B. A. Weisbrod. 1986. Tax Policy and Volunteering. In Independent Sector, *Philanthropy, Voluntary Action and the Public Good*, pp. 623-633. Spring Research Forum Working Papers. Washington, DC: Independent Sector.

Schlesinger, M. 1985a. *Ownership and Access to Health Care: New Evidence and Policy Implications*. Center for Health Policy Working Paper. Cambridge, MA: Harvard University, JFK School of Government.

Schlesinger, M. 1985b. The Rise of Proprietary Health Care. *Business and Health*, 2(3), 7-12.

Schlesinger, M., J. Bentkover, D. Blumenthal, R. Musacchio, & J. Willer. 1987. The Privatization of Health Care and Physician's Perceptions of Access to Hospital Services. *Milbank Memorial Fund Quarterly/Health and Society*, 65, 25-58.

Schlesinger, M., & R. Dorwart. 1984. Ownership and Mental Health Services: A Reappraisal of the Shift Toward Privately Owned Facilities. *New England Journal of Medicine*, 311, 959-965.

Schlesinger, M., T. R. Marmor, & R. Smithey. 1987. Nonprofit and For-Profit Medical Care: Shifting Roles and Implications for Health Policy. *Journal of Health Politics, Policy and Law,* 12, 427-457.

Schorr, A. 1980. *Thy Father and Thy Mother: A Second Look at Filial Responsibility and Family Policy.* Washington, DC: U.S. Department of Health and Human Services.

Schrager, J. 1978. Impediments to the Course and Effectiveness of Discharge Planning. *Social Work in Health Care,* 4(1), 65-79.

Schramm, C. J., & J. Gabel. 1988. Prospective Payment: Some Retrospective Observations. *New England Journal of Medicine,* 318, 1681-1683.

Schreiber, H. 1981. Discharge Planning: Key to the Future of Hospital Social Work. *Health and Social Work,* 6, 48-53.

Schreter, C. A. 1990, July/August. How to Tap Private Funding Sources During Rapidly Changing Times. *Perspectives on Aging,* pp. 9-13.

Schreter, C. A., & S. W. Brummel. 1988. Primer on Private Philanthropy and Aging. *Journal of Applied Gerontology,* 7, 530-541.

Scott, W. R. 1987. *Organizations: Rational, Natural, and Open Systems,* 2nd ed. Englewood Cliffs, NJ: Prentice Hall.

Seay, J. D., & R. M. Sigmond. 1989. The Future of Tax-Exempt Status for Hospitals. *Frontiers of Health Services Management,* 5(3), 3-39.

Seay, J. D., & B. C. Vladeck. 1988. *In Sickness and in Health: The Mission of Voluntary Health Care Institutions.* New York: McGraw-Hill.

Secord, L. J. 1986. *Institution or Home Care? Predictors of Long-Term Care Placement Decisions.* Excelsior, MN: InterStudy Center for Aging and Long-Term Care.

Shaughnessy, P. W., & A. M. Kramer. 1990. The Increased Needs of Patients in Nursing Homes and Patients Receiving Home Health Care. *New England Journal of Medicine,* 322, 21-27.

Shaughnessy, P. W., A. M. Kramer, & R. E. Schlenker. 1987. *Preliminary Findings from the National Long Term Care Study.* Paper presented at the Health Care Financing Administration.University of Colorado, Center for Health Services Research, Denver.

Shaughnessy, P. W., R. E. Schlenker, & A. M. Kramer. 1990. Quality of Long-Term Care in Nursing Homes and Swing-Bed Hospitals. *Health Services Research,* 25, 65-96.

Sherwood, S. J., N. Morris, & H. S. Ruchin. 1986. Alternative Paths to Long-Term Care: Nursing Home, Geriatric Day Hospital, Senior Center, and Domiciliary Care Options. *American Journal of Public Health,* 76, 37-44.

Shortell, S. M., E. M. Morrison, & B. Friedman. 1990. *Strategic Choices for America's Hospitals.* San Francisco: Jossey-Bass.

Shortell, S. M., E. M. Morrison, S. Hughes, B. Friedman, & J. Vitek. 1986. Diversification of Health Care Services: The Effects of Ownership, Environment and Strategy. In L. Rossiter, R. Scheffler, G. Wilensky, & N. McCall (Eds.), *Advances in Health Economics and Health Service Research.* Greenwich, CT: JAI Press.

Simon, J. G. 1987. The Tax Treatment of Nonprofit Organizations: A Review of Federal and State Policies. In W. W. Powell (Ed.), *The Nonprofit Sector: A Research Handbook,* pp. 67-98. New Haven, CT: Yale University Press.

Simon, W. E. 1980. Reaping the Whirlwind. *Philanthropy Monthly,* 13(1), 5-8.

Simonen, L. 1990. *Contradictions of the Welfare State: Women and Caring.* Tampere, Finland: University of Tampere.

Simpson, K. N. 1991. *Market Rationing or Needs-Based Rationing: Comparing Access and Biases.* Paper presented at the American Public Health Association Annual Meeting, Atlanta.

Sjoberg, G., R. A. Rymer, & B. Farris. 1966. Bureaucracy and the Lower Class. *Sociology and Social Research*, 50, 325-337.

Skloot, E. 1987. Survival Time for Non-Profits. *Foundation News*, 28(1), 38-42.

Sloan, F., M. Morrisey, & J. Valvona. 1988. Case Shifting and the Medicare Prospective Payment System. *American Journal of Public Health*, 78, 553-556.

Sloan, F., J. Valvona, & R. Mullner. 1986. Identifying the Issues: A Statistical Profile. In F. Sloan, J. Blumstein, & J. Perrin (Eds.), *Uncompensated Hospital Care: Rights and Responsibilities*. Baltimore, MD: Johns Hopkins University Press.

Sloan, F., & R. Vraciu. 1983. Investor-Owned and Not-for-Profit Hospitals: Addressing Some Issues. *Health Affairs*, 2, 25-37.

Smith v. Heckler, 747 F.2d 583 (10th Cir. 1984).

Smith, D. B., & R. Picard. 1986. Evaluation of the Impact of Medicare and Medicaid Prospective Payment on Utilization of Philadelphia Area Hospitals. *Health Services Research*, 21, 529-546.

Smith, D. H. 1983. The Impact of the Voluntary Sector on Society. In B. O'Connell (Ed.), *America's Voluntary Spirit*, pp. 331-344. New York: Foundation Center.

Smits, H. L., J. Feder, & W. Scanlon. 1982. Medicare's Nursing-Home Benefit: Variations in Interpretation. *New England Journal of Medicine*, 307, 855-862.

Smucker, B. 1991. *The Nonprofit Lobbying Guide*. San Francisco: Jossey-Bass.

Society for Hospital Social Work Directors. 1987. Social Work Administration: Survey Shows Social Work Gains in Staffing, Discharge Planning. *Society for Hospital Social Work Directors Newsletter*, 13(2), 1-6.

Soldo, B. 1984. Supply of Informal Care Services: Variations and Effects on Service Utilization Patterns. In W. Scanlon (Ed.), *Project to Analyze Existing Long-Term Care Data*, Vol. 3, pp. 56-97. Washington, DC: Urban Institute.

Soldo, B., & J. Myllyluoma. 1983. Caregivers Who Live with Dependent Elderly. *The Gerontologist*, 23, 600-611.

Sommers, T., & L. Shields. 1987. *Women Take Care: The Consequences of Caregiving in Today's Society*. Gainesville, FL: Triad.

Spence, D. A., & Wiener, J. M. 1989. *Estimating the Extent of Medicaid Spend-Down in Nursing Homes*. Washington, DC: Brookings Institution.

Spiegel, A. D. 1987. *Home Health Care*, 2nd rev. ed. Owings Mills, MD: National Health Publishing.

Spitze, G., & J. Logan. 1989. Gender Differences in Family Support: Is There a Payoff? *The Gerontologist*, 29, 108-113.

Spohn, P. H. 1988. Discharge Planning in the Post-PPS Era: Findings from the DRG Impact Study. In C. L. Estes, J. B. Wood, et al., *Organizational and Community Responses to Medicare Policy: Consequences for Health and Social Services to the Elderly*, Vol. 1, pp. 71-92. Final Report. San Francisco: University of California, Institute for Health & Aging.

Spohn, P. H. 1989. Convergence of Form and Function Between Nonprofit and For-Profit Hospitals: The Case of Discharge Planning (Doctoral Dissertation, University of California, Berkeley). *Dissertation Abstracts International*, 51/01-B, 135.

Spohn, P. H., L. A. Bergthold, & C. L. Estes. 1987-1988. From Cottages to Condos: The Expansion of the Home Health Care Industry Under Medicare. *Home Health Care Services Quarterly*, 8(4), 25-55.

Spohn, P. H., L. A. Bergthold, C. L. Estes, & S. C. Goldberg. 1988. Community-Based Long Term Care in Philadelphia: The Interaction of Federal Policy and Community Environment. In C. L. Estes, J. B. Wood, et al., *Organizational and Community Responses to Medicare Policy: Consequences for Health and Social Services to the*

Elderly, Vol. 2, pp. 1-39. Final Report. San Francisco: University of California, Institute for Health & Aging.

Spohn, P. H., M. Holstein, & C. L. Estes. 1986. *A Community Grantmaking Strategy for the Frail Elderly in the San Francisco Bay Area*. Paper prepared for the Henry J. Kaiser Family Foundation. University of California, Institute for Health & Aging, San Francisco.

Stark, F. H. 1987a. Testimony. In *Medicare Hospital DRG Margins: Introduction*. Hearing before the U.S. House of Representatives Committee on Ways and Means, Subcommittee on Health. Washington, DC: Government Printing Office.

Stark, F. H. 1987b. Testimony. In *Unrelated Business Income Tax Hearings*, Part 2. Hearing before the U.S. House of Representatives Committee on Ways and Means, Subcommittee on Oversight. Washington, DC: Government Printing Office.

Starr, P. 1982. *The Social Transformation of American Medicine*. New York: Basic Books.

Stearns, S. C. 1991. Hospital Discharge Decisions, Health Outcomes, and the Use of Unobserved Information on Case-Mix Severity. *Health Services Research*, 26, 27-51.

Stephens, S. A., & J. B. Christianson. 1985. *Informal Care of the Elderly*. Lexington, MA: Lexington/Heath.

Stevens, R. 1989. *In Sickness and in Wealth: American Hospitals in the Twentieth Century*. New York: Basic Books.

Stoller, E. P., & L. L. Earl. 1983. Help with Activities of Everyday Life: Sources of Support for the Noninstitutionalized Elderly. *The Gerontologist*, 23, 64-70.

Stone, R. 1991. Defining Family Caregivers of the Elderly: Implications for Research and Public Policy. *The Gerontologist*, 31, 724-725.

Stone, R., G. L. Cafferata, & J. Sangl. 1987. Caregivers of the Frail Elderly: A National Profile. *The Gerontologist*, 27, 616-626.

Stone, R., & P. Kemper. 1989. Spouses and Children of Disabled Elders: How Large a Constituency for Long Term Care Reform? *Milbank Memorial Fund Quarterly/Health and Society*, 67, 485-506.

Strahan, G. 1987. Nursing Home Characteristics: Preliminary Data from the 1985 National Nursing Home Survey. *NCHS Advancedata*, 131, 1-7.

Strawbridge, W., & M. Wallhagen. 1991. Impact of Family Conflict on Adult Child Caregivers. *The Gerontologist*, 31, 770-777.

Swan, J. H. 1990. The Share of Medicaid for Nursing Home Care. *Journal of Health and Social Policy*, 1(3), 35-53.

Swan, J. H., & A. E. Benjamin. 1990a. Home Health Utilization as a Function of Nursing Home Market Factors. *Health Services Research*, 25, 479-500.

Swan, J. H., & A. E. Benjamin. 1990b. Nursing Costs of Skilled Nursing Care for AIDS. *AIDS and Public Policy Journal*, 5, 64-67.

Swan, J. H., & A. E. Benjamin. 1990c. *Nursing Home Queues and Home Health Users*. Paper presented at the conference, "Home Health Care in the 90's," Los Angeles, CA.

Swan, J. H., A. E. Benjamin, & A. Brown. In press. Skilled Nursing Facility Care for Persons with AIDS: Comparison to Other Patients. *American Journal of Public Health*.

Swan, J. H., A. E. Benjamin, & P. J. Fox. 1991. *PT and OT Service Use During the Medicare Home Health Period*. Paper presented at the Long Beach Research Symposium, Long Beach, CA.

Swan, J. H., A. de la Torre, & R. Steinhart. 1990. Ripple Effects of PPS on Nursing Homes: Swimming or Drowning in the Funding Stream? *The Gerontologist*, 30, 323-331.

Swan, J. H., & C. L. Estes. 1990a. Changes in Aged Populations Served by Home Health Agencies. *Journal of Aging and Health*, 2, 373-394.

Swan, J. H., & C. L. Estes. 1990b. *Nursing Home Access for the Elderly: Waiting Lists and Waits for Admission.* Paper presented at the American Public Health Association Annual Meeting, New York.

Swan, J. H., C. L. Estes, & J. B. Wood. 1982. *Fiscal Crisis: Impact on Aging Services.* Final Report to the U.S. Administration on Aging. San Francisco: University of California, Aging Health Policy Center.

Swan, J. H., C. L. Estes, & J. B. Wood. 1983. Fiscal Crisis: Economic and Fiscal Problems of State and Local Governments. In C. L. Estes, R. J. Newcomer, et al., *Fiscal Austerity and Aging: Shifting Government Responsibility for the Elderly*, pp. 113-132. Beverly Hills, CA: Sage.

Swan, J. H., P. J. Fox, & C. L. Estes. 1986. Community Mental Health Services and the Elderly: Retrenchment or Expansion? *Community Mental Health Journal*, 22, 275-285.

Swan, J. H., P. J. Fox, & C. L. Estes. 1989. Geriatric Services: Community Mental Health Centers: Boon or Bane? *Community Mental Health Journal*, 25, 327-339.

Swan, J. H., & C. Harrington. 1985. Medicaid Nursing Home Reimbursement Policies. In C. Harrington, R. Newcomer, C. L. Estes, et al., *Long Term Care of the Elderly: Public Policy Issues*, pp. 125-152. Beverly Hills, CA: Sage.

Swan, J. H., & C. Harrington. 1986. Estimating Undersupply of Nursing Home Beds in the United States. *Health Services Research*, 21, 57-83.

Swan, J. H., & C. Harrington. 1990. Certificate of Need and Nursing Home Bed Capacity in the States. *Journal of Health and Social Policy*, 2(2), 87-106.

Swan, J. H., C. Harrington, & L. A. Grant. 1988. State Medicaid Reimbursement for Nursing Homes, 1978-86. *Health Care Financing Review*, 9(3), 33-50.

Swan, J. H., C. Harrington, L. A. Grant, & S. D. Preston. 1991. *Recent Trends in Medicaid Nursing Home Reimbursement.* Paper presented at the American Public Health Association Annual Meeting, Atlanta.

Swan, J. H., C. Harrington, & L. Miller. 1991. *Estimating State Nursing Home Bed Undersupply: 1978-1988.* Paper presented at the Association for Health Services Research Annual Meeting, San Diego, CA.

Swan, J. H., & M. E. McCall. 1987. Mental Health System Components and the Aged. In E. E. Lurie, J. H. Swan, et al., *Serving the Mentally Ill Elderly: Problems and Perspectives*, pp. 111-138. Lexington, MA: Lexington/Heath.

Szasz, A. 1990. The Labor Impacts of Policy Change in Home Health Care: How Federal Policy Transformed Home Health Organizations and Their Labor Policies. *Journal of Health Policy, Politics and Law*, 15, 191-210.

Taylor, H. 1986, April 8. Testimony before the U.S. House of Representatives Select Committee on Aging, Washington, DC.

Taylor, H. 1992. *Consumer Perspectives on Health Care Reform.* Paper presented at the National Health Care Reform Lecture Series, School of Nursing, University of California, San Francisco.

Thornton, P. 1991. Subject to Contract? Volunteers as Providers of Community Care for Elderly People and Their Supporters. *Journal of Aging Studies*, 5, 181-194.

Townsend, P. 1981. The Structured Dependency of the Elderly: The Creation of Social Policy in the Twentieth Century. *Ageing and Society*, 1, 5-28.

Traska, M. R. 1988. Tax Issues Could Plague Not-For-Profits. *Hospitals*, 62, 24-27.

Ungerson, C. 1987. *Policy Is Personal: Sex, Gender and Informal Care.* London: Tavistock.

United Hospital Fund of New York. 1986. *New Directions in Health Care: Consequences for the Elderly.* New York: Author.

United Hospital Fund of New York. 1987a. *Mission Matters.* Summary of report presented by J. D. Seay and B. C. Vladeck. New York: Author.

United Hospital Fund of New York. 1987b, October 15. *Voluntary Hospitals Urged to Recapture Historic Purposes of Charity, Community Service.* Press release. New York: Author.

United Hospital Fund of New York. 1990. *Policy and Practice: Certified Home Health Care in New York City.* New York: Author.

U.S. Bureau of the Census. 1990a. *Current Population Reports,* Ser. P-25. Washington, DC: U.S. Department of Commerce.

U.S. Bureau of the Census (C. Nelson & K. Short). 1990b. *Health Insurance Coverage, 1986-88* (Current Population Reports, Ser. P-70, No. 17). Washington, DC: U.S. Department of Commerce.

U.S. Bureau of the Census. 1990c. *Statistical Abstract of the United States: 1990.* Washington, DC: Government Printing Office.

U.S. Congressional Research Service. 1988. *Health Insurance and the Uninsured: Background Data and Analysis.* Washington, DC: U.S. Library of Congress.

U.S. Congress, Office of Technology Assessment (COTA). 1985. *Medicare's Prospective Payment System: Strategies for Evaluating Cost, Quality, and Medical Technology.* Washington, DC: U.S. Office of Technology Assessment.

U.S. Department of Health and Human Services (DHHS). 1985. *The Impact of the Medicare Prospective Payment System: The 1984 Report.* Report to Congress. Washington, DC: Government Printing Office.

U.S. Department of Health and Human Services (DHHS) (Task Force on Long-Term Care Policies). 1987. *Long-Term Health Care Policies: Report to Congress and the Secretary.* Washington, DC: Author.

U.S. Department of Health and Human Services (DHHS). 1990. Long-Term Care for the Functionally Dependent Elderly. *Vital and Health Statistics,* Ser. 13, No. 104.

U.S. General Accounting Office (GAO). 1982. *The Elderly Remain in Need of Mental Health Services.* Washington, DC: U.S. General Accounting Office.

U.S. General Accounting Office (GAO). 1983. *Medicaid and Nursing Home Care: Cost Increases and the Need for Services Are Creating Problems for States and the Elderly.* Washington, DC: U.S. General Accounting Office.

U.S. General Accounting Office (GAO). 1985. *Information Requirements for Evaluating the Impacts of Medicare Prospective Payment on Post-Hospital Long-Term Care Services.* Preliminary Report. Washington, DC: U.S. General Accounting Office.

U.S. General Accounting Office (GAO). 1986. *Post-Hospital Care: Efforts to Evaluate Medicare Prospective Payment Effects Are Insufficient.* Report by E. Chelimsky to the Chairman, U.S. Senate Special Committee on Aging. Washington, DC: U.S. General Accounting Office.

U.S. General Accounting Office (GAO). 1987a. *Medicare and Medicaid: Stronger Enforcement of Nursing Home Requirements Needed.* Report to the Chairman, U.S. House of Representatives Select Committee on Aging, Subcommittee on Health and Long Term Care. Washington, DC: U.S. General Accounting Office.

U.S. General Accounting Office (GAO). 1987b. *Post-Hospital Care: Discharge Planners Report Increasing Difficulty in Placing Medicare Patients.* Report to the Chairman, U.S. House Select Committee on Aging, Subcommittee on Health and Long Term Care. Washington, DC: U.S. General Accounting Office.

U.S. Health Care Financing Administration (HCFA). 1986. *Health Care Financing Program Statistics: Analysis of State Medicaid Program Characteristics, 1986.* Washington, DC: U.S. Department of Health and Human Services.

U.S. Health Care Financing Administration (HCFA). 1987a. *Home Health Agency by Type of Facility, 1978-86.* Washington, DC: U.S. Department of Health and Human Services.

U.S. Health Care Financing Administration (HCFA). 1987b. *Program Statistics: Analysis of Medicaid Program Characteristics, 1986.* Washington, DC: U.S. Department of Health and Human Services.

U.S. House of Representatives (Select Committee on Aging). 1986a. *The Attempted Dismantling of the Medicare Home Care Benefit.* Washington, DC: Government Printing Office.

U.S. House of Representatives (Select Committee on Aging). 1986b. *The "Black Box" of Home Care Quality.* Report prepared by the American Bar Association. Washington, DC: Government Printing Office.

U.S. House of Representatives (Select Committee on Aging). 1986c. *Out "Sooner and Sicker" Myth and Medicare Crisis?* Washington, DC: Government Printing Office.

U.S. House of Representatives (Committee on Ways and Means). 1987a. *Medicare Quality Protection Act of 1986.* Hearing. Washington, DC: Author.

U.S. House of Representatives (Select Committee on Aging). 1987b. *Long Term Care and Personal Impoverishment: Seven in Ten Elderly Living Alone Are at Risk.* Washington, DC: Government Printing Office.

U.S. House of Representatives (Committee on Small Business). 1988a. *Nonprofit Competition.* Hearing. Washington, DC: Government Printing Office.

U.S. House of Representatives (Select Committee on Aging). 1988b. *Exploding the Myths: Caregiving in America.* Washington, DC: Government Printing Office.

U.S. House of Representatives (Select Committee on Aging). 1989. *Mental Health and the Elderly: Issues in Service Delivery to Asian Americans, Hispanics, and Blacks.* Washington, DC: Government Printing Office.

U.S. House of Representatives (Select Committee on Aging). 1990. *Emptying the Elderly's Pocketbook: Growing Impact of Rising Health Care Costs.* A Report by the Chairman. Washington, DC: Government Printing Office.

U.S. House of Representatives (Committee on Energy and Commerce, Subcommittee on Health and Environment). 1991. *Community Mental Health Services.* Hearing. Washington, DC: Government Printing Office.

U.S. Senate (Special Committee on Aging). 1974-1976. *Nursing Home Care in the U.S.: Failure in Public Policy.* An Introductory Report and Supporting Papers. Washington, DC: Government Printing Office.

U.S. Senate (Special Committee on Aging). 1984. *Discrimination Against the Poor and Disabled in Nursing Homes.* Washington, DC: Government Printing Office.

U.S. Senate (Special Committee on Aging). 1985. *Impact of Medicare's PPS on the Quality of Care Received by Medicare Beneficiaries.* Staff Report. Washington, DC: Government Printing Office.

U.S. Senate (Special Committee on Aging). 1986a. *Developments in Aging: 1985.* Washington, DC: Government Printing Office.

U.S. Senate (Special Committee on Aging). 1986b. *Crisis in Home Health Care: Greater Need, Less Care.* Hearing. Washington, DC: Government Printing Office.

U.S. Senate (Special Committee on Aging). 1986c. *Nursing Home Care: The Unfinished Agenda.* Special Hearing and Report. Washington, DC: Government Printing Office.

U.S. Senate (Special Committee on Aging). 1989. *Developments in Aging: 1988,* Vol. 1. Washington, DC: Government Printing Office.

U.S. Senate (Special Committee on Aging). 1991. *Developments in Aging: 1990,* Vol. 1. Washington, DC: Government Printing Office.

U.S. Senate (Special Committee on Aging), American Association of Retired Persons, Federal Council on Aging, & U.S. Administration on Aging. 1988. *Aging America:*

Trends and Projections. Washington, DC: U.S. Department of Health and Human Services.

U.S. Small Business Administration, Office of Advocacy. 1983. *Unfair Competition by Nonprofit Organizations with Small Business: An Issue for the 1980s.* Washington, DC: Government Printing Office.

Van Gelder, S., & J. Bernstein. 1986. Home Health Care in the Era of Hospital Prospective Payment: Some Early Evidence and Thoughts About the Future. *Pride Institute Journal of Long Term Home Health Care,* 5(1), 3-11.

Van Til, J. 1987. The Three Sectors: Voluntarism in a Changing Political Economy. In S. A. Ostrander, S. Langton, & J. Van Til (Eds.), *The Shifting Debate: Public/Private Sector Relations in the Modern Welfare State,* pp. 50-63. New Brunswick, NJ: Transaction Books.

Van Til, J. 1988. *Mapping the Third Sector: Voluntarism in a Changing Social Economy.* New York: Foundation Center.

Verbrugge, L. M. 1984. Longer Life But Worsening Health? Trends in Health and Mortality of Middle Aged and Older Persons. *Milbank Memorial Fund Quarterly/Health and Society,* 62, 475-519.

Verbrugge, L. M. 1989. Recent, Present, and Future Health of American Adults. In L. Breslow, J. E. Fielding, & L. B. Lave (Eds.), *Annual Review of Public Health,* Vol. 10, pp. 333-361. Palo Alto, CA: Annual Reviews Inc.

Vesperi, M. 1985. *City of Green Benches.* Ithaca, NY: Cornell University Press.

Vladeck, B. 1980. *Unloving Care: The Nursing Home Tragedy.* New York: Basic Books.

Von Behren, R. 1986. *Adult Day Care in America: A Summary of a National Survey.* National Institute of Adult Day Care, National Council on the Aging. Washington, DC: Government Printing Office.

Von Behren, R. 1988. *Adult Day Care: A Program of Services for the Functionally-Impaired.* National Institute of Adult Day Care, National Council on the Aging. Washington, DC: Government Printing Office.

Von Behren, R. 1989. Adult Day Care: A Decade of Growth. *Perspectives on Aging,* 18(4), 14-19.

Waerness, K. 1990. Informal and Formal Care in Old Age: What Is Wrong with the New Ideology in Scandinavia Today? In C. Ungerson (Ed.), *Gender and Caring.* London: Harvester Wheatsheaf.

Wagner, L. 1988. Nursing Homes Buffeted by Troubles. *Modern Healthcare,* 18(12), 33-42.

Waldo, D. R., K. R. Levit, & H. Lazenby. 1986. National Health Expenditures, 1985. *Health Care Financing Review,* 8(1), 1-21.

Walker, A. 1980. The Social Creation of Poverty and Dependency in Old Age. *Journal of Social Policy,* 9, 49-75.

Walker, A. (Ed.). 1982. *Community Care: The Family, the State and Social Policy.* Oxford: Basil Blackwell & Martin Robertson.

Walker, A. 1983. Care for Elderly People: A Conflict Between Women and the State. In J. Finch & D. Groves (Eds.), *A Labour of Love: Women, Work, and Caring,* pp. 106-128. London: Routledge & Kegan Paul.

Walker, A. 1985. *The Care Gap: How Can Local Authorities Meet the Needs of the Elderly?* London: Local Government Information Unit.

Walker, A. C., & C. Phillipson. 1986. *Ageing and Social Policy.* Brookfield, VT: Gower.

Wallace, S. P. 1990a. The No-Care Zone: Availability, Accessibility, and Acceptability in Community-Based Long-Term Care. *The Gerontologist,* 30, 254-261.

Wallace, S. P. 1990b. Race Versus Class in the Health Care of African-American Elderly. *Social Problems,* 37(4), 101-119.

Wallace, S. P., & C. L. Estes. 1989. Health Policy for the Elderly: Federal Policy and Institutional Change. In R. C. Rist (Ed.), *Policy Issues for the 1990's: Policy Studies Review Annual*, Vol. 9, pp. 591-613. New Brunswick, NJ: Transaction Books.

Wallack, S. 1989. *Financing Long-Term Care: Private Initiatives*. Paper presented at the conference, "The Economics and Politics of Long-Term Care," Irvine, CA.

Wan, T. T. H., & K. F. Ferraro. 1991. Assessing the Impacts of Community-Based Health Care Policies and Programs for Older Adults. *Journal of Applied Gerontology*, 10, 35-52.

Watkins, V., & W. Kirby. 1987. Health Care Facilities Participating in Medicare and Medicaid Programs, 1987. *Health Care Financing Review*, 9(2), 101-105.

Weber, M. 1946. *From Max Weber: Essays in Sociology* (H. H. Gerth & C. W. Mills, Trans. & Eds.). New York: Oxford University Press.

Weinstein, I. 1984. The Future of the MIO in a Price-Competitive, Price-Driven Market. *Topics in Health Care Financing*, 11, 84-92.

Weissert, W. G. 1976. Two Models of Geriatric Day Care: Findings from a Comparative Study. *The Gerontologist*, 16, 420-427.

Weissert, W. G. 1977. Adult Day Care Programs in the United States: Current Research Projects and a Survey of 10 Centers. *Public Health Reports*, 92, 49-56.

Weissert, W. G. 1978. Costs of Adult Day Care: A Comparison to Nursing Homes. *Inquiry*, 15, 10-19.

Weissert, W. G. 1982. *Size and Characteristics of the Noninstitutionalized Long-Term Care Population*. Washington, DC: Urban Institute.

Weissert, W. G. 1985. Estimating the Long-Term Care Population: Prevalence Rates and Selected Characteristics. *Health Care Financing Review*, 6(4), 83-91.

Weissert, W. G. 1988. The National Channeling Demonstration: What We Knew, Know Now, and Still Need to Know. *Health Services Research*, 23, 175-187.

Weissert, W. G., C. M. Cready, & J. E. Pawelak. 1988. The Past and Future of Home- and Community-Based Long-Term Care. *Milbank Fund Memorial Quarterly/Health and Society*, 66, 309-388.

Weissert, W. G., J. M. Elston, E. J. Bolda, et al. 1989. Models of Adult Day Care: Findings from a National Survey. *The Gerontologist*, 29, 640-649.

Weissert, W. G., J. M. Elston, M. C. Musliner, & E. Mutran. 1991. Adult Day Care Regulation: Déjà Vu All over Again? *Journal of Health Politics, Policy and Law*, 16, 51-66.

West, P., R. Illsley, & H. Kelman. 1984. Public Preferences for the Care of Dependency Groups. *Social Science and Medicine*, 18, 417-446.

Whiteis, D. G., & J. W. Salmon. 1990. The Proprietarization of Health Care and the Underdevelopment of the Public Sector. In J. W. Salmon (Ed.), *The Corporate Transformation of Health Care: Issues and Directions*, pp. 117-131. Amityville, NY: Baywood.

Willging, P. 1986. Postacute Care Gaps: Fueling Discharge Debate. *Hospitals*, 60(5), 88-89.

Williams, J., G. Gaumer, & M. Cella. 1984. *Home Health Services: An Industry in Transition*. Home Health Agency Prospective Payment Demonstration. Cambridge, MA: Abt Associates.

Wingard, D. L., D. Williams-Jones, J. McPhillips, R. M. Kaplan, & E. Barrett-Connor. 1990. Nursing Home Utilization in Adults: A Prospective Population-Based Study. *Journal of Aging and Health*, 2, 179-193.

Wolch, J. 1990. *The Shadow State*. New York: Foundation Center.

Wong, W., S. R. Ingman, & J. B. Wood. 1988. The Effects of Hospital Cost Containment on the Delivery of Hospice Care. In C. L. Estes, J. B. Wood, et al., *Organizational*

308								THE LONG TERM CARE CRISIS

and Community Responses to Medicare Policy: Consequences for Health and Social Services for the Elderly, Vol. 1, pp. 156-177. Final Report. San Francisco: University of California, Institute for Health & Aging.

Wood, J. B. 1984. Public Policy and the Current Effect on Home Health Agencies. *Home Health Care Services Quarterly*, 5(2), 75-86.

Wood, J. B. 1985. Federal Funding Cutbacks Hard on Increasingly Popular Senior Center. *Perspective on Aging*, 14(5), 14-17.

Wood, J. B. 1985-1986. The Effects of Cost-Containment on Home Health Agencies. *Home Health Care Services Quarterly*, 6(4), 59-78.

Wood, J. B. 1989. The Emergence of Adult Day Care Centers as Post-Acute Care Agencies. *Journal of Aging and Health*, 1, 521-537.

Wood, J. B., & C. L. Estes. 1985. Private Nonprofit Organizations and Community-Based Long Term Care. In C. Harrington, R. J. Newcomer, C. L. Estes, et al., *Long Term Care of the Elderly: Public Policy Issues*, pp. 213-232. Beverly Hills, CA: Sage.

Wood, J. B., & C. L. Estes. 1986. The Nonprofit Sector and Community-Based Care for the Elderly: A Disappearing Resource? *Social Science and Medicine*, 23, 1261-1266.

Wood, J. B., & C. L. Estes. 1988. The Medicalization of Community Services for the Elderly. *Health and Social Work*, 13, 35-42.

Wood, J. B., & C. L. Estes. 1990. The Impact of DRGs on Community-Based Service Providers: Implications for the Elderly. *American Journal of Public Health*, 80, 840-843.

Wood, J. B., C. L. Estes, P. R. Lee, & P. J. Fox. 1983. *Public Policy, the Private Nonprofit Sector and the Delivery of Community-Based Long Term Care Services for the Elderly*. Year 1 Report. San Francisco: University of California, Institute for Health & Aging.

Wood, J. B., P. J. Fox, C. L. Estes, P. R. Lee, & C. W. Mahoney. 1986. *Public Policy, the Private Nonprofit Sector and the Delivery of Community-Based Long Term Care Services for the Elderly*. Year 2 Report. San Francisco: University of California, Institute for Health & Aging.

Wood, J. B., & S. R. Ingman. 1988. Adult Day Care. In C. L. Estes, J. B. Wood, et al., *Organizational and Community Responses to Medicare Policy: Consequences for Health and Social Services for the Elderly*, Vol. 1, pp. 156-177. Final Report. San Francisco: University of California, Institute for Health & Aging.

Young, A. T. 1987. Discharge Planning and Ethical Dilemmas. *Discharge Planning Update*, 7(5), 3-9.

Zawadski, R. T. 1983. The Long Term Care Demonstration Projects: What They Are and Why They Came into Being. *Home Health Care Services Quarterly*, 4(3/4), 5-19.

Zawadski, R. T., & M. L. Ansak. 1983. Consolidating Community-Based Long Term Care: Early Returns from the On Lok Demonstration. *The Gerontologist*, 23, 364-369.

Zelman, W. M., J. M. Elston, & W. G. Weissert. 1991. Financial Aspects of Adult Day Care: National Survey Results. *Health Care Financing Review*, 12(3), 27-36.

Zev, H., L. Noelker, & B. F. Blake. 1985. Comprehensive Services for the Aged: Theoretical and Empirical Perspectives. *The Gerontologist*, 25, 644-649.

Zinn, J. 1991. *Competition and the Quality of Nursing Home Care*. Paper presented at the Association for Health Services Research Annual Meeting, San Diego, CA.

Zola, I. K. 1975. In the Name of Health and Illness: On Some Socio-Political Consequences of Medical Influence. *Social Science and Medicine*, 9, 83-88.

Zola, I. K. 1986. The Medicalization of Aging and Disability: Problems and Prospects. In C. W. Mahoney, C. L. Estes, & J. E. Heumann (Eds.), *Toward a Unified Agenda, Proceeding of a National Conference on Disability and Aging,* pp. 20-40. San Francisco: University of California, Institute for Health & Aging.

Zola, I. K. 1988. Policies and Programs Concerning Aging and Disability: Toward a Unifying Agenda. In S. Sullivan & M. E. Lewin (Eds.), *The Economics and Ethics of Long Term Care and Disability,* pp. 90-130. Washington, DC: American Enterprise Institute for Public Policy Research.

Zones, J. S., C. L. Estes, & E. A. Binney. 1987. Gender, Public Policy and the Oldest Old. *Ageing and Society,* 7, 275-302.

Index

About the Authors

Linda A. Bergthold, Ph.D., Associate, Medical Audit Services Unit, William M. Mercer, Inc., San Francisco, California, was until 1988 Assistant Research Sociologist, Department of Social and Behavioral Sciences and Institute for Health & Aging, University of California, San Francisco (UCSF). She is the author of *Purchasing Power in Health: Business, the State, and Health Care Politics* (1990) and a member of Insurance Commissioner John Garamendi's Health Care Reform Advisory Task Force, 1991-1992.

Elizabeth A. Binney, doctoral student, Department of Social and Behavioral Sciences, and Research Associate, Institute for Health & Aging, UCSF, cowrites articles and book chapters and participates in two national studies of community-based long term care for the elderly. A former National Institute on Aging Predoctoral Fellow, she is conducting research on the political economy of aging and health policy, older women's issues, including the social construction and political economy of osteoporosis, and the State and nonprofit sectors.

David S. Carrell, Ph.D., National Institute on Aging Fellow, Institute for Health & Aging, and Pew Health Policy Fellow, Institute for Health Policy Studies, UCSF, completed dissertation research in political science (1990) examining state-level political and economic correlates of long term care policy effort (1977 to 1986). Currently on the faculty, University of Washington, School of Nursing, his research interests include health promotion and disease prevention policy, specifically, breast cancer prevention and tobacco control policy.

Monica J. Casper, doctoral student, Department of Social and Behavioral Sciences, and Research Assistant, Institute for Health & Aging,

UCSF, is involved in research on the emergence of fetal therapy as a biomedical concern and in a historical sociology of the Pap smear as technology. Academic interests include the sociology of science and technology, organizations and professions, feminist theory, and medical sociology, especially women's health.

Adela de la Torre, Ph.D., Associate Professor, Health Care Administration and Chair, Chicano and Latino Studies Department, California State University, Long Beach, focuses her research on Latina health and health care financing. Appointed Pew Postdoctoral Fellow from 1986 to 1988, Institute for Health & Aging and Institute for Health Policy Studies, UCSF, she collaborated on major health policy research projects.

Carolinda Douglass, doctoral student, Department of Social and Behavioral Sciences, and Research Assistant, Institute for Health & Aging, UCSF, received the M.S.G. and M.P.A. degrees from the University of Southern California. Her dissertation research is on the appropriateness of community-based long term care and the use of geriatric assessment teams in appropriateness research. She is also affiliated with the Rand Graduate School in Santa Monica, California.

Carroll L. Estes, Ph.D., Professor and Chairperson, Department of Social and Behavioral Sciences, and Director, Institute for Health & Aging, School of Nursing, UCSF, is consultant to federal and state legislative committees, a member of the Institute of Medicine, and past president of both the American Society on Aging and the Association for Gerontology in Higher Education. Recipient of an Honorary Doctorate in Human Letters from Russell Sage College (1986), the American Society on Aging Award (1988), and the Kent Award of the Gerontological Society of America (1991), among others, she conducts research on social policy and aging, health and long term care, the nonprofit sector, older women, and generational equity. Best known for *The Aging Enterprise* (1979) and *Political Economy, Health and Aging* (1984), she is author and coauthor of five other books and more than 100 articles.

Patrick J. Fox, Ph.D., Assistant Professor in Residence, Institute for Health & Aging, and Department of Social and Behavioral Sciences, UCSF, conducts research examining the emergence of Alzheimer's disease as a social and health problem, the rate of disease progression, comorbid conditions and causes of death for persons with Alzheimer's disease, the cost of care, and the evaluation of California diagnostic centers. His publications include an article in *Milbank*

Memorial Fund Quarterly and a book (in process) on Alzheimer's disease for Johns Hopkins University Press.

Sheryl C. Goldberg, Ph.D., M.S.W., Program Analyst and Specialist in Aging, San Francisco Commission on the Aging, and Vice-Chair, Marin County Commission on the Status of Women, completed her doctorate in Sociology (1990) at UCSF. Her dissertation on changes in access to health and social services is a community case study of San Francisco based on survey data from the Institute for Health & Aging DRG study, in which she participated as a research associate.

Charlene Harrington, Ph.D., R.N., F.A.A.N., Professor, and Vice-Chairperson, Department of Social and Behavioral Sciences, and Associate Director, Institute for Health & Aging, UCSF, specializes in research on long term care use and expenditures. In addition to extensive publications in *Health Care Financing Review* and *Health Services Research,* among other journals, she recently cowrote "A National Long-Term Care Program for the United States," published in the *Journal of the American Medical Association.*

Susan E. Humphers, doctoral student, Department of Social and Behavioral Sciences, and Post-Graduate Researcher, Institute for Health & Aging, UCSF, received her B.A. in sociology from the University of California, San Diego. A National Institute on Aging Predoctoral Fellow and the data manager for a survey of community-based care providers, she is conducting dissertation research on the diffusion of technology in home health care for the elderly.

Stanley R. Ingman, Ph.D., Professor and Director, Texas Institute for Research and Education on Aging, University of North Texas and Texas College of Osteopathic Medicine, Denton, is coeditor with Derek Gill of "Generative Cure and Distributive Justice: Cross-National Perspectives," a special issue of *Social Science and Medicine,* and coauthor with Gill of *The Aged, Distributive Justice, and the Welfare State: Retrenchment or Development?* (SUNY Press, forthcoming). As a Mid-Career Pew Fellow, Institute for Health & Aging, UCSF (1986-1987), he participated in the DRG study.

Lorraine M. Kramek, Ph.D., Program Director, Sacramento's Homeless Havens Program, Sacramento Food Bank Services, Sacramento, California, directs an innovative transitional housing program for homeless families. After completing dissertation research at Northwestern University on human development and social policy, she was appointed Pew Postdoctoral Research Fellow, Institute for Health

& Aging and Institute for Health Policy Studies, UCSF (1987 to 1989), collaborating on two major studies of Medicare policy.

Carol C. McKetty, doctoral student, Department of Social and Behavioral Sciences, UCSF, was awarded the President's Health Sciences Fellowship at UCSF, 1990-1991. As Research Associate, Institute of Medicine (IOM), National Academy of Sciences, 1986-1989, she contributed to IOM studies of physician staffing for the Veterans Administration and the role of allied health personnel. Her current research interest is probing the interwoven construction of race and the biomedical sciences through the discourse on hypertension.

Ellen M. Morrison, Ph.D., Associate Director, Health Care Program, Institute for the Future, Menlo Park, California, is a contributing author to *System in Crisis: The Case for Health Care Reform* (1991). After completing dissertation research at the University of Chicago on the interdependence of HMOs and health care providers, she was a National Center for Health Services Research Postdoctoral Fellow in health services research at UCSF and the University of California, Berkeley (1989 to 1990), and collaborated on Institute for Health & Aging studies of Medicare policy.

Ida VSW Red, M.A., M.S.L.S., Resource Director, Institute for Health & Aging, and Senior Public Administration Analyst, Department of Social and Behavioral Sciences, UCSF, directs the multidisciplinary Institute for Health & Aging research library and publications program. Editorial credits include *Critical Perspectives on Aging* (1991); *The Nation's Health* (3rd ed., 1990); *Cost of Injury: Report to Congress* (1989), which she designed and desktop published; and, for the Older Women's League, *"Resources" in Women Take Care: The Consequences of Care-giving in Today's Society* (1987).

Douglas S. Sebesta, doctoral student, Department of Social and Behavioral Sciences; Research Associate, Human Development and Aging Program, Langley Porter School of Psychiatry; and Predoctoral Fellow, Center for AIDS Prevention Studies, UCSF, is involved in research focused on the developing integrated systems of AIDS-related health care as well as the direct medical and social service needs of persons living with HIV disease and their informal care providers and advocates.

Pamela Hanes Spohn, Ph.D., M.S.W., Assistant Professor, School of Social Work, University of Wisconsin, Madison, currently is conducting research on the efficacy of expanded eligibility under Medicaid for working-age persons with disabilities and low-income and non-AFDC families. She was a Research Associate, Institute for Health & Aging, UCSF, participating in the DRG study and writing her dissertation on discharge planning, based on IHA data (1985-1989). In tandem with her current research on alternative financing mechanisms, she is studying a range of nonfinancial health care access barriers, including the effects of alternative models of organizing and delivering services.

James H. Swan, Ph.D., Associate Professor, Department of Health Administration and Gerontology, College of Health Professions, the Wichita State University, Wichita, Kansas, while working on this volume was until 1989 Associate Research Sociologist, Institute for Health & Aging, UCSF, and from 1989 to 1992 was Associate Professor, Health Care Administration Program, College of Health and Human Services, California State University, Long Beach. He is a health services researcher, specializing in long term care for more than 15 years, with recent publications including "Home Health Utilization as a Function of Nursing Home Market Factors" in *Health Services Research* (1990), "Ripple Effects of PPS on Nursing Homes" in *The Gerontologist* (1990), and "Skilled Nursing Facility Care for Persons with AIDS" in *American Journal of Public Health* (1992).

Augusta M. Villanueva, Ph.D., Assistant Professor of Medicine and Director of Community Programs in Medical Education, Office of Medical Education, Medical College of Pennsylvania, Philadelphia, is seeking funding to foster the development and implementation of an agenda aimed at linking the Medical College of Pennsylvania with appropriate community networks. A former Pew Postdoctoral Fellow, Institute for Health & Aging and Institute for Health Policy Studies, UCSF, she is currently initiating a program to increase the number of graduates entering generalist residency programs, the number of practicing generalist physicians, and financial incentives for practitioners committed to primary care.

Juanita B. Wood, Ph.D., Public Policy Analyst, Institute for Health & Aging, and Associate Adjunct Professor, Department of Social and Behavioral Sciences, UCSF, has served as Co-Principal Investigator and Project Director on a number of long term national studies at the Institute for Health & Aging to detail the effects of federal policy changes on the aged and on service delivery agencies at the community level. Her publications have appeared in *Health and Social Work* and *Home Health Care Services Quarterly,* among other journals.

DATE DUE		
Jul 12/8/93		
FEB 22 2001		

Demco, Inc. 38-294